The Measurement of Work Performance

Methods, Theory, and Applications

ORGANIZATIONAL AND OCCUPATIONAL PSYCHOLOGY

Series Editor: PETER WARR
MRC/SSRC Social and Applied Psychology Unit, Department of Psychology.
The University, Sheffield, England

A complete list of titles in this series appears at the end of this volume.

The Measurement of Work Performance

Methods, Theory, and Applications

FRANK J. LANDY

JAMES L. FARR

Department of Psychology
The Pennsylvania State University
University Park, Pennsylvania

WITHDRAWN

ACADEMIC PRESS   1983
A Subsidiary of Harcourt Brace Jovanovich, Publishers
New York   London
Paris San Diego San Francisco São Paulo Sydney Tokyo Toronto

ACADEMIC PRESS, INC.
111 Fifth Avenue, New York, New York 10003

United Kingdom Edition published by
ACADEMIC PRESS, INC. (LONDON) LTD.
24/28 Oval Road, London NW1 7DX

Library of Congress Cataloging in Publication Data

Landy, Frank J.
 The measurement of work performance.

 (Organizational and occupational psychology)
 Bibliography: p.
 Includes index.
 1. Employees. Rating of. I. Farr, James L.
 II. Title. III. Title: Work performance. IV. Series.
 HF5549.5.R3L35 1983 658.3'125 82-22657
 ISBN 0-12-435660-5

PRINTED IN THE UNITED STATES OF AMERICA

83 84 85 86   9 8 7 6 5 4 3 2 1

Contents

chapter five

Integrating Empirical Research
with the Process Model of Performance Judgment   119

part three

Uses of Performance Data

chapter six

Performance Information and Employee Motivation   163

chapter seven

Performance Evaluation for Research and
Administrative Purposes   187

part four
New Areas for Examination and Application

chapter eight
Cognitive Aspects of the Process Model
of Performance Rating: Theory and Research   217

chapter nine
The Utility of Performance Measurement   247

chapter ten
Concluding Comments   275

Appendix: Wherry's Theory of Rating   283
ROBERT J. WHERRY

Preface

Human performance represents a projective device for applied psychologists. As a dependent variable, it can be used to satisfy virtually every urge or hunch of researcher and administrator alike. If your interests are psychometric, you may be challenged to develop a new method for gathering performance ratings. If your interests are cognitive, you might consider working with attribution theory. For those interested in macroanalysis, the organizational personality can be found in its response to ineffective performance.

The point is that performance is behavior of the broadest variety. The seeming comfort of thinking of work behavior as somehow more contained or narrow than behavior in general dissolves quickly when one decides to write a book about it. In 1976 we decided to write a quick review of the performance rating literature. In 1980 it was published. The lion's share of that time was spent not in gathering or reading the literature but in deciding how to structure the review. That experience provided our first inkling that perhaps a book was in order. Not satisfied with the rating review, we decided to take on a bigger task and consider the whole issue of performance and its measurement. This meant moving in some new directions: We could no longer consider only "how" questions; we now had to ask "what" and even "why" questions. The pages that follow contain our attempts to answer these additional questions.

We have tried to be equally sympathetic to the concern of the practitioner for salience and the plea of the researcher/theoretician for structure and logic. We freely admit to accepting a cognitive approach in our consideration of how one person evaluates another. This is hardly breaking new ground, for virtually all of psychology is in the sway of cognitive models. Nevertheless, over the years, industrial and organizational psychology has tended to skirmish at the perimeter of a paradigm shift rather than accept a comprehensive framework for theory and research. This makes Robert Wherry's Appendix to our book almost ironic, for in the late 1940s and early 1950s Wherry was deducing a set of propositions to help understand one aspect of performance measurement that anticipated the cognitive shift by a good 20 years. Unfortunately, his work simply did not get much exposure. In the last 5 years, however, much of this lost time has been made up. In the next 5 years we may well go beyond what he suggested more than 30 years ago.

It is our hope that this book will be a useful tool in making progress in performance theory and measurement in several ways. First, we have tried to present a well-balanced and representative history of the area through the research that has been conducted in the past several decades. We would hope that the literature reviewed will save the reader some time and effort. Next, we have tried to point out the areas in which little is known, and there are an alarming number of such areas. Finally, we have tried to present some novel ways of thinking about performance issues. Some of these are substantive, some methodological, and others administrative. We hope the reader will encounter many new ideas, and that this will lead to administrative action or new research programs.

As is always the case, we have many people to thank for their generosity in helping us produce the book. The late Robert Wherry thought long and hard before deciding to contribute the appendix. We are flattered that he decided to help, and we hope that we have maintained the theme that characterized his research. Peter Warr, our series editor, provided a critical review of the entire manuscript. Peter is part cheerleader and part schoolmaster, and these two elements are in perfect balance. Joy Creeger, Ellen Trumbo, and Helen Gardner typed, cut, pasted, cursed at, and otherwise massaged our efforts until they finally resembled the pages of a manuscript. Our graduate students, particularly Jan Cleveland and Janet Barnes-Farrell, were enormously helpful in completing various literature reviews.

part one

The Measurement of Performance

In Chapters 1–3, we discuss the technological and measurement aspects of performance measurement. Chapter 1 is concerned with the conceptual and methodological demands of any type of measurement. These demands include reliability, validity, and accuracy. Chapters 2 and 3 provide a sample of various types of performance measures. These measures range from the obvious indexes such as output to the indirect indexes such as ratings.

chapter one

Introduction to the Measurement of Work Performance

The measurement of work performance has been a concern of applied psychologists for over 60 years. Performance description and prediction play a major role in all personnel decisions and many other types of organizational decisions. Recent concerns over the declining productivity of organizations and the resulting boost to inflation rates highlight the importance of work performance. Unfortunately, the recognition of the importance of performance measurement and the accurate measurement of such performance are different matters. The difficulty of accurately measuring work performance, or the "criterion problem" as it has been labeled, is still one of the most vexing problems facing industrial– organizational psychologists today.

PURPOSES OF PERFORMANCE MEASUREMENT

Performance information in work settings may be gathered for administrative purposes, guidance and counseling purposes, and research purposes. Administrative purposes include promotion, lateral transfer, demotion, and retention decisions; merit compensation decisions; training program assignments; and the establishment of cutting scores for selection procedures. Guidance and counseling uses of performance information may include supervisory feedback to subordinate personnel regarding their relative and absolute strengths and weaknesses. Such information can also be used in career planning and preparation. An often-intended goal of this general use of performance data is the improvement of job satisfaction and work motivation through providing information regarding current performance level and probable, and possible, future assignments in the organization. Performance information may also be obtained as part of various personnel research projects such as the validation of selection procedures, the evaluation of training programs, and the evaluation of motivation- and satisfaction-oriented interventions such as compensation plans and job enrichment programs.

CLASSIFICATION OF PERFORMANCE MEASURES

There are many conceptual and operational approaches to the measurement of work performance. Smith (1976) has developed a three-dimensional framework that is useful for classifying different forms of performance measures. This framework is illustrated in Figure 1.1. The three dimensions are the time span covered by the measure, the specificity of the measure, and the closeness of the measure to organizational goals.

The time span covered by the measure refers to the fact that performance measures can be obtained shortly after the actual on-the-job behavior has occurred or following a delay of a few hours up to many years. A sports example may serve to illustrate this dimension. The offensive performance of a basketball player can be measured in terms of whether a particular shot went in the basket (immediate), the number of points scored in a game (more distant), the scoring average for a season (still more distant), and the scoring average for the player's career (most distant).

The second dimension along which performance measures may vary is specificity–generality. A particular measure may refer to a specific aspect of job performance or to some index of overall performance. In terms of the basketball example, the performance (for a season, e.g., in order to keep the time span fixed) of a player can be measured by free-throw percentage (specific), by scoring average (more general), and by whether the player was selected to an all-star team (most general).

The most important dimension in Smith's (1976) classification framework is that of closeness to organizational goals. As shown in Figure 1.1,

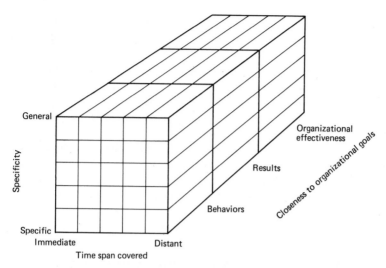

Figure 1.1. Smith's three-dimensional framework for classifying different forms of performance measures. (Adapted from P. C. Smith, Behaviors, results, and organizational effectiveness: The problem of criteria. In M. D. Dunnette [Ed.], *Handbook of industrial and organizational psychology.* Chicago: Rand McNally, 1976, p. 749.)

this dimension has three levels: behaviors, results, and organizational effectiveness. The behaviors level refers to the direct observation of work behavior such as the timing of the movement elements required in the assembly of some product. The results level refers to a summary measure of the effectiveness of work behaviors of an individual. Observations from several points in time are combined to yield an inference about the work performance of the individual. These results measures may be objective (e.g., absence rate, production rate) or subjective (e.g., supervisory rating). Finally, the organizational effectiveness level consists of measures that result from another inferential step. The measures at the results level are combined or aggregated to tell us how well the organization is functioning vis-à-vis its goals. Again, a basketball example may be used. One could measure the average distance from the apogee of the jump at which a player releases the ball in a jump shot (behavior level). The scoring average for the player represents the results level. The organizational effectiveness level could be represented by the winning percentage for the player's team.

THE FOCUS OF THIS BOOK

It is evident from Smith's (1976) taxonomy that a wide variety of different performance measures exist. We will not attempt to treat all of these types of measures exhaustively, but we will concentrate on the behaviors and results levels of Smith's dimension of closeness to organizational goals. Because the level of organizational effectiveness is itself worthy of lengthy exposition (and has received it, e.g., Cameron, 1978; Cameron & Whetten, 1983; Connolly, Conlon, & Deutsch, 1980; Goodman, Pennings, & Associates, 1977; Snyder, Raben, & Farr, 1980), we will not discuss it here. From our perspective, when we consider organizational effectiveness the unit of analysis moves away from the individual to larger aggregates, and it is our intention here to focus on the measurement of the performance of individual employees. We also do not discuss the methods engineering approaches to measuring performance standards. These techniques are discussed in Neibel (1982), among others. The methods engineering approaches are generally limited to repetitive, physical tasks. We intend to focus on measurement methods and procedures that are more broadly applicable to different types of work activities.

Our focus on only the results level and part of the behaviors level leaves many kinds of performance measures to be considered. In the next two chapters in this part, we describe the common forms of performance measures and summarize the research literature concerned with them. Chapter 2 covers the "objective" or countable measures of performance such as absenteeism, accident rate, and productivity, although it is later shown that these measures contain considerable evaluative components. Chapter 3 examines the explicitly evaluative or judgmental measurement techniques such as ratings, rankings, and paired comparisons.

Because of the ubiquitous use of performance ratings for personnel evaluation, Part II of this book presents an expanded version of the authors' process model of performance rating (Landy & Farr, 1980). Chapter 4 describes the components of the model, and Chapter 5 presents the empirical research foundations of the model.

Part III is concerned with using performance data. Chapter 6 discusses the motivational and developmental applications of performance information including performance feedback and goal setting. Chapter 7 elaborates on the use of such data in personnel research studies, including selection procedure validation and training evaluation, and discusses the use of performance measures in making administrative decisions such as promotions and transfers.

In Part IV, future directions that performance measurement may take are examined. Chapter 8 looks at several theoretical frameworks that have developed in other areas of psychology (primarily in social and cognitive psychology) that appear to have relevance for the area of performance measurement. Chapter 9 presents a utility-based analysis about the economic benefits to be derived from performance measurement and feedback. Finally, Chapter 10 summarizes our views on performance measurement and offers some concluding comments about the area.

The appendix contains an updated version of Wherry's classic 1952 theory of rating, written especially for this volume by the late Robert J. Wherry, Sr. This seminal work is the earliest attempt to integrate what is now known as cognitive psychology and traditional mental test theory into a systematic examination of performance ratings. It is a document worthy of reading and rereading for those interested in better understanding the rating process and, indeed, in better understanding performance measurement procedures. It has profoundly affected our thinking, and we hope it will have a similar effect on the readers of this volume.

GENERAL MEASUREMENT ISSUES

Work performance measurement may be considered to be a special case of psychological measurement. *Psychological measurement* is concerned with the procedures or operations that provide quantitative descriptions of the extent to which individuals demonstrate or have certain characteristics, properties, or traits (Ghiselli, 1964). *Work performance measurement* then involves the methods or procedures that provide quantitative indexes of the extent to which employees demonstrate certain work behaviors and of the results of those behaviors.

Work performance measurement procedures, like the more general psychological measurement methods, are predicated on the existence of individual differences. Most of the theoretical and applied work in the measurement area has been concerned with interindividual differences in behavior or properties. This is also true of work performance measurement, although intraindividual differences are of importance, especially in the uses of such measurement in the counseling and development of employees. The bulk of our discussion in this chapter focuses on interindividual differences. A related discussion emphasizing intraindividual differences is presented in Chapter 6. In the remainder of this chapter the term *individual differences* is used to mean interindividual differences.

SOURCES OF VARIANCE IN THE MEASUREMENT
OF WORK PERFORMANCE

Even a cursory examination of the work performance of a group of individuals employed in a common job reveals considerable individual variation. McCormick and Tiffin (1974) report that the ratio of the least productive worker's productivity to that of the most productive worker varied from about 1:2 to 1:3 for various kinds of production jobs. Clearly such a wide range of work performance is probably not attributable to a single cause but to multiple causes.

Figure 1.2 is a simple representation of the major groups of factors that influence the measurement of work performance. Figure 1.2 shows that characteristics of the individual and the situation interact to yield the work performance of the individual (in both the global and specific sense). Individual characteristics include ability (such as cognitive, physical, social, and emotional factors; past work experience; education; training), motivation (level of effort expenditure), and role perceptions (the individual's beliefs about what constitutes effective performance of his or her job; cf. Porter & Lawler, 1968). Situational characteristics are broadly defined here as all aspects of the work setting other than the single individual whose performance we are considering. These characteristics include the supervisor, peers, work design, reward system, organizational structure and policies, etc. An important element of the model shown in Figure 1.2 is the distinction between the work performance of the individual and the work performance "score" of the individual as obtained by the use of a performance measurement procedure. Performance measurement procedures act as imperfect translators of behavior into some quan-

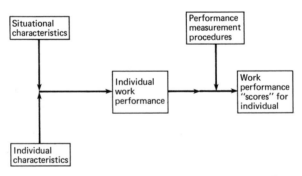

Figure 1.2. Factors influencing the measurement of work performance.

tified index of work performance. A major goal of performance measurement is to reduce those imperfections to a minimum.

Psychometric Indexes of Performance Measures

Several psychometric indexes are related to the adequacy of any psychological measure; these include reliability, validity, and accuracy. Although these concepts are central to the value of any psychological measure, there are specific aspects of these concepts that are especially relevant for work performance measurement. The following discussion addresses both general and specific concerns.

RELIABILITY. *Reliability* may be defined as the extent to which a set of measurements is free from variance due to random error or the extent to which the variance in a set of measurements is due to systematic sources. In the case of work performance measurement, there are really two questions that could be asked (and answered) concerning reliability (Ronan & Prien, 1966). The first is whether job performance itself is reliable; the second is whether the observation or measurement of that work performance is reliable. At a conceptual level it is easy to make this distinction, but in actual research studies it is often difficult to separate these questions.

Ronan and Prien (1971) note that performance reliability has received very little attention in the research literature. The evidence that they reviewed suggested that performance is not especially reliable. For example, Rothe and Nye (1958) examined the weekly productivity of a group of coil winders over a 38-week period. The median intraindividual ratio of the best weekly productivity to the worst weekly productivity was over 2:1. That is, on the average the workers produced over twice as much in their best week as in their worst week. This was interpreted as indicative of considerable unreliability in individual work performance. It should be noted that one does not really know how much of this variability is truly random variation and how much is due to systematic but unknown (at least in terms of being measured in this study) factors. Figure 1.2 suggests that many situational and individual factors affect performance. All of the performance variance associated with those factors that are not controlled or measured in a particular study must be labeled as unexplained variance, but it may not all be nonsystematic.

An additional factor to be considered is the period of time over which each performance measurement is taken. It is well known from psychological measurement theory (e.g., Ghiselli, 1964) that, all else being equal, the larger the sample of behavior that is measured the more reliable that measure is. It may be that, because of the large number of situational and individual factors influencing work performance, such performance may appear to be unreliable over relatively short periods of time due to fluctuations in these other variables. Thus, performance measured over longer blocks of time may be of greater reliability (Landy & Trumbo, 1980; Rothe, 1978).

As noted previously, it is often difficult to separate in an operational sense the questions of the reliability of performance and of the observation of that performance. Particularly with judgmental methods of performance measurement (such as ratings), the two questions are irretrievably confounded. Even with objective or countable kinds of performance measures, the methods of recording such data and adjusting the data for various kinds of situational constraints (e.g., material outages, machine breakdowns) suggest that one rarely has a pure measure of work performance. Thus, although it makes good conceptual sense to consider both of these reliability questions, in most situations, research or applied, we should realize that we can only attempt to assess the reliability of some combination of performance and its observation.

For any set of measurements we can never be sure exactly what proportion of total variance in the measurements is systematic and what is error. This means that we can never compute directly *the* reliability of the set of scores resulting from a measurement procedure. There are several ways that we can *estimate* the reliability of such a set of scores. These estimation procedures can be thought of as *operational definitions* of the reliability of the measurement technique (Guion, 1965). The estimates of reliability may be grouped into three general classes: (*a*) measures of stability; (*b*) measures of equivalence; and (*c*) measures of internal consistency.

Measures of stability are often referred to as *test–retest reliability estimates.* They are obtained by the correlation of measurements gathered at one time with measurements gathered at a later time on the same group of individuals with the same measurement instrument. For example, Cheloha and Farr (1980) obtained measures of absenteeism for a sample of state government employees for 2 consecutive years. The correlations between the data from the 2 years yielded estimates of the stability of the absenteeism measures. Dickinson and Tice (1973) and Kafry, Jacobs, and Zedeck (1979) gathered supervisory ratings of subordinate work performance at two and three points in time, respectively. The correlations between the ratings provided evidence related to the test–retest reliability of the supervisory judgments.

The stability or consistency of performance measures over time is an important property for such measures. If performance measures are highly erratic over time, then we cannot place faith in any single measurement of that performance with regard to its representativeness of the individual's effectiveness. However, there are several important additional points that must be considered in evaluating estimates of the stability of performance. The length of time between the measurements is critical. Too short a period may result in spuriously high estimates of reliability for some types of performance measures. For example, with supervisory ratings, the rater may be able to remember the ratings given to the ratee at the prior measurement and simply reproduce them the second time. With too long a period of time between measurements, estimates of stability may be spuriously low if true performance change has occurred. No precise statement regarding the optimal length of the period between measurements can be given, although 6–12 months is common (Guion, 1965). It would appear that in choosing an interval length one should consider the general type of performance measure (objective or judgmental), the length of job tenure of those being evaluated, the possible existence of seasonal variations in performance constraints or facilitators, and the purpose for which the measures are being obtained.

If the estimate of performance stability is high, we are normally pleased, but the sensitivity of the performance measure must be considered. It is possible that high measurement stability results not from stable performance but from the crudity of the measurements. Some measures may be insufficiently sensitive to actual change in job performance. One needs to investigate whether the performance is actually stable or whether the measure cannot detect systematic change. If multiple measures of performance exist and are obtained at the two points in time, then the correlations among the measures within the same period of measurement and between the two measurements can be examined. A measure that demonstrates high test–retest reliability but that is not significantly correlated with changes in other performance measures is likely to be insensitive to actual performance change. One should also expect that, in general, individuals with less work experience or less experience on a particular job should show more performance change (usually in the direction of improved performance) than those individuals with greater work and job experience. Greater change among the less experienced should be particularly expected for jobs that are complex and varied, as they should take a longer period of time to master. Again, the purpose for which the performance measurements are being obtained is important. For some purposes, a relatively insensitive measure (e.g., a rating of the overall performance of each individual as below average, average, or above average) may be sufficient and the most cost effective to develop and obtain.

Measures of equivalence or *parallel-forms estimates of reliability* are commonly used with psychological tests. Two sets of test items are developed that cover the same content domain and have equivalent degrees of difficulty and variability. The correlation between the two sets of items (or test forms) is an estimate of the parallel-forms reliability of each. The basic issue is whether the measurements obtained generalize beyond the specific test items to the content domain from which the items were drawn. In job performance measurement, the direct analogy to the procedures used with psychological tests to estimate parallel-forms reliability would be the use of two sets of equivalent performance items to assess effectiveness. For example, Zedeck, Jacobs, and Kafry (1976) developed parallel forms of behavior anchored rating scales in which the performance dimensions were identical across the two forms but the behavior examples anchoring each dimension differed for the two forms. With objective measures of job performance, Guion (1965) has suggested that correlations between contiguous brief periods of counting such data (for example, daily productivity or attendance) could be interpreted as estimates of equivalence or parallel-forms reliability. However, such an operationalization could also be interpreted as a way of estimating the internal consistency of a measure. Internal consistency approaches to estimating reliability are discussed in more detail later in this section.

A form of reliability estimation that might be considered a type of parallel-forms reliability is interrater reliability. Often used with judgmental performance measures as the principal way of estimating reliability, interrater reliability is generally operationalized as the correlation between the judgments of two raters each independently evaluating the same set of individuals. To maintain the logic of equivalence, the two raters should have the same or highly similar relationship with the ratee (e.g., both raters are supervisors of the ratee or both are peers of the ratee). (When two raters occupy different organizational roles vis-à-vis the ratee, the relationship between the judgments is usually considered evidence of the validity of the judgments. This will be discussed in more detail later in this chapter.)

The *internal consistency* approach to the estimation of reliability is concerned with the question of whether all parts of a total measure are measuring the same thing. Logically, if we combine into a single measure various elements or parts (e.g., test items to form a total test score or various supervisory ratings to yield a rating of overall job performance), then all of those elements or parts should be assessing the same characteristic or attribute of the individual. Otherwise, the composite measure makes little sense; rather it is akin to the proverbial addition of apples and oranges.

The most common operational approaches to estimating the internal consistency of a measure involve the intercorrelations of parts of the total measure. The necessary data for the estimate of internal consistency can be obtained from one administration of the measurement instrument. In the case of a psychological test or attitude scale composed of a number of items, a typical procedure is to correlate the scores or responses on one-half of the items with the scores or responses on the other half for some samples of individuals. This is referred to as a *split-half reliability estimate.* Often the two halves of the tests that are used for estimating the internal consistency of the total measure are the odd-numbered items and the even-numbered items. This particular form of split-half reliability estimate is usually referred to as *odd–even reliability.* The direct analogue of this form of reliability estimation for measures of work performance is to correlate, for example, productivity on odd-numbered days with productivity on even-numbered days for some period of time. Similarly, if one had a number of specific rating scale items purporting to assess effectiveness on some performance dimension, then one could logically correlate the ratings on the odd-numbered items with those of the even-numbered items as an estimate of the internal consistency of the total of the ratings of that dimension of performance.

One problem with split-half estimates of internal consistency is that there are many ways to divide a multi-item measure into two halves. Our estimate of reliability is likely to be affected by the particular choice that is made. A procedure developed by Cronbach (1951) allows us to avoid this problem. Cronbach's estimate of reliability, known as *coefficient alpha,* is based on average item variances and covariances with other items and does not require that the measure be divided into halves. Coefficient alpha can be interpreted as the correlation of a measure with a *hypothetical* parallel form (Nunnally, 1978).

Internal consistency estimates of reliability are logical only if the content of the items of the measure are assumed to be homogeneous. If a work performance measure is heterogeneous in content (e.g., rating dimensions of quantity of production, interpersonal relations, and safety behavior), then an internal consistency estimate of the reliability of the total sum of ratings on these three performance dimensions would not make sense.

The various approaches to estimating reliability have particular advantages and disadvantages for various purposes and types of performance measurement. Coefficients of stability are most meaningful only when it is presumed that level of performance is not likely to change over the time interval between measurements. Coefficients of equivalence are useful if errors in the sampling of what is to be measured or observed are likely to be substantial. If the principal concern is whether the items comprising a measure are heterogeneous in content, then a coefficient of internal consistency is the best estimate.

Table 1.1 suggests how different factors that contribute to performance measurement scores (see Figure 1.2) are treated by different estimates of reliability as being either systematic or error variance. In this table, individual, situational, and performance measurement procedure characteristics are each categorized as either relatively permanent or relatively transient, as this temporal factor affects how the source of variation is treated. Also, each of the three major methods for estimating reliability (test–retest, parallel forms, and internal consistency) are subdivided into immediate and delayed categories, as the time lapse between measurements affects whether a particular estimate treats certain sources of variation as systematic or error. (The delayed internal consistency category is unusual, as we generally consider all internal consistency estimates as immediate. However, with some performance measures, the various measurements could occur over a considerable length of time. For example, we might wish to estimate the internal consistency of a set of weekly production rates or of absence measures for several time blocks.)

A number of factors are likely to influence any estimate of the reliability of a performance measure and should be taken into consideration in the interpretation of such estimates. These factors include characteristics of the sample such as size, representativeness, homogeneity, and average performance level and characteristics of the measure itself such as number of items or length of performance period. (For more complete treatments of reliability estimates and related issues, see Allen & Yen [1979], Ghiselli, Campbell, & Zedeck [1981], Guion [1965], Lord & Novick [1968], and Nunnally [1978], among others.)

VALIDITY. Although adequate reliability is necessary for a performance measure to be useful, it is not sufficient to ensure the worth of such a measure. Reliability estimates provide information about whether the variance in a measure is systematic, but they do not inform us about whether the source or sources of the systematic variance is (are) relevant for the purpose of the measurement. The reliability of a set of measure-

Table 1.1

Allocation of Sources of Variation by Different Estimates of Reliability[a]

Sources of variation in individual performance scores	Immediate test–retest	Delayed test–retest	Immediate parallel form	Delayed parallel form	Immediate internal consistency	Delayed internal consistency
Work performance factors						
Individual characteristics						
Relatively permanent	S	S	S	S	S	S
Relatively transient	S	E	S	E	S	E
Situational characteristics						
Relatively permanent	S	S	S	S	S	S
Relatively transient	S	E	S	E	S	E
Performance measurement procedure						
Characteristics						
Relatively permanent	S	S	E	E	S	S
Relatively transient	S	E	E	E	S	E
Other factors	E	E	E	E	E	E

[a]S = treated as systematic source of variation; E = treated as error source of variation.

ments does set an upper limit to its possible validity because the maximum validity coefficient is equal to the square root of the reliability coefficient. Validity addresses this question of relevance. A psychological measure traditionally has been said to be valid if it measures what it is intended to measure. Validation is a process of investigation (or research) through which the degree of validity of a measure can be estimated.

As with reliability, most of the theoretical and conceptual developments related to validity have evolved in the context of psychological tests. In that context the principal concern is one of making inferences about an individual (e.g., capacity for academic achievement, likelihood for being successful in an occupation) on the basis of a score or scores on a psychological test or tests. The issue of validity fundamentally becomes one of the appropriateness of the inferences made on the basis of some set or sets of scores on the measure. Thus, it is not really appropriate to describe a measure as being valid or not valid. Rather, we should recognize that the validity of the inferences made on the basis of a measure is likely to vary with different uses and purposes of measurement (Dunnette & Borman, 1979).

In the specific case of work performance measures, we use the scores obtained on these measures to make inferences about the job incumbents. These inferences differ dependent on the purpose of the measurement. For example, we may infer that certain incumbents are likely to be successful in a higher position in the organization whereas others are not, or that some should be retained in their jobs but others fired, or that some should attend one type of training program and others should attend another type. Thus, a particular work performance measure could be thought of as possessing many validi*ties*, one for *each* possible use of the information.

There are several strategies or procedures for estimating validity. Traditionally (e.g., Guion, 1965), these have been labeled as content validity, criterion-related validity, and construct validity. *Content validity* is concerned with the degree to which a measure is representative in terms of content. Since performance data are only samples of a much larger population, some estimate of the content validity of a performance measure is necessary. The usual estimation procedure for content validity is the judgment of individuals who are in some way "experts" about the job in question (e.g., supervisors, job incumbents, and job analysts). That a performance measure is representative of the population of data that might have been obtained is important whether we are considering objective measures such as absenteeism and productivity or judgmental measures such as checklists and rating scales. With objective measures we would be concerned with the possible existence of atypical conditions (e.g., machine breakdowns, product-line changeovers, influenza epidemics) that would distort the performance indexes. With judgmental measures, the concern would be with such factors as the particular items on a checklist, the performance dimensions in a rating system, or the performance observation schedules. A consideration with either objective or judgmental measures is whether the job tasks and activities are relatively static or dynamic. Somewhat general, rather than specific, measures are more likely to retain content validity if the job is dynamic in nature.

The key to many content-validity questions is job analysis. *Job analysis* is some systematic procedure for describing a job in terms of tasks performed and the knowledges, skills, and abilities required to perform the tasks successfully. We will not attempt to review extensively the various techniques of job analysis and related issues. (For reviews and descriptions of job-analysis methods, see Cornelius, Carron, & Collins [1979], McCormick [1979], and Prien & Ronan [1971].) The important point is that, although the content validity is determined by judgmental means, the judgments should be systematically obtained as such by job analysis. Lawshe (1975) has recently proposed a quantitative index to assess the content validity of test items that could be applied to performance measures.

Criterion-related validity refers to the relationship (usually expressed in the form of a correlation coefficient) between the scores on the measure of interest and the scores on some behavioral measure. Since, for our purposes, the measure of interest (a measure of work performance) is also a behavioral measure, we are really concerned with criterion–criterion (or behavior–behavior) relationships when we estimate the criterion-related validity of a performance measure.

Behavior–behavior relationships can be examined in two principal time-related paradigms. *Predictive validity* refers to the relationship between a measure at one point in time and another behavioral measure at a later time. *Concurrent validity* refers to the relationship between a measure obtained at one point in time and another behavioral measure obtained at essentially the same time. Figure 1.3 illustrates these two validity paradigms.

Predictive validity is most important for work performance measures when they are used as predictors of future performance or as part of any personnel decision procedure. Unless it can be demonstrated empirically that the scores on the prior performance measure are significantly related

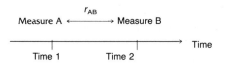

(a) The correlation (r_{AB}) between A and B is an estimate of *predictive validity.*

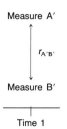

(b) The correlation ($r_{A'B'}$) between A' and B' is an estimate of *concurrent validity.*

Figure 1.3. Predictive (a) and concurrent (b) validity paradigms.

to scores on the subsequent measure, then the prior performance measure should not be a part of the input to the personnel decision.

(The distinction between reliability and validity can become most fuzzy when we examine the validity of performance measures. When we are estimating the degree of relationship between two measures of work performance, should that degree of relationship be labeled as a validity estimate or a reliability estimate? To answer this question is often not easy. For many practical purposes, the conceptual distinction may be unimportant. How we label the degree of relationship between two performance measures is probably better based on our purpose than on the operations used. If we want to determine how much systematic variance exists in two sets of absence measures [e.g., Year 1 versus Year 2], then we are estimating the reliability [stability] of the data. If we want to know if Year 1 absence data can be used to predict Year 2 so that personnel decisions can be made [e.g., fire those with absence rates because we can predict that they will continue to have high absence rates in the future], then we are estimating the [predictive] validity of the set of absence measures.)

It is common for personnel researchers to correlate concurrent performance measures, although the purpose of obtaining estimates of the concurrent validity of the measures may not always be articulated. Furthermore, although usually one desires (and hopes for) validity coefficients that are large, there are instances in which large correlations among concurrent measures are looked on with dismay. In particular, high correlations among supervisory ratings on various performance dimensions are usually treated as an error (called halo error) committed by the raters. Thus, no simple decision rule or operational standard, such as "validity is demonstrated when the correlation between two concurrent work measures is statistically significant," can be stated. The inconsistency of the desirability of strong intercriterion correlations leads us to consider the third strategy for the estimation of validity, namely, construct validity.

A work performance or criterion construct can be thought of as an attribute or characteristic of employees, not directly observable or measurable, that is inferred from observable job behaviors in one situation or occasion and that underlies performance in other situations or occasions. *Construct validity* is the extent to which a measure actually assesses the construct that it was designed to measure. This approach to estimating validity does not lend itself to easy operationalization or to the calculation of a few statistics. Rather, construct validity can be better considered as an ongoing process, with data accumulating over time regarding how well a construct is being measured.

It has been noted (e.g., American Psychological Association, 1980) that to separate validation estimation into the three traditional categories of content, criterion related, and construct is not fully logical. Indeed, we would agree with James (1973) and Smith (1976) who argue that construct validity is the desired strategy for estimating the validity of performance measures. Content and criterion-related validity strategies can best be thought of as ways of obtaining data about the construct validity of a measure, rather than as validity strategies that can stand alone.

James (1973) has presented in some detail the rationale for the use of a construct approach to the validation of performance measures. We will outline his major points here and refer the interested reader to his article for further discussion and for additional references. As noted by James, Cronbach and Meehl (1955) presented a classic discussion of the development of construct validity for psychological tests that can be extended to cover other types of measures. The fundamental step in ascertaining the construct validity of a measure is the development of a nomological network (Feigl & Scriven, 1956). The nomological network is composed of a P plane representing perceptual or observable data and a C plane representing hypothetical constructs.

Several conditions are necessary for the existence of a nomological network (James, 1973). The observable measures in the P plane must be where a series of technical steps can be followed that will necessarily result in the network. Cronbach and Meehl (1955) suggested a number of methodological approaches that could offer evidence for the construct validity of a measure. These include investigations of group differences (or the known groups method), correlational and factor analyses, examination of the internal structure of the measure (including internal consistency estimates of reliability), studies of time-related change (including test–retest reliability estimates), and studies of process.

The most commonly used method for construct validation has probably been the multitrait–multimethod matrix suggested by Campbell and Fiske (1959). This procedure requires at least two different operational methods that are used to measure at least two different traits or characteristics. Evidence for the construct validity for each trait is obtained from the discriminant and convergent validity estimates available in the matrix of correlations among all the variables. *Convergent validity* is shown when two or more methodologically distinct measures of the same trait are significantly correlated with each other. *Discriminant validity* is shown when the correlations among traits measured by different methods are larger than the correlations among different traits measured by the same method.

The multitrait–multimethod procedure for construct validation has been applied in the area of performance measurement. For example, Lawler (1967) modified the approach somewhat in the construct validation of performance ratings. He substituted the type of rater (supervisor, peer, or self) for the method factor and formulated a multitrait–multirater matrix for obtaining convergent and discriminant validity estimates. Kavanagh, MacKinney, and Wolins (1971) advocated the use of multitrait–multimethod procedures to assess the construct validity of various operational measures of managerial performance.

It should be noted that the multitrait–multimethod approach to construct validation is limited and does not represent a sufficient methodology for developing construct validity (James, 1973). The multitrait– multimethod procedures are primarily concerned with developing rules of correspondence (or epistemic definitions) between operational measures in the P plane and the underlying constructs in the C plane. Information to assess the relationships among constructs in the C plane (the constitutive definitions) is not fully available in a multitrait–multimethod matrix. The Campbell and Fiske (1959) criteria for the determination of construct validity have also been criticized and alternative methodologies proposed (e.g., Alwin, 1974; Kalleberg & Kluegel, 1975). The interested reader can refer to these sources for details of the criticisms and suggested alternative approaches.

Campbell (1976) has noted that construct validation should be properly considered as both a deductive and inductive process. In the specific case of performance measures, a model or theory of work performance in a given job or job family could give rise to hypotheses about the connections among variables and constructs. Farr (1980), among others, has argued for the need to theorize about work performance, particularly about the relationships among components of such performance. However, deductive approaches alone are too limiting. The use of inductive reasoning (e.g., giving substantive meaning to a particular measure or set of measures) may also be crucial, especially in the exploratory stages of research in an area.

ACCURACY. Accuracy of performance measurement is often confused with the concepts of reliability and validity. Indeed, accurate measurement implies both reliable and valid measurement, but the reverse is not necessarily true. Accuracy is concerned not only with consistency of measurement (reliability) and with the construct being measured (validity) but also with the absolute level of performance. Does the "score" that an individual receives on a performance measure reflect the "true" performance level of that individual? The question of accuracy is often a vexing one, because we usually have no objective way of assessing "true" performance. (If we did, we would not worry about using our probably inaccurate measures!)

Accuracy is a more salient issue with judgmental measures of performance, especially ratings, than with objective measures. One can conceive of a set of ratings that are reliable (either in the sense of interrater argument or consistency over time) and that are valid (in that the ratings correlate highly with the "true" performance levels of the ratees), but that are inaccurate due to a severe or lenient rater. That is, a particular rater may rate everyone too highly in terms of level of performance, although the proper order of the individuals' performance is maintained, or everyone may be rated as a poorer performer than he or she actually is. Figure 1.5 illustrates valid (and, by definition, reliable) ratings that are inaccurate.

Accuracy has recently become a topic of research in the performance rating area (e.g., Bernardin & Pence, 1980; Borman, 1979; Vance, Kuhnert, & Farr, 1978). Further work is needed on this problem. Much of the research has been, and probably will be in the future, conducted in the

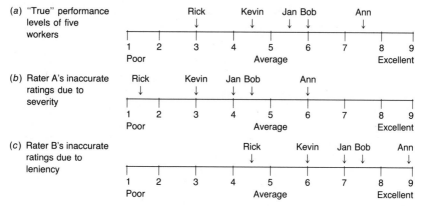

Figure 1.5. Valid but inaccurate performance ratings.

laboratory because of the inherent problem of the "true" performance levels of the ratees. In laboratory settings the researcher is able to control the performance levels of the ratees and, thus, can know what the actual rating should be. Such research must be well designed so as to permit generalization to field settings and operational uses of performance measures. We need to create innovative ways of studying accuracy in realistic settings. We must also be sensitive to the fact that accuracy is dependent on the intended use of the information (Farr, 1980). Only inaccuracies that change a personnel decision (either on the part of the organization or of the individual) are really important. Thus, an inaccuracy such as that shown in Figure 1.5 does not matter if the sole purpose of the ratings is to validate a selection test because constant errors or changes in scores of the entire sample do not affect the correlation between the ratings and the test scores. Such an inaccuracy would affect the cutting score that we might set to establish an eligibility list for selection, however, and for that purpose the inaccuracy would be important.

Other Requirements of Performance Measures

In addition to the psychometric properties just described in some detail, most researchers and users of performance measures suggest that the measures possess other desirable properties. These properties are usually evaluated in qualitative terms, as they may not be amenable to quantitative assessment. We will not treat these in great detail here since discussions are available elsewhere (e.g., Blum & Naylor, 1968; Jacobs *et al.*, 1980; Landy & Trumbo, 1980; McCormick & Ilgen, 1980).

Jacobs *et al.* (1980) have proposed two broad classes of criteria for criterion measures other than psychometric ones, namely, qualitative and utilization indexes. *Qualitative* criteria may be thought of as guidelines by which performance measurement procedures are *judged* to be adequate and beneficial. These guidelines involve a consideration of organizational constraints, interactions between individuals (e.g., raters and ratees), the implications of the evaluations, and other logical concerns that an evaluator of a performance measure may consider when assessing the measure.

Specific qualitative criteria mentioned by Jacobs *et al.* (1980) include relevancy, data availability and practicality, and equivalence. *Relevancy* is the extent to which important and/or frequent job behaviors are assessed by the performance measure while unimportant and infrequent behaviors are excluded. *Data availability and practicality* refer to possible organizational constraints. Can the data necessary for a performance measure be obtained from appropriate sources without undue interruption or interference with the performance of the individual performer, work group, or organization? *Equivalence* is akin to standardization of observation and judgment. Does the procedure yield performance data that are logically equivalent and comparable for different work performers?

Utilization criteria refers to how well suited a particular performance measure is for various possible uses or purposes of the performance evaluation. Purposes of evaluation include, as noted before, administrative decisions (disciplinary action, promotion, awards, etc.), research data (selection procedure validation, training evaluation, etc.), and counseling and feedback for development of the individual work performer. Some performance data clearly are more useful for certain purposes than others (e.g., specific behavioral data are better for feedback to a work performer whereas general, overall ratings may be useful for an administrative decision).

Finally, the utilization criteria for a performance measure also include its potential value to the job incumbent, the supervisor, and to the organization in terms of organizational diagnosis. Jacobs *et al.* (1980) have discussed the benefits that may accrue to the ratee, rater, and organization from a performance measurement system. These include increased satisfaction and motivation of the ratee, improved clarity of work goals, focusing the time and energy of the supervisors on those aspects of performance of their subordinates that require improvement or deserve commendation, improved manpower analysis and personnel information systems, and an increase in organizational communication concerning objectives and standards of performance.

SUMMARY

Performance information may be obtained for several general uses, including administrative, guidance and counseling, and research purposes. Performance measures can be classified according to the time span covered by the measure, the specificity of the measure, and the closeness of the measure to organizational goals. Performance measures should be reliable, valid, and accurate, in addition to being practical and useful. Proper consideration to measurement issues is important. The reliability of work performance measures concerns two issues. Is work performance reliable? Is the measurement of such performance reliable? Validity can best be treated within the framework of construct validity in which the relationships among various performance measures and other variables are examined for their logic. Accuracy is often confused with reliability and validity but more properly is concerned with the deviation of measured performance from the "true" level of performance. Performance measures should provide sufficient information for their cost of attainment, should be meaningful to those whose performance is being assessed, and should be related to personal and organizational goals.

chapter two

Nonjudgmental Measures of Performance

As we indicated in the introductory chapter, there are many different ways to measure performance. At the simplest levels, we have two categories of performance data—judgmental measures and nonjudgmental measures. Ratings are examples of judgmental measures. The rating process requires one individual to make a judgment about the performance level of another. This involves collecting information, weighing its value, and using it to make a statement about the performance of the person being rated. In a sense, ratings deal in abstractions. The other class of performance measures—nonjudgmental measures—consists of measures that do not require abstraction or synthesis, or at least not by the person collecting the measures. These data consist of things that can be counted, seen, and compared directly from one employee to another. Traditionally, these nonjudgmental measures have included such things as production output, scrap rate, and time to complete a task. These are fairly obvious and in many instances define the individual's performance for the organization. There are other nonjudgmental measures that do not directly represent performance but are clearly involved in any definition of overall effectiveness. These variables include absence, accidents, grievances, and turnover or quits. In this chapter, we will consider both types of nonjudgmental measures.

ABSENTEEISM

The concept of absence as an index of efficiency is a seductive one. Who could argue with a straight face that an absent employee was a productive one? It seems intuitively obvious that one of the preconditions for good performance is attendance. Thus, it is understandable that a popular dependent variable or criterion in organizational research is absenteeism. Unfortunately, it seems that it may be as difficult to measure absence rate in any meaningful way as it is to reduce it.

There are several excellent reviews of both the research and administrative aspects of measures of absenteeism. Gaudet (1963) did an excellent job of describing the various types of measures available as well as their strengths and weaknesses. He catalogued no less than 41 alternative measures. Still more have appeared since 1963. In the past several years, there has been renewed interest in absence by psychologists because of the implications that it has for understanding work motivation. This has led to several reviews (Muchinsky, 1977; Steers & Rhodes, 1978) as well as models of absence or attendance behavior (Chadwick-Jones, Nicholson, & Brown, 1982; Fitzgibbons & Moch, 1980; Mowday, Porter, & Steers, 1981; Steers & Rhodes, 1978). It is not our task in this chapter to understand or explain absence behavior. The interested reader can easily tap into that literature from the references just cited. Instead, we will try to outline the typical motivations for gathering absence data, the most common measures employed, the psychometric characteristics of those measures, and some strategies for effective research and administrative use of absence data.

Some Points of View

There are two different perspectives that can be taken with respect to the phenomenon of absenteeism. The first is organizationally based and the second individually based. The organizational perspective considers absenteeism to be a "cost" that must be reduced through various control activities. Steers and Rhodes (1978) put a price tag of 24.6 billion dollars on absenteeism in the United States for the period of 1 year. Fitzgibbons and Moch (1980) report the cost of absenteeism in one department in a medium-sized manufacturing organization in a particular year to be $66,000. These are substantial costs and most organizations are anxious to reduce them. From the organizational perspective, the reasons for absence are less important than the fact of absence. Accordingly, the measures that are employed seldom involve statistics at any level lower than the work group. In addition, those measures seldom distinguish between excused and unexcused absences. As an example, the United States Bureau of Labor Statistics (BLS) suggests a standard absence formula that is used by many organizations:

$$\text{Incidence rate} = \frac{\text{Number of workers absent}}{\text{Number of workers employed}} \times 100$$

Similarly, BLS suggests some additional measures:

$$\text{Severity rate} = \frac{\text{Average number of hours lost by absent workers}}{\begin{array}{c}\text{Average number of hours usually worked}\\ \text{by absent workers}\end{array}} \times 100$$

$$\text{Inactivity rate} = \frac{\text{Number of hours absent}}{\text{Number of hours usually worked}} \times 100$$

Other variations include formulas for computing average number of days absent per employee, average number of days lost per absence, absences computed as cost, and average absence frequency rate. All of these measures have one thing in common—they are unconcerned with the reason for absence. As an organizational phenomenon, absence is usually handled administratively when the perspective is a simple economic one. The company might take a harder line on personnel policies governing absence. If the company employees are represented by a union, management might bargain for fewer sick days when the next contract rolls around. Whatever the "treatment," there is little concern for individual differences in absence circumstances.

The individual perspective is quite different. This perspective implies that the "treatment" will be one applied to a specific subgroup of employees rather than across the board. Thus, the individual perspective distinguishes between excused and unexcused absences, sick leave versus nonsick leave. Gaudet (1963) has provided a staggering list of qualitative distinctions that have been applied to absences as viewed from the individual perspective. This list, plus some distinctions that have appeared since 1963, appears in Table 2.1. Many of the terms in this list have strong motivational connotations. They suggest that some people are "lazy" or "irresponsible" or "disloyal." The clear implications of lists such as these are that certain types of absences can be more easily reduced than others.

Table 2.1
Some Commonly Used Categories of Absence

Scheduled versus unscheduled absence
Authorized versus unauthorized absence
Certified versus uncertified absence
Avoidable versus unavoidable absence
Justified versus unjustified absence
Contractual versus noncontractual absence
Sickness versus nonsickness absence
Disability versus nondisability absence
Medical versus personal absence
Injury versus noninjury absence
Chronic illness versus acute illness absence
Long-term versus short-term absence
Repeater versus nonrepeater absence
Voluntary versus involuntary absence
Intentional versus unintentional absence
Explained versus unexplained absence
Excused versus unexcused absence
Official versus unofficial absence
Compensable versus noncompensable absence
Insured versus noninsured absence
Occupational versus nonoccupational absence
Legal versus illegal absence
Reasonable versus unreasonable absence
Illness versus self-induced illness absence
Certified illness versus casual illness absence
Monday/Friday absence versus midweek absence
Reported versus unreported absence
Employee-centered versus management-centered absence

Common Measures of Absenteeism

Most of the measures of absence employed by psychologists are of the individual rather than organizational variety. Personnel psychologists look for hints in test scores, interview results, or background data that might provide some indication of which applicants might make dependable employees. Organizational psychologists look for variations in supervisory attitudes, job satisfaction, or job-induced stress that might account for the absence history of various individuals in the organization.

The commonly used measures of absenteeism at the individual level are deceptively few in number. The most common are frequency (the number of periods or "spells" of absence) and duration or severity (the average or total number of days absent). Other measures have been used on occasion (Chadwick-Jones, Brown, Nicholson, & Sheppard, 1971) and include (*a*) attitudinal: frequency of short absences; (*b*) time lost: number of days lost in a week regardless of any reason except leave; (*c*) blue Monday: occurrence of a 1-day absence on a Monday; and (*d*) worst day: the incidence of absence for an indiviudal on the week's "worst" day (as computed from plant-wide absence figures). To be sure, there are other measures of absence that are occasionally used, but the six measures just listed are the most common.

There are two major problems with these measures. The first problem involves the relative reliability of these measures, and the second issue concerns their operational definitions.

From an individual perspective, the reliability of the index of absence is critically important. If we are going to make inferences about the relative satisfaction of employees, if we plan to reward those with "outstanding" performance records, if we would like to identify administrative variables that might be contributing to high absence rates such as the work or shift schedules, we must start with a good, solid measure of absence. At the very least, this means that it must be reliable. As shown in Table 1.1, reliability can mean many different things and can be reduced by many different variables. In Table 2.2, we have identified several sources of

Table 2.2
Sources of Unreliability in Absence Data

Individual
    General health and resistance to illness
    Work-induced fatigue
    Nonwork-induced fatigue
    Current hobbies, leisure activities
    Shift
Environmental
    Ambient flu, virus, etc.
    Fluctuations in atmospheric conditions
Suborganizational
    Accuracy of supervisor in recording incident and reason
Administrative
    Accuracy of personnel office in transcribing supervisory attendance reports
    Administrative categories used for attribution of absence
    Level of aggregation of absence data (day, week, month, quarter; individual, work group, shift, plant, etc.)
    Index of absence used (i.e., number of total days per unit time, number of periods, ratio of total days to periods)

unreliability in absence data. These are only examples of the variables that might add error variance to our absence data. Thus, the list is neither exhaustive nor representative. It is presented to give a feel for the problems of measurement inherent in absence data.

The list in Table 2.2 suggests that unreliability in the data may be just as much a problem in dealing with legitimate absences as illegitimate ones. There are occasions when lots of people are out sick. In the winter, these absences often involve respiratory illnesses. In the summer, we might find a higher proportion of gastrointestinal illnesses. But the incidence of an illness and an absence may have nothing to do with the "constitution" or general state of health of the individual. It may be more closely linked to a transient flu epidemic or a pattern of social interactions. The same might be true of nonillness absences. The occasional absence due to reduced motivation to work may be a terribly unreliable phenomenon, seldom occurring.

The most common threat to reliability of absence measures is the period of time during which data are gathered. As an example, if we were to collect absence data for a period of 1 week, we would find the reliability very low. In other words, for any group of individuals, the correlation between the frequency of absence in two randomly chosen weeks would be very low. This suggests that a longer period is required for a more reliable measure.

How long a period should be used? The few studies that have reported reliabilities suggest relatively long periods of time—possibly as long as 1 year. The stability of absence measures over a 3-month period was appallingly low in a study described by Ilgen and Hollenback (1977). Reliability coefficients for several measures did not exceed .20. Chadwick-Jones et al. (1971) report reliabilities hovering in the .30 range for several measures gathered over a 1-year period. Farr, O'Leary, and Bartlett (1971) report similar values for a 6-month period. Latham and Pursell (1975) report reliabilities averaging .32 for a 12-week period of data collection.

Of all of the available measures, the frequency measure seems to be the most reliable (Muchinsky, 1977), but by conventional standards, even this reliability is poor, seldom exceeding .50. A more serious problem in interpreting research related to absenteeism is that few authors even bother to report the reliabilities of their absence indexes. This would not be as serious a problem if there were some general body of research that allowed for the calculation of some "expected value" of the reliability. Unfortunately, the fact that reliabilities are seldom reported places an extra burden on both the researcher and the administrator to develop local reliability data. This might not be particularly hard to do. If data are available on a group of employees randomly chosen from the work force for a substantial time period (e.g., 36 months), those data might be sequentially aggregated for progressively larger blocks of time and the reliabilities computed at each level of aggregation. For example, one might start looking at the reliability of data gathered for 1-week periods. The next step might be to look at data collected for 1-month periods, then for 2-, 4-, 6-, 8-, and 12-month periods, and so on until the largest block of time is used (in this case, 18 months for a split-half estimate of the reliability). A graph depicting the results of such an analysis is presented in Figure 2.1. This figure suggests that reliability is asymptotic, reaching its highest level at 12 months and leveling off after that point. This, in turn, suggests that we should use absence data aggregated over a 12-month period. Any shorter time period carries with it reduced reliability. As reliability data appear with more frequency in the literature, it will be possible to use estimates of reliability derived from other studies to make a decision about the necessary time period for data collection for various indexes. But until then, researchers and administrators should determine the most stable time period through local normative research.

A second, equally serious problem in interpreting research that is currently available concerns the operational definitions used to measure ab-

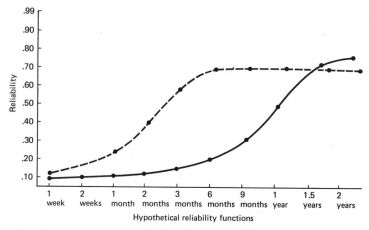

Figure 2.1. This graph depicts hypothetical reliability curves for two different absence measures. The solid line indicates unexcused absences; the broken line indicates excused absences. These were proposed in a study that examined absence patterns in a group of 70 clerical employees (Landy, Hedrick, & Bellamy, 1982).

sence. The indexes vary wildly from one study to another—there is no consistency in definition. For example, the period of time for which data are gathered might vary from 1 week to several years. The number used to represent an absence might be based on hours of work or weeks of work missed. Some studies deal with any absence, regardless of reason, whereas others exclude absence for medical reasons, and still others exclude from consideration days involving jury duty, union activities (presumably including strikes and other job actions), bereavement, and vacation. Thus, the conceptual characteristics of the index vary at the whim of the researchers. Muchinsky (1977) has termed this a problem of the "validity" of the measure.

A recurring finding is that many absence measures are unrelated to each other. For example, excused and unexcused absences tend to be uncorrelated. The number of vacation days taken is unrelated to the number of days charged as unexcused absences. This suggests two things: (a) broad measures of the number of people at work on a given day are relatively useless to the psychologist since they do not represent a unitary concept; and (b) one should think carefully about the object of the research or administrative procedure before choosing a specific absence measure.

Some have suggested that an attendance measure be used instead of an absence measure, since there is little ambiguity about a warm body in a work place on any given day (Latham & Pursell, 1975). This suggestion has been attacked as simpleminded and illusory (Ilgen, 1977; Smulders, 1980). The argument against this measure is that it gains its reliability from ignoring qualitative differences in type of absence (Smulders, 1980). In essence, when properly interpreted, the attendance measure is identical to the absence frequency (if the number of periods of attendance are counted) or absence severity/duration (if the number of days in a row at work are counted). As Smulders suggests, there is a problem, however, in the attendance measure with respect to how one might count 10 years of perfect attendance!

We feel obliged to offer a warning with respect to accepting any findings that are currently available in the literature. Do not draw inferences from summary descriptions of findings, abstracts of studies, or non-methodological reviews of literature dealing with absence. *Go and read the reports yourself.* Unless you can be sure that the index is reliable and fits the conceptual mold you have in mind for your use of those results, ignore the findings of the study. This is a terribly pessimistic prescription, but the current state of absence research does not warrant much optimism.

TURNOVER

Like absenteeism, turnover is one of those "countable" organizational indexes that is commonly used to represent performance. The logic is simple. Turnover costs money. It is expensive to recruit, select, and train individuals to take the places of those who have left. At its simplest level, a turnover statistic represents individuals who have decided to leave the organization, or organizational decisions to eliminate (either permanently or temporarily) certain employees. The simplicity is illusory here, as with absenteeism measures. We will consider the definitions, measurement, and conceptual issues related to measures of turnover.

Definitions

Turnover rate is generally defined as the ratio of quits per unit time to the average number of individuals in the work force for that time period. That seems simple enough. The complexities are introduced when we consider three parameters: (*a*) what is the definition of *quit*, or more generally the number in the numerator; (*b*) what is the period of time considered; and (*c*) are we considering all individuals in the work force or some special subgroup. We will deal with these three parameters in order.

The specification of what is to go into the numerator of the turnover equation is just as problematic as defining an absence. Most studies specify that only "voluntary" turnover was used, but the definition of *voluntary* is often missing, occasionally questionable, and frequently bizarre. In addition, it is often impossible to distinguish between *voluntary* turnover (e.g., leaving for a better position) and *involuntary* turnover (e.g., fired due to poor performance), thus *all* separation data often are included in the turnover statistic. In one study (Porter, Crampon, & Smith, 1976), the initial sample consisted of 212 individuals. Of that number, 56 joined a branch of the armed services, thus leaving a residual total of 156. The reader is told that 37 "voluntarily" left the organization over a 15-month period and 119 stayed. One is left to wonder if there were no terminations for cause or if all who left, regardless of reason, were classified as "voluntary." Similarly, some studies specify what was done with death, retirement, and layoffs, whereas others simply state that figures were taken from company records (without specifying *what* figures). This problem makes it virtually impossible to interpret the results of research without carefully examining the operational definition of *turnover* employed in the particular study. We would not contend that one definition of *turnover* is "correct" and others are in error, but we would caution the reader to be sensitive to finding out exactly what was used to construct the index.

A second problem in computing turnover rates concerns the period of time being considered. As we suggested in absence measurement, the time period may have substantial effects on the reliability of the index. This problem is compounded by the fact that in turnover studies, we have *one* observation per subject—they have either left or stayed. This is in contrast to an absence index, which would consider each scheduled work day as another observation. Thus, we have a range of time periods from 2 months (Newman, 1974) through 6 or more years (Hellreigel & White, 1973). Most studies seem to settle on 1 year as an appropriate time period, although why that is the case is unclear.[1] The time period is even more problematic than just the absolute amount of time. Turnover data are seldom gathered by a random selection of time units. Rather, turnover data temporally relate to the administration of a particular questionnaire. Thus, we read that turnover data were monitored from April 15 to July 31 (Kilbridge, 1961). The fact that this 3.5-month period of time is not a random selection from a larger population of all possible 3.5-month periods presents some rather formidable interpretation and inference problems. These problems are universally ignored.

The third problem relates to the focus of the turnover studies. Some deal with turnover rates in the work force as a whole. Thus, turnover for a 1-year period has at least some limited meaning even though the 1-year period was not randomly chosen. Other studies, however, concentrate on a specific 1-year period—the first year of employment for members of the organization. These studies usually are contrasting short-term and long-term turnover. As an example, Robinson (1972) has defined short-term turnover as turnover that occurs in the first 15 months of employment, whereas long-term turnover is that which occurs after 15 months. The logic is understandable—the research is interested in the phenomenon of "job hopping" or some similar concept. Unfortunately, it is not always clear whether this specific instance of turnover is being considered or a more general approach is being taken.

A final concern with indexes of turnover is distinguishing between absenteeism and turnover. This is a particularly acute problem when

[1]We suspect that it has more to do with the experimenter's concern for temporal symmetry or the manner by which companies collect and store data than it does with the implications of that time period for reliability of the index.

company records are being used as the data source. Some supervisors will record a termination on the first day or two of absence. Others will wait heroic periods of time (sometimes as long as 2 months) before they finally admit that a valued employee is not coming back to work. Latham and Pursell (1975) have documented these problems with respect to the recording of absence data; in fact it is part of their rationale for using an attendance statistic rather than an absence measure. Company records are notoriously poor representations of turnover and absence data if accepted uncritically. These records require some translation or interpretation before they can be of value.

We would advise the researcher or administrator to collect as specific an information set as possible surrounding each instance of turnover. These data should be kept regularly over extended periods of time, and the probable reason for the separation coded in as refined a form as possible. One can always collapse data across these categories, but one cannot decompose undifferentiated turnover rates at a later date. With respect to the currently available literature on turnover, we must urge the same caution as was suggested with the absence data: Do not accept summaries, reviews, or abstracts uncritically: Go and read the studies in their original form before accepting the findings.

GRIEVANCES

A *grievance* is an employee's complaint about some aspect of personnel administration or procedure. As such, it might be considered either a measure of the effectiveness of a supervisor or of the subordinate. As a supervisory performance index it is thought to represent the capacity of the supervisor to maintain harmonious relations with subordinates or to settle complaints at an informal level. As a performance index of the subordinate, in theory it represents a measure of the unwillingness of employees to listen to reason, the tendency to complain too much, and other negative behaviors. Most organizations feel that grievances should be minimized. The real issue is how this will be accomplished.

Grievance indexes as measures of performance have several problems. The most serious is that, almost by definition, grievances are filed exclusively by union members or their elected representatives. This means that grievance indexes are seldom available for nonunion workers or for supervisory or technical/professional personnel. There are some organizations that maintain a grievance mechanism for nonunion workers, but this is usually in the case of organizations that have both union and nonunion hourly workers. It is meant to be a parallel system to the union mechanism and would often not exist if there were not a represented group in the same environment.

Grievances are usually defined by the process that governs their filing. If an employee has a complaint about some aspect of personnel administration, the employee may file an appeal on a particular decision that affected him or her. For example, an employee might be suspended for a day due to a violation of company policy. The employee may claim that the decision was an unfair one and file an appeal. This appeal is known as a grievance, and most labor agreements or union contracts spell out in gory detail the procedure that must be followed for such an appeal. The first step is usually a discussion between the employee and the immediate supervisor (the individual who presumably imposed the punishment or at least approved of it). If the employee is not satisfied, the appeal is taken to the next level of supervision, usually a shift supervisor, department head, or plant manager. If the employee is still not satisfied, it might be sent on to a joint labor/management committee or a management hearing board for discussion and approval or rejection. If the employee is still not satisfied, the last step is to submit the appeal to arbitration. In this instance, an arbitrator is chosen or appointed to hear the appeal and the result is usually binding on both labor and management. Commonly, the union and management share in the cost of the arbitration. Thus, there is reason to try to settle disputes at the lowest possible level.

As a result of the procedure just outlined, most organizations consider a grievance as something that has not been settled by discussion. In the scheme described in the preceding paragraph, this would be at the third step in the process. Organizations commonly discard records of grievances that do not reach this step. This means that we might have, at best, a somewhat incomplete record of grievance behavior. Nevertheless, some organizations consider every formal complaint, regardless of the level it reaches, a grievance. Thus, we are once again faced with the problem of indexes that are not comparable from one study to another.

There have been some distinctions made over the years in the nature of grievances. Ash (1970) distinguishes between group grievances and name grievances. Group grievances are similar to class action suits in which all workers of a particular type (e.g., production workers, third-shift employees) complain about a personnel procedure that adversely affects all members of that group. Name grievances are usually complaints by a particular person concerning a particular decision that adversely affected him or her. Eckerman (1948) took a subordinate orientation in suggesting a distinction. He suggested that grievances could be either *initial* (the first one filed by an individual) or *other* (subsequent grievances filed by that individual). There is a "grievance proneness" flavor to that distinction. Turner (1960) took the opposite point of view and defined grievance rate as a characteristic of a supervisor.

Like several of the other countable measures of performance, there is no clear time period that has been identified as the most reliable for gathering such data; nor is there a clear indication of whose performance it represents. There are many other factors that mitigate the value of grievance indexes. To mention but two: (*a*) there is a tendency for unions to use the grievance procedure as a weapon in times of dissatisfaction (managers, with some justification, accuse union stewards of "papering the walls" with grievances just to waste the time of the supervisor); and (*b*) grievances are often withdrawn, as part of a negotiated "truce" between labor and management, even though they were formally filed. This is a form of "revisionism" of personnel records. Thus, the statement that data were collected from company files does not always tell the whole tale. If a grievance measure is of some interest to an organization, the questions of who is characterized by a grievance and over what time period data will be collected must be dealt with. If those issues can be resolved, it might make sense to count grievances that have reached some secondary level of discussion as measures of performance.

ACCIDENTS

It has been estimated that in the United States more than 12,500 workers die and over 2,200,000 workers are disabled by industrial accidents each year (Komaki, Barwick, & Scott, 1978). By any standard, this is a staggering rate. Anything that an organization might do to reduce or eliminate accidents would be of benefit both to the organization and the work force.

Accident data are gathered in many different forms. The most common of these forms is an index of lost time. Typically, an accident is recorded on the personnel record of an individual worker if a shift or a work day is lost. Accident data are often reported as injuries and may vary with respect either to the number of accidents/injuries or to the severity of that injury (measured as shifts or hours lost). The organizational index of accident rates is similar to absence and turnover indexes—the number of hours or shifts lost divided by the number of hours or shifts scheduled.

As was the case with other objective measures, there is confusion with respect to whether accidents are properties of jobs or workers. For example, most job evaluations include a factor called *hazard* in determining the pay class of a particular hourly job. Thus, an individual in a "dangerous" job will receive higher pay than an individual in a "safe" job, all other things being equal. This clearly implies that accidents are at least partially determined by the job duties. On the other hand, it has been popular over the years to consider the concept of accident proneness (Suchman & Scherzer, 1960) or the probability that some individuals will have more accidents than others when job duties are held constant. Over the years, investigators have examined psychomotor skills, personality traits, intelligence, and many other factors in an attempt to demonstrate that some individuals are more likely to have accidents than others. Thus, this second approach implies that an accident reflects characteristics of the worker rather than the job.

To be computed, an accident must usually appear in a medical record of some type. It may be dispensary visits, workman's compensation claims, or appointments with the industrial nurse. In research studies, the period of time over which these data are gathered varies widely, from several months to the entire time an employee is with an organization. Similarly, some studies record only that there was at least one accident during the period of time in question but not whether another accident occurred during that time.

The major problem with accident data relates to their validity. On an organizational level, it is obvious that accidents are costly and should be reduced. But at an individual level, the issue is not quite so clear. An accident is an instance of unsafe behavior that interacts with environmental conditions to produce an injury. The same unsafe behavior in one setting might result in death or serious injury, whereas that behavior might not cause even discomfort in another setting. If we would like to consider the performance of the individual independent of the environment effects on that performance, we would be better off to document and reduce instances of unsafe behavior. Since the interaction between unsafe behavior and environmental conditions is most likely multiplicative, the fewer the instances of unsafe behavior, the less likely it is that an accident will occur. Thus, we are arguing that accident statistics are often misleading at an individual level and should be reconsidered in light of the reasons for measuring them in the first place. At the risk of being seen as common scolds, we must also point out once again that the reliability of accident indexes for research purposes has not been addressed to date.

MEASURES OF OUTPUT

The "Holy Grail" of performance measurement is an index of output or production. In a free enterprise system, it is this index that ultimately determines the health and life expectancy of any single organization. As a result, there is a good deal of lip service paid to gathering output data as they relate to single individual or group performance. We will not go into great detail with respect to specific indexes. In part this is due to the fact that each index is determined, to some extent, by local conditions rather than individual behaviors. An equally important reason for not dealing with specific measures of productivity is that there are some more general considerations that are often obscured by such a listing or taxonomy of measures. We will try to deal with these general principles here. In later sections of this chapter, we will discuss approaches to operational definitions of output measures for specific occupations, as well as from industrial engineering principles. We will not do a detailed analysis of output measures that have appeared in studies over the years, but since it would be a shame not to at least list the measures that we have found in the course of our review, we have presented these measures, as well as the reference for each, in Table 2.3.

There are two ways to collect indexes of output. They can be gathered in absolute terms such as number per unit time, time per unit, pounds of scrap, or rejected units. They can also be gathered in comparative terms such as percentage of standard time, percentage of standard output, or percentage of mean shift performance. This difference is an important one because it suggests two parameters of output measures. One parameter might be labeled an optimization parameter and the other parameter is an absolute–comparative one. These two parameters are independent of one another and are both critical for utilizing output data for personnel research and administration.

The Optimization Parameter

A question that is seldom asked in performance measurement is "what is the *best* level of performance?" We generally assume that more is better.

Table 2.3
Representative Performance Measures from Varied Job Titles

Job Title	Measure	Reference
Typist	Lines per week	Yukl and Latham (1978)
Forester	Cords cut	Latham and Kinne (1974)
Keypuncher	Number of characters; number of errors	Johnson (1975)
Service representative	Errors in processing customer orders	Hackman and Porter (1968)
Toll collector	Dollar accuracy/axle accuracy	Farr, O'Leary, and Bartlett (1971)
Clerk	Errors per 100 documents checked; number of documents processed	Bassett (1979)
Wood harvesters	Number of cords delivered	Latham and Locke (1975)
Tree planters	Bags of tree seedlings planted	Yukl and Latham (1975)
Typist	Number of strokes; number of errors	West (1969)
Skateboard makers	Number produced; number rejected	Newman, Hunt, and Rhodes (1966)
Sewing machine operators	Minutes per operation	Lefkowitz (1970)
Loggers	Weight of wood legally hauled	Latham and Baldes (1975)
Dentists	Errors in reading radiographs	Goldstein and Mobley (1971)
Foreman in open hearth	Time between "taps"	Cleven and Fiedler (1956)
Inspectors	Errors detected in finished product	Chaney and Teel (1967)
Tool makers–die makers	Dies produced	Ivancevich (1978)
Helicopter pilots	Deviations from proper instrument readings	Isley and Caro (1970)
Bank tellers	Number of shortages; number of overages	Bass and Turner (1973)
Air traffic controllers	Speed of movement of aircraft through the system Correction of pilot error Errors in positioning aircraft for final approach Errors in aircraft separation	Kidd and Christy (1961)

This is not necessarily the case. Even Frederick W. Taylor, the apostle of scientific management, realized that Schmidt might burn out if he worked too fast or hard as we can see in the following instructions given to Schmidt by Taylor. "You will do exactly as this man tells you tomorrow from morning till night. When he tells you to pick up a pig and walk, you pick it up and walk and when he tells you to sit down and rest, you sit down. [Taylor, 1947, p. 44]." This simple principle is not evident in most performance indexes. This is true independent of whether we are considering absolute or comparative performance. Things to consider in defining "best" levels of performance would include employee turnover, satisfaction and accidents, performance consistency, equipment efficiency, and possibly even market "saturation" indexes. The point is that performance might be better indexed as a deviation from optimal rather than a deviation from maximum.

The Absolute–Comparative Parameter

One can clearly distinguish between absolute and comparative indexes of performance. Thus, one study will report that the measure of typing productivity was number of words per minute averaged over a number of randomly selected periods, whereas a second study will report that output was indexed as the number of units over or under the "standard" established for that job. The first measure is an absolute one, whereas the second is comparative. Note that both measures ignore the notion of the optimal level of performance. There are good reasons for choosing a comparative measure of performance over an absolute one, even if the optimization parameter is ignored. A wide range of discrimination-learning research suggests that comparative evaluations are easier to make, more accurate, and more reliable than absolute evaluations. In addition, when comparative measures are gathered, there is less interpretation required in terms of levels such as "high," "average," or "low" levels of performance. Finally, comparative indexes are more easily communicated to the performer and thus can play a more significant directive role than absolute measures. Absolute measures represent a type of "do your best" exhortation that has been shown to be inefficient in many situations (Locke, Shaw, Saari, & Latham, 1981). There seems to be a growing tendency among organizations to develop "performance standards." This is a healthy development and will eventually lead to more reliable data. The question of the validity of those data will be addressed more directly by the optimization parameter, and as far as we can tell, there is little research activity on that topic.

Another way of categorizing output or productivity measures might be in terms commonly used in educational settings to characterize test performance measures. Tests are described as either "norm referenced" or "criterion referenced." A norm-referenced test is one that is scored by comparing an observed score to norm tables derived from the performance of some appropriate standardization sample. A criterion-referenced test, on the other hand, is scored in terms of whether an individual was able to meet or exceed some required level of performance. A similar distinction might prove valuable in measuring work performance. Thus, a measure such as *percentage of standard time* might be considered a norm-referenced index, whereas the *time required to complete an operation* might represent a criterion-referenced index (particularly if the operation is machine paced and some estimate of "adequate" performance can be obtained).

OCCUPATIONAL MEASURES OF PERFORMANCE

In addition to examining nonjudgmental measures of performance according to conceptual category, we can also look at measures that are peculiar to particular occupations. Some of these measures come to mind immediately; measures such as sales success for sales representatives, or arrests for police officers. Other measures are not so obvious. In this section, we will consider a small number of particular occupations that have received some attention from researchers regarding objective measures of performance.

Sales

One of the most ubiquitous job titles is that of sales representative. A measure of sales success would seem obvious—number of sales or dollar volume of those sales. Such measures are common and have intuitive appeal. But measures of dollar volume or number of sales agreements must often be qualified or adjusted to account for factors outside of the control of the sales representative. We will consider some of these adjustments as well as additional indexes of sales performance.

There are two distinct categories of sales measures: outcome measures and behavioral measures. The outcome measures are the traditional ones—sales volume, type of sale, sale renewal, etc. The behavioral measures deal more with what the sales representative actually does and to a lesser degree with the outcome of those behaviors.

OUTCOME MEASURES. Some organizations use the most primitive of measures—dollar volume of sales over a fixed period of time (e.g., 6 months or 1 year). Other organizations use a dozen or more measures to represent the productivity of a sales representative. Roach and Wherry (1970) derived 36 different measures of sales performance for various categories of insurance sales representatives. These measures included new policies, new premiums, company cancellations, new coverages, nonpay cancellations, loss ratio (claims losses/premiums), and face amount of new policies. Kirchner (1965) considered the performance of sales representatives selling outdoor advertising on several dimensions including number of signs sold, amount of materials sold, delinquent accounts collected, and property leases obtained for outdoor sign erection. Harris and Vincent (1967) considered the performance of new insurance sales representatives with respect to the number of insurance premiums produced, the average size of the life insurance policy produced, the number of policies produced, the length of time that a policy remained in effect, and some ancillary measures of automobile and fire insurance policy sales.

Most sales managers and sales representatives will tell you that the indexes described in the preceding paragraph are anything but "objective." They would contend that many factors other than the performance of the individual sales representative affect those numbers. As a result of such objections, many attempts have been made to "clean up" those indexes so that they more accurately reflect the contribution of the individual sales representative. Ronan and Prien (1971) suggest that sales success be measured in terms of the percentage of the monthly quota achieved by the individual. This suggests that sales managers can accurately set goals or quotas that take into account differences in territory, product line, and so on. They also suggest that the sales volume figure be adjusted for the number of months that the individual has been in the territory such that the same sales volume would be more impressive if an individual had just recently picked up the territory than if the individual had worked that territory for several years. Miner (1972) examined the sales performance of sales representatives for oil companies and suggested that sales figures be adjusted for economic conditions in the territory of the representative. Cravens and Woodruff (1973) proposed that raw sales figures tell us more about the sales territory performance than the sales representative performance. They suggest that sales figures be corrected for industry market potential, territory workload, sales representative experience, company experience in the territory, and company effort in the territory.

These adjustments form quite a list. Nevertheless, they tell us something important: Raw sales figures do not always tell us what we want to know. But some of the adjustments create their own problems. For example, we mentioned that Ronan and Prien (1971) proposed a measure of sales success that included time in territory. They suggested the following ratio:

$$\text{Sales success} = \frac{\text{Net sales}}{\text{Months in territory}}$$

Consider the individual who moves quickly into an area, immediately makes all sales available, and maintains those sales forever after. That representative's sales success index must inevitably decline over time as a simple result of the increasing size of the denominator. A similar result occurred in past measures of intelligence in which an intelligence quotient (IQ) was computed as some ratio of mental to chronological age. Intelligence appeared to decline with age simply because the denominator had increased while the numerator remained constant. This may have been how our stereotypes regarding older individuals developed. In the area of sales success, such a measure would guarantee that sales representatives would appear to "burn out."

As an alternative to sales volume measures, some have suggested that sales performance be measured in terms of what the sales representative does rather than the outcome of those behaviors. Baker and Schuck (1975) studied life insurance sales representatives and defined successful performance in terms of the presence or absence of the following behaviors: (a) presence of a smile before speaking; (b) use of proper remarks in introduction; (c) use of correct response to objections of prospect; (d) promptness of response to objections; (e) perseverance in seeking an interview with a prospect; (f) reminding prospect of appointment time; (g) using correct name in addressing prospect; (h) thanking the prospect regardless of outcome; and (i) concentrating on selling the interview rather than insurance. These behaviors beg a question in the sense that they imply that if each is correctly carried out a sale is likely. If we assume that such a relationship had been established by past research, the Baker and Schuck dimensions will produce quite reasonable criterion-referenced performance indexes as described earlier. If, on the other hand, these measures have been simply pulled out of the air either by the researchers or the organization, they represent not criterion measures but simply potential predictors. In the case where the organization would *prefer* that the representative act this way regardless of impact on sales, then these behaviors could hardly be considered measures of sales success. Instead, they might represent measures of willingness to comply with company policy (a much broader criterion) or even measures of learning.

Some measures imply an interaction between behaviors and outcomes. Pace (1962) defined sales success as a ratio of the dollar value of sales divided by the number of hours of active selling. This suggests that the best sales representatives spend the least amount of time selling. Although this proposition might be heartily endorsed by experienced representatives who have been in well-established regions for long periods of time, it is unlikely that such a relationship would form the core of a training program for new hires. Kirchner (1960) suggests that sales performance might be measured in terms of several ratios. For example, he considers the number of orders to calls made, the number of calls to the number of days worked, the number of new account calls to days worked, and the number of orders taken to the number of new account calls made. These indexes suggest some very complicated relationships among and between behavioral and outcome measures of sales success.

In the sales representative position, the number of potential objective measures is encouraging, but little or no work has been done to date on either the reliability or the validity of those measures. In addition, the lion's share of available research has been done on insurance sales. Little has appeared describing industrial sales and even less on retail sales. This is a fruitful area for further consideration.

Management

Another popular occupational grouping for study has been that of manager. A disturbingly common measure of management success (at least in levels above first-level supervisor) has been either rate of promotion or salary growth (Ghiselli & Siegal, 1972; Hulin, 1962; Kraut, 1969; Srinivasan, Shocker, & Weinstein, 1973; Tenopyr, 1969). As pointed out by Klimoski and Strickland (1977), there is no necessary relationship between salary–advancement measures and performance. Rusmore (1973) operationalized the bias implicit in these measures. He suggested that a management advancement quotient be computed by dividing the individual's "management age" (the mean age of managers at the individual's level in the organization) by his or her chronological age and multiplying by 100. Time in rank becomes a definite handicap for managers when measures such as these are used, particularly if colleagues are being replaced with younger additions.

Other attempts to measure management success have fallen into two specific categories: those that consider management process and those that consider management substance. The management process measures would include things such as the number of grievances in the work group, the rate of turnover, the number of absences, the number of suggestions offered by workers, the number of injuries, or the number of hospital passes requested (Turner, 1960). These approaches assume that if a manager were doing a good job, "bad" things would not happen (e.g., accidents, absences, quits). The implication is that management is a matter of handling (managing) the context or the process of work. It suggests that management is a series of roles that must be filled either sequentially or simultaneously by the manager. Figure 2.2 is a representation of such a role approach. This figure shows why measures such as grievance rate,

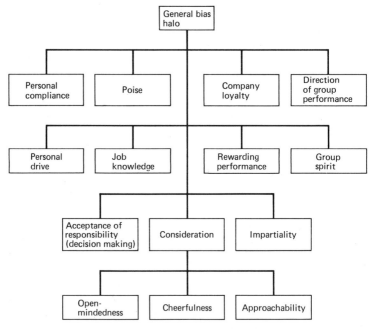

Figure 2.2. A hierarchy of supervisory evaluation factors. (From D. E. Roach, Factor analysis of rated supervisory behavior. *Personnel Psychology,* 1956, *9,* p. 491.)

absence, and turnover would be considered objective measures of a manager's performance.

A different point of view is presented by Lamouria and Harrell (1963). They suggest that there are certain substantive responsibilities that describe management duties (and by extension, management success). These responsibilities include profit, diversification, growth, and welfare. This approach suggests that management success has less to do with the process of managing a group and more to do with the productivity of that group. There are many theories and taxonomies of management or supervision that take this approach. For example, Hemphill (1960) studied a number of executives and developed a series of nine components that comprise a manager's job. These dimensions and their constituent parts are described in Table 2.4. As you can see from examining this table, each component suggests its own criterion measure. Some of these measures might fall into the objective grouping whereas others would be considered "judgmental." For example, in the internal business control component (Cluster C), one should be able to get a number that represents cost reduction over some period of time. On the other hand, the business reputation component (Cluster H) would seem to require a judgment by someone with respect to manager adequacy rather than an objective measure of some sort.

With the exception of salary growth and advancement rate, there has been little concerted effort in developing criteria of management success. In recent years, management by objectives (MBO) has become a popular way of motivating managers and nonmanagers alike. In this system, work-related goals are set and progress toward those goals recorded. It may be that a content analysis of this type of data will tell us something about the aspects of a manager's performance that can be measured with nonjudgmental indexes. At this point, we can only describe the potential of measuring success rather than the reality of the phenomenon.

Police Officers

During the 1960s, the Law Enforcement Assistance Administration (LEAA) was formed in order to aid municipal and state law enforcement agencies in carrying out their duties. The LEAA was engaged in everything from supplying weapons to conducting research in police officer selection and training. It was this latter category of activity that stimulated interest in measures of police officer performance. These measures were thought to have relevance for several different issues. In the first place, the LEAA was interested in knowing how efficient individual departments

Table 2.4
Dimensions of an Executive Job

Cluster A: Providing a staff service in nonoperational areas
  Is considered a staff rather than a line position
  Be capable of performing the jobs of all subordinates
  Selection of new employees
  (Services such as gathering information, interviewing, selecting employees, briefing superiors, checking statements, verifying facts, or making recommendations)
Cluster B: Supervision of work
  Troubleshoot special problems as they arise
  Plan the best use of available facilities
  Involves firsthand contact with machines and their operation
  (Planning, organization, and control of the work of others, direct contact with workers and with the machines they use, and concern with getting work done effectively and efficiently)
Cluster C: Internal business control
  Maintenance of proper inventories
  Reduction of costs
  Review budgets for operations
  (Cost reduction, inventory control, budget preparation, justification of capital expenditures, determination of goals, definition of supervisory responsibilities, payment of salaries, or enforcement of regulations)
Cluster D: Technical aspects with products and markets
  Anticipate new or changed demands for products and services
  Assist salesmen in securing important accounts
  Involves firsthand contact with customers of the company
  (Concern with product–market–customer details and relations, development of new business, checking on activities of competitors, changes in demand, customer contact, data analysis, and assistance in sales)
Cluster E: Human, community, and social affairs
  Be active in community affairs
  Nominate key personnel in the organization for promotion
  Take a leading part in local community projects
  (Working well with others, both in and out of the organization; concern for company goodwill; public speaking; evaluating people and their performance; and participation in community and civic affairs)
Cluster F: Long-range planning
  Keep informed about the latest technical developments in a professional area
  Long-range solvency of the company
  Long-range objectives of the organization
  (Oriented toward the future of the organization; thinking about, and planning for, the future in industrial relations, management development, organizational objectives, corporate solvency, new ventures, new ideas, and new legislation relevant to the organization)
Cluster G: Exercise of broad power and authority
  Provides opportunity for actually managing an important part of the business
  Offers an opportunity to gain experience in management

Continued

Table 2.4 (*continued*)

Make recommendations on matters at least as important as the construction of a new plant
    (Status, independence, and power are the key characteristics of this dimension)
Cluster H: Business reputation
    Directly affects the quality of the company products or services
    Involves activities that are not closely supervised or controlled
    Avoid any public comment critical of a good customer or supplier
    (Responsibility for reputation of the organization's products or services; for both product
        design and public relations, requiring little in the way of attention to details but making
        rather stringent demands on personal behavior)
Cluster I: Personal demands
    Refrain from activities that might imply sympathy for unions
    Involves spending at least 10 hours per week in direct association with superiors
    Spend at least 50 hours per week on the job
    (Constraints upon the personal behavior of the incumbent, calling for propriety of behav-
        ior, fulfilling the stereotype of the conservative businessman)

Source: Campbell, J., Dunnette, M., Lawler, E., & Weick, K. *Managerial behavior, performance, and effectiveness.* New York: McGraw-Hill, 1970. Pp. 86–88.

were in some absolute sense. But before this could be done, it was necessary somehow to define the concept of departmental "efficiency." A secondary purpose for developing measures of police officer performance was
for the validation of various selection devices and the evaluation (validation) of training programs, both academy and on-the-job components. As
a result of this interest, a number of studies examined the potential indexes
of performance, both objective and judgmental (Landy & Farr, 1976).
We were heavily involved in the judgmental effort, as were several other
psychologists. Reviews of these measures can be found in several sources.
In this section, we will deal exclusively with nonjudgmental measures.

The first measure of police performance that springs to mind is *number
of arrests*. This is one of the most obvious and sensational of police activities. Unfortunately, as is the case with almost every other objective
index of performance, it is ambiguous. For example, if we wanted to
maximize arrests, we would simply ask officers to walk out the door of
their precinct and arrest every individual they came in contact with until
their shift was over. For the sake of department morale, we might ask
them to refrain from arresting each other. It is obvious that there is such a
thing as a "good" arrest and a "bad" arrest. A good arrest might be one
that involved proper procedures and eventually resulted in a conviction.
But if the case resulted in an acquittal because a crucial witness failed to
appear for the trial, we might still want to consider the arrest a "good"
one. These are but a few of the problems plaguing the measurement of
police officer output. In Table 2.5 we list most of the common objective

Table 2.5
Common Measures of Police Officer Performance

Number of arrests for felony offenses	Number of chargeable accidents
Number of arrests for misdemeanor offenses	Danger-tension index: Number of arrests divided by sick days taken × 100
Number of traffic citations issued	
Number of accident reports taken	Clearance rates: Number of incidents reported divided by number of arrests for such incidents
Number of nontraffic cases in court	
Number of convictions on court cases	
Number of letters of commendation from the public	Average time required to respond to calls in various categories (felony, traffic, etc.)
Number of trial board hearings	
Number of written reprimands	Percent of crimes solved in less than "x" days
Number of sick days used	
Number of department citations	Time required to solve a crime
Number of precinct citations	Number of arrests without use of force
Number of shots fired in line of duty	Number of resisting arrest charges filed by officer[a]
Number of citizen complaints sustained	

[a]This may seem like an unusual measure of police officer performance, but some suggest that this index, at least when abnormally high, represents brutality on the part of the officer. The charge is filed by the officer to shift the focus to the suspect.

measures of police performance. Reviews and discussions of these measures can be found in Spielberger (1979) and Cohen and Chaiken (1972).

As shown in this list, there are quite a few indexes to choose from in describing police performance. The job of a police officer is terribly complex and involves being a doctor, lawyer, social worker, crime buster, and dozens of other major and minor work roles. As the number of distinct activities in a job increases, it is likely that the number of potential objective indexes will also increase. Simple jobs will be more easily characterized than complicated ones. Unfortunately, with respect to the measures of police performance, little information is generally available regarding reliability, validity, or sensitivity.

Scientists and Engineers

The productivity of engineers and scientists was central to the cold war between the Eastern bloc nations and the United States that began with the launching of Sputnik. Effective performance of individuals in those particular job titles was equated with winning that "war." As a result, there were many studies of the productivity of scientific personnel. Most of the attention was focused on the predictors of success, but the criterion variable came under examination as well. In the section on the productivity of managers, a study by Lamouria and Harrell (1963) was cited. The managers in this study were supervising the work of research scientists, and their measures of the effectiveness of these scientists included the number of papers written, the number of publications, the number of patent disclosures, and similar indexes. These are some of the most commonly used indexes of scientists' productivity or output, particularly in the physical sciences. Chaney (1966) measured the number of patent specifications published and the number of technical articles accepted for publication as his measure of industrial research scientist performance in a cross-cultural study. Friedlander (1971) examined scientists in research and development units and characterized their performance in terms of number of articles published in journals, number of articles appearing in local–internal publications, number of papers at professional meetings, and the number of societies in which the scientist was a member. Judgment as to the quality of the articles and papers was presumably left to editorial boards.[2] Barnowe (1975) suggested an additional consideration. He suggested that the extent to which the individual was solely or principally responsible for the product (paper, publication) rather than jointly responsible (as a co-author) be taken into account. This would suggest a concern for "adjusting" the measure similar to those encountered in sales or production success so that the individual's unique contribution could be identified.

It seems reasonably clear that research scientists are expected to produce ideas that are both unique and of value to others. These ideas are documented in the form of papers, articles, patents, and devices. As was the case with many other objective measures, the psychometric characteristics (e.g., reliability, validity, sensitivity) of these measures remain unknown.

Other Occupations

It is obvious that we have overlooked literally thousands of job titles in our treatment of performance indexes for particular occupations. This was not inadvertent. It was not our purpose to write the "Encyclopedia of

[2]When performance is measured in this manner, it is difficult not to think of the admonition of an apocryphal reviewer that given the choice of "publish or perish," some authors might well choose the latter.

Performance Indexes." Nevertheless, in the occupations that have attracted some broad attention from behavioral researchers, we have tried to describe the performance measures. There are many other single studies that have produced unique definitions of objective performance. We presented a sample of those definitions in Table 2.3. We make no claims on behalf of these measures; we simply list them for your consideration. We did not list in that table any studies of general production workers in manufacturing organizations. The objective index used almost uniformly is percentage of standard. This standard is usually set by the industrial engineering department, and you should carefully consider the normative–criterion–referenced distinction made earlier in the chapter before choosing such an index.

Some Issues to Consider

The importance of nonjudgmental measures of performance is obvious. Variables such as production speed and accuracy, accident rates, and absenteeism all play an important role in the ultimate survival of any enterprise. Despite the fact that there are problems in measuring many of these variables at the individual level, at higher levels of aggregation such as the work group, the shift, or the department or the plant level they can be reliable, useful, and sensitive. In other words, even though we may not completely understand all of the variables that influence performance and behavior at the individual level, we may still be able to affect these behaviors at an aggregate level.

At the individual level of measurement, certain basic improvements can be made that might add to our understanding of industrial behavior. One improvement that should be made is at the taxonomic level. Our review of the literature in the absence and turnover area demonstrated how capricious these data were. The definitions of categories such as "voluntary absence," "quit," and "mutually agreed upon departure" leave much to be desired. At the very least, researchers should endeavor to provide good descriptions of how categorization was done. Perhaps we might even come to some agreement on a standard set of definitions. Such a conceptual standardization might go far in improving prediction and reliability at the individual level of analysis.

Another simple improvement that might be made in the area of nonjudgmental measures of performance is the simple reporting of basic psychometric data that characterize the specific measures under consideration. This would include means, standard deviations, departures from normality (or symmetry), and reliability estimates. At least this might provide the reader with some feel for how "trustworthy" and/or generalizable the results of the study are.

There is a great debate raging in psychology today. This debate concerns the consistency and predictability of behavior. The trait theorists suggest that behavior is consistent from one setting to another and from one time to another. The interactionists, on the other hand, suggest that behavior may vary dramatically from one time to another depending on the nature of the situation. If the interactionists are "right," it makes the search for consistency in production rates, absence, and accidents somewhat quixotic. Since the debate is likely to continue unabated for some time before the issue is resolved, no final statement can be made about the ultimate value of nonjudgmental measures of performance at the level of the individual worker. Nevertheless, we can suggest that these measures of performance can be effectively used as intraindividual data. It may be quite informative to look at changes in an individual's performance on various dimensions over time. Such longitudinal examinations might provide useful information about trends in behavior (i.e., changes that are not obvious in single-occasion data collection). This may even make the issue of reliability irrelevant, or at least less important.

In any event, there are many uses for these types of data at both the individual and group level. It is likely that our conceptual understanding and our measurement capabilities will improve rapidly in the next decade. Organizations are not likely to lose interest in absenteeism or productivity in the near future.

SUMMARY

There are many different ways that might be used to describe the performance of a given individual. We might look at the behavior of the individual, record it, and later attach values to what we saw. Another possibility might be simply to look at the results of the behavior of that individual: This is commonly referred to as output. We can record how long it took, how much it weighed, how many pieces were perfect, and so forth. Finally, we might look at both behavior and output but record neither. We might simply use this information to make a judgment about the individual in question. These are the choices we have. In this chapter, we have examined methods for observing and recording the first two forms of performance data—behavior and results of behavior. In the next chapter we will consider judgments.

There are many limiting conditions to performance—conditions that either add to or detract from the overall efficiency of both the individual and the organization. Some of these limiting conditions would be accidents, absence, turnover, and grievances. Since each of these variables is in turn affected by many others, there are problems in collecting and using these data as measures of performance at the individual level. These problems include both statistical ones and conceptual ones. Often the data are unreliable; equally often, we do not know what they are telling us. Nevertheless, they are important indicators of efficiency and can be quite useful when aggregated across time and individuals.

Output measures are often thought of as "objective." The implication is that they are not open to interpretation, that they are unambiguous and reliable. Unfortunately, there are problems in collecting these data as well. The results of behavior are influenced by co-workers, supervisors, machinery, supplies, and dozens of other variables. This means that a particular output measure is only partially a property of a given individual. It also "belongs" to co-workers, machines, and so forth. It is important that we know the degree to which these nonworker factors are affecting output rates.

In the past, the pressure on the production floor has been for maximization. Turn out as many as possible in as short a time as possible with as few rejections as possible. Given the nature of the human organism, this may not be the most appropriate strategy for peak efficiency. It might be more appropriate to adopt an optimization principle that stresses ideal rates for man and machine. Most of our measures of output imply maximization. In selection, we are trying to identify the individual who will produce the most, or the best, or the fastest. The optimization principle might suggest very different selection, training, and motivation programs.

In measuring performance, many different pieces of information will be required to describe a given worker reasonably. This will include both judgmental and nonjudgmental data. It is important that we recognize both the capacities and the limitations of these data.

chapter three

Judgmental Measures of Work Performance

By far the most widely used performance measurement techniques are judgmental ones. As noted in Chapter 2, for many occupations objective performance measures other than absenteeism and turnover are rarely developed or used. Most reviews of the popularity of various performance measures in *published* research studies suggest that about three-quarters of such investigations used judgmental criteria as the primary criterion variable (e.g., Guion, 1965; Landy & Trumbo, 1980). In actual practice in organizations we would estimate a similar popularity for judgmental measures.

Despite the widespread use of judgmental performance measures, it appears that everyone involved is generally dissatisfied with them, including researchers, administrators, raters, and ratees. The dissatisfaction appears to arise from the fact that judgmental measures are vulnerable to both intentional and inadvertent bias (Landy & Farr, 1980). This dissatisfaction has been an impetus for an enormous amount of research aimed at improving existing measures and at creating new formats or techniques that are more resistant to bias.

In this chapter we present descriptive information about various kinds of judgmental performance measures. We then present research findings related to the various measures as well as to several format questions that cut across specific kinds of measures. In the second section of the chapter, we also address the question of the criteria that can be used to evaluate judgmental criterion measures. A third major section then presents a brief discussion of some general issues in the judgment of work performance.

TYPES OF JUDGMENTAL MEASURES

Judgmental measures of work performance may be classified in a number of ways. One of the simplest classifications is similar to that proposed in Chapter 2 for nonjudgmental, criterion-referenced, and norm-referenced performance measures. Criterion-referenced measures attempt to describe or evaluate the work performance of an individual employee without reference to other individuals but with reference to some standard or standards of performance. Norm-referenced measures are concerned with comparing the performance of an individual with that of another individual or a group of other employees.

Criterion-Referenced Measures

GRAPHIC RATING SCALE. Donald Paterson introduced the graphic rating scale to the general psychological community in 1922. In his opinion, this new method was characterized by two things: (a) the rater was freed from quantitative judgments; and (b) the rater was able to make as fine a discrimination as desired. The scales consisted of trait labels, brief definitions of those labels, and unbroken lines with varying types and number of adjectives below. A variety of graphic scales have since been used as shown in Figure 3.1. These scales vary along several factors: (a) the degree to which the meaning of the response categories is defined or is ambiguous; (b) the degree to which the rater is able to convey his or her intended rating response; and (c) the degree to which the performance dimension is defined for the rater. The relative ambiguity or meaningfulness of response categories is addressed through what can be termed the process of "anchoring." Anchors are an attempt to convey meaning about the various points on the rating scale, just as markings on a ruler convey information about length. As shown in Figure 3.1, there is considerable variation in the anchors that have commonly been used with graphic rating scales. Some graphic rating scale anchors are merely numbers or only transmit information about the directionality of the scale (e.g., "high" and "low" as anchors for the scale endpoints). Other anchors, such as those in scales (c)

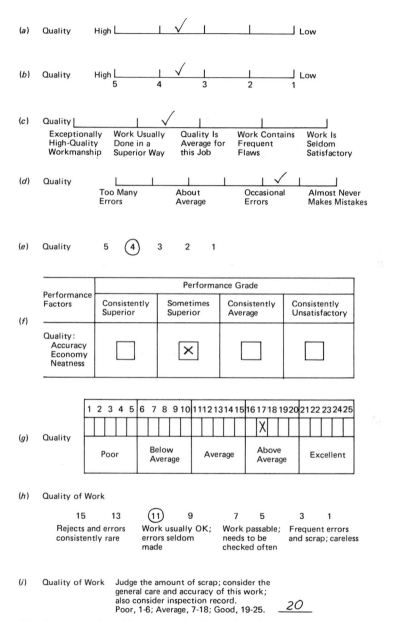

(a) Quality   High |___|_√_|___|___| Low

(b) Quality   High |___|_√_|___|___| Low
         5   4   3   2   1

(c) Quality |___|_√_|___|___|

| Exceptionally High-Quality Workmanship | Work Usually Done in a Superior Way | Quality Is Average for this Job | Work Contains Frequent Flaws | Work Is Seldom Satisfactory |

(d) Quality

| Too Many Errors | About Average | Occasional Errors √ | Almost Never Makes Mistakes |

(e) Quality   5 (4) 3 2 1

(f)

Performance Factors	Performance Grade			
	Consistently Superior	Sometimes Superior	Consistently Average	Consistently Unsatisfactory
Quality: Accuracy Economy Neatness	☐	☒	☐	☐

(g) Quality

1 2 3 4 5	6 7 8 9 10	11 12 13 14 15	16 17 18 19 20	21 22 23 24 25
Poor	Below Average	Average	Above Average X	Excellent

(h) Quality of Work

   15   13   (11) 9   7   5   3   1

| Rejects and errors consistently rare | Work usually OK; errors seldom made | Work passable; needs to be checked often | Frequent errors and scrap; careless |

(i) Quality of Work   Judge the amount of scrap; consider the general care and accuracy of this work; also consider inspection record.
Poor, 1-6; Average, 7-18; Good, 19-25.   _20_

Figure 3.1. Examples of graphic rating scales. (From R. M. Guion. *Personnel testing.* New York: McGraw-Hill, 1965, p. 98.)

and (i) in Figure 3.1, are more informative regarding the various response points along the scale.

The clarity to another individual of the intended rating response given by a rater also varies among the scales shown in Figure 3.1. Scales (a) to (d) in Figure 3.1 can be ambiguous, as the rater can check any point on the scale continuum, but another individual may not be sure exactly what was intended. Scales (e) to (h) are reasonably clear with regard to the rater's intended rating.

The meaning of the particular dimension of work performance being evaluated can also vary in clarity. In Figure 3.1 it can be seen that in scales (a), (b), (e), and (g) the rater must define the dimension in the absence of any guidance from the scale itself. This can obviously be a major source of disagreement among raters regarding ratee performance. Scales (f) and (i), and to some extent (h), do a better job of defining the performance dimension.

Dissatisfaction with graphic rating scales has led to efforts to develop other types of criterion-referenced judgmental measures. Several of these are described in the following sections.

BEHAVIORALLY ANCHORED RATING SCALES (BARS). Among the more systematic attempts to improve graphic rating scales were those that attempted to reduce the ambiguity of scale anchors. The most common attempt was to replace simple numerical and adjectival anchors with descriptions of actual job behaviors that reflected varying levels of effectiveness on the performance dimension under consideration. Coupled with an emphasis on behavioral anchors was the use of scaling procedures, borrowed from psychophysics and attitude measurement, and designed to improve the psychometric properties of the resulting measures.

The seminal work on BARS was that of Smith and Kendall (1963). The Smith and Kendall format and developmental procedure have become widely used either in the original form or with variations. Not all of the variations have adhered to the fundamental elements of the Smith and Kendall approach (Bernardin & Smith, 1981). Table 3.1 presents the procedural sequence suggested by Smith and Kendall for the development of BARS.

As shown in Table 3.1, the procedure for developing BARS is quite complex and demanding in terms of time and the number of job experts (usually incumbents and/or supervisors) required. In the ideal case each step of the procedure uses a separate group of job experts. The number of experts in each group has varied widely with 15–30 being common. Fig-

Table 3.1
Procedure for Development of Behaviorally Anchored Rating Scales (BARS)

Identification and definition of performance dimensions	Group A of job experts identifies all important dimensions of performance for job in question. They also define conceptually each performance dimension and define high, average, and low performance on each dimension.
Generation of behavior examples	Group B of job experts gives examples of good, average, and poor job behaviors for each performance dimension. (Examples are edited by personnel researchers to reduce redundancy and to place each example in the expectation format.)
Retranslation and allocation	Group C of job experts is presented with a randomized list of behavioral examples and a list of the performance dimensions. They each independently allocate or classify each behavioral example to the performance dimension that it best represents. (A behavioral example is eliminated by the personnel researcher unless a large majority [e.g., 70%] of the group assigns it to the same performance dimension.)
Scaling	Group D of job experts evaluates the behavioral examples meeting the allocation criterion in the previous step in terms of the effectiveness of the performance described.
Scale anchor selection	Personnel researcher computes the mean and standard deviation of the ratings given to each behavioral example in the scaling step. Examples are selected as anchors for each performance dimension such that items have mean values that provide anchors for the entire performance scale (from low to high) and that items have relatively small standard deviations.

ure 3.2 shows BARS for the performance dimension of skill in human relationships for the job of nurse.

The behavioral anchors on the BARS shown in Figure 3.2 are worded in a "could be expected to" format. Smith and Kendall believed this feature solved certain possible problems with behaviorally anchored scales. The rater is not being asked whether he or she had actually observed the ratee behaving in a manner indicated by one of the example anchors. Rather, the rater is asked to infer or predict the behavior of the ratee in terms of the scale authors based on the rater's past observations of the ratee's work performance. Because the specific job behaviors used to anchor a rating scale can only be a small sample of the population of job

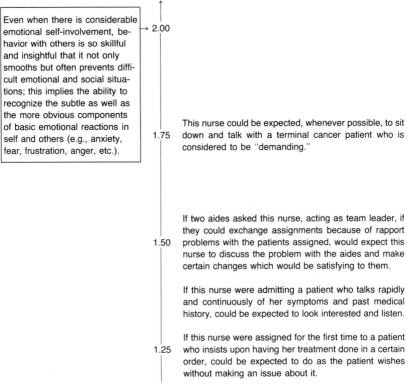

Skill in human relationships (*with patients, families, and co-workers*)
behaves in a manner appropriate to the situation and individuals involved.

Even when there is considerable
emotional self-involvement, be-   → 2.00
havior with others is so skillful
and insightful that it not only
smooths but often prevents difficult emotional and social situations; this implies the ability to
recognize the subtle as well as
the more obvious components
of basic emotional reactions in   This nurse could be expected, whenever possible, to sit
self and others (e.g., anxiety,   1.75 down and talk with a terminal cancer patient who is
fear, frustration, anger, etc.).   considered to be "demanding."

                                         If two aides asked this nurse, acting as team leader, if
                                         they could exchange assignments because of rapport
                                   1.50 problems with the patients assigned, would expect this
                                         nurse to discuss the problem with the aides and make
                                         certain changes which would be satisfying to them.

                                         If this nurse were admitting a patient who talks rapidly
                                         and continuously of her symptoms and past medical
                                         history, could be expected to look interested and listen.

                                         If this nurse were assigned for the first time to a patient
                                   1.25 who insists upon having her treatment done in a certain
                                         order, could be expected to do as the patient wishes
                                         without making an issue about it.

Figure 3.2. Example of behavior-anchored rating scale for describing nurses' skills in human relationships. (From National League for Nursing, Research and Studies Service. *A Method for Rating the Proficiency of the Hospital General Staff Nurse; Manual of Directions.* New York, 1964, p. 16.)

behaviors, it is quite likely that for a given ratee the rater will not have had the opportunity to observe whether the ratee behaved in such a manner as described by the anchors. Asking the rater to make a prediction about the ratee's expected job performance (as defined by the anchors) avoids this problem.

Unfortunately, many applications of BARS have instructed the raters to pick the most "typical" job behavior for the ratee from among the set of behavioral anchors (Bernardin & Smith, 1981). Thus, the advantage of the expectation format is lost in these instances.

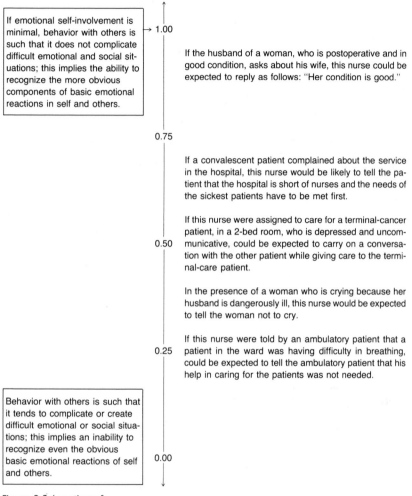

If emotional self-involvement is minimal, behavior with others is such that it does not complicate difficult emotional and social situations; this implies the ability to recognize the more obvious components of basic emotional reactions in self and others.

→ 1.00

If the husband of a woman, who is postoperative and in good condition, asks about his wife, this nurse could be expected to reply as follows: "Her condition is good."

0.75

If a convalescent patient complained about the service in the hospital, this nurse would be likely to tell the patient that the hospital is short of nurses and the needs of the sickest patients have to be met first.

0.50

If this nurse were assigned to care for a terminal-cancer patient, in a 2-bed room, who is depressed and uncommunicative, could be expected to carry on a conversation with the other patient while giving care to the terminal-care patient.

In the presence of a woman who is crying because her husband is dangerously ill, this nurse would be expected to tell the woman not to cry.

0.25

If this nurse were told by an ambulatory patient that a patient in the ward was having difficulty in breathing, could be expected to tell the ambulatory patient that his help in caring for the patients was not needed.

Behavior with others is such that it tends to complicate or create difficult emotional or social situations; this implies an inability to recognize even the obvious basic emotional reactions of self and others.

0.00

Figure 3.2 (*continued*)

The expectation format, even when used as suggested by Smith and Kendall, may have another problem. Asking raters to make predictions about the ratee's work performance rather than having the rater describe and evaluate the past work behavior of the ratee may incur legal difficulties. It can be difficult to justify in legal proceedings predictions of job performance made in reference to behavioral anchors that may not have been observed for the ratee. Justification to the ratee, independent of legal proceedings, may be strained when the scale anchors are worded in the expectation format; yet the performance appraisal is concerned with *past* performance. A partial solution to this is requiring written statements from the rater documenting the specific ratee job behaviors that support the evaluations on the various performance dimensions. Nonetheless, there may be instances in which the expectation format is not desirable.

An additional problem often encountered when using BARS is the objection of raters to the order of the behavioral anchors on a given scale. In most applications of BARS, such as in Figure 3.2, the scale anchors are ordered in terms of the mean effectiveness rating obtained in the scaling phase of the developmental procedure. Although anchors are selected with small standard deviations for these ratings, it is common for the confidence intervals for the means of adjacent anchors to overlap. This can result in a rater believing that a lower placed anchor describes more effective performance than a higher placed anchor. The credibility of the scales can easily be badly damaged when this occurs. This may be avoided by grouping behavioral examples into broad performance-level categories, such as more than adequate, adequate, and less than adequate. Though there is potentially a loss of information to the rater about the meaning of the performance scale, the reduced credibility loss is likely to overcome this. An example of a BARS designed in this way is presented in Figure 3.3.

The scale shown in Figure 3.3 was developed for the purpose of assessing the technical performance and skill updating of engineers employed in industry (Farr, Enscore, Dubin, Cleveland, & Kozlowski, 1980). In addition to grouping the scale anchors into three categories, the expectation format for the anchors is also dropped and the rater is required to indicate a specific example of performance that documents the evaluation. The instructions for this scale emphasize that the anchors are a sample of possible job behaviors that may or may not have been observed for a particular ratee.

MIXED STANDARD SCALES (MSS). Blanz and Ghiselli (1972) proposed a rating format that they labeled as the mixed standard scale. The format consists of three specific behavioral examples (much like, if not identical to, the anchors in a BARS format) per performance dimension. One of the three examples describes above average performance on the performance dimension, one describes average performance, and the last describes below average performance. (Usually the examples have been scaled regarding performance level in a manner similar to that employed in the develop-

Factor K. *Technical Interest and Curiosity*—The interest and curiosity shown by the engineer regarding recent developments in science and technology

Numerical scale		Examples of activities related to this factor
9	More than usual amount of typical activity or effort related to this factor	Seeks information about all technical areas
8		Seeks involvement in relevant technical developments
7		Works extra hours on own initiative to learn about new developments
6	Usual amount of typical activity or effort related to this factor	Occasionally reads journals in related technical areas
5		Interest in new technology is usually limited to own area only
4		Sometimes displays a negative attitude toward new ideas
3	Less than usual amount of typical activity or effort related to this factor	Is pessimistic and cynical about new technical developments
2		Has little curiosity about technologies related to own specific area
1		Adopts an attitude of "if it's important, someone will tell me about it" toward developments

Specific instances of this individual's work activities related to this factor:

_____Numerical description for this factor

Figure 3.3. BARS with scale anchors grouped into three categories. (From Farr *et al.*, 1980, p. 39.)

ment of BARS.) The behavioral examples are arranged randomly and the performance dimensions are not identified. The rater is to make one of three responses to each example: The ratee's performance is poorer than that described by the example; the ratee's performance is equal to that described by the example; or the ratee's performance is better than that described by the example. Figure 3.4 presents an example of a MSS for the job of police officer.

It was suggested by Blanz and Ghiselli (1972) that the disguised nature of the performance dimensions and of the levels of performance described by the examples would result in reduced rating errors such as halo and leniency. A ratee's "score" on each performance dimension is calculated

---

Listed below are a number of descriptions of behavior relevant to the job of patrol officer. Your task is to carefully examine each example, and then to determine in your own mind the answer to the following question: Is the patrol officer to be rated "better than this statement," "worse than this statement," or "does this statement fit this patrol officer?"

If you believe that the person you are rating is "better than the statement," put a + in the space to the right of the statement. If you believe that the person is "worse than the statement," put a − in that space. If you believe that the statement "fits" the patrol officer, put a 0 in that space.

Be sure that you write either a +, a −, or a 0 after each of the statements listed below.

	Rating
(II) 1. The officer could be expected to misinform the public on legal matters through lack of knowledge. (P)	+
(III) 2. The officer could be expected to take the time to carefully answer a rookie's question. (G)	0
(II) 3. This patrol officer never has to ask others about points of law. (G)	−
(I) 4. The officer could be expected to refrain from writing tickets for traffic violations which occur at a particular intersection which is unusually confusing to motorists. (G)	+
(I) 5. The patrol officer could be expected to call for assistance and clear the area of bystanders before confronting a barricaded, heavily-armed suspect. (A)	+
(III) 6. The officer could be expected to use racially-toned language in front of minority-group members. (P)	+
(II) 7. This officer follows correct procedures for evidence preservation at the scene of a crime. (A)	0
(I) 8. The patrol officer could be expected to continue to write a traffic violation in spite of hearing a report of a nearby robbery in progress. (P)	+
(III) 9. This officer is considered friendly by the other officers on the shift. (A)	+

Note: (I), (II), and (III) to the left of the items indicate the performance dimension; (G), (A), and (P) following the items refer to Good, Average, and Poor performance levels, respectively.

Figure 3.4. Mixed standard scale for job of police officer. (This figure and subsequent figures from Landy & Trumbo, 1980, have been adapted from F. J. Landy & D. Trumbo. *Psychology of work behavior* (revised ed.). Homewood, Ill.: Dorsey, 1980, pp. 124–25. Copyright © 1980 The Dorsey Press. Reprinted with permission.)

on the basis of the pattern of rater responses to the three items comprising the dimension. Saal (1979) has noted several problems in the original scoring scheme suggested by Blanz and Ghiselli, including the omission of possible response patterns and inconsistencies among scores assigned to certain patterns. Saal has proposed a more rational and complete scoring scheme that is shown in Table 3.2 along with the original Blanz and Ghiselli scoring procedure.

The 27 rater response patterns shown in Table 3.2 vary in consistency and transitivity of the judgments. Analyses of rater response patterns can identify those raters whose use of the scales appears to be haphazard. These raters can be targeted for training or their judgments removed from the data set of a research study or from the information set used to make personnel decisions. The ability to determine objectively the frequency of rater errors, defined as inconsistent rating responses, was noted as a major advantage of MSS by Blanz and Ghiselli (1972). The finding of high rater error rates for a particular performance dimension or particular items may be useful for refinement of the instrument itself.

FORCED-CHOICE RATING SCALES (FC). The forced-choice rating scale format, similar to the mixed standard scale, disguises the rating scale continuum (Zavala, 1965). The rater is presented with some number of sets of examples of job performance. From each set of examples the rater's task usually is to select some specified subset that best describes the particular ratee's job performance. Some variations of the procedure ask the rater to choose the most and least descriptive examples from the set.

As with BARS and MSS, there are critical developmental steps that must be followed in the construction of an FC scale. Behavioral examples must be generated for the job in question. Each example is twice scaled by job experts. Job experts are asked to judge the favorability (or social desirability) of an example as a description of a job performer. The mean of these expert judgments is termed the preference index score for the example. Job experts are also asked how descriptive the example is for high performers and for low performers on the job. A discrimination index score is calculated that indicates how well the example differentiates between high and low performers. Thus, for each behavioral example, the scaling procedure results in a measure of the favorability of the behavior (the preference index score) and in a measure of whether good job performers are more or less likely to display the behavior than poor performers (the discrimination index score).

In the most common (and the one generally considered to be best,

Table 3.2
Original and Revised Numerical Ratings for the Twenty-Seven
Possible Mixed Standard Scale Response Combinations[a]

	Response combination[b]			Numerical ratings	
Number	Superior behavior	Average behavior	Inferior behavior	Original	Revised[c]
1	+	+	+	7	7
2	+	+	0	7	6
3	+	+	—	7	5
4	+	0	+	4	6
5	+	0	0	3	5
6	+	0	—	4	4
7	+	—	+	3	5
8	+	—	0	2	4
9	+	—	—	1	3
10	0	+	+	6	6
11	0	+	0	6	5
12	0	+	—	6	4
13	0	0	+	Omitted	5
14	0	0	0	4	4
15	0	0	—	4	3
16	0	—	+	5	4
17	0	—	0	2	3
18	0	—	—	1	2
19	—	+	+	5	5
20	—	+	0	5	4
21	—	+	—	5	3
22	—	0	+	4	4
23	—	0	0	Omitted	3
24	—	0	—	3	2
25	—	—	+	3	3
26	—	—	0	2	2
27	—	—	—	1	1

[a]From Saal, F. E. Mixed standard rating scale: A consistent system for numerically coding inconsistent response combinations. *Journal of Applied Psychology*, 1979, *64*, 424. Copyright 1979 by the American Psychological Association. Reprinted by permission of the author.

[b]+ indicates "ratee is better than this behavior"; 0 indicates "ratee is the same as this behavior"; — indicates "ratee is worse than this behavior."

[c]Revised numerical ratings were derived as follows: numerical equivalent of response to superior behavior (+ = 8, 0 = 7, — = 6) + numerical equivalent of response to average behavior (+ = 5, 0 = 4, — = 3) + numerical equivalent of response to inferior behavior (+ = 2, 0 = 1, — = 0) − 8.

Berkshire & Highland, 1953) format, four favorable examples with appropriately equal preference index scores are chosen for each set or tetrad of examples. (There are a number of such sets of examples or tetrads.) Two of these four examples have a low discrimination index score and two have high discrimination scores. In each tetrad of examples, the rater selects the two examples that best describe the job performance of the ratee. Since the rater does not know which items differentiate between high and low performers, a rater trying to give a ratee a positive evaluation is equally likely to choose differentiating and nondifferentiating items since they are matched on favorability. Thus, the expected number of differentiating items that might be chosen in any single tetrad is one. Typically, a ratee's evaluation is the number of differentiating (or valid) examples chosen across the various tetrads. In most cases a ratee receives only an overall job performance evaluation or rating, although forced-choice scales could be developed for various dimensions of performance (Bartlett, 1959; Wherry, 1959).

In the late 1940s, the United States Army initially developed FC scales for evaluating job performance because of difficulties with the graphic rating scale system then in use (Travers, 1951). The major difficulty with the graphic ratings was that the mean rating was almost at the most favorable endpoint of the scale. These extremely lenient ratings were of no value in differentiating among ratees. A major assumed advantage for FC scales was less lenient mean ratings because of the disguised nature of the scoring procedure.

The disguised nature of how the rater's responses are translated into a performance evaluation score for the ratee also has its weaknesses. Foremost among these is lack of rater acceptability. Raters are often quite resistant to the FC technique because they do not know what evaluations they are giving to the various ratees. They do not want to give inadvertently a "good" rating to a "poor" performer or a "poor" rating to a "good" performer. If the FC scale has been properly constructed, the rater cannot be sure of the actual evaluation (relative or absolute) that a ratee will receive. Also, it would be extremely difficult for a rater to give reasonable feedback to a ratee or to explain the performance rating received by the ratee. This can create interpersonal stress for the rater and also increase resistance to the FC format.

Rater resistance seems to be related to the specific FC format employed. Berkshire and Highland (1953) found the least rater resistance when raters chose the two most descriptive items from a tetrad of all favorable examples. More resistance occurred if raters were to choose from among unfavorable examples or if raters were to pick the most and least descriptive item from either all favorable, all unfavorable, or a mixture of favorable and unfavorable examples.

OTHER CHECKLISTS. Although the forced-choice scale, and perhaps the mixed standard scale, can be categorized as checklists, the organization of the FC items into sets and the scoring of the MSS result in formats that differ in important ways from other checklists. A common format for checklists is simply a listing of relatively specific items that describe possible work behaviors or individual characteristics. The rater either makes a response to each example or chooses some of the examples as most descriptive of the ratee. The examples during scale development have typically been scaled according to one of two procedures borrowed from attitude measurement methodology, Thurstone's method of equal-appearing intervals and Likert's method of summated ratings.

The *method of equal-appearing intervals* (see Edwards, 1957, for a detailed presentation) requires that judges (or job experts in our specific case) sort or rate a series of statements (about job behaviors in our case) according to a 7-, 9-, or 11-point scale. Highly favorable job performance might be judged in Category 10 or 11 (on an 11-point scale) and extremely poor performance in Category 1 or 2. Each judge is instructed to sort the statements into the categories so that the differences in level (of job performance in our case) between neighboring categories seem to him or her to be equal. If one can accept the assumption that the judges can keep the categories (or intervals on a continuum of job performance) psychologically equal, then the resulting scale can be treated as an interval scale. After many such judgments have been collected, item means and standard deviations are computed. Relatively unambiguous statements (using the standard deviation criterion as with BARS) with means representing the full range of levels of job performance are placed in a checklist format. The rater's task is to check for each ratee those items (usually a fixed number) that best describe the individual. The means of the items checked for an individual (or the algebraic deviations of the item means from the scale midpoint) are summed to yield a score for the individual.

Uhrbrock (1950, 1961) has presented over 2700 statements that have been scaled according to this procedure. Although it would be desirable to compute new item means and standard deviations in reference to performance of the particular job(s) one is concerned with, this large pool of items serves as a useful starting point for creating a checklist.

The *method of summated ratings* requires the rater to judge a ratee with regard to each of a number of items that describe job behaviors. The judgment scale typically has five categories with category anchors of "strongly agree" to "strongly disagree." Items that describe favorable job behaviors are scored so that a "strongly agree" response receives an item score of "5" and a "strongly disagree" response a score of "1." Items describing unfavorable behavior are scored in the reverse fashion. An overall rating is obtained by summing the item scores (hence the method's name).

The development of a summated rating checklist usually involves the use of item analyses to ensure the reliability of the resulting scale. The reliability of a summated rating checklist is usually assessed by an internal consistency estimate. Internal consistency reliability exists when there is a high degree of interrelatedness among the items on the scale (Crano & Brewer, 1973). The summation of item responses makes psychological sense only if the various items are measuring the same construct. If the items measure a common construct, then the item responses should show significant intercorrelations.

The specific steps in conducting the item analysis and estimation of the internal consistency reliability of a summated rating scale are as follows. Judgments on a sample of work performers for a preliminary set of items are obtained. The correlation between an item score and the total scale score (minus the particular item score) is generally used as the statistical criterion for item inclusion or exclusion. If the item-total correlation fails to reach statistical significance, the item is dropped from the scale. The internal consistency reliability (see p. 12, Chapter 1, this volume) of the set of remaining items is then computed (usually using coefficient alpha; Cronbach, 1951). If coefficient alpha exceeds .80, then the scale is generally of sufficient internal consistency. If less than .80, more items may need to be added. The purpose of the item analyses is to obtain a scale that is unidimensional so that the unrestricted addition of items is not desirable. Scales with a very large number of items may yield a high coefficient alpha but may still be multidimensional (Crano & Brewer, 1973).

Recently, Latham and Wexley (1977, 1981; also Latham, Fay, & Saari, 1979) have proposed for the appraisal of work performance a variant of the summated rating scale that they have labeled as *behavioral observation scales* (BOS). The BOS are developed using the item-analytic approach discussed earlier for summated rating scales. The principal change from more usual summated rating scales that Latham and Wexley have made is in the nature of the response categories for each item. The five response categories in a BOS are defined in terms of the frequency with which the rater has observed the ratee engaged in the behavior described by each item. The categories are typically 0–64%, 65–74%, 75–84%, 85–94%, and 95–100% of the time, although the exact rationale for these percentage limits is unclear in the writings of Latham and Wexley. In some works (e.g., Latham & Wexley, 1977) the authors suggest using 0–19%, 20–39%, 40–59%, 60–79%, and 80–100%.

Latham et al. (1979) used factor analytic procedures to develop BOS for four dimensions of the job performance of first-level foreman. Thus, the problem of having only an overall rating, common to most checklists, can be handled if sufficient numbers of initial behavioral items, and job experts to rate them, are available. If sample size limitations prevent the use of factor analytic procedures, a rational grouping of items, followed by empirical item analyses, might still be feasible and be able to yield BOS for various performance dimensions.

Among the advantages of the use of BOS claimed by Latham and Wexley (1981) and Latham et al. (1979) are content validity, reliability, and relevance to the job. Such claims made on the basis of a few studies conducted by one group of researchers may be premature, but the continued *careful* use of such developmental procedures is to be encouraged.

Latham and Wexley (1981) and Latham et al. (1979) also suggest that BOS are to be preferred over other judgmental performance measures because of the simpler task asked of the rater by BOS. These authors have suggested that with a BOS the rater is required merely to indicate the frequency with which he or she has observed each behavior, whereas BARS and graphic rating scales involve complex judgments about performance. The assumption that BOS response requirements are simple does not appear tenable (Murphy, Martin, & Garcia, 1982). Since BOS data would usually be gathered only on a periodic basis (e.g., every 6 months or 1 year), BOS must measure not only the raters' observations of work behaviors but also the *recall* of these observations. It would appear that the cognitive operations required of the rater by BOS and BARS (and other judgmental formats) would converge as the interval between the observation of behavior and the judgment task increases.

Bernardin and Kane (1980) and Latham, Saari, and Fay (1980) have argued the relative merits of BARS and BOS. It appears to us that many of the arguments are premature, as insufficient data are available to reach any reasonable decision about the desirability of their use. We further suspect that after more data are in, the answer will be "it depends," with dependency based on the purpose or purposes of the judgments, the carefulness of the scale developmental procedures, and the preferences of the raters, among other factors.

Norm-Referenced Measures

In many applications of performance information, the fundamental question is often "who is the best work performer in this group?" or "who are the best four people to assign to a given task?" For these kinds of questions an evaluation procedure that yields information about the relative performance of various work performers is appropriate. There are two commonly used measures of norm-referenced performance, paired comparisons and rank order.

PAIRED COMPARISONS. One approach to making relative judgments about individuals is to compare every possible pair of the individuals. The rater is presented with all possible pairs of individuals and is asked which of each two is better. Most frequently, "better" is defined in terms of overall job performance, but the basis for the decision may be more specific, such as a single performance dimension. A rank order of the individuals can be obtained by counting the number of times each individual is selected as being the better of a pair.

Several potential problems can arise in the use of paired comparisons. If the number of individuals to be compared is very large, the number of comparisons can be unwieldly. There are $N(N-1)/2$ total comparisons, where n is the number of individuals. Thus, for 20 individuals, there are 190 comparisons. There are several ways for reducing the number of comparisons that are necessary (Guilford, 1954). For example, names can be listed randomly and a systematic pattern for sampling pairs of names can be developed. McCormick and Bachus (1952) and McCormick and Roberts (1952) have shown that partial paired comparisons using only about one-half of the total comparisons yield rank orderings highly similar to those resulting from the total set of comparisons.

Intransitivity of judgments is another potential problem with paired comparisons. Judgments are said to be transitive if, for every A, B, and C, it is true that, if $A > B$ and $B > C$, then $A > C$. A considerable amount of intransitivity can be expected to occur if the individuals to be compared are quite similar to each other so that the choice approaches randomness. More often, intransitivity may occur if there are multiple dimensions on which the people may vary, such as the components of overall job perfor-

Table 3.3
Scores of Three Individuals on Two
Performance Factors

Individual	Performance factor	
	I	II
A	20	30
B	22	25
C	24	20

mance. Tversky (1969) has noted that under certain conditions intransitivity in preferences can be reliably predicted. These conditions include the situation in which a particular factor is the sole initial basis for the preference choice and another factor or factors are considered only when two individuals do not differ (significantly or more than some margin of error on the initial factor).

Table 3.3 presents an example in which intransitivity might be expected to occur. Three individuals have scores on two performance factors. They are to be compared pairwise on overall performance. Assume a rater discriminates solely on the basis of Factor I, but the rater assumes that any difference on Factor I of less than 3 points is not reliable. When the Factor I score difference for a pair of individuals is less than 3, the rater uses Factor II scores to determine the better individual. The data in Table 3.3, using the decision strategy outlined earlier, would result in $A > B$, $B > C$, but $C > A$. Although understandable from the point of view of this decision strategy, the occurrence of many different decision strategies by various raters can yield what in the aggregate may appear to be uninterpretable data.

From the standpoint of the intransitivity issue, it would be desirable in paired comparisons to make decisions on the basis of relatively unidimensional components of job performance. Unfortunately, many times we are interested in the best overall performer. Thus, we have a paradox that does not have a simple solution if we use the paired-comparison procedure.

RANKING. One way to avoid the intransitivity problem is to use a ranking procedure that directly yields a single ordering of individuals. Since multiple comparisons of individuals are not asked for, intransitivity is a moot issue. Ranking procedures can be as simple as asking a judge to place a group of individuals in order of merit. This can usually be accomplished if there are not many individuals in the group. More complex procedures may be necessary if there are substantial numbers of work performers to be ranked.

One recommended procedure for handling many individuals is *alternation ranking*. The evaluator is told to select the best person in the group and assign that individual the rank of "1" and to select the worst person and assign that individual the rank of "N" (the number of people in the group). Then, from the $N - 2$ remaining people, the evaluator selects the best person and assigns him or her a rank of "2" and selects the worst person and assigns that individual a rank of "$N - 1$." Ranking is generally most difficult when the individuals are average in performance and similar to each other. Alternation ranking, by removing the extreme performers from the group before these difficult decisions are made, reduces the complexity of the ranking task.

ISSUES CONCERNING NORM-REFERENCED MEASURES. The most critical problems facing the user of norm-referenced performance measures are that no information regarding the absolute level of performance is available nor is any information regarding the absolute similarity of the performance of any two individuals available. Since paired-comparison and ranking procedures yield only ordinal information, we do not know if the best performer in a group is, on an absolute basis, an excellent, average, or poor employee. Further, we do not know if two individuals with adjacent ranks are quite similar or quite disparate in their performance levels. Thus, for certain kinds of personnel decisions, relative performance measures may not be very useful.

A further complication arises if we want to compare individuals from different groups. We cannot easily do this since norm-referenced performance measures can be interpreted only in the context of the ranked group. If there are certain individuals who are well known to all evaluators, these individuals can be included in all groups of work performers and used as common reference points for the rankings in the various groups (Uhrbrock & Richardson, 1933). When groups are of different sizes, we have an additional comparability problem. Ranks in different-sized groups can be transformed into scale values in a normal frequency distribution (e.g., see Ghiselli, 1964, pp. 80–82) and compared more directly if we are willing to make the assumptions of normally distributed performance within each group as well as comparable mean levels of performance in the groups.

There are instances in which a fairly crude ranking or grouping of individuals is all that is needed. A *forced distribution rating* procedure could then be used. This is a combination of rating and ranking procedures. Individuals receive a rating of absolute performance level, but the rater must also assign individuals to rating categories (or ranked performance levels) according to some predetermined distribution, usually a percentage of the group of individuals to be rated that must be placed in each category. The distribution is often rectangular or normal with five or seven categories. The number of categories is somewhat arbitrary although logical, if one considers the findings on the number of judgment categories that are optimal (e.g., Lissitz & Green, 1975).

RESEARCH ON TYPES OF JUDGMENTAL MEASURES

Considerable research attention has been paid to the question of finding the best format for the judgmental measurement of work performance. Before we can review such research in an intelligent fashion, we need to consider the bases by which the judgment formats are typically evaluated. Generally, judgment formats have been evaluated on the basis of several psychometric indexes, namely, halo, leniency, central tendency, range restriction, and interrater reliability or agreement.

Psychometric Indexes of Rating Scale Quality

As noted by Saal, Downey, and Lahey (1980), the psychometric properties of ratings have each been defined, conceptually and operationally, in a number of ways in the research literature. We will briefly review the varieties of conceptual and operational definitions and refer the reader to Saal *et al.* for details.

HALO. *Halo* has been usually defined as a tendency to attend to a global impression of each ratee rather than to distinguish carefully among performance levels on different work dimensions. Thus, a rater may fail to discriminate among conceptually different and possibly empirically independent components of a ratee's job behavior.

Saal *et al.* (1980) found four operational definitions of halo in the recent literature. These were (*a*) magnitude of intercorrelations among different dimension ratings; (*b*) percentage of variance accounted for by the first factor in a factor analysis of the dimension incorrelation matrix; (*c*) the variance of a particular rater's ratings of a given ratee across all dimensions; and (*d*) the statistical significance of the Rater × Ratee interaction in an analysis of variance of a Rater × Ratee × Dimension data matrix.

LENIENCY. *Leniency* (and its conceptual opposite, severity) refers to a displacement of a particular rating or the mean rating from some "ideal" point. The ideal has been defined in several ways (e.g., that warranted by the ratee's behavior [for a particular rating] or the midpoint of the rating scale [for mean ratings]). Some discussions also focus on "hard" and "easy" raters in the sense of a response set bias leading to a systematic shift in ratings for a particular rater.

Three operational definitions of leniency have been described by Saal *et al.* (1980). The most frequent was the comparison of the mean dimension ratings with the scale midpoint. The next most frequently used was a significant Rater main effect in a Rater × Ratee × Dimension analysis of variance. The least frequently used was the degree of skewness in the frequency distribution of the ratings for a particular performance dimension.

CENTRAL TENDENCY AND RESTRICTION OF RANGE. *Central tendency* is characterized as the avoidance of extreme (favorable or unfavorable) ratings or a preponderance of ratings at or near the scale midpoint. Saal *et al.* (1980) found that central tendency was rarely used in empirical research articles as a criterion of rating-scale quality, but that restriction of range was frequently used. *Restriction of range* has been defined as the extent to which obtained ratings discriminate among ratees in terms of level of performance. Although both of these concepts are related to the variance of a distribution of ratings, they are not completely synonymous (or, at least, they should not be). Range restriction could occur at any part of the rating continuum, whereas central tendency can occur only at the scale midpoint.

Operational definitions of range restriction identified by Saal *et al.* (1980) include: (*a*) the standard deviation of the dimension ratings; (*b*) the kurtosis of the rating distribution; and (*c*) the absence of statistical significance for the Ratee main effect in a Rater × Ratee × Dimension analysis of variance. Central tendency has been assessed by the proximity of the average rating to the scale midpoint.

INTERRATER RELIABILITY OR AGREEMENT. A frequently used index of the quality of a rating scale is *interrater reliability or agreement*, which is the extent to which two or more raters give similar ratings to a ratee or group of ratees. Interrater reliability may represent only shared bias or commonly observed but irrelevant behavior (e.g., Buckner, 1959; Freeberg, 1969; Wherry, Appendix, this volume), but its use in the research literature warrants its mention here. Operational definitions found by Saal *et al.* (1980) include: (*a*) the standard deviation of ratings assigned to a given ratee by several raters for each performance dimension; (*b*) correlations between pairs of raters who evaluate the same ratee on several performance dimensions; (*c*) the intraclass correlation coefficient; (*d*) a statistically significant Ratee main effect in a Rater × Ratee × Dimension analysis of variance; and (*e*) the absence of a significant Rater × Ratee Interaction in an analysis of variance.

Comparative Rating Format Research

Despite the large number of judgmental formats, most of the comparative studies have focused on just a few of the possible comparisons. We will present a brief review of such research organized by the types of formats compared, followed by a presentation of some "format-free" research on scaling procedures.

COMPARISON OF GRAPHIC SCALES AND BARS. There has been a good deal of careful work attempting to assess the relative effectiveness of BARS in relation to traditional graphic methods of rating. Campbell, Dunnette, Arvey, and Hellervik (1973) compared the BARS method to summated ratings and concluded that the BARS format yielded less method variance, less halo, and less leniency in ratings.

Borman and Vallon (1974) found that the BARS technique yielded ratings that were superior in reliability and rater confidence in ratings, but that simpler numerical formats resulted in less leniency and better discrimination among ratees.

Burnaska and Hollman (1974) compared three different formats. The first format was the standard behaviorally anchored scale. The second format consisted of the same dimensions and definitions but adjectival anchors were substituted for behavioral ones. The third format was a traditional graphic rating format with a priori dimensions. Leniency and composite halo were present in all three formats, but the BARS method reduced leniency and increased the amount of variance attributable to ratee differences. Nevertheless, Burnaska and Hollman, in concluding that improvements in some aspects of rating using the BARS method were accompanied by problems in other areas, stated "innovations in rating, although plentiful, are likely to result in robbing Peter to pay Paul [p. 307]." Each format seemed to have its own unique problems.

Keaveney and McGann (1975) compared the student ratings of college professors on behaviorally anchored and graphic rating scales. Behaviorally anchored scales resulted in less halo but did not differ from graphic scales in terms of leniency. Their general conclusion was that neither format could be judged superior to the other.

Borman and Dunnette (1975) compared the standard BARS format to rating scales with identical dimension labels and definitions, but with numerical anchors, and to traditional graphic rating scales with trait labels and numerical anchors. They concluded that, in spite of the fact that the standard BARS format was psychometrically superior (in terms of halo, leniency, and reliability), format differences accounted for trivial amounts of rating variance (approximately 5%).

Bernardin, Alvares, and Cranny (1976) compared summated ratings with BARS ratings. They concluded that summated ratings were characterized by less leniency and greater interrater agreement than were BARS ratings. They hypothesized that the rigor of scale development was a crucial issue in the resistance to rating errors, regardless of the format of the scales. In a follow-up study, Bernardin (1977) demonstrated that, when item analysis procedures are used for choosing anchors in the BARS method, there is no difference between BARS ratings and summated ratings.

Friedman and Cornelius (1976) compared ratings from three groups: (a) a group that participated in developing BARS; (b) a group that participated in developing graphic rating scales; and (c) a group that did not participate in scale development. There was no difference in the psychometric properties of the ratings made by subjects in Groups 1 and 2. The ratings of Group 3 were characterized by significantly higher levels of halo than the ratings of either of the other two groups.

Other comparative studies of BARS and other formats have been reported and are noted in two reviews of BARS (Jacobs et al., 1980; Kingstrom & Bass, 1981). Both reviews noted few consistent indexes of rating-scale quality (halo, leniency, etc.). However, neither review was willing to conclude that BARS were an unnecessary expense in terms of time, effort, and money.

Kingstrom and Bass (1981) noted a number of methodological problems in the various studies comparing BARS and other formats. These included different operationalizations of the psychometric indexes (cf. Saal *et al.*, 1980), the use of different numbers of scale points with the different formats, and the possible lack of comparability of corresponding scale points on the different formats (even if the number of scale points was constant). Kingstrom and Bass also reported that in two-thirds of the studies they reviewed a common procedure (namely, the BARS method) was used to develop the dimensions and/or examples for the two (or more) formats. Thus, these studies actually contrasted only the actual presentation modes and did not compare the total BARS methodology with another independent means of developing rating scales. This confounds the comparison of BARS versus other methodologies. A strength of the BARS method appears to be the development of performance dimensions and behavioral examples. Thus, other presentation modes that use the BARS technique for dimension and example development may not be expected to differ much from BARS in terms of the various psychometric indexes.

Although Jacobs *et al.* (1980) concluded that BARS and other formats differ little on psychometric (or quantitative, in their terms) criteria, they did indicate that BARS may be superior with regard to two other classes of criteria, *qualitative* and *utilization* (see Chapter 1, this volume). Qualitative criteria are guidelines or "rules of thumb" by which one can *judge* rating formats to be useful. Qualitative criteria include relevancy, data availability, practicality, and equivalence. Utilization criteria refer to whether a particular rating procedure can be used for particular purposes of performance evaluation, such as feedback to the employee, administrative purposes (e.g., promotion, disciplinary action), and personnel research (e.g., selection procedure validation, training evaluation, organizational diagnosis).

Jacobs *et al.* (1980) also noted that most comparative studies of BARS and other formats have collected their data during scale development and a single use of the scales (usually a research use and not an operational use). They indicated that many of the potential advantages of BARS might occur only over time as the BARS were used as an ongoing part of the personnel appraisal and feedback system. A study by Ivancevich (1980) supports this. Ivancevich reported that in comparison with engineers rated on a trait-evaluation form, engineers who were evaluated with a BARS had more favorable attitudes regarding performance appraisal, had less job-related tension, and demonstrated improved performance in some aspects. These results were sustained for 18 months following the BARS implementation.

COMPARISON OF FORCED-CHOICE WITH OTHER FORMATS. More is learned from the comparison of the forced-choice format with other formats than from an examination of variations within the forced-choice format. Staugas and McQuitty (1950) compared the forced-choice technique to both graphic ratings and peer rankings. Since the correlations between forced-choice ratings and the other two performance measures were higher than similar indexes for the other two methods, it was concluded that forced-choice methodology was "superior." Were they to rewrite the discussion section today, the authors would undoubtedly use the term *convergent validity* to describe advantages of the method. A number of other studies used a similar logic for supporting the superiority of the forced-choice format. Berkshire and Highland (1953) demonstrated that forced-choice ratings had higher correlations with an overall ranking than did graphic ratings. Taylor, Schneider, and Clay (1954) found the correlations between forced-choice ratings and graphic ratings to be quite high, but found that forced-choice ratings showed less leniency bias. Cotton and Stoltz (1960) showed less range restriction on forced-choice ratings than on graphic ratings. It would seem that these studies point to one major advantage of forced-choice ratings: They seem to maximize interindividual variance, although little is known about their effects on intraindividual variance. Since forced-choice scales were introduced primarily in an attempt to control positive bias or leniency, little attention was paid to the problem of halo error. Nevertheless, there is some peripheral evidence available. Sharon and Bartlett (1969) examined the relative resistance of forced-choice and graphic ratings to leniency bias under four conditions: (*a*) rater anonymous, research purposes only; (*b*) rater anonymous, feedback to instructor; (*c*) rater identified, research purposes only; and (*d*) rater identified, follow-up discussion with ratee. The ratings represented student evaluations of college instructors. Although the results showed significant leniency for all graphic rating conditions, the forced-choice ratings were uniformly resistant to leniency bias.

In one of the few comparative studies dealing with reliability, Lepkowski (1963) found that graphic ratings and forced-choice ratings yielded equal reliability when scales were developed from critical incidents. From the earlier studies of descriptors just summarized, it might be concluded that these descriptors worked to the disadvantage of the forced-choice format because of the inclusion of negative items.

Taylor and Wherry (1951) compared forced-choice and graphic rating systems in a military setting. In one condition, they told raters that the ratings were for "experimental" purposes; in a second condition, they implied that the ratings would be used to make administrative decisions. They found an increase in the mean ratings for both formats under the "for keeps" condition. Nevertheless, the impact seemed to be greater on the graphic ratings. In addition, there was poorer discrimination among ratees at the top of the scale in the graphic, "for keeps" condition. They suggested that graphic rating scales that followed forced-choice scales might be less biased.

In 1959, Cozan reviewed the studies addressing the validity of the forced-choice format and concluded that, unless a new system was clearly superior to an existing system, the costs of organizational change argued in favor of the old system. Since the studies to that date had not presented any compelling reason for choosing forced-choice formats over alternative formats, he suggested that traditional graphic rating schemes be retained. The argument is similar to that made against the increased cost of developing BARS formats. Nevertheless, there does seem to be evidence that the forced-choice format reduces range restriction. Unfortunately, sufficient data are not available to determine whether this psychometric advantage is accompanied by other disadvantages.

MIXED STANDARD SCALES VERSUS OTHER FORMATS. A small number of studies have contrasted MSS and other rating formats. Saal and Landy (1977) compared MSS and BARS. Both types of scales had been developed by a common procedure (the retranslation of the expectation approach of Smith & Kendall, 1963). The MSS format resulted in lower levels of leniency and halo, but the scale reliabilities were lower than those of the BARS. Saal and Landy also noted problems with the scoring procedure suggested by Blanz and Ghiselli (1972). As noted earlier, Saal (1979) has developed a more logical and consistent scoring procedure.

Dickinson and Zellinger (1980) also compared MSS and BARS by multitrait–multimethod procedures, which had been developed by retranslation of expectations procedures. The MSS and BARS demonstrated equivalent discriminant validity, but the MSS had less method bias than the BARS. The raters preferred the BARS as an instrument to aid in giving performance feedback to the ratees. This preference was probably due to the identification of the performance dimensions and to the opportunity the raters had for providing commentary related to the numerical judgments.

In a related study, Arvey and Hoyle (1974) found that scales developed by Guttman scaling techniques (the methodological foundation of the

MSS) demonstrated good convergent and discriminant validity, but that attempts to use the technique to identify poor raters were not successful. There was only slight evidence to suggest that raters who made rating errors on one job dimension also rated poorly on other dimensions, or that raters who made errors in rating one individual also made errors when rating other individuals. The Guttman-based scales also exhibited higher rating intercorrelations than more traditional behavioral-based scales.

Methodological Research Relevant to Many Formats

Some research studies have examined characteristics of rating scales that are important to the design of any type or format of scale. The results of these research efforts are described in the following section.

NUMBER OF RESPONSE CATEGORIES. A series of careful studies by Bendig (1952a, 1952b, 1953, 1954a, 1954b) provide firm evidence concerning the most efficient number of response categories for rating formats. There is no gain in reliability when the number of categories increases from 5 to 9; reliability drops with 3 categories or less and with 11 categories or more. Finn (1972) studied the effect of number of categories on reliability of rating and found that reliability dropped with less than 3 or more than 7 response categories. Lissitz and Green (1975) in a Monte Carlo study of the effect of response categories on scale reliability concluded that there was little increase in reliability when there were more than 5 scale points or response categories. Bernardin, LaShells, Smith, and Alvares (1976) compared a continuous to noncontinuous 7-point response format and found no differences in rating errors. Finally, Jenkins and Taber (1977), in another Monte Carlo study of factors affecting scale reliability, agreed with Lissitz and Green that there is little utility in adding scale categories beyond 5.

Since several studies have found that an excessive number of categories can have negative effects on scale reliability, the studies on number of response categories would seem to have serious implications for scales that allow the rater to define the number of categories of response. Specifically, the format should require the individual to use one of a limited number of response categories, probably less than 9. In spite of the fact that the Bernardin et al. (1976) results do not support the generalization, the weight of evidence suggests that individuals have limited capacities for dealing with simultaneous categories of heterogeneous information. This was suggested long ago by Miller (1956) in his now-famous "seven, plus or minus two" dictum, and appears to generalize to rating behavior.

ANCHORS: TYPE. Rating scales typically have one of three types of anchors: numerical, adjectival, or behavioral. There have been several studies directed toward determining the relative merits of these alternative anchoring systems with regard to traditional psychometric indexes. This, of course, begs the question of whether there should be any anchors at all. Several studies have demonstrated the positive effect increasing the degree of scale anchoring. Bendig (1952a, 1952b, 1953) found that the reliability of ratings improved with increased anchoring. Barrett, Taylor, Parker, and Martens (1958) demonstrated the increased effectiveness of anchored scales compared to unanchored ones. Campbell, Hunt, and Lewis (1958) examined the effect of shifting context on ratings of cognitive organization present in responses of schizophrenics. They found that a 9-point scale with detailed anchors was less susceptible to distortion than a similar scale with a minimum of descriptive anchoring.

A number of studies have suggested a positive effect on psychometric indexes of behavioral anchors as compared to simple numerical or adjectival anchors (Barrett et al., 1958; Bendig, 1952a, 1952b; Maas, 1965; Peters & McCormick, 1966; Smith & Kendall, 1963). Since the BARS format has relied heavily on the behavioral nature of the scale anchors, almost all studies positive toward the BARS format might also be thought of as positive toward behavioral rather than adjectival or numerical anchors. Nevertheless, there have been some studies that have cast some doubt on the nature of elaborate anchors. Finn (1972) found no difference in means or reliabilities of ratings as a function of the manner of defining scale levels. It did not seem to matter if the anchors were numerical or descriptive. Kay (1959) found that using critical incidents to anchor rating scales depressed reliability values. He suggested that critical incidents were too specific and context bound for use as anchors. Shapira and Shirom (1980) found that behavioral anchors that frequently occurred on the job resulted in more lenient ratings than scales composed of less frequently occurring anchors.

The importance of the type and number of anchors probably covaries with the adequacy of the dimension definition. In the absence of adequate definitions of the dimensions to be rated, the rater must depend on the anchors to supply the meaning of the scale. In the Barrett et al. (1958) study, it was found that scales with good behavioral anchors and no dimension definitions (only trait labels) had higher reliability, less halo, and less leniency than either scales with definitions and anchors or scales with definitions but no anchors. In general, it seems as though anchors are important, and there is some evidence to suggest that behavioral anchors are better than numerical or adjectival ones.

ANCHORS: SCALING. Traditionally, one of the weaker procedures in the development of rating scales has been the process of assigning scale values to anchors. Although there have been some attempts at modifying scale intervals with numerical and adjectival anchors (Bendig, 1952a, 1952b), for the most part there has been little research on the nature of the psychological scale of measurement implied by traditional graphic rating scales.

In the forced-choice format, indexes of discrimination and favorability are determined for each item to be used. The *discrimination index* is the degree to which the particular item or phrase discriminates between high and low performers; the *preference value* is the degree to which the trait or behavior represented by the item is valued by the typical rater. Both Isard (1956) and Obradovic (1970) found that neutral items were superior to positive or negative items in terms of psychometric characteristics of the resulting ratings. By implication, one might conclude that items with intermediate scale values on the preference dimension were more useful than high or low preference items.

Smith and Kendall (1963) used item analysis to determine the ability of particular behavioral anchors to discriminate good from poor nurses. Unfortunately, few studies that followed the Smith and Kendall lead were as rigorous in terms of either anchor selection or placement. The most common technique for anchoring in the BARS method is the use of judges to estimate "how much" of a particular dimension a behavioral example represents. This is usually accomplished with graphic ratings on adjectivally or numerically anchored graphic rating scales. These items have been previously judged for content. The final selection of anchors is based on the resulting mean value of the item and its standard deviation. The decision rule is frequently arbitrary (choose items that represent as many points along the continuum as possible and have standard deviations less than a specified value). Bernardin has demonstrated (Bernardin, 1977; Bernardin, Alvares, & Cranny, 1976) that the resistance of rating scales to traditional rating errors depends, to some degree, on the rigor of scale development and anchoring. He suggests that this rigor can be introduced through rather standard item analysis procedures. Barnes and Landy (1979) demonstrated that a Thurstone solution of a pair-comparison scaling of behavioral anchors produces anchor scale values that are significantly different from those produced by the graphic rating method common to BARS development. It may very well be that the reason for the relatively disappointing showing of the BARS format to other formats has been due to a lack of rigor in the selection and scaling of anchors. This has been suggested by Schwab, Heneman, and DeCotiis (1975), Bernardin (1977), Landy (1977), and Bernardin and Smith (1981).

There are some data which suggest that the anchoring process itself is susceptible to the same kinds of biases that new rating formats, such as BARS, are attempting to eliminate. Thus, the situation becomes one of infinite regress; the anchoring procedure introduces the very type of error variance that the format attempts to eliminate. Wells and Smith (1960), Rotter and Tinkleman (1970), Landy and Guion (1970), and Barnes and Landy (1979) have all demonstrated that anchoring procedures affect ultimate item scale values and standard deviations. These data suggest that anchoring be accomplished by means of some method based on firm psychometric theory (such as Thurstone's Law of Comparative Judgment).

SOME GENERAL ISSUES

Rating Dimensions

The nature of what dimensions are to be rated has created some controversy. Kavanagh (1971) has argued that the empirical literature does not allow one to choose unequivocally the type of content of rating scales (i.e., performance results versus observable job behaviors versus personal traits of the incumbent). Brumback (1972) has called for the elimination of personal traits (e.g., emotional stability, initiative, honesty, cooperation), as rating dimensions in preference to performance factors (defined in terms of observable job behaviors). Kavanagh (1973) has rejoined that the question of appropriate rating dimensions can only be answered by a consideration of the nature of the job requirements, the relevance of personal and performance factors for that job, and the empirical defensibility of each content type in terms of reliability, resistance to rating bias, and construct validity.

Kane and Lawler (1979) contend that traits have no place in performance appraisal systems. They argue that traits (if we can measure them) are only characteristics of individuals that serve as causes or limiters of performance level and do not constitute performance per se. In one sense Kane and Lawler are suggesting that, if certain traits are theoretically related to job performance, they may be useful as selection devices or predictors of future job success, but that they are not legitimate substitutes for performance dimensions since performance level is affected by factors other than the traits.

Further points made by Kane and Lawler (1979) are that the appropriate content of appraisal system is limited to work behaviors and work outcomes (see Figure 1.1 in Chapter 1, this volume). They suggest that, when a job's desired outcome can be reached by only a single means or set of procedures, it is more appropriate to assess the work behaviors of incumbents. When there are two or more ways to succeed, Kane and Lawler suggest that work outcomes are more appropriate as the content of the appraisal system.

It would appear that there is not an easy solution to the issue of the content of performance ratings. Traits seem too subjective, yet we seem likely to organize our evaluations of others around such traits (see Chapter 8, this volume). We find traits useful (or perceive them to be useful at least) in predicting the behavior of individuals in new situations (e.g., when considering someone for a job transfer or promotion). Behavioral performance dimensions are more objective but may not seem to offer us the transsituational generalizability that may be desired when we want to predict the behavior of an individual in a new situation.

The solution, or our best approximation to a solution, may be a compromise. Dimension labels may be trait names whereas the dimension definitions and scale anchors may be task and behavior oriented. This may allow us the objectivity of measurement we desire while providing a form of relatively standardized information about traits. The operational definition of traits in terms of job behaviors does not perfectly solve the content issue but it seems better than a strict reliance on just traits or just job behaviors.

Sources of Judgments

The most frequent source of performance judgments is the immediate supervisor of the work performer. However, several other sources of judgments are available, including higher levels of supervision, peers, the actual work performer, subordinates, customers, and trained obser-vors–evaluators. Much of the comparative research literature on sources of judgments is reviewed in Chapter 5. Here we will briefly discuss the uses of judgment sources other than the immediate supervisor that have been noted in the literature.

Peer assessment has been widely used. A review by Kane and Lawler (1978) was generally positive in its conclusions about the value of peer assessment, although Brief (1980) questioned whether that judgment was overly optimistic (but see the rebuttal to Brief by Kane & Lawler, 1980).

There are three peer-assessment techniques, peer nominations, peer rankings, and peer ratings. Peer rankings and ratings are identical to their supervisor counterparts previously discussed. Peer-nomination procedures consist of having each member of a work group designate some specified number of group members as best or highest on some performance dimension or characteristic. Sometimes group members are also asked to designate the lowest or worst N members of the group on the dimension or characteristic. Self-nominations are generally banned.

Kane and Lawler (1978) concluded that peer assessments can be reliable and valid. They also concluded that peer nominations appear to have the highest reliability and validity, that peer ratings are most useful for feedback but least valid and reliable, and that peer rankings are not well researched but potentially the most discriminating method. (Considerable detail regarding the psychometric properties and usefulness of peer-assessment techniques is presented in Kane & Lawler [1978] and will not be repeated here.) Kane and Lawler suggested that peer assessment is most likely to be useful in situations in which work-group members have access to unique information about each other's job performance and are capable of accurately observing and judging that performance information.

Brief (1980) noted the lack of operational definitions concerning the conditions for the successful application of peer techniques suggested by Kane and Lawler (1978). He further noted that there may be conditions that are antagonistic to the use of peer assessment, including lack of interpersonal trust in the work group and the existence of a competitive reward system analogous to a zero-sum game (Cummings & Schwab, 1973). Of course, the suggestions of both Kane and Lawler and Brief need to be operationalized and empirically tested, but they should serve as useful hypotheses for research.

It is likely that the purpose of assessment is a major factor influencing the usefulness and acceptance of peer assessments as a performance evaluation technique. The use of such data in administrative decisions is more likely to be resisted (by all elements of the organization) than are uses concerned with the development of personnel or research studies.

Self-appraisal of performance was one focus of several articles. Levine (1980), Thornton (1980), and Meyer (1980) presented evidence that self-appraisals are likely to be more lenient than judgments from other sources and to be problematic if used for certain purposes such as administrative decision making, diagnosis of training needs, and selection. Self-appraisals are congruent with participative styles of organizational decision making (see, e.g., McGregor, 1957, 1959) and may be useful in reducing defensiveness about performance-appraisal interviews (feedback sessions) (Bassett & Meyer, 1968; Meyer, Kay, & French, 1965). Self-appraisals may also be informative for understanding motivational phenomena (Thornton, 1980), as motivational constructs are often better at predicting self-appraisals than more objective performance measures or judgments from other sources.

The other possible sources of performance judgments have been seldom studied with the exception of higher levels of supervision. Research on higher supervision is discussed in Chapter 5, usually in contrast to immediate supervision. In general, a good strategy regarding sources would be to include as many as possible, considering the likely redundancy of the information obtained and the purposes for which the information will be used. Each source is biased in some way and diversity of input is likely to be valuable.

Typical Performance versus Performance Distribution

As noted by Kane and Lawler (1979), most performance-judgment systems seek information about *typical* performance displayed by a work performer over some period of time. Thus, the rater must in some fashion integrate a number of instances of performance and arrive at a single judgment. This single judgment may or may not be well representative of a given individual's performance dependent on the variability of the individual's distribution of performance and other performance distribution characteristics such as skewness or kurtosis. To the extent that differences in individual performance distributions are reliable characteristics of work performers, the ignoring of such distributional properties is a loss of valuable information.

Kane and Lawler (1979) have suggested an approach to performance measurement that they call *distributional measurement* that attempts to elicit ratings in terms of the frequency or rate at which each individual has exhibited a given performance dimension at a series of "benchmark" levels of performance (along the whole continuum of performance). These judgments are scored via profile similarity techniques that use the profile parameters of elevation, shape, and scatter. Details of the logic and the actual steps of this procedure are presented in Kane and Lawler (1979). Although the technique requires much research to assess its applicability, it represents an interesting approach to performance measurement.

SUMMARY

After more than 30 years of serious research, a generally accepted, efficient, and psychometrically sound alternative to the traditional graphic rating scale has not yet been developed. Nevertheless, we have learned some things about rating formats in general. Despite the fact that people may have preferences for various physical arrangements of high and low anchors and of graphic numbering systems, these preferences seem to have little effect on actual rating behavior. The number of response categories available to the rater should not exceed nine. If multiple response categories are desired for a rating scale, it would be wise to conduct some pilot studies to determine how many response categories are *perceived* by the potential raters. There is some advantage to using behavioral anchors rather than simple numerical or adjectival anchors. This advantage is probably increased in the absence of good dimension definitions. Finally, it is important that rigorous item selection and anchoring procedures be used in the development of rating scales, regardless of the particular format being considered. It may be that new techniques, such as BARS or MSS, will show improvements over more traditional methods if more rigorous developmental procedures are used.

It appears likely that greater progress in understanding performance judgments will come from research on the rating process than from a continued search for the "Holy Format." In the next chapter we offer an initial attempt at modeling this process.

part two

A Model of Rating

Many forms of performance measurement involve a judgment that one person makes about the efforts or output of another person. Since rating is the single most common form of performance measurement found in applied settings, it is considered as a separate topic.

As is the case with any judgment, there is the possibility of inaccuracy that results from both random and systematic error. Chapter 4 presents a model of the performance-rating process as manifested in work settings. The components of the model highlight the dynamic properties of performance rating. Chapter 5 reviews the literature supporting the model.

chapter four

A Model of Performance Judgment

As we saw in the previous two chapters, there are many different ways to measure the performance of individual workers. The nonjudgmental methods would include counts of units produced, time elapsed, errors, scrap, absences, accidents, and so forth. The judgmental methods might involve ranking, rating, or simply prose descriptions. To the psychologist, the latter methods—judgmental measurements—have provided the greatest theoretical and administrative challenges. This is the result of a rather simple and obvious fact: A *rater* is involved. This rater may be compared to a little computer. This little computer collects information, stores it, retrieves it, uses it to make decisions, and replaces some form of that information in memory. The problem seems to be that, like computers, there are many different "brands" of raters. These raters are affected to differing degrees by internal capacities and limitations as well as external forces. These differences can be disruptive to both the administrative and the research enterprise since they influence the quality of the data that represent behavior or performance.

In the past decades, an enormous amount of research has been directed toward eliminating or controlling variables that were thought to influence ratings. These variables included such things as scale format and rater training. They were somewhat limited in scope and tended toward the trivial. For example, many studies addressed the issue of the appropriate number of response categories on a rating scale (see Landy & Farr, 1980 for a review of these studies). Although an issue such as the number of scale points is relevant for understanding and using rating data, many other issues, equally relevant, had been ignored during 30 years of research.

We reviewed the literature on performance rating (Landy & Farr, 1980) and concluded that the needs of practitioners and researchers alike would be best served by developing a model to guide future efforts in rating research. We felt that a model would be an efficient method for pointing out the diverse sources of influence in rating behavior and for highlighting those areas that needed more attention. The only previous attempt to model the rating process had been carried out by Wherry in 1952. His model was based on logical, methodological, and statistical principles rather than on empirical data. It was an outstanding contribution from the deductive perspective. Many of his propositions have been confirmed. Unfortunately, his reports were not widely circulated and have never been published. Since his work is as timely now as the day it was completed, we have reproduced one of his technical reports in the Appendix to this book.

Even though Wherry's efforts were both salient and outstanding, they did not address many variables that have been shown to affect the rating process. This encouraged us to develop and present our model of the rating process. This chapter reviews that model. In the discussion, we will attempt to place current rating research in both theoretical and historical perspective. In Chapter 8, we will use the model as a basis for discussing some of the cognitive activities that are related to performance measurement.

THE DEVELOPMENT OF THE MODEL

We chose to develop a model of performance evaluation based on ratings for several reasons. As indicated earlier, ratings are by far the most ubiquitous forms of performance estimates (Guion, 1965; Landy & Farr, 1976; Landy & Farr, 1980; Landy & Trumbo, 1980). As a result, the research on ratings overwhelms (at least in quantity if not quality) research on other approaches to performance evaluation.

Additionally, performance judgment rather than simple counts of the results of behavior (i.e., production measures) is more fascinating from the strictly psychological point of view. It includes aspects of cognitive psychology, learning theory, social psychology, personality theory, and scaling measurement theory, just to mention a few substantive areas of investigation implied in the study of the process.

Finally, we chose to limit our model building to rating rather than other judgmental operations such as ranking, pair-comparison estimation, and other forms of worker-to-worker comparison because it was our feeling that these other estimation procedures implied a qualitatively different discrimination process on the part of the rater. In traditional learning terms, pair-comparison judgments comprise a series of simultaneous discriminations, whereas graphic ratings involve successive (and occasionally absolute rather than relative) discriminations.

The very nature of performance rating in industrial settings places some constraints on the definition of "appropriate" literature to be used in building a model. Such constraints are a blessing in disguise for both the reviewer and the reader. Such was the case in the effort to develop a model of performance rating. In the most common case, a supervisor is asked to consider the past performance of a subordinate. "Past" performance usually means in the last year. It is likely that the supervisor and the subordinate have interacted frequently during that period of time and may have even developed some social relations that transcend the work setting (e.g., they may belong to the same bowling team, or church, or softball team, or book club). In short, they are far from strangers to each other. For that reason, we have excluded the more artificial variations of laboratory research using students. Similarly, we have not considered the research on the selection interview, at least directly, since the applicant is typically not well known to the judges who will evaluate the interview "performance." Finally, we have chosen not to consider the rating behavior of evaluators of "paper people" in building our model. There is something special about the interaction of real individuals with real dependencies on each other (emotional, economic, political, etc.) that cannot be captured by the examination of the behavior of a college junior role playing a manager watching a videotape, or reading a description of performance. As you will see in our model, we believe that the typical performance rating represents a very different type of cognitive activity, one that depends heavily on memory, synthesis, and stereotypes. Most paper-people experiments are deficient in their potential generalizability. Rather than throwing the baby out with the bath water, they ultimately drown the baby with experimental control. We consider performance rating to be a retrospective synthesis by one individual of the efforts of another. This implies the evaluation of a long string of events rather than a single one. In addition, the rater is most often dealing with a constellation of activities rather than a single physical or mental operation on the part of the ratee. We do not feel that this in any

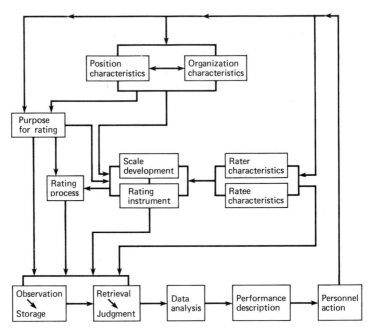

Figure 4.1. A process model of performance rating. (From Landy, F. J., & Farr, J. L. Performance rating. *Psychological Bulletin*, 1980, *87*, p. 94. Copyright 1980 by the American Psychological Association. Reprinted by permission of the publisher and author.)

way burlesques or trivializes the behavior to be modeled. On the contrary, we feel that our conception of the prototypic performance rating closely matches reality.

With all of those qualifications, we offer Figure 4.1 as a representation of the factors influencing the typical performance rating. We will now describe each of these factors in some detail. As a heuristic aid, it might help to think of each of the factors as a possible "filter" through which an individual's actual behavior passes. These filters have the capacity to alter dramatically the eventual performance description rendered by the rater.

RATER CHARACTERISTICS

To restate the obvious, rating is done by raters. These raters inevitably bring their characteristics with them to the rating task. These characteristics vary in relevance to the rating task. As far as many ratees are concerned, every characteristic that the rater brings to the task is some variation on a personal bias. The rater is white, or male, or older, or younger, or well educated. It is assumed that these characteristics play a major role in the resulting evaluations. These are personal characteristics. In a sense, they are the characteristics that the individual carries around that may influence any interpersonal evaluation—not just work-related ones. Table 4.1 presents various classes of variables that might be thought of as rater characteristics having the potential to influence ratings.

In addition to these variables, we must consider the influence of the level of the rater with respect to the ratee. One might expect peer ratings to differ from subordinate and supervisor ratings of the same individual. All of these characteristics are somehow "possessed" by the raters. The rater cannot leave them at home when evaluating the performance of others. The demographic variables are gross and artificial indicators of influence. Some have labeled them "boxcar variables" since they simply transport other variables of greater interest to the psychologist. For example, age per se is more interesting to the sociologist than the psychologist. The psychologist is more interested in knowing how age influences thought processes. Nevertheless, it is the boxcar variables that have received major attention in the last decade. This is undoubtedly due to the influence of legislation such as Equal Employment Opportunity (EEO) guidelines and the Age Discrimination Act. It is hard to believe that there are structural differences that might account for differences in the evaluations done by men and women, blacks and whites, older and younger workers. We must not lose sight of the fact that demographic characteristics represent the beginning of the search, not the end. It is ultimately the psychological and job-related variables that will lead to a better understanding of the nature of performance evaluation. A final and obvious characteristic that might be "possessed" by the rater is the extent to which he or she has been trained to carry out the rating. Of course, this is a process of the organization, but when it has been accomplished, it becomes a property of the rater.

RATEE CHARACTERISTICS

Ratees also bring certain characteristics to the rating task. In an idealized world, ratees would present only performance indicators to the rater for consideration, estimation, and recording. Unfortunately, this is probably not the case in the real world. In the process of presenting performance data for consideration, ratees also unwittingly (or sometimes

Table 4.1
Rater Characteristics

Demographic	Psychological	Job related
Gender	Personality variables	Job satisfaction
Race	Intellectual skills	Leadership style
Age	Life satisfaction	Level of performance
Education	Perceived similarity to ratee	Tenure
		Knowledge of the job rated
		Job involvement
		Supervisory expertise
		Knowledge of the individual rated
		Ability to appraise performance (training)

wittingly) present data on demographic and psychological dimensions that have no direct relevance to the performance evaluation being conducted.

Ratee characteristics that might influence the ratings assigned are slightly different from those attributed to raters. Table 4.2 lists some of these characteristics.

A comparison of Tables 4.1 and 4.2 suggests that physical characteristics of ratees may play a larger role in performance ratings than similar characteristics of raters. Although it is difficult to conceive of any direct relationship between the weight of a rater and the score assigned to a given ratee, many believe that overweight employees are discriminated against in work settings.

In Table 4.2, the term *identification with the rater* is substituted for the term *perceived similarity to ratee*, which appears in Table 4.1. This suggests

Table 4.2
Ratee Characteristics

Demographic	Psychological	Job related
Age	Personality variables	Job satisfaction
Gender	Intellectual skills	Satisfaction with supervision
Race	Life satisfaction	Level of performance
Education	Identification with rater	Tenure
Color	Social deviance	Performance deviance
Religion		Reaction to performance appraisal
National origin		Job involvement
Physical attractiveness		

that ratees who actively imitate raters affect the perceptions of those raters (i.e., raters perceive those ratees as similar to themselves).

Finally, Table 4.2 suggests that there is a deviance–conformity continuum that may play a major role in the ratings that are assigned to a ratee. This deviance may be of a general nature: The ratee may be simply seen as not fitting in with the other workers or the typical employee population. The deviance may also be of a more specific, work-related variety: The worker may stand out in the work group as the best or the worst. Both the general and the specific forms of deviance may have a contrast effect on the ratings assigned to that individual, making the performance estimates either higher or lower than warranted. There is one comforting suggestion in Table 4.2. The variable titled *level of performance* implies that there is *some* relationship between the worker's effectiveness and the ratings assigned.

RATER–RATEE INTERACTION

The boxes representing the rater characteristics and the ratee characteristics in Figure 4.1 are shown to interact. This interaction suggests that in addition to the main effect of rater and ratee characteristics, *certain* ratee characteristics are treated differentially by *certain* raters. For example, it is widely believed that white supervisors show favoritism toward white subordinates, that younger supervisors prefer younger subordinates, and that male supervisors prefer male subordinates. Each of these would be an example of a rater–ratee interaction. It is not simply the race, age, or sex of the rater that makes a difference in the ratings; rather it is the interaction of the race, age, and sex of the ratee with the race, sex, and age of the rater that is important.

SCALE DEVELOPMENT

One of the most popular rating techniques to appear in the last decade has been the Behaviorally Anchored Rating Scale (BARS). As described in the previous chapter, the BARS technique involves collecting examples of behavior from those who will ultimately rate or be rated. It is hoped that by such a process, the anchors on each scale will have maximum salience and generality to the raters and maximum face validity or credibility to those being rated.

One of the inevitable consequences of using the BARS technique is the involvement of the rater–ratee population in scale development. Not only do they provide examples but they may also be called upon to (*a*) identify the basic dimensions of performance; (*b*) define these performance dimensions; (*c*) judge the adequacy of behavioral anchors supplied by others; (*d*) assign scale values to anchors; and (*e*) help in field testing newly developed rating scales. In the briefing that precedes BARS procedures, participants are usually told that *they* are experts, that *they* will be building the scales, that this will be *their* system. In short, every attempt is made to motivate these individuals to take the rating-scale construction personally. The assumption underlying this involvement is that individuals who have something of themselves invested in the scale construction will do a better job and will be more likely to use the rating scales in an appropriate manner when they become operational.

The BARS technique is the most extreme with respect to the involvement of rater–ratee populations in scale development. At the other extreme is a more common procedure. An organization becomes aware of a rating instrument currently being used in another location and simply introduces it as the "new" procedure. A variation on this theme is the situation in which a division is told by the corporate personnel officer that as of a particular date a new format *will* be used. In both of these instances the scale development occurs outside rather than inside the organizational unit in question. Intermediate to these extremes of total involvement and no involvement, we have situations in which general discussions are conducted with the possibility for procedural modification of the system to be introduced. Several studies have pointed to the importance of the "acceptability" of an evaluation system (Landy, Barnes, & Murphy, 1978; Landy, Barnes-Farrell, & Cleveland, 1980; Lawler, 1967). This acceptability is very likely to be affected by the manner in which the rating scales are developed. Often, organizations are faced with the choice among alternative sets of rating scales rather than having to develop their own from scratch. The principle would be the same in those situations. A single individual, such as the vice-president for personnel, might make the choice, or the ultimate "consumers" (raters and ratees) might be consulted.

Some of the issues to be considered with respect to the scale development component include:

1. Rater involvement: Will the raters who will eventually use the scales take part in the scale development? If so, will they take part directly

(i.e., every rater will have a say in the development) or be represented by peers (i.e., only a subset of the raters will help develop the scales)?

2. Ratee involvement: Will those to be evaluated have any involvement in scale development? If so, will this involvement be direct or representative?

3. How long a time period will intervene between scale development and actual use of the scales for rating? 3 weeks? 3 months? 3 years?

4. Will the scale development be guided by someone from inside the organization (e.g., vice-president for human resources, personnel director) or an outsider such as a consultant or researcher who has no ties to the organization other than those developed in the course of constructing the rating scales?

Keep in mind that these issues are independent of the type of scale being developed or chosen. The same decisions about involvement must be made regardless of whether the scale is a traditional graphic one or a summated rating checklist.

RATING INSTRUMENT

The enormous amount of research on the topic of rating format clearly indicates the assumed importance of the actual rating scales in the performance evaluation process. Hundreds of studies have varied every conceivable aspect of the rating-scale format. These studies have examined the number of scale points, the types of anchors, the spatial orientation of the scale, instructions, and countless other parameters. Table 4.3 presents a sample of the variables that would define this component of the model.

There is a clear logic that underlies most of this research. It is assumed that the individual processes performance information and that the actual scales can affect this processing. Rating forms either allow or discourage certain processing capabilities by the individual rater. If we request limited information on a few number of performance areas with yes/no response alternatives, we should expect limited value from that information. On the other hand, if we are able to elicit information of a sophisticated nature from a broad sampling of performance areas, that information should prove more generally useful. In that sense, the rating scale is similar to a computer language. Just as a computer language cannot "create" data, a rating scale cannot "create" a judgment. The computer

Table 4.3
Rating Instrument

Format variables	Content variables
Number of scale points	Type of anchor (numerical, adjectival, or behavioral)
Number of dimensions	behavioral)
Requirement for documentation for rating	Dimension definitions
Number of anchors	Type of decision required (continuous versus discrete)
Spatial orientation of response scale	discrete)
Presence of "not applicable" category	Rater awareness of "scoring procedures"
	Number of judgments required of rater
	Nature of dimensions to be rated

language helps analyze data—the rating scale helps the rater synthesize individual judgments.

In a broad sense, the assumed function of a rating format is to encourage certain cognitive operations on the part of the rater. We ask the rater to consider one set of dimensions and not another; we ask the rater to assign ratings within certain limits; we ask the rater to consider specific definitions when assigning ratings. It is becoming increasingly obvious that rating formats themselves are less important than their effects on the cognitive operations of raters. Unfortunately, we know very little about these cognitive operations. Nevertheless, it is clear that a rating-scale format must be an integral part of any model that purports to explain performance evaluation.

RATING PROCESS

In many respects, the administration of the performance evaluation system may be as important to the actual instrument. It has been suggested that the concept of organizational climate may be defined as the process by which an organization carries out its functions (Landy & Trumbo, 1980; Lawler, Hall, & Oldham, 1974). In a sense, the climate of the organization is its personality. It can be personal or impersonal, supportive or punitive, responsive or unresponsive. Just as the personality of an individual is perceived by others on the basis of the individual's "style" of behavior, so is the personality or climate of an organization perceived on the basis of how its policies are carried out. Thus, the climate of an organization can be seen in its recruitment and selection programs, in the nature of its training procedures, in reward and promotional policies, and in performance evaluation processes. It is for that reason that the model includes a component dealing specifically with the rating process. Certainly the rating process will be affected by the instrument used, but of equal importance is the effect that the rating process has on the individual rater.

When considering the rating process or the administration of the performance-rating procedures, there are many variables that might play a role. Table 4.4 lists some examples of these variables. There are two basic classes of variables: task-relevant variables (i.e., relevant to the task of *rating*) and environmental variables. These two classes are suggested only for heuristic convenience. We do not mean to imply any real independence of the variables listed in each column. It is easy to see that many of the variables that we have listed as "environmental" would be expected to have direct effects on the "task-relevant" variables, and vice versa.

One might also expect that the rating process would have some effect on the acceptability of the performance evaluation system. If an organization budgets little or no time for its managers to complete evaluations on subordinates, those managers will place a low priority on that activity. When the personnel department requests those evaluations, the managers will comply with minimally acceptable effort, dashing the evaluations off over a lunch break. Ratees are fully aware of such procedures and respond with appropriate cynicism about the value of the ratings (and any feedback that is based on those ratings). On the other hand, in an organization that backs up evaluations with rater training, instruction booklets, with a block of time budgeted specifically for evaluation, and similar credible measures for accomplishing the performance evaluation, the effect on rater and ratee will probably be considerably different.

Table 4.4
Rating Process Characteristics

Environmental variables	Task-relevant variables
Physical location of rating	Prerating training
Time pressure for completion of rating	Instructions
Temporal rating schedule	Anonymity of rater
(anniversary date of hire versus	Knowledge of ratings by ratee
common time for all)	Number of ratings to be completed at one time
Logistic support from personnel	Position of ratee in rating sequence
department	Knowledge of previous ratings of ratee

We do not mean to suggest that the only effect of the rating process is on attitudes or motivations of raters and ratees. Recently, there have been suggestions that the actual cognitive operations involved in rating can be affected by the rating process as we have described it. For example, we might expect that asking raters to keep specific dimensions of performance in mind in the months preceding actual rating would have an effect on the resulting ratings. In a sense, the rater has been given some instruction in separating the important from the trivial (at least from the organization's point of view). Similarly, it is hard to believe that 25 minutes stolen in the midst of a hectic day for completing some ratings will yield the same results as several hours devoted to nothing but the consideration of the efficiency of a set of ratees. It is reasonable to expect that cognitive operations can be significantly affected by environmental and procedural variables.

ORGANIZATIONAL CHARACTERISTICS

We implied earlier that organizations had "personalities." This meant that organizations have habitual or ritualized ways of responding to their members. One of those rituals is performance evaluation (or the dogged avoidance of evaluation). We would expect both the substance and the process of performance evaluation to be affected by organizational characteristics. In a sense, these characteristics, like process characteristics, help comprise the organizational personality.

An organization that employs thousands of workers is likely to carry out performance differently than an organization with less than 100 members; organizations with large spans of control will evaluate differently than those with a small subordinate–supervisor ratio; organizations that have union representation for some or all of its nonsupervisory members will evaluate the effectiveness of these members differently than those with no collective-bargaining units. These are all examples of variables that might be thought of as organizational characteristics. Many of them are traditional ones that are thought to comprise the "shape" of the organization. Many others are nontraditional and may be more aptly applied to the environment in which the organization is embedded. Table 4.5 lists examples of the variables that belong to these two classes of organizational characteristics.

This component is based on the premise that many of these characteris-

Table 4.5
Organizational Characteristics

Intraorganizational characteristics	Environmental characteristics
Size	Market share
Span of control	Profitability
Number of supervisory personnel	Market predictability
Line–Staff ratio	Local unemployment
Number of levels between rater and ratee	National unemployment
Direction of information flow	Demands for diversification
Participation in decision making	Restrictions imposed by local, state,
Goods versus service orientation	and federal legislation (e.g., EEO
Union representation	guidelines)
Tenure of current performance appraisal system	
Turnover	
Seasonal variation in production	
Part-time/full-time ratio	
Percentage minority/female employees	

tics affect both the rating process and the instrument that is used. For example, many smaller organizations, in which all supervisors know all subordinates, use supervisor conferences to assign ratings. In these conferences, all of the supervisors get together as a group and discuss the performance of each employee in turn. After the discussion of each subordinate, a rating is assigned that is thought to represent the level of performance of that employee. This is a luxury afforded by a small organization. This type of evaluation procedure would be much more difficult in a larger organization. Similarly, many union contracts prescribe the substance, timing, and process of performance evaluation. As an example, a recent contract demand of a municipal workers' union was that a 5-point (outstanding to poor) rating scheme be eliminated in favor of a simple binary (satisfactory/unsatisfactory) rating scheme.

There is another important aspect of organizational characteristics. Some organizations use performance evaluation as a punitive mechanism, depriving the lowest $X\%$ of salary increases. Other organizations use performance evaluation as a means of motivation, providing the feedback that employees need for setting goals for future performance. To a certain extent these purposes are affected by the physical and psychological characteristics of the organization. We will discuss these uses (or purposes) in greater detail shortly.

POSITION CHARACTERISTICS

Independent of the characteristics that the ratee possesses, and the characteristics of the organization to which the ratee belongs, the particular job or position that the ratee holds has characteristics of its own. Much like the other characteristics just reviewed, the characteristics of the position also have the potential to influence the ratings that an individual receives. Many think of the job of patrol officer as a "male" job; for years, the upper age limits on the job of stewardess made it a "younger" person's job. It is possible that many, if not most, jobs have some stereotypic properties. Thus, it is possible to conceive of characteristics that are specific to the job title of the ratee in question. These characteristics might be loosely grouped into two categories—those intrinsic to the tasks that define the job and those that are part of the context in which the job is performed. Table 4.6 presents examples of these variables. As has been the case with several other components, no claim is made for the functional independence of these variables. It is not hard to see how they might be influenced by other variables that have already been described. Nevertheless, conceptually, position characteristics are meaningful to consider in attempting to list the impediments to accurate performance evaluation.

PURPOSE FOR RATING

Researchers and practioners alike agree that the intended use of ratings probably has some effect on performance evaluation. In a sense, this component represents the "motivation to rate." To this point, we have dealt with the rater as a rather passive component of the system, reacting to characteristics that impinge on the actual rating process. We have suggested that the rater can be influenced by format, can be inadvertently swayed by stereotypes and prejudices, and can be confused by conflicting demands and pressures to complete the ratings. The purpose-for-rating component, however, places the rater directly in the driver's seat with respect to the accuracy of the ratings. This component implies that the rater evaluates the possible impact of the ratings on the ratee, on the organization, and any unwanted "backlash" effects on the rater.

Consider the implications of different purposes. If ratings were gathered simply to play the role of criterion measures for the validation of a selection device or an evaluation of the impact of a training program, one

Table 4.6
Position Characteristics

Intrinsic	Contextual
Prevailing job stereotypes (age, sex, etc.)	Valid selection procedures
Job difficulty (physical)	Effective training procedures
Type of technology	Number of levels between rater and ratee
Workload predictability	Method of payment
Autonomy	Boundary uncertainty
Feedback opportunities	
Skill variety	
Task complexity	
Task significance	
Work-group dependence	

might expect raters to be as accurate as possible, within limits imposed by components already mentioned. In other words, the individual might have the appropriate "motivation to rate." On the other hand, suppose that the rater was told that the ratings were to be used to make decisions about who would be laid off, or who would receive merit increases, or who would be allowed to apply for company-subsidized training. It is reasonable to look for differences between ratings completed for administrative purposes and those done for "research only."

The same point can be made in a slightly different way. It might make sense to assume that raters are operating on the environment when carrying out evaluations. The question to answer is which aspect of the environment are they directing their efforts toward. It is by no means assured that raters will accept the reasons for rating as provided by the organization. Many organization members have well-developed conspiracy theories with respect to the hidden agenda for performance ratings. The challenge then becomes one of estimating the motivational forces on the rater. Certainly, the stated purpose for the ratings is a beginning. But this obscures the more realistic component, the purpose for ratings *as perceived by the rater.*

OBSERVATION–STORAGE

In the description of the model, we have addressed the issue of cognitive operations obliquely several times. We have suggested that stereotypes affect judgments, that rating dimensions may act as "prepackaged concepts" for the rater, and that the general atmosphere surrounding the appraisal process may affect the quality of judgment made about an individual's performance. All of these suggestions imply some rather important cognitive operations. These operations can be divided into several distinct processes. The first of these consists of the process of observing and storing information. Figure 4.2 is an attempt to describe more specifically the actual process involved in observation and storage. There are two real issues to consider. The first is the "quality" of the observation. This would include the representativeness of the behavior observed, the number of distractions present during observation, and the motivation of the observer. The second issue is a more traditional one and deals with the notion of memory. At least at a heuristic level, it is generally accepted that there are two kinds of memory—short term and long term. It is also generally assumed that there is some mediating mechanism that is involved in the transfer of information from short-term to long-term memory. At some basic level we must be concerned with the person's capacity to carry out this transfer as well as the conditions that might aid or hinder that transformation. Thus, storage is a functional term and memory is a structural term. It is reasonable to assume that the components in Figure 4.2 labeled *stimulus preprocessing* and *stimulus categorization* are relevant for considerations of both observation and storage.

In the most common performance evaluation scenario, the observations and storage activities are occurring constantly, right up to the moment of evaluation. Nevertheless, it is assumed that all of the information to be considered in the evaluation has been transferred to long-term memory

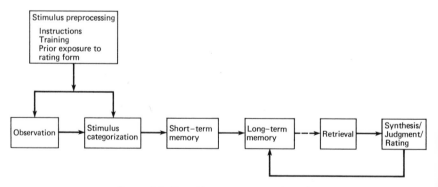

Figure 4.2. Cognitive components in rating.

mation. As we have seen in earlier sections of this chapter, there are many filters through which the "true performance" of the ratee passes on the way to the performance description. This filtering process is reminiscent of a whispering game that children play. A number of children are arranged in a line. A "secret" is whispered quickly to the first child, who in turn whispers that secret quickly to the second, who whispers it to the third, and so on. By the time the secret reaches the end of the line, it is hopelessly garbled. It has passed through a number of distorting filters in the process of transmission. Our model proposes that performance evaluation suffers from similar filtering problems. Once the judgments are made, it may be necessary to screen *out* certain distracting influences.

This process can be thought of in a different way. We might consider the actual ratings to be a puzzle that must be solved to be useful. The rater is trying to tell us something. It is our task to discover what that is. Like a jigsaw puzzle in a box, we have all the pieces, but we must still assemble them. This is not particularly new for psychology. Scaling procedures perform exactly that function. There are two ways to look at scaling research. We might assume that it has as its object the arrangement of a set of stimuli. This is a common interpretation of scaling activities. But at a much more basic level, scaling studies are directed toward discovering the underlying dimension that led to that arrangement. In a sense, scaling studies are carried out to solve the riddle of the arrangement of the objects. Performance ratings represent a similar riddle of arranged objects—the objects happen to be ratees. We may have done everything possible to eliminate the riddle using instructions, training, formats, conditions of administration, and so on. Nevertheless, the riddle may remain. There is one final set of variables that may either deepen the riddle or solve it. These variables are subsumed in the component that we have labeled *data analysis*. This component implies a statistical control (or filtering) of distracting influences in the actual ratings. There are several operations that might be performed on data. First, we might consider reducing the ratings to some nonredundant subset. This implies that much of the information that we receive in ratings is overlapping. A rating scale may ask for as many as 200 separate decisions about the performance of an individual. It is unlikely that 200 independent dimensions are necessary to describe essentially the performance of an individual, or to separate the performance of that individual from the performance of another individual. The most common form of data reduction is component analysis, although factor and cluster analysis are also used frequently. These analyses are intended to produce a new set of performance scores, fewer in number than the old (or "raw") scores, yet having basically the same or greater information value. This type of analysis presumably allows for easier interpretation of seemingly complex or conflicting data. It is a step toward solving the riddle of performance.

There are other statistical techniques that might be employed to clean up the performance ratings. If ratings are available from multiple ratees, we might assume that each of these ratings has a certain amount of random (uncorrelated) error but that the average of these ratings is closer to the expected value of the "true" performance score. Thus, we might improve the technical characteristics by taking the mean of the ratings from multiple raters on a single performance dimension. This would be done for each performance dimension on which ratees were considered. We might also weight each performance rating by its "reliability" (Passini & Norman, 1969).

Finally, we might use partial correlational techniques for eliminating unwanted influences in ratings. For example, we might find that the height of ratees has a positive influence on all of their performance ratings. If height is unrelated to successful performance of the job in question, we might simply statistically subtract (or partial out) the influence of height on the ratings by trying to predict performance ratings from height, subtracting the predicted rating from the actual rating and treating the resulting (residual) score as a performance rating that is free of the influence of height. Height is a silly example, but there are other characteristics that could be handled in a similar manner, such as the rater's overall view of the ratee (Landy, Vance, & Barnes-Farrell, 1982; Landy, Vance, Barnes-Farrell, & Steele, 1980), the job level (Myers, 1965), or the extent to which the rater likes the ratee. In each case, however, it is essential that we have a real number that represents the variable to be controlled or partialed.

PERFORMANCE DESCRIPTION AND PERSONNEL ACTION

These two components are necessary to complete the flow chart of performance rating. After the data are analyzed, they must be presented in some organizationally acceptable form. The form will depend on the use for which the information was originally intended. Thus, if counseling were the intended purpose, the form might be a narrative description of performance; if administrative decisions were to be made on the basis of ratings, a set of numbers might be produced. On the basis of this performance description, some personnel action is taken (either directly by commission or indirectly by omission). This action or inaction will have implications for future evaluations, as suggested by the feedback loops. Personnel actions represent salient information for learning the "rules" and the personality of the organization.

COMPONENT INTERACTIONS

The easiest thing to do with a model such as the one we have proposed is to attach each component to every other component with arrows running in both directions. This is a safe but trivial exercise. On the other hand, the area is so chaotic, with research and logic missing for many components, that a doctrinaire or prescriptive set of component relationships would be bizarre. We have tried to affect a compromise. We present some suggestions with respect to the manner in which the components interact. It should be easy enough to frame these suggestions as hypotheses. We expect that many of these suggested relationships will change as data become available. In short, we suggest the directional relationships as points of departure for subsequent research rather than an answers to unasked questions.

For expository ease, we will simply present the components one at a time with a brief description of how each is affected by other components.

Rater Characteristics

This component is most immediately affected by personnel actions that have been taken in the past as a result of performance evaluations.

Ratee Characteristics

It is not uncommon for ratees to try to guess what the rater considers to be good performance. "Good" may be defined as bootlicking or productivity. No matter how it is defined, the preferences, attitudes, and behavior of the rater can have a significant influence on the ratee. It is much less likely that the ratee characteristics will significantly alter a rater characteristic. If a ratee acts in a manner pleasing to the rater, the rater's definition of good performance is not likely to change.

Scale Development

The manner by which a rating scale is developed or chosen is influenced by both rater and ratee characteristics. If raters and/or ratees are unfamiliar with the concepts and operations of performance rating, it might be best to involve them heavily in scale development, as would be the case with a BARS procedure. On the other hand, if they are relatively sophisticated with respect to performance evaluation, it might be sufficient simply to have them review the suggestions of a personnel research group. If the ratees belong to a union, they may request formal inclusion in the development process. These are some examples of the impact of rater–ratee characteristics on scale development.

Scale development is also affected by organizational and position characteristics. Large organizations are less likely to encourage direct involvement of raters and ratees in scale development. Mechanistic organizations will approach scale development differently than dynamic organizations. It is more likely that incumbents and supervisors will be involved in scale development as one moves into the higher levels of the organizations.

Finally, the purpose for rating (administrative, counseling, and/or research) will likely have an influence on scale development. Administrative purposes usually require scales that are capable of distinguishing among individuals on the basis of overall strength or performance. On the other hand, one might look for scales that will help to suggest actual changes in behavior to a ratee for counseling purposes. Thus, if the ratings are to be used for administrative purposes, we might want to develop a set of scales that maximally discriminate among individuals; on the other hand, for counseling, we might prefer scales that highlight intraindividual strengths and weaknesses. For research purposes, we might want criterion measures in the form of ratings that have maximum reliability. For counseling or administrative purposes, reliability may be a relatively minor issue.

Rating Instrument

The scales that are eventually used are most clearly affected by the development or selection process. The scales are also influenced by the rater and ratee characteristics. Sophisticated rating procedures are problems for unsophisticated audiences. Inexperienced raters are likely to push for simple scales. The same organizational, position, and purpose-for-rating influences that were thought to affect the scale development are also likely to affect the characteristics of the instrument itself.

Organization Characteristics

Aspects of the organization are most clearly affected by the personnel actions that result from the performance ratings. One would hope that profitability would be directly affected. Similarly, turnover, size, and span of control might be directly affected by performance-contingent personnel actions.

Organization characteristics are also influenced by position characteristics. For example, positions that are linked through the production chain such that a production unit passes sequentially from one position to another create organizations with very different communication and allocation systems than organizations with independent positions. Similarly, an organization that makes selection decisions for certain positions on the basis of valid predictor data will function differently than one that makes decisions capriciously. We might also expect the climate of the organization to vary as a function of how well the human resource needs are met by job incumbents.

Position Characteristics

In a manner similar to organizational characteristics, position characteristics are influenced by the nature of the personnel action taken. The prevailing job stereotype will probably be affected by reward and punishment patterns. Similarly, the very nature of the duties and responsibilities will be affected by personnel actions (or inactions).

Purpose for Rating

As indicated earlier, it might be better to think of this component as the *perceived* purpose for rating. Both the position and organization characteristics will have influences on this perception. Big organizations want performance information for different reasons than small organizations. The level of the position is also likely to influence the perceived purpose for rating. This variable probably has the greatest influence, however, in a historical or retrospective context. If I am told that ratings are being done for counseling purposes and later discover that pay increases were based on those ratings, my perception of the purpose for rating is likely to be different the next time I complete these ratings.

Rating Process

If the purpose for rating is simply to determine who is "expendable" in the organization, it is likely to be a "quick and dirty" process. If the ratings are to be used for counseling, the process is likely to be slower and more personal. Similarly, simple scales are likely to be accompanied by simple procedures, whereas complicated formats may require more elaborate instructions and preparation.

Cognitive Components (Observation–Storage—Retrieval–Judgment)

These components represent the actual ratings or judgments of the rater. As such, they cannot help but be influenced by the perceived purpose for rating, the rating procedure, the instrument that is actually used to assign the ratings, and individual differences variables that are characteristic of both the rater and the ratee.

Data Analysis, Performance Description, and Personnel Action

As indicated earlier, these are more activities that result from completed ratings rather than formal components that are influenced by other components of the model. Thus, they are arranged in a temporal rather than functional sequence. One exception may be the performance description component. The actual representation of performance that is produced for consumption by the ratee or by the organization is heavily influenced by the data analysis. As a simple example, a data-reduction technique (such as factor analysis) will allow broader and more consistent statements to be made with respect to performance of the individual being considered.

SUMMARY

The rating that one person assigns to another appears simple enough. That simplicity is deceptive. There are an enormous number of influences that have affected that value. In the past few decades, research on ratings concentrated on the effect of rating format on evaluations. This was, of course, the most obvious place to start. Nevertheless, there are many other sources of influence such as rater characteristics, organizational climate, and the intended use of the ratings. There has been some difficulty in planning research in these diverse areas in proper perspective due to a lack of any coherent framework or model of rating.

A model of performance rating should include some consideration of the roles involved in the process (rater and ratee), of the context in which the rating is done (the organization, the job title), of the vehicle used to accomplish the ratings (the rating instrument), of the rating process, and of the cognitive operations involved in making judgments of this type. In addition, this model should, at least at some preliminary level, suggest interrelationships among these elements. We have presented such a model in this chapter. The model is based on an examination of the theoretical, logical, and empirical underpinnings of performance rating. We hope that the model will serve two purposes. First, we feel that it is a good guess about the nature of performance evaluations. As such, we plan to embark on programmatic research that might lead to refinement and general acceptance of the model. Second, we hope that the model will provide some taxonomic guidance to future research. At the very least, those who do research in the area of performance rating might converse more easily as a result of the framework we have presented.

We think of a rating as a piece of data that has passed through many different filters before it is actually recorded. Each of these filters has the potential to distort the rating. The most obvious filter is the mind of the rater. In addition to the capacity of the rater to observe and assess the behavior of the ratee accurately, there are also predispositions or attitudes that the rater possesses that might also play a role. The rater might not like women, or people with dark skin, or young people, or loud people. All of these attitudes may influence the eventual rating given to the employee.

The organization itself represents another filter. One organization may be large, impersonal, and bottom-line oriented. Another organization might be small, personal, and effort oriented. These two different organizations will appraise performance differently. A given behavior in one organization may be valued. The same behavior in another organization may be grounds for dismissal. Even the particular job in question represents a filter—a possible distortion. It is very hard to judge the effectiveness of a manager. It is much easier to judge the effectiveness of a riveter. The probability that your performance can be accurately measured may depend, to some extent, on the job you hold.

Finally, the actual rating form that is used and the process imposed on rating activities are filters. The form can be long or short, with good or poor instructions. It might have descriptive or behavioral anchors. Similarly, rating might be done quickly, in a chaotic environment, or slowly, in a conducive environment. Each of these elements has the potential to influence the final number used to represent the performance of a given individual.

The model that we have presented should be a help in understanding the variables that influence ratings. In turn, this increased awareness of the potential influences on ratings can provide certain principles of caution to the administrator–manager and areas for research to the scientist. More will be said about the model in later chapters.

chapter five

Integrating Empirical Research with the Process Model of Performance Judgment

In this chapter we review the empirical research literature that is related to the various components of the process model of performance judgment presented in Chapter 4. Since clarity of presentation suggested that the rating instrument research should be presented in Chapter 3 along with the descriptions of various judgmental techniques, we will refer the reader back to that chapter for a discussion of the instrument-related components of the model (scale development and rating instrument).

A discussion of the cognitive component of the process model is delayed until Chapter 8. There are virtually no empirical research studies that have directly addressed the cognitive processes of performance raters. There are sufficient suggestions from published reports in the performance-rating area, as well as in other areas of psychological inquiry, that attention to cognitive processes is necessary and overdue. Chapter 8 will present the theoretical rationale for several directions that empirical performance-rating research should take in the near future.

We will limit our discussion in this chapter, for the most part, to studies that were directly concerned with performance ratings and that have gathered data relevant to one or more components of our model. Some empirical investigations not directly concerned with performance ratings, but which have relevance for our model, will be discussed in

Table 5.1
Studies Investigating Rater Characteristics

Variable investigated	Study	Summary of results concerning variable
I. Demographic factors		
A. Rater gender	Centra and Linn, 1973 Dipboye et al., 1977 Elmore and LaPointe, 1974 Elmore and LaPointe, 1975 Gupta et al., 1980 Hamner et al., 1974 Jacobson and Effertz, 1974 Lee and Alvares, 1977 London and Poplawski, 1976 Mai-Dalton et al., 1979 Mischel, 1974 Rose, 1978 Rosen and Jerdee, 1973 Schmitt and Lappin, 1980	Rater gender in most studies had little or no effect on the performance ratings, although there are some data suggesting that female raters may be more lenient than males. Most of the studies are laboratory or simulation experiments; more data are needed from actual work settings.
B. Rater race	Cox and Krumboltz, 1958 Crooks, 1972 DeJung and Kaplan, 1962 Hamner et al., 1974 Schmidt and Johnson, 1973 Schmitt and Lappin, 1980 Wendelken and Inn, 1981	Raters often give higher ratings to same-race ratees than to cross-race ratees, although this effect may be affected by the degree of interaction among members of the different races.
C. Rater age	Barnes, 1980 Cleveland and Landy, 1981 Klores, 1966 Mandell, 1956 Schwab and Heneman, 1978	Rater age does not appear to have a substantial main effect on performance ratings.
D. Rater education	Cascio and Valenzi, 1977	Although a statistically significant effect of education was found, Cascio and Valénzi concluded that it was so small as to have little or no practical significance.
II. Psychological factors		
A. Personality variables	Lewis and Taylor, 1955 Mandell, 1956 Rothaus et al., 1965	A lack of systematic research effort makes general comments impossible. See text.
B. Cognitive variables	Bernardin, Cardy, and Carlyle, 1982 Lahey and Saal, 1981 Saurer and Pond, 1981 Schneier, 1977	Zedeck and Kafry found no effect of several cognitive measures on rating strategies. Schneier found that cognitive complexity af-

Continued

Table 5.1 (*continued*)

Variable investigated	Study	Summary of results concerning variable
	Vance and Kuhnert, 1980 Zedeck and Kafry, 1977	fected the psychometric properties of ratings. Subsequent research has failed to replicate Schneier's findings regarding cognitive complexity.
III. Job-related factors		
A. Job experience	Cascio and Valenzi, 1977 Jurgensen, 1950 Klores, 1966 Mandell, 1956	Job experience seems to affect positively the quality of ratings, but it is not clear exactly why experience functions in this way.
B. Job performance level	Bayroff *et al.*, 1954 Kirchner and Reisberg, 1962 Mandell, 1956 Mullins and Force, 1962 Schneider and Bayroff, 1953	Better performers seem to provide performance ratings of higher quality, but no recent work in this area.
C. Leadership style	Bernardin, 1980 Klores, 1966 Taylor *et al.*, 1959	Production-oriented leaders seem to be less lenient than interaction-oriented leaders. The causal relationship between ratings and leadership may be complex and reciprocal.
D. Type of rater	Bartlett, 1959 Booker and Miller, 1966 Borman, 1974 Centra, 1975 Fiske and Cox, 1960 Freeberg, 1969 Gordon and Medlund, 1965 Heneman, 1974 Kirchner, 1965 Klieger and Mosel, 1953 Klimoski and London, 1974 Kraut, 1975 Landy *et al.*, 1976 Lawler, 1967 Parker *et al.*, 1959 Rothaus *et al.*, 1965	Different types of raters (i.e., supervisors, peers, self, subordinates) are likely to have different perspectives on and information about the ratee's job performance. Thus, cross-rating correlations are usually low to moderate in magnitude. No one type of rater appears to be more valid than any other type. The differences among types may be useful for organizational problem diagnosis.

Continued

Table 5.1 (*continued*)

Variable investigated	Study	Summary of results concerning variable
E. Organizational level relative to ratee	Springer, 1953 Zedeck *et al.*, 1974 Berry *et al.*, 1966 Borman and Dunnette, 1975 Campbell *et al.*, 1973 Whitla and Tirrell, 1953 Zedeck and Baker, 1972	Usually only low to moderate agreement has been found among ratings from supervisors at differing levels in the organization vis-à-vis the ratee. Whitla and Tirrell and Zedeck and Baker found higher quality in ratings by first-level supervisors than by higher level supervisors.
F. Knowledge of job requirements	Amir *et al.*, 1970 Wagner and Hoover, 1974	More knowledgeable raters gave more valid ratings (Amir *et al.*) and were less affected by serial position of ratees (Wagner and Hoover).
G. Amount and type of rater–ratee contact	Amir *et al.*, 1970 Brown, 1968 Ferguson, 1949 Fiske and Cox, 1960 Freeberg, 1969 Gordon and Medland, 1965 Hollander, 1957 Hollander, 1965 Klieger and Mosel, 1953 Klores, 1966 Landy and Guion, 1970 Suci *et al.*, 1956 Waters and Waters, 1970	Frequency of contact does not appear to be as important as the relevancy of the contact with regard to the performance being evaluated.

Chapter 8 along with the related theoretical frameworks that suggest their applicability to performance ratings.

Little of the research reviewed in this chapter was conducted after the initial publication of the process model of performance judgment (Landy & Farr, 1980). In fact, most of these investigations were used inductively in the development of the model. Thus, we are primarily using the model as a heuristic device to aid in the organization of the large body of research concerned with performance ratings.

The discussion in this chapter will parallel the presentation of the model components in Chapter 4. Tables summarizing the research related to the various components are presented in addition to the text discussions for those model components for which substantial research exists. The following section discusses rater characteristics literature as summarized in Table 5.1.

RATER CHARACTERISTICS

Demographic Factors

GENDER OF RATER. Since 1970 there has been a large number of studies investigating the possible effect of rater gender on personnel ratings. In the majority of those studies there has been no consistent main effect of rater gender on ratings obtained in various contexts, including instructional settings (Centra & Linn, 1973; Elmore & LaPointe, 1974, 1975), simulated work settings (Dipboye, Arvey, & Terpstra, 1977; Mai-Dalton, Feldman-Summers, & Mitchell, 1979; Rose, 1978; Rosen & Jerdee, 1973; Schmitt & Lappin, 1980), laboratory research settings (Jacobson & Effertz, 1974; Mischel, 1974), and actual work settings (Gupta, Beehr, & Jenkins, 1980). Lee and Alvares (1977) found that the rater's sex affected the description of supervisory behavior but not the evaluation of such behavior. In a simulated work setting, London and Poplawski (1976), studying college students' evaluations in appraisal and interview situations, found that female subjects gave higher ratings than males on some dimensions but not on overall performance. Hamner, Kim, Baird, and Bigoness (1974) found that females gave higher ratings than males when evaluating performance in a simulated work setting, especially for high levels of performance.

There is a relative lack of data in actual work settings. Whereas obtaining data on gender effects in laboratory and simulation settings has the advantage of greater experimental control over actual performance levels of ratees (and other ratee characteristics), the settings and the subject samples typically used in these studies may result in more null findings than would occur if more heterogeneous jobs, organizations, and subjects were studied.

RACE OF RATER. Several studies have examined the effect of the race of the rater on ratings. Research conducted by the Educational Testing Service in conjunction with the United States Civil Service Commission

(Crooks, 1972) found that in a majority of cases supervisory raters gave higher ratings to subordinates of their own race than to subordinates of a different race. Hamner *et al.* (1974) found results similar to those reported in Crooks (1972), but the effect accounted for only 2% of the rating variance. DeJung and Kaplan (1962) and Cox and Krumboltz (1958) also obtained results comparable to Crooks (1972), with stronger effects for black raters. Schmitt and Lappin (1980) found that black raters gave higher mean ratings to black ratees than to white ratees. They also found that both black and white raters gave more variable ratings to ratees of their own social group, and that raters were more confident of the accuracy of ratings given to members of their own racial group. Schmitt and Lappin also noted that in this simulation study with a college-student subject sample the white raters were more accurate than black raters in evaluating the work performance of the ratees. Wendelken and Inn (1981) found a statistically significant effect of rater race in a study of police oral board ratings, but only a very small percentage of the total variance in these ratings was accounted for by rater race.

Schmidt and Johnson (1973), examining peer ratings in an industrial setting, found no race-of-rater effect. The work setting in which this research took place was highly integrated with subjects who had been exposed to human relations training. The ratings were gathered for research purposes only and required a prescribed distribution. It is likely that some or all of these factors influenced the results of this study. It would be of interest to compare supervisory and peer ratings regarding rater-race effects (as well as effects of other demographic variables).

AGE OF RATER. In two relatively early studies, Mandell (1956) and Klores (1966) examined the effects of rater age on performance ratings. Mandell found that younger supervisors were less lenient in their ratings of subordinates, whereas Klores found no effect of supervisor age in his study of forced-distribution ratings. For over a decade there were no further studies of rater-age effects. Recently, there have been several investigations of these effects, probably initiated by changes in federal legislation regarding age discrimination in employment. Schwab and Heneman (1978) investigated rater-age effects using written descriptions of secretaries as the stimuli and individuals holding personnel specialist positions as the subjects. The subjects were dichotomized at the median age for the sample (33 years) and no main effect of rater age on ratings was found.

Cleveland and Landy (1981) examined actual performance ratings obtained in a large corporation for possible rater-age effects. There were no

rater-age effects on overall performance ratings. Of six more specific ratings, there was one significant rater-age effect on the performance dimension of interpersonal skills. Younger raters tended to give more favorable
ratings on this dimension than did older raters. Barnes (1980), in a field
correlational study of age effects on performance ratings, did not find any
significant relationship between rater age and performance ratings.

RATER EDUCATIONAL LEVEL. The educational level of raters was examined
by Cascio and Valenzi (1977). They found a significant effect of rater
education on supervisory ratings of the job performance of police officers,
but the effect accounted for such a small percentage of total rating variance
that Cascio and Valenzi concluded that rater education was of no practical
importance in their study. No other studies of this variable have been
reported.

Psychological Factors

A relatively small number of psychological characteristics of raters
have been studied as possible influences on performance ratings. Unfortunately, in most instances, there has been only a single study investigating
any one variable. Thus, general conclusions are difficult, if not impossible,
to make about their effects. These investigations may suggest variables
worthy of more research effort.

PERSONALITY VARIABLES. Mandell (1956) found that raters who were low
in self-confidence were less lenient in their ratings of subordinates than
raters high in self-confidence. Lewis and Taylor (1955) reported that individuals high in anxiety tended to use more extreme response categories
than those lower in anxiety. Rothaus, Morton, and Hanson (1965) found
that increased psychological distance of the rater tended to result in more
critical and negative ratings.

COGNITIVE VARIABLES. Cognitive variables have rarely been examined as
characteristics of raters that might effect ratings. Schneier (1977) found
that the cognitive complexity of raters had an effect on ratings. *Cognitive
complexity* is the degree to which a person possesses the ability to perceive
behavior in a multidimensional manner (Schneier, 1977). The cognitively
complex individual has more differentiated systems of dimensions for
perceiving, storing, and recalling information about others than does the
cognitively simple person. Cognitively complex raters were less lenient

and demonstrated less restriction of range with behaviorally anchored scales than did cognitively simple raters. The cognitively complex raters also exhibited less halo in their ratings than did the simple raters with both behavioral scales and a simpler form of rating scale. Cognitively complex raters also preferred the behaviorally anchored scale to the simpler format.

Several studies have attempted to replicate and/or extend the findings of Schneier (1977). In general, these attempts have been unsuccessful (Bernardin, Cardy, Carlyle, 1982; Lahey & Saal, 1981; Sauser & Pond, 1981; Vance & Kuhnert, 1980). Lahey and Saal have concluded that the weight of evidence certainly argues against cognitive complexity, as usually measured, as an important factor in the rating process. They stress that cognitive variables are still likely to be important in understanding performance judgment, but that we have not yet identified (or properly measured) the critical ones.

In a study of rater policy capturing using regression and cluster analytic methodology, Zedeck and Kafry (1977) investigated whether several psychological variables would be related to how a rater used performance information to form overall ratings of performance. Their results indicated that neither interest measures, social insight, nor intelligence measures (verbal or nonverbal) were significantly related to the rating strategies of the subjects.

Job-Related Factors

PERSONAL CHARACTERISTICS OF RATER. Among the personal characteristics of the rater that can be thought of as job-related variables are the rater's job experience, performance level, and leadership style. The results of studies examining the rater's length of job experience are mixed. Jurgenson (1950) found more experienced raters to have more reliable ratings, and Mandell (1956) noted that raters with more than 4 years of experience as supervisors tended to be more lenient in their ratings than raters with less experience. Klores (1966) obtained no significant effect of rater experience. Cascio and Valenzi (1977) found a significant effect of rater experience, but noted that it accounted for only a very small percentage of total rating variance. The range and distribution of rater job experience is probably important. There may not be a simple linear relationship between rating characteristics and length of job experience throughout the entire possible range of job experience length. There may be substantial effects of increases in job experience up to some point after which only minimal changes occur. Certainly, length of job experience influences the rater's knowledge of the ratee and the job; research on that variable is reviewed in a subsequent section of this chapter.

Several studies have found that the performance level of the rater affects the nature of the ratings assigned to others by that rater. Schneider and Bayroff (1953) and Bayroff, Haggerty, and Rundquist (1954) reported that United States Army trainees who received high aptitude test scores and were rated positively during training gave ratings of their fellow trainees that were more valid in predicting subsequent job performance. Mandell (1956) found no difference in central tendency between good and poor job performers but did find that those raters who were poor performers tended to disagree more with consensus ratings of subordinates than did the more favorable performers. Kirchner and Reisberg (1962) found that the ratings given to subordinates by supervisors high in job performance were characterized by greater range, less central tendency, and by more emphasis being placed on the independent action of subordinates as the basis for ratings. In a related study, Mullins and Force (1962) obtained evidence for a generalized ability to rate others accurately. Peer raters who were more accurate in judging one skill of their co-workers also were accurate in judging another performance dimension (accuracy assessed by comparing the ratings with scores on paper-and-pencil tests).

The performance level of the rater has not received research attention in the past 2 decades, despite the generally significant results noted in earlier studies. One's own performance level may be an anchor for one's evaluation of others or function in more complex ways. It is likely to influence judgments and attributions about task difficulty, ratee motivation, and ratee ability. The implications of these effects will be discussed in Chapter 8, which is concerned with future theoretical and research directions.

The effects of the rater's leadership style on the ratings have been examined by Taylor, Parker, Martens, and Ford (1959). They found that production-oriented supervisors gave lower ratings to subordinates. Klores (1966) reported that raters who were high in consideration were more lenient in their ratings of subordinates than raters who were high in initiation of structure. Those raters high in initiation of structure exhibited more range in their ratings and gave more weight to the planning and organization function when evaluating their subordinates' overall job performance. Bernardin (1980) reported results generally consistent with Taylor et al. (1959) and Klores (1966). He found that raters who were described by their subordinates as lower in consideration gave on the average more unfavorable ratings. Bernardin raised an interesting question of cause and effect in the relationship between leadership style and rating characteristics. Does the nature of ratings given by a supervisor (particularly the mean favorability of those ratings) affect the way in which subordinates describe the leadership style of the supervisor? Or does the ("objective") leadership style of a supervisor effect the nature of the ratings that the supervisor makes? Or is it a complex, reciprocal causation model incorporating leadership style, subordinate response to leadership style, and the supervisor's response to the subordinate response? Clearly, many interesting research questions remain unanswered.

TYPE OF RATER. The studies reviewed in this section are concerned with rating differences obtained with raters who differed in the type of relationship they held in regard to the ratee (e.g., supervisor, peer, self, or subordinate). Studies that focused on only one type of rater are generally not reviewed here. A discussion of the various types of raters was presented in Chapter 3.

The most frequent rater type comparison has been that of supervisory rating versus peer rating. These studies have generally demonstrated differences between the two rater types. Springer (1953), Rothaus et al. (1965), and Zedeck, Imparato, Krausz, and Oleno (1974) found that supervisors were less lenient in their ratings than were the peers of the ratees. Klieger and Mosel (1953) and Springer (1953) both found that there was more interrater agreement with supervisory ratings than with peer ratings, but Gordon and Medlund (1965) reported greater reliability for peer ratings of leadership than for similar supervisory ratings.

Although Booker and Miller (1966) obtained general agreement between peers' and instructors' ratings of United States Reserve Officers Training Corps (ROTC) students, Springer (1953) and Borman (1974) reported less supervisor–peer agreement than was found within either type of rater group. Data reported by Borman (1974) and Zedeck et al. (1974) suggest that supervisory–peer rating differences may be expected and do not necessarily suggest that either type of rating is invalid or unreliable. Borman (1974), as well as Landy, Farr, Saal, and Freytag (1976), found that the dimensions of job performance resulting from the development of behavior-anchored scales for use by peers and supervisors differed. Zedeck et al. (1974) obtained similar dimensions of performance for the two rater types when developing behavior-anchored scales, but did find that the specific examples of job behaviors used to anchor the dimensions differed between the two rater types. Thus, supervisory and peer ratings may represent two distinct views of a common individual's job performance and may be equally valid even though they are not highly correlated.

Supervisory ratings have also been compared with the ratees' self-ratings. Parker, Taylor, Barrett, and Martens (1959) and Kirchner (1965) found that self-ratings were more lenient than supervisory ratings, but Heneman (1974) found less leniency with self-ratings than with supervisory ratings. Heneman's data were gathered for research purposes via a mail questionnaire returned to the researcher. These factors may have affected his results. Kirchner (1965) and Heneman (1974) reported more halo in supervisory ratings than in self-ratings, whereas Parker *et al.* (1959) found no differences in halo. Both Kirchner (1965) and Parker *et al.* (1959) reported only moderate agreement between supervisory and self-ratings.

Lawler (1967) and Klimoski and London (1974) examined supervisory, peer, and self-ratings of performance. Lawler found that supervisory and peer ratings exhibited greater convergent and discriminant validity than self-ratings. Klimoski and London reported that each rater type was distinct with regard to use of information and that supervisory- and peer-rating strategies were more similar than self-ratings. Supervisory ratings demonstrated a strong correlation between effort and performance ratings, whereas peer and self-ratings differentiated between effort and performance.

A few studies have compared peer ratings to other nonsupervisory ratings. Bartlett (1959) reported that, whereas peer ratings on a forced-choice scale of leadership were useful for both evaluative and diagnostic purposes, self-ratings on a similar scale were adequate only for diagnostic purposes. Centra (1975) compared peer and student ratings of college instructors. Peer ratings were found to be more lenient and to have lower interrater agreement than the student ratings.

Freeberg (1969), Fiske and Cox (1960), and Rothaus *et al.* (1965) all compared peer ratings with observer ratings in various role-playing and group activities. Fiske and Cox and Rothaus *et al.* found that peer ratings were more lenient than observer ratings. Freeberg reported that, when peers and observers had similar relevant contact with the ratee, peer ratings were more valid predictors of cognitive skills than were the observer ratings. Kraut (1975) also found that peer ratings in a month-long management training program were more predictive of promotion and future performance appraisals than were ratings by the training staff.

RATER KNOWLEDGE OF RATEE AND JOB. Although some minimum rater knowledge of the ratee's job performance and of the job in question is certainly necessary before valid ratings can be obtained, the necessary extent of such knowledge has been a focus of much research. Several studies have found only low to moderate agreement among the ratings made by supervisors at differing organizational levels relative to the ratee (Berry, Nelson, & McNally, 1966; Borman & Dunnette, 1975; Campbell, Dunnette, Arvey, & Hellervik, 1973). Whitla and Tirrell (1953) found that first-level supervisors' ratings more accurately predicted job knowledge test scores of subordinates than did the ratings of second- or third-level supervisors. Zedeck and Baker (1972) reported better construct validity for ratings by first-level supervisors than for those of second-level supervisors. Individuals with more knowledge of the requirements of the particular job have been found to be less influenced by serial position (Wagner & Hoover, 1974) and to be more valid in predicting future performance (Amir, Kovarsky, & Sharan, 1970) than individuals with less knowledge of the job requirements.

The amount and type of contact between the rater and ratee has also been of concern to performance appraisal researchers. Although Ferguson (1949) reported that reliability of ratings increased as the amount of rater-reported acquaintance with the ratee increased, more recent research has not generally supported this finding. Klieger and Mosel (1953) found no effect of rater-reported "opportunity to observe the rater" on rating reliability. Fiske and Cox (1960), Gordon and Medlund (1965), and Klores (1966) found no effect of length of rater acquaintance with ratee. Hollander (1957, 1965) found no differences in peer-rating reliability or validity for ratees who had been acquainted for 3, 6, or 12 weeks. Brown (1968) found that peer raters were not influenced by degree of acquaintance, but that untrained peer raters' ratings were characterized by increased halo for less well-known ratees. Waters and Waters (1970), Amir et al. (1970), and Suci, Vallance, and Glickman (1956) reported little or no effect on the validity or reliability of ratings when the rater's friendship with the ratee was considered. Finally, Freeberg (1969) reported that the relevance of the rater–ratee acquaintance was important in terms of the validity of the ratings. Raters who interacted with the ratees in a situation relevant to the dimension being rated were more valid in their evaluations than raters who interacted with the ratees in a nonrelevant situation. Similarly, Landy and Guion (1970) reported that raters with daily but peripheral contact with ratees had a median interrater reliability of .24 in contrast to a median reliability of .62 for those raters with more relevant contacts with the ratees. Thus, relevancy, rather than frequency, of contact appears to be the critical factor. It is likely that the relevancy of rater contact with ratees can be enhanced through the training of raters in observational skills and in the relevance of specific behavior for assessments of performance dimensions. This will be discussed more fully in the section on rater training later in this chapter.

Summary

The research on rater characteristics provides relatively few general conclusions. Since most studies examine only one or very few characteristics, it is likely that unmeasured or unreported variables have had some effect on the results of any single study. This results in a rather chaotic pattern of findings in many instances. Nevertheless, some generally consistent effects can be described. Rater gender does not generally affect ratings, although female raters may be somewhat more lenient. Few field studies of rater gender are reported. Raters usually give higher ratings to same-race ratees, although this may be moderated by the degree of contact members of each race have with each other. Rater age does not appear to have a substantial main effect on performance ratings, although relatively few studies on this have been conducted. Rater education has been studied too infrequently to make general statements about its effects.

Psychological characteristics of raters have not been systematically researched, but it appears that cognitive complexity, although initially promising, does not appear to impact on ratings in a simple and direct fashion. The measurement of cognitive complexity is problematic and, thus, there may yet be value in considering this variable. Other cognitive variables should be researched for possible impact on performance judgments.

Rater job experience appears to have a positive effect on the quality of performance ratings, but the mechanism responsible (e.g., more training or experience with the rating form, better observation skills, or better knowledge of the job requirements) is not known. The general job performance of the rater is related to rating quality, with better performers also providing higher quality ratings. Production-oriented raters (versus interaction-oriented) seem to be less lenient and pay more attention to planning activities. The causal relationships between the rater's leadership style and characteristics of ratings given by the rater may be complex and reciprocal.

Comparisons of different types of raters suggest that, in general, one should expect only low to moderate correlations among raters of different types (e.g., peer, supervisory, self). It cannot be stated that any one type of rater is more valid than any other, although peer ratings appear to be especially useful for predicting promotion potential. Peer ratings appear to be more lenient than supervisory ratings. As Borman (1974) and others have suggested, the best conclusion may be that different types of raters have different perspectives on performance that influence their ratings. Lawler (1967) and Blood (1974) have noted that these differences may provide valuable information for the diagnosis of organizational problems.

Raters require knowledge of the individual ratee and of the requirements of the ratee's job to evaluate job performance in an adequate manner. It appears that the relevance of the rater–ratee interaction is more important than the simple amount of interaction. The following section discusses the research that has been conducted on ratee characteristics; Table 5.2 presents a summary of this research.

RATEE CHARACTERISTICS

Demographic Factors

GENDER OF RATEE. Much of the research concerned with ratee gender is supportive of the hypothesis that the gender stereotype of the occupation (i.e., whether a particular job is typically perceived as masculine or feminine) interacts with the gender of the ratee. Studies in which the occupation would be likely to be perceived as masculine (e.g., managerial positions, program auditors) have found that females received less favorable evaluations than males (Schmitt & Hill, 1977; Schneier & Beusse, 1980), although in a simulation study with college students as subjects, raters gave equivalent ratings to male and female managers (Rose, 1978). In addition, Terborg and Ilgen (1975) found in an in-basket exercise that, while female ratees received ratings similar to males, females received lower salary and less challenging job assignments. Gupta et al. (1980) in a field study found no main effect for ratee gender when ratings were examined, but females received fewer promotions than males. Rosen and Jerdee (1973) and Bartol and Butterfield (1976) reported in simulation studies that the gender of a supervisor influenced the rater's perceptions of the appropriate behavior of the supervisor in a gender stereotypic fashion. Similarly, Mai-Dalton et al. (1979) found that in a simulation study hypothetical female banking officers who behaved in an emotional and angry fashion were evaluated more favorably than hypothetical male banking officers who behaved in the same manner. Males and females who be-

Table 5.2
Studies Investigating Ratee Characteristics

Variable investigated	Study	Summary of results concerning variables
I. Demographic factors		
A. Ratee gender	Bartol and Butterfield, 1976 Bigoness, 1976 Elmore and LaPointe, 1974 Elmore and LaPointe, 1975 Gupta et al., 1980 Hamner et al., 1974 Jacobson and Effertz, 1974 Lee and Alvares, 1977 Mai-Dalton et al., 1979 Pulakos and Wexley, 1982 Rose, 1978 Rosen and Jerdee, 1973 Schmitt and Hill, 1977 Schmitt and Lappin, 1980 Schneier and Beusse, 1980 Terborg and Ilgen, 1975	Much of the data suggests that the gender stereotype of the occupation often interacts with the ratee gender such that males receive more positive ratings in "male" occupations and females in "female" occupations. Recent work does suggest that a simple gender stereotype hypothesis is insufficient. More data from actual work settings are also needed.
B. Ratee race	Bass and Turner, 1973 Bigoness, 1976 Crooks, 1972 DeJung and Kaplan, 1962 Farr et al., 1971 Fox and Lefkowitz, 1974 Greenhaus and Gavin, 1972 Hamner et al., 1974 Huck and Bray, 1976 Kirkpatrick et al., 1968 Landy and Farr, 1976 Schmidt and Johnson, 1973 Schmitt and Hill, 1977 Schmitt and Lappin, 1980 Toole et al., 1972 Wendelken and Inn, 1981	Ratees tend to receive higher ratings from same-race raters. Ratings may be correlated with different performance factors for members of different races. Race and performance level may jointly influence ratings in complex ways.
C. Ratee age	Barnes, 1980 Bass and Turner, 1973 Cleveland and Landy, 1981 Klores, 1966 Schwab and Heneman, 1978	Ratee age is not generally related to ratings of overall performance, but may be related to ratings on more specific performance dimensions.
D. Ratee education	Cascio and Valenzi, 1977	No effect of ratee education was found in this study of a po-

Continued

Table 5.2 (*continued*)

Variable investigated	Study	Summary of results concerning variables
		lice officer sample. More data are needed before any general statements can be made.
II. Job-related factors		
A. Performance level of ratee	Baker and Schuck, 1975 Bigoness, 1976 Gordon, 1970 Gordon, 1972 Hamner *et al.*, 1974 Kaufman and Johnson, 1974 Lay *et al.*, 1973 Leventhal *et al.*, 1977 Schmitt and Lappin, 1980 Schneier and Beusse, 1980	In several simulation and laboratory experiments, actual performance level was the primary influence on performance ratings. Gordon (1970, 1972) has found that good performance is more accurately rated than poor performance, although this may not hold for all dimensions of performance.
B. Variability of performance	Brehmer, 1972 Grey and Kipnis, 1976 Scott and Hamner, 1975 Willingham, 1958	Variability of individual performance may increase ratings of ability but decrease ratings of motivation, although data are limited. Relative performance vis-à-vis co-workers may affect ratings.
C. Ratee tenure	Bass and Turner, 1973 Cascio and Valenzi, 1977 Jay and Copes, 1957 Klores, 1966 Leventhal *et al.*, 1977 Rothe, 1949 Schneier and Beusse, 1980 Svetlik *et al.*, 1964 Zedeck and Baker, 1972	Generally, job tenure and performance ratings are positively but weakly correlated; it has been suggested that situational factors may influence this relationship but insufficient research has been reported to make a general statement.

haved in a calm and unemotional manner were evaluated more favorably than those acting in the angry and emotional fashion.

Elmore and LaPointe (1974, 1975) found that students gave essentially equal ratings to male and female college instructors, an occupation perhaps perceived as less gender specific than management jobs. Lee and Alvares (1977) obtained no effect of ratee gender on evaluations of interviewers. Once again, perhaps the job of interviewer could be considered to be neither masculine nor feminine. Schmitt and Lappin (1980) found that white females received lower ratings from raters of all gender and race groups in a simulation study involving college students' observations of videotapes of individuals shelving books in a library. Bigoness (1976) and Hamner *et al.* (1974) also examined ratee gender effects in semiskilled and low-skilled tasks. However, Bigoness and Hamner *et al.* both found that females received higher ratings than males in a simulation study in which objective performance was controlled. Again, since gender stereotypes were not measured, it is difficult to determine if these studies support the interaction hypothesis. Jacobson and Effertz (1974) obtained results opposite to those predicted by the gender-role stereotype hypothesis. They found that male leaders were evaluated more negatively than female leaders, but that male followers received higher ratings than female followers. It should be noted that many of the studies examining the effects of ratee gender on evaluations were simulations. Relatively few studies (Elmore & LaPointe, 1974, 1975; Gupta *et al.* 1980; Pulakos & Wexley, 1982; Schmitt & Hill, 1977) have been conducted in which "real-world" performance of the ratee was being rated. It also appears that a simple gender-role stereotype explanation does not explain all of the research results to date. More complex models of these effects are necessary.

RACE OF RATEE. The effect of the race of the ratee has been examined in several studies. Most of these investigations have used ratings of the "real-world" performance of ratees as the behavior of interest, whereas some have used simulation methodology. Ratees have been found to receive higher ratings from same race raters by Crooks (1972), DeJung and Kaplan (1962), and Hamner *et al.* (1974), whereas Schmidt and Johnson (1973) found no such effect with peer ratings obtained in a highly integrated setting. Landy and Farr (1976) reported that on four of eight rating dimensions predominantly white supervisors rated the performance of white police officers more favorably than that of black officers. Schmitt and Lappin (1980) found that black ratees received higher ratings from black raters than from white raters, but that the ratings of white ratees were equivalent for both white and black raters.

Other studies have demonstrated an interaction between ratee race and ratee performance level. Bigoness (1976) and Hamner *et al.* (1974), both using videotaped task performance controlled for level, found interactions of race and objective performance levels. Bigoness reported that among low performers blacks were rated more favorably than white ratees, whereas there were no racial differences for the high performers. Hamner *et al.* found that raters significantly differentiated between high and low white performers, but did not for black ratees.

Huck and Bray (1976) and Schmitt and Hill (1977) both examined ratings gathered in assessment center settings. Huck and Bray found that black female assessees received lower ratings than white female assessees. The validities of those ratings for predicting future job performance were about equal for blacks and whites. The black women also received somewhat lower criterion ratings than the white women. Schmitt and Hill reported that black female assessees tended to receive lower ratings when their assessment center group was composed principally of white males than if the group was better integrated in terms of race and sex.

Several studies that were primarily interested in the validity of selection devices for black and white workers have reported data for performance ratings for the racial subgroups. Farr, O'Leary, and Bartlett (1971) found that white employees received higher performance ratings than blacks in 13 of 22 comparisons. The other 9 comparisons revealed no differences in the rating means for the two groups. Greenhaus and Gavin (1972) reported that white employees were rated higher than blacks on all three supervisory ratings used in their study. Toole, Gavin, Murdy, and Sells (1972) split their workers into younger and older subgroups by dividing their sample at age 35. There were no racial differences on a rating measure for the older workers, but white workers received higher ratings than blacks in the younger group. Kirkpatrick, Ewen, Barrett, and Katzell (1968) found only one significant difference among 8 possible comparisons of rating means for black and white workers. In that one case the white workers received a higher rating than black workers. Crooks (1972) reported that white employees were rated more favorably than black employees, but that white employees also received a higher mean score on an objective test of job knowledge. Fox and Lefkowitz (1974) found no mean racial difference for a supervisory rating measure. Wendelken and Inn (1981) found a statistically significant effect of ratee race for police oral board ratings. Black candidates received higher ratings than white candidates (the majority of the raters were white). However, the ratee-race effect accounted for a very small percentage of the total variance in the ratings.

Bass and Turner (1973) found no significant mean differences for black and white raters when age and job tenure were held constant for full-time employees and small, but statistically significant, racial differences (white ratees evaluated more favorably) for part-time workers. However, ratings of black and white employees were differentially related to more objective criterion measures. The ratings of black employees were more strongly related to attendance and error data than were those of white employees. Crooks (1972) reported that black ratees received more valid ratings from black and white raters. Validity of the ratings was measured by their relationship with scores on a job knowledge test. These results suggest that the "meaning" of performance ratings may differ for members of different racial groups. In terms of our model, the possible differential meaning of performance ratings for various groups of ratees suggests that raters may have operational definitions of work performance that differ for the various ratee groups. Thus, the rater attends to and/or recalls different information when making performance judgments concerning members of the different ratee groups. This may not be a conscious process. Indeed, we will discuss theory and research in Chapter 8 that argues that this process is likely to be automatic without conscious control.

AGE OF RATEE. Klores (1966) found that ratee age had no relationship with performance ratings. No ratee-age effect for part-time workers was reported by Bass and Turner (1973), who did find significant positive relationships between age and supervisory ratings for white full-time workers on one-half of the dimensions being evaluated. No significant correlations between age and ratings were found for black full-time employees. In other field studies, Barnes (1980) found that ratee age was positively related to supervisory ratings on several performance dimensions (communication skills, use of time, and cost effectiveness), but found no ratee-age effect on other performance dimensions. Cleveland and Landy (1981) found no effect of ratee age on overall supervisory ratings, but did find significant effects of ratee age on two of six more specific performance ratings. Older workers received lower ratings on the dimension of self-development and older workers received lower ratings on the dimension of interpersonal skills, especially from younger raters. In two simulation experiments, Barnes (1980) and Schwab and Heneman (1978) found no main effect of ratee age on ratings.

EDUCATION LEVEL OF RATEE. Cascio and Valenzi (1977) found no effect of ratee education on supervisory ratings of police officers. This variable has not been investigated (or, at least, reported in the research literature) in other occupations. Perhaps in many occupations the range of incumbent education is rather restricted, limiting the likelihood of significant results.

Psychological Factors

Generally, relatively few studies have been conducted on the effects of various psychological factors of ratees on ratings of job performance in which the primary interest of the investigation has been possible "biases" introduced into the ratings by the level of the ratees' psychological factors. There is, of course, a considerable literature that has assessed the validity of various personality, interest, and cognitive measures as predictors of job performance. For our immediate purpose, we are not concerned with the "valid" effects of psychological factors on job performance (and, hence, on judgmental measures of that job performance). Rather, we are interested in "invalid" effects of these factors. The question of interest might be phrased as "are there psychological characteristics of raters that influence performance ratings, but not true job performance?"

This is not an easy question to answer as it requires both judgmental and nonjudgmental indexes of performance. It appears to be a research question best attacked initially in simulation studies. Certainly we often talk about "style, but no substance"; it would be interesting to investigate this possible phenomenon.

Job-Related Factors

Job-related ratee characteristics include the level and variability of the ratees' job performance and the job and organizational tenure of the ratee.

LEVEL OF RATEE'S JOB PERFORMANCE. Obviously, the ratees' level of job performance should be related to performance ratings. However, as noted in Chapter 1, this is not always easy to assess, particularly in field settings. There have been a relatively small number of simulation studies in which actual performance levels of various ratees are known. We review these studies in this section. Some related work concerned with the effect of rater training on the accuracy of ratings are reviewed later in this chapter.

In simulation studies, Bigoness (1976) found that actual performance has the largest effect on performance ratings. Task performance was experimentally manipulated and videotaped to standardize the stimuli for the subjects. Leventhal, Perry, and Abrami (1977) manipulated lecture quality in addition to other variables and found that student ratings of the instructor were consistently affected by the lecture quality level. Hamner *et al.* (1974) also found that actual performance accounted for the largest percentage of variance in performance ratings (30%), although the sex and race of the raters and ratees accounted for an additional total of 23% of the rating variance. Schneier and Beusse (1980) found that high performers received higher ratings than did low performers. Schmitt and Lappin (1980) found that actual performance level accounted for about 70% of the total variance in performance ratings, with other systematic factors accounting for another 12% of the total variance. Random error accounted for the remaining 18% of variance. In general, these data suggest actual performance level is the primary influence on performance ratings. This is heartening; however, it must be noted that there is not a large data base on this question and it may be easier to find such relationships between actual and rated performance in the controlled setting of a simulation experiment than in an actual work setting.

Gordon (1970, 1972) has identified what he has termed the *differential accuracy phenomenon*. He has reported that ratings were more accurate when the behavior in question was favorable rather than unfavorable. Baker and Schuck (1975) reanalyzed Gordon's data from the framework of signal detection theory and noted that the differential accuracy phenomenon appeared to be limited to only some rating dimensions and not others. The reason why the effect was observed for some but not all performance dimensions was unclear, but deserves more research attention. In a related finding, Kaufman and Johnson (1974) found that negative peer nominations (individuals name the worst of their peers) add little to the predictiveness of positive peer ratings. This finding is compatible with the differential accuracy phenomenon. The effect may be explainable in terms of base rates of information. Negative performance information is probably less frequent than positive information. Lay, Burron, and Jackson (1973) found that low base rate information led to more certainty of judgment than high base rate information. These findings combined with those of Gordon (1970, 1972) suggest that unfavorable information may be less accurately perceived but given more weight in the judgment process.

VARIABILITY OF RATEE'S PERFORMANCE. The effects of variability of the level of ratee performance were examined in an interesting study conducted by Scott and Hamner (1975). They manipulated the variability of subordinate performance as well as changes in the average level of performance. Variability of performance resulted in more favorable ratings of ability to do the task and less favorable ratings of task motivation, but had no effect on ratings of overall task performance. A descending order of performance level led to less favorable rating of task motivation, but did not affect the other two ratings. In a related study that specifically focused on the decision-making process of human judges, Brehmer (1972) found that an inconsistent cue (as variable performance could be considered) received less weight than its actual validity in a prediction task.

In a correlational field study of supervisory ratings of the performance of clerical workers, Grey and Kipnis (1976) found that the proportion of compliant and noncompliant members of a work group affected the performance ratings. A compliant worker was defined as one who had no basic job weaknesses related to lack of ability or to an inappropriate work attitude. Ratings tended to be higher for compliant members in work groups with a large proportion of noncompliant workers than in work groups with few or no noncompliant workers. Also, ratings of noncompliant workers tended to be lower in work groups where there were many compliant workers than in work groups with few compliant workers. The data of Grey and Kipnis (1976), as well as those of Willingham (1958), suggest that more attention be paid to ratee group composition in research on performance rating.

JOB AND ORGANIZATIONAL TENURE. Organizational and job tenure have been investigated as possible influences on performance ratings. Jay and Copes (1957) reviewed the results of 47 studies with a total sample size of 2462 and found that the average correlation between measures of tenure and evaluations of job performance was .17. There was a stronger relationship between tenure and performance ratings as the skill level and organizational level of the job increased. Much of the more recent research in this area has supported the general findings of Jay and Copes. Bass and Turner (1973), Cascio and Valenzi (1977), and Zedeck and Baker (1972) found positive but low correlations between tenure measures and performance ratings. Leventhal et al. (1977) manipulated the level of perceived task experience of the ratee and found that ratings of performance were higher in the condition of higher perceived experience. Some research has obtained contradictory results. Klores (1966) found no relationship between organization tenure and performance rating, although he did find a significant positive relationship between skill level within a job family and ratings. Schwab and Heneman (1978) found no effect for job tenure in a simulation study. Svetlik, Prien, and Barrett (1964) found a negative relationship between supervisory ratings and the job tenure of the ratee. Schneier and Beusse (1980) in a simulation study found that hypothetical job incumbents who had been in grade for a longer period were evaluated more negatively than those who had been in grade for less time, especially if they were female.

Rothe (1949) noted that the relationship between tenure and performance ratings appeared to be affected by such factors as the organizational reward system, the intended use of the ratings, and the raters' acceptance of the rating system and its application to organizational problems. This suggestion has not been explicitly investigated to date.

Summary

The research on the effects of ratee characteristics on performance ratings offers some general conclusions. It appears that the gender stereotype of an occupation often interacts with the gender of the ratee in such a way that males receive more favorable evaluations than females in traditionally masculine occupations, but that no differences or smaller differences in favor of females occur in traditionally feminine occupations. There are findings that suggest that a simple gender hypothesis will not always hold. Ratees tend to receive higher ratings from raters of their same race, although this may not occur in highly integrated situations. Race and performance level of the ratee appeared to interact in complex ways. Further research is needed to determine if performance ratings have the same meaning for ratees of different races. Ratee age is not consistently related to overall performance ratings but may affect some more specific performance dimension ratings. Other personal characteristics of ratees have been studied too infrequently to yield conclusions about their general effects.

Experimental studies of the effect of the performance level of the ratee on performance ratings generally support the validity of the ratings. Performance level and ability have been found to have the strongest effect on ratings in these studies, although other ratee variables also significantly affect ratings. Raters may evaluate favorable performance more accurately than unfavorable performance, but not for all performance dimensions. Performance variability also appears to influence rating accuracy and reliability. Contrast effects may be important in performance ratings and need further investigation. Tenure and performance ratings are generally positively but weakly correlated, although situational variables may moderate this relationship.

This section and the preceding section have been concerned primarily with the main effects of rater and ratee characteristics. The following section examines the research literature that has investigated whether certain combinations of rater and ratee characteristics have effects on performance ratings. A summary of these studies appears in Table 5.3.

Table 5.3
Studies Investigating the Interaction of Rater–Ratee Characteristics

Variable investigated	Study	Summary of results concerning variables
Gender	Bartol and Butterfield, 1976 Elmore and LaPointe, 1974 Elmore and LaPointe, 1975 Gupta et al., 1980 Hamner et al., 1974 Jacobson and Effertz, 1974 Lee and Alvares, 1977 Rose, 1978 Rosen and Jerdee, 1973 Schmitt and Lappin, 1980 Wexley and Pulakos, 1982	Laboratory and simulation have typically found no gender interactions. One field study (Gupta et al.) found that raters gave higher ratings to cross-gender ratees, although male subordinates of male supervisors received more organizational rewards. In another field study, Wexley and Pulakos found that females gave more variable ratings to male ratees than to female ratees, whereas male raters gave equally variable ratings to male and female ratees.
Race	Crooks, 1972 DeJung and Kaplan, 1962 Hamner et al., 1974 Schmidt and Johnson, 1973 Schmitt and Lappin, 1980 Wendelken and Inn, 1981	Raters tend to give same-race ratees higher ratings, although the degree of integration of the setting may affect this. Schmitt and Lappin found little effect on this interaction on the validity of ratings given by various race raters.
Age	Barnes, 1980 Cleveland and Landy, 1981 Schmitt and Lappin, 1980 Schwab and Heneman, 1978	Data on the age stereotype of occupations may be necessary to organize the mixed results found to date.
Psychological similarity	Frank and Hackman, 1975 Pulakos and Wexley, 1982	Similarity affected the judgments with more favorable ratings given to "similar" ratees.
Agreement on job requirements	Barrett, 1966a	No effect of supervisor–subordinate agreement on the subordinate's job duties was found.

INTERACTION OF RATER AND RATEE CHARACTERISTICS

RATER AND RATEE GENDER. A number of studies have been reported in which the interaction of the gender of the rater and the gender of the ratee has been investigated. Most of these studies found no interaction effect of rater gender and ratee gender on ratings (Bartol & Butterfield, 1976; Elmore & LaPointe, 1974, 1975; Hamner *et al.*, 1974; Jacobson & Effertz, 1974; Lee & Alvares, 1977; Mai-Dalton *et al.*, 1979; Rose, 1978; Rosen & Jerdee, 1973; Schmitt & Lappin, 1980). It should be noted that the majority of these studies have involved laboratory tasks. There have been reported only a few studies of the effects of a rater gender and ratee gender interaction on performance ratings in which both rater and ratee were actual employees of an organization. Gupta *et al.* (1980) found that supervisors gave higher ratings to cross-gender subordinates, although male subordinates who had male supervisors received more promotions than others. In addition, Elmore and LaPointe (1974, 1975) did investigate the ratings of college instructors by students, but, as just noted, found no significant interaction. Wexley and Pulakos (1982) found that female raters gave more variable evaluations to male ratees than to female ratees, whereas male raters gave equally variable ratings to male and female ratees.

The general lack of rater–ratee gender interaction suggests that, if the gender-role stereotype hypothesis described in the ratee characteristics section of this chapter is correct, it appears that it holds for both male and female raters. Schein (1973, 1975) has reported data consistent with this interpretation. She found that both male and female managers perceived that successful middle-level managers possessed traits more commonly ascribed to men in general than to women in general. Thus, men and women seem to share common gender-role stereotypes about work-related variables and could be expected to evaluate male and female ratees with common biases.

RATER AND RATEE RACE. The interaction of rater race and ratee race has been investigated in several studies. The results of these studies are mixed. Schmidt and Johnson (1973) found no interaction effect of race on peer ratings in a study conducted in a highly integrated setting with individuals who had completed a human relations training program. Crooks (1972), DeJung and Kaplan (1962), and Hamner *et al.* (1974) found that raters tended to give ratees of their same race higher ratings than ratees of a different race. Schmitt and Lappin (1980) and Wendelken and Inn (1981) found that black raters tended to give higher ratings to black ratees than to white ratees, but that white raters gave comparable ratings to both white and black ratees. However, raters have been found to be more confident of ratings given to members of their own racial group and to give more variable ratings to members of their own group (Schmitt &

Lappin, 1980). The validity of the ratings in this simulation study were not substantially affected by the rater–ratee race interaction. Crooks (1972) also found that the validity of ratings, as measured by a job knowledge test, was affected by the rater–ratee race interaction, but the results were complex. For black raters there were more valid ratings for black ratees, but for white raters nonwhite ratees received more valid ratings.

RATER AND RATEE AGE. Several recent studies have looked at the interaction of rater and ratee age in a performance rating context. In a simulation study, Schwab and Heneman (1978) found that for three of six rating dimensions older raters tended to give lower evaluations to older incumbents than to younger incumbents, whereas younger raters gave the opposite pattern of results. These findings are quite surprising and contrary to a similarity hypothesis prediction. In a field study, Barnes (1980) found that perceived age similarity was positively related to some performance ratings (interpersonal problem solving and promotability) but not others. Generally, as the perceived age of the ratee relative to the rater increased, the ratings were lower. Cleveland and Landy (1981) found no interaction of rater and ratee age for overall performance ratings, but did find an interaction effect for some more specific ratings. On interpersonal skills, younger raters gave younger ratees more favorable evaluation than older ratees, but older raters gave comparable ratings to all ratee age groups. Older raters gave older ratees more positive ratings on self-development, but younger raters gave comparable ratings on this dimension to all ratee age groups.

It appears that the age stereotype of various occupations may help to make sense of the rather mixed bag of research results, as has been suggested by Schwab and Heneman (1978) and Cleveland and Landy (1981). To date, data on occupational age stereotypes have not been gathered in studies of age effects on performance ratings. Such data will be of interest.

OTHER FACTORS. A few studies have examined the hypothesis that the similarity (biographical, attitudinal, etc.) of judges and ratees affects evaluations. Frank and Hackman (1975) examined similarity effects in actual college admission interviews conducted by three college officials. They found considerable individual variation in the effect of rater–ratee similarity. One interviewer showed no similarity effects, one showed positive but weak effects, and one showed strong, positive effects of similarity. The similarity hypothesis has only been directly examined in one performance-rating setting (Pulakos & Wexley, 1982), although the data on racial similarity effects fit into this conceptual framework. Pulakos and Wexley found that perceived similarity between rater and ratee resulted in more favorable ratings than when dissimilarity was perceived in a sample of manager–subordinate dyads. Research on the similarity effect and its individual correlates would appear to be a fruitful area for performance-rating work.

Barrett (1966a) found that supervisor–subordinate agreement on the requirements of the subordinate's job had no effect on the mean rating or reliability of the supervisor's rating of the job performance of the ratee.

Table 5.4
Studies Investigating Rating Process Variables

Variable investigated	Study	Summary of results concerning variables
Prerating rater training	Bernardin, 1978 Bernardin and Pence, 1980 Bernardin and Walter, 1977 Borman, 1975 Borman, 1979 Brown, 1968 Ivancevich, 1979 Latham et al., 1975 Pursell et al., 1980 Spool, 1978 Taylor et al., 1970 Thornton and Zorich, 1980 Vance et al., 1978 Wexley et al., 1973	The content of rater training should include more than the traditional psychometric rating errors. Observational skills and rating accuracy should also be stressed. The effects of rater training are probably short term; thus, such training may need to be repeated.
Rater anonymity	Bayroff et al., 1954 Creswell, 1963 Sharon and Bartlett, 1969 Stone et al., 1977	Little effect of rater anonymity has been reported.
Rating by dimension or by ratee	Blumberg et al., 1966 Brown, 1968 Johnson, 1963 Taylor and Hastman, 1956	No effect on performance ratings has been reported in these studies.
Ratee sequence	Bayroff et al., 1954 Wagner and Hoover, 1974 Willingham, 1958	Serial position effects have been reported, but the results are mixed.
Time pressure to complete ratings	Wright, 1974	With less time to complete ratings, raters used less information and weighted negative information more heavily.

Summary

Rater sex and ratee sex do not appear to interact in their effects on evaluative judgments. More research in actual work settings is needed, however. Both male and female raters may have common sex-role stereotypes that affect judgments. Raters often give more favorable ratings to same-race ratees although situational factors may moderate this effect. Age effects are mixed and data on age stereotypes of occupations may be needed. It was suggested that the similarity of rater and ratee on background and attitudinal factors may affect ratings, although no direct results are available that bear on this question.

Another class of variables affecting performance ratings are those factors related to the process by which ratings are obtained, exclusive of the rating instrument itself. These variables can be categorized as task relevant or environmental and are discussed in the following section. Table 5.4 summarizes these studies.

RATING PROCESS VARIABLES

Task-Relevant Process Variables

PRERATING TRAINING OF RATERS. A large number of studies have examined the effect of rater training on rating errors and validity, following the suggestions for such research from Borman and Dunnette (1975), Moore and Lee (1974), and Schneier (1977) among others. Most investigations have found that training raters reduces rating errors, although some data suggest no differences between trained and untrained raters (Taylor, Haeffele, Thompson, & O'Donoghue, 1970; Vance et al., 1978) or only short-term effects (Bernardin, 1978; Ivancevich, 1979). Wexley, Sanders, & Yukl (1973) found that only rather extensive training was effective in reducing rating errors, a finding corroborated by Borman (1974), Brown (1968), Latham, Wexley, and Pursell (1975), and Bernardin and Walter (1977). Borman (1975) reported decreased halo with no reduction in the validity of ratings with only a brief training program.

Although rater training programs have concentrated on the avoidance of the typical rating errors such as halo and leniency, only Bernardin (1978) has demonstrated a correlation between knowledge of such errors, as measured by a test, and a reduction of the errors in actual ratings. This suggests that rater training programs may have internal validity in that the learning of training content was directly linked to improved performance on the rating task.

Quite recently the content of rater training programs has been shifting away from a sole concern for traditional psychometric rating errors such as halo, leniency, and central tendency. The impetus for this work has come from growing evidence that a reduction in psychometric rating errors may not improve rater accuracy (Borman, 1979) and may even accompany a *reduction* in rater accuracy (Bernardin & Pence, 1980). Bernardin and Pence, for example, found that subjects who received training focused on the definitions and examples of leniency and halo errors did reduce leniency and halo errors more than control-group subjects. However, the subjects receiving rater-error training also less accurately rated the performance of classroom instructors described in written vignettes. Apparently, the trained subjects developed a response set of avoiding halo and leniency errors that itself led to the distortion of ratings away from the actual performance levels described in the stimulus materials.

Data from a few earlier studies, as well as concepts presented in the broader context of training for observation accuracy and interpersonal judgment (e.g., Campbell, 1958; Spool, 1978), have suggested additional focuses of rating training. Gordon (1970) found that greater experience with a particular rating instrument improved rater accuracy, and Friedman and Cornelius (1976) found that rater participation in rating-scale development resulted in decreased rating errors regardless of scale format. These studies can be interpreted as pointing to the inclusion of detailed instruction in the use of whatever scale format has been selected. Klieger and Mosel (1953) noted that better interrater agreement among supervisory raters, when compared to peer raters, might be the result of supervisory training that gave raters a common frame of reference for the evaluation of performance.

Two reports of more extensive rater training programs illustrate what topics should be covered in such training. Thornton and Zorich (1980) focused on observation accuracy improvement. Drawing on work by Campbell (1958) on the specification of systematic errors made when processing information from an input source to some response or output, Thornton and Zorich designed a three-group experiment in which all subjects viewed a 45-minute videotape of a group decision-making discussion and then answered a 75-item questionnaire concerning objective facts about the discussion group members and their discussion. A control group was told to watch the discussion, take notes, and be prepared to answer questions about the taped discussion. One other group received behavioral instructions that included what was told to the control group, as well as instructions to observe carefully, to note specific verbal and nonverbal behaviors, and to take complete notes on the tape. The third group received the behavioral instructions just mentioned, the control-group instructions, and instructions on eight observation errors. The error instructions included labels, definitions, examples, and avoidance tips on these errors: (*a*) loss of detail through simplification; (*b*) over dependence on a single source; (*c*) middle message loss; (*d*) categorization error; (*e*) contamination from prior information; (*f*) contextual errors; (*g*) prejudice and stereotyping; and (*h*) halo effect. Results indicated that the group that received all instructions performed better on the questionnaire than did the group receiving the behavioral instructions which, in turn, performed better than the control group.

Pursell, Dossett, and Latham (1980) conducted an extensive rater training program with a group of supervisors after initial performance ratings assigned by these supervisors to a sample of journeyman electricians were not predicted by a carefully selected test battery. The rater training program was like that described by Latham *et al.* (1975) and lasted 8 hours. The training consisted of the observation, recording, and evaluation of job behaviors from videotapes, the discussion of such ratings with the group, the receiving of feedback about the accuracy of the ratings, and a group brainstorming discussion about the minimization of various rating errors. Ratings obtained 1 month after training (and 1 year after the initial, unpredictable ratings) were now predictable by four of five tests and the distributions of ratings were less negatively skewed than before. Although the experimental design permits some alternative explanation of the data because of the lack of a control group, the rating distribution changes in the direction of less rating error suggest that the training reduced rating errors, thus resulting in more predictable ratings.

The Thornton and Zorich (1980) and Pursell *et al.* (1980) studies suggest that rater training programs need to cover observation and recording skills, evaluation skills, and errors of observation and evaluation that can be made by a rater. Further, it appears that active participation by the raters in training, feedback about rating accuracy, and practice are also desirable (Pursell *et al.*, 1980).

RATER ANONYMITY. Bayroff *et al.* (1954), Sharon and Bartlett (1969), and Stone, Rabinowitz, and Spool (1977) found no difference in rating errors or validity between identified and anonymous raters. Creswell (1963) reported no effect on leniency of ratings, but did find somewhat more variance with confidential ratings as opposed to ratings that were to be shown to the ratees or to the rater's superior.

RATING BY DIMENSION OR BY RATEE. A suggestion for the reduction of halo error by Guilford (1954), among others, was to rate all ratees on a given trait or dimension, then to rate all ratees on the next trait, etc. This was predicted to result in less halo error than the process of rating a given ratee on all traits, then rating the next ratee on all traits, etc. However, studies that have compared these two rating processes have found no differences (Blumberg, DeSoto, & Kuethe, 1966; Brown, 1968; Johnson, 1963; Taylor & Hastman, 1956).

RATEE SEQUENCE EFFECTS. Several studies have reported data concerning the question of whether position of the ratee in a sequence affects the rating of the ratee. Bayroff et al. (1954) found that ratings early in a sequence were more valid than those later in the sequence. Wagner and Hoover (1974) reported that raters who were not especially knowledgeable about the technical aspects of the task performance being evaluated tended to be more favorable to ratees early in the sequence. Finally, Willingham (1958) found that ratings tended to be biased in the direction of the previous rating and that this tendency increased as the number of response categories increased.

Environmental Process Variables

As noted in Chapter 4, rating process variables include those factors that are not directly associated with the rating task per se, but which still are a part of the rating process. These include the physical location in which the rating occurs, the time pressure to complete the ratings, and the degree of logistical support from the personnel department. These factors have not been researched in any substantial way. Indeed only a single study of one of these variables has been located. Wright (1974) found that, when faced with less time to reach a judgment, individuals tended to use fewer sources of information and to weigh unfavorable information more heavily in making evaluations.

Summary

Rater training has generally been found to reduce traditional psychometric errors, although the duration of such effects is not considerable.

Furthermore, training that focuses only on the elimination of psychometric rating error may not affect, or negatively impact on, rater accuracy. Training that emphasizes observation accuracy, recording accuracy, and rating accuracy (including the minimization of traditional rating errors) may result in more accurate judgments of work performance.

Identified versus anonymous raters appear to give equivalent ratings. There appears to be no reduction in halo error when all ratees are evaluated on one trait, then all ratees are evaluated on the next trait, and so on. Serial position appears to have some effect on ratings, but no general pattern has emerged from the research to date.

ORGANIZATIONAL CHARACTERISTICS

Few studies have been conducted to examine the effects of organizational characteristics. Indeed, systematic comparative organizational studies are nonexistent in the area of performance ratings. Cascio and Valenzi (1977) hypothesized that the expectation of favorable performance, because the ratees had passed selection and training hurdles, might cause raters to be lenient in their judgments. It would be interesting to examine this hypothesis both at the individual rater level through perceptual measures and at more aggregate levels through the use of either perceptual or objective measures of selection and training validity.

Rothe (1949) found that the nature of the incentive system could affect ratings. When the ratees were given pay increases based on performance ratings, and the pay for each job had a ceiling, supervisors gave more favorable ratings to less senior subordinates who had not yet reached the pay maximum.

POSITION CHARACTERISTICS

A few investigations of the effect of position or job characteristics on performance ratings have been conducted. Much of this literature has been concerned with the gender-role stereotype hypothesis discussed in previous sections of this chapter. In general, the data suggest that ratings are influenced by the interaction of the gender of the ratee and the gender-role stereotype of the job or task, although not all studies support this general conclusion (e.g., Jacobson & Effertz, 1974). Rosen and Jerdee (1973) found that observer ratings of the effectiveness of supervisors' leadership styles were affected by the gender of the supervisor and the gender of the subordinates. In general, ratings were more favorable when the leadership style of the supervisor was appropriate for traditional gender-role stereotypes. Rose (1978) found that managers in a simulation study were judged to be higher in effort expenditure if they had cross-gender subordinates than if they had same-gender subordinates. Actual performance level of the managers was controlled in this study. These gender-related position characteristics variables seem worthy of more research attention, particularly in actual work settings.

In other research looking at position characteristics, Svetlik et al. (1964) found that job difficulty, as measured by a job evaluation point system,

Table 5.5
Studies Investigating Organizational and Position Characteristics

Variable investigated	Study	Summary of results concerning variables
Organizational factors		
Perception of selection and training validity	Cascio and Valenzi, 1977	Authors suggested that the perception of such validity may cause more lenient ratings, but they reported no data on this issue.
Incentive system	Rothe, 1949	When pay and ratings were linked organizationally and when there was a pay ceiling, raters gave higher ratings to those not yet at the pay ceiling.
Position factors		
Gender-role stereotype	Rose, 1978 Rosen and Jerdee, 1973 (also, see studies under Ratee gender, Table 5.2)	Supervisors with cross-gender subordinates received higher ratings than those with same-gender subordinates. Gender-role stereotypes affected the evaluation of leadership style appropriateness.
Job and skill level	Klores, 1966 Myers, 1965 Svetlik et al., 1964	Job and skill level weakly but positively correlated with performance ratings. Removing such variance statistically may result in less halo and better factor structure.

was weakly but positively related to a supervisory rating of job competence, although not to a rating of overall effectiveness. Klores (1966) reported that performance ratings were positively correlated with skill level within a job classification. Myers (1965) partialed job level from rating intercorrelations and found a reduction of halo effects in the correlation matrix and a more meaningful factor structure. Table 5.5 summarizes studies of organizational and positional characteristics.

PURPOSE OF THE PERFORMANCE RATINGS

A number of studies have investigated the effect of the intended use of the ratings on various psychometric properties of the ratings. Table 5.6 summarizes this research. Several studies have shown that ratings are more lenient under conditions of administrative use than under conditions of research use (Borresen, 1967; Centra, 1975; Heron, 1956; Taylor & Wherry, 1951), whereas Sharon (1970) and Sharon and Bartlett (1969) found a similar effect for graphic rating scales but not for a forced-choice scale. Bernardin (1978) found that leniency decreased in conditions in which the importance of the ratings was stressed. Kirkpatrick *et al.* (1968) reported that, whereas ratings on three scales intended for research purposes only did not differ for black and white ratees, ratings for the same sample of ratees on a scale intended for administrative use were more favorable for the white employees. Hollander (1957, 1965) found no difference between administrative and research conditions in terms of the reliability or validity of ratings.

Table 5.6
Studies Investigating the Purpose of Ratings

Study	Summary of research
Bernardin, 1978 Borresen, 1967 Centra, 1975 Heron, 1956 Hollander, 1957 Hollander, 1965 Kirkpatrick *et al.*, 1968 Sharon, 1970 Sharon and Bartlett, 1969 Taylor and Wherry, 1951	Administrative uses of ratings often results in more leniency than research uses, especially for direct performance ratings. The raters' perceptions of the uses of performance ratings may be of interest, although not researched to date.

Unfortunately, since most of the published research was done in the "research purposes" context, too little information is currently available to draw firm conclusions about impact of "purpose for rating." The intuitive importance of purpose, especially perhaps of *perceived* purpose, demands more research effort in this area.

DATA ANALYSIS

After one gathers ratings of performance, decisions must still be made concerning the manner in which these data might be analyzed to produce accurate and reliable performance descriptions. It is possible that various analytic techniques are more successful at reducing or eliminating rating errors than other techniques. In this section, we review the research that addresses this issue. Table 5.7 summarizes these research studies.

Dimension Reduction

Traditionally, the performance of individuals is considered with respect to a number of presumably independent dimensions. We use the term *presumably* because, in spite of the attempt by the research to identify and define independent aspects of performance, the intercorrelations among ratings on these dimensions are often high; this problem is usually introduced as one of halo error. A number of studies have examined the effect of combining ratings across dimensions into some smaller number of homogeneous subsets. The process of combination is assumed to produce new, derived performance scores that are more reliable and that better describe important aspects of work-related performance. The use of these derived criteria may allow the construction of more efficient selection and training programs.

The most common technique for data reduction and combination in the area of performance ratings has been factor analysis. Factor scores have been computed and used as the criteria for various administrative, counseling, and research purposes. Grant (1955) suggested that factor analysis was a useful device in determining the degree of halo present in ratings, as well as the degree to which discriminations might be made among individuals on performance dimensions. Guilford, Christenson, Taaffe, and Wilson (1962) proposed that certain marker tests and variables be included in a factor analysis of performance ratings in order to better understand exactly what was being rated. Schultz and Siegel (1964) gathered esti-

Table 5.7
Studies Investigating Data Analytic Techniques

Technique investigated	Study	Summary of results concerning technique
Dimension reduction	Dickinson and Tice, 1977 Grant, 1955 Guilford et al., 1962 Kane and Lawler, 1978 Kavanagh et al., 1971 Norman and Goldberg, 1966 Schultz and Siegel, 1964	Although most studies suggest that the number of rating dimensions can be reduced resulting in less halo, a question can be raised whether the reduced data matrix represents ratee job performance or the raters' perceptions of dimension interrelationships.
Weighting and grouping methods	Jurgensen, 1955 Naylor and Wherry, 1965 Passini and Norman, 1969 Wherry and Naylor, 1966	Group weights are not likely to be effective in weighting performance dimensions due to individual differences in judgment strategies.
Multiple ratings	Buckner, 1959 Carter, 1952 Einhorn, 1972 Overall, 1965 Windle and Dingman, 1960	Although often advocated, multiple ratings may confound rather than improve if raters have different strategies for making judgments.
Scoring schemes	Bass, 1956 Meyer, 1951	Little research on this topic has been reported and the results may be confounded with the particular rating format and instructions.
Partialing and standardization	Harvey, 1982 Hulin, 1982 Landy et al, 1982 Landy et al., 1980 Murphy, 1982 Myers, 1965 Ritti, 1964	Several promising techniques for improving the factor structure, discriminability, and validity are presented. Further work with these appears to be promising.

mates of judged similarity among performance dimensions from raters and used those judgments as the basis for identifying more basic performance dimensions through multidimensional scaling procedures. Dickinson and Tice (1977) used factor-analytic techniques to improve the discriminant validity in performance ratings. They suggested that factor analysis could be used to eliminate complex anchors (anchors loading on more than one dimension) and, thus, to reduce trait intercorrelations. Kane and Lawler

(1978) suggested that performance ratings be factor analyzed and the first unrotated factor score be used as a measure of overall performance for administrative purposes.

Unfortunately, there have been no rigorous tests of the hypothesis that "reduced" scores tell us more about the performance of the ratee than raw scores. As a matter of fact, there are several studies that have implied that a factor analysis of ratings tells us more about the cognitive structure of the raters than the behavior patterns of the ratees. Grant (1955) suggested that factor analysis might tell us how the raters interpreted the items on the rating scale. Norman and Goldberg (1966) instructed raters to evaluate individuals with whom they had little familiarity and individuals with whom they were quite familiar. The factor structures derived from a factor of the two data sets independently were very similar. They concluded that the similarity among these dimensions was more a property of the raters' views of performance than the ratees' actual behaviors. This has serious implications for the use of factor-analytic results for developing selection or training programs. Kavanagh, MacKinney, and Wolins (1971) demonstrated the difficulties in determining the number of performance dimensions represented in managerial ratings. Using multitrait– multimethod procedures (Campbell & Fiske, 1959), they had serious difficulties in identifying independent aspects of managerial performance. They were able to identify "personality dimensions" suitable for rating. They imply that for the first time a procedure was available for identifying and measuring personality-based performance aspects in managers. This begs the question of the existence of these dimensions in the behavior patterns of the ratees. It may be that they "exist" in the cognitive framework of the raters and have little or no "reality" with respect to ratees!

In general, this particular area of research raises many more questions than it answers. The identification of behavioral patterns in ratees is an extremely complex issue. Data reduction techniques such as factor analysis and cluster analysis of ratings seriously confound dimensions of rater cognitive structure with ratee behavior. More will be said about this in Chapter 8.

Weighting and Grouping Methods

Factor analysis might be thought of as one technique for assigning weights to performance dimensions. These weights would represent "relative importance" and could be calculated on the basis of variance accounted for by a particular component or factor. Jurgensen (1955) suggested that statistical weights might help improve the relationship between performance ratings on specific dimensions and overall performance. He found that statistical weights were no better than arbitrarily assigned weights. In light of the research of Dawes and Corrigan (1974), this finding might be extended to include unit weights. Naylor and Wherry (1965; Wherry & Naylor, 1966) were able to describe distinctly different rater "policies" in rating behavior. Each of these different policies could be described by a unique set of relative weights. Consequently, if different raters have different policies, it is likely that computing statistical weights on a group basis will not be effective in weighting specific dimensions. Rather, some initial subgrouping of raters is required. Passini and Norman (1969) suggest a complicated weighting scheme for improving the reliability of peer nominations and rankings that might be extended to cover ratings as well. They suggest that indexes of agreement be computed within and across ratees. Dimensions with greater agreement across raters would receive heavier weights, and dimensions that have highest interobserver agreement within ratees would also receive heavier weights.

The Passini and Norman (1969) procedure assumes that two or more raters are available for each ratee. Several researchers have suggested that multiple ratings are desirable. Carter (1952) suggested that multiple ratings would improve criterion reliability. Windle and Dingman (1960) found that perceptions shared by two raters were more predictive of an independent criterion than perceptions unique to each judge. This study was in response to an earlier study by Buckner (1959), which proposed that unique views of individual judges were ultimately more valuable than common views of a ratee. Overall (1965) suggested an optimal weighting scheme based on the reliability and variance of individual raters. He was concerned with methods for combining ratings from multiple judges. He developed a scheme for weighting judgments by factors that represented the reliability and variance of individual raters. Einhorn (1972) proposed combining components of expert judgment to take advantage of differential validity of individual judges. All of these suggestions assume the existence of multiple ratings on a single ratee. This is seldom the case in applied settings. Nevertheless, even if it were possible to accumulate multiple ratings, the results of Naylor and Wherry (1965; Wherry & Naylor, 1966), and Passini and Norman (1969) imply that there are significant differences among raters in rating policies. This, in turn, implies that "gains" produced by collapsing ratings across judges may be illusory.

There have been some suggestions that scoring schemes might be developed for improving various types of rating data. Meyer (1951) suggested a binary scoring scheme based on the absolute number of items checked in a checklist-type rating scale. He found no differences between this simple technique and more complicated ones. Bass (1956) suggested a binary scoring system that was based on the relative distribution of superior and inferior performers on a 5-point scale. The simple binary recoding system reduced leniency without significantly reducing internal consistency. There have been some studies in scoring procedures, but they have been confounded with scale format and instructions (Bernardin, LaShells, Smith, & Alvares, 1976; Blanz & Ghiselli, 1972; Zedeck, Kafry, & Jacobs, 1976) and the results do not easily generalize to weighting and grouping principles.

Other Techniques of Statistical Control

A number of authors have suggested statistical techniques for reducing the level of intercorrelation (or halo) among ratings on various performance dimensions. These techniques are described here.

Myers (1965) attempted to remove halo from the ratings of job factors in a job-analysis study of 82 different jobs on 17 dimensions. He partialed out the effect of organizational level on these ratings and substantially reduced dimension intercorrelations. As a result, he suggested that researchers look for demographic factors that correlate highly with ratings and remove the influence of those factors statistically, thereby reducing unwanted halo.

Ritti (1964) substantially reduced halo in supervisory ratings by standardizing both the rows and the columns of the rating matrix. He was able to demonstrate through factor-analytic results that the simple structure was improved, the within-factor correlations remained high, and the between-factor correlations were substantially reduced.

Landy, Vance, Barnes-Farrell, and Steele (1980) partialed out an overall rating from ratings on 15 specific performance dimensions and found a substantial reduction in factor correlation, a reduction in variance accounted for by the first unrotated factor (a possible measure of method variance), an improved simple structure factor solution, and greater discriminant validity. The Landy et al. (1980) procedure has created some controversy. Several authors (Harvey, 1982; Hulin, 1982; Murphy, 1982) have criticized the procedure, and Landy, Vance, and Barnes-Farrell (1982) have rejoined.

Murphy (1982) and Hulin (1982) both noted that it is probably unreasonable to attempt to reduce rating dimension correlations to .00, since the actual performance on job dimensions is likely to be positively correlated. Landy *et al.* (1982) agreed with this criticism but noted our current ignorance regarding the true level of performance dimension intercorrelations. Landy *et al.* also note that it is important to distinguish between the behaviors of work performers and the ratings of those behaviors. If the ratings of behaviors are more highly intercorrelated than the behaviors being rated, then the partial correlation techniques suggested by Landy *et al.* are appropriate for some purposes. These purposes do not include using the residual ratings as substitutes for the raw performance ratings when making individual decisions.

Summary

    The research on dimensional combination strategies resulting from data reduction algorithms have been equivocal. A substantial amount of research still must be done before it will be possible to specify what those performance factors represent—behavioral patterns of ratees or cognitive constructs of raters. The research on the combination of multiple ratings is also equivocal. If distinct patterns of rating exist among raters (i.e., policies), the presumed gains in reliability may represent a hollow victory. On a practical basis, it seems unlikely that techniques based on multiple ratings will prove useful in applied settings, although they may be of value in cataloging sources of error. The research by Myers (1965), Ritti (1964), and Landy *et al.* (1980) suggests a possible avenue for continued research in the data analysis of performance ratings.

USEFULNESS OF THE PROCESS MODEL OF PERFORMANCE RATING

The literature review presented in this chapter provides support for the value of considering how the various components of the process model presented in Chapter 4 affect performance ratings. This model does not make detailed predictions about the specific influences that the various components have on performance ratings. Thus, it is not feasible to test the empirical validity of the model. However, it does appear that the model can serve at least as a heuristic device for organizing research and thought about performance ratings.

An examination of the tables in Chapter 4 that suggest specific examples for the various components of the model and of the tables and text of this chapter (and instrument-related research in Chapter 3) that describe the published research in the area is revealing. Many of the variables suggested in Chapter 4 have been rarely or never examined (at least in the published literature). Furthermore, the major areas of published research concern rating formats or instruments and variables such as rater and ratee demographics that are not really the psychological variables of interest. Relatively little attention has been paid to the truly psychological variables of interest such as attitudinal, perceptual, and cognitive factors. There appears to be increasing interest in these variables. It is welcomed.

part three

Uses of Performance Data

There are many different ways in which performance data might be used after it is collected. Three broad classes of use are administration, research, and counseling. The types of information used vary by category of use and intended effect. Chapter 6 considers motivational, counseling, and developmental uses of performance information. Chapter 7 deals with administrative and research uses of performance data.

chapter six

Performance Information and Employee Motivation

An important goal for work organizations is the improved job performance of its members. It is generally agreed that performance information or feedback is a necessary part of any successful performance improvement approach. However, not until recently have we moved in our understanding much beyond the general statement that "feedback improves performance," as established by the literature reviews and research of Ammons (1956) and Payne and Hauty (1955), among others.

One purpose of a work performance measurement system is to provide the basic information about performance that can be used by the individual to change his or her behaviors. It is necessary to understand as much as possible about the factors that affect the usefulness of performance information in improving performance in order to design a performance measurement system that well serves this purpose. Performance information that may be appropriate as the criterion variable in a test validation study may be useless as feedback information. In this chapter we will examine recent models and research about feedback that can be brought to bear on the issue of designing performance measurement systems for feedback purposes.

Ilgen, Fisher, and Taylor (1979) have noted several factors that have contributed to the relatively few generalizations that can be made about

163

the effects of performance feedback. First, feedback is often treated as a unidimensional concept, but it is in fact quite complex. This complexity, and the accompanying variability in what is contained in "feedback" from one situation to another, makes generalizations difficult. Second, there has been little development of theoretical frameworks that specify relationships among the characteristics of feedback, the psychological processes of the individual, and the behavioral changes of the individual. Particularly, much of the laboratory-based research on feedback was concerned with demonstrating the empirical link between one or two dimensions of feedback and some behavioral response (or set of responses). This research paid little attention to the psychological processes of the individual. This omission especially limits the value of the bulk of the laboratory research on feedback as a contributor to the understanding of feedback processes in work organizations. Feedback about work performance takes place in a social context that introduces a myriad of factors not usually relevant to the laboratory research. Of particular importance are interpersonal interactions, power, and the esteem and achievement needs of the employee.

There have been two major attempts to advance our present state of understanding about the impact of work performance feedback on individuals' attitudes and behavior. Ilgen et al. (1979) have conceived of feedback as a special case of the general communications process in which a *message* (feedback) is conveyed to a *recipient* (work performer) from some *source* (e.g., a supervisor or co-worker). They have developed a process model that attempts to integrate human performance and information-processing research findings from laboratory studies with the social context in which feedback occurs in organizational settings. Ashford and Cummings (in press) have taken a different perspective and have argued that performance feedback is a valued resource for the individual work performer and, as such, is actively sought by the individual. They have developed a theoretical framework that attempts to explain how individuals seek and respond to feedback in their work environments.

We will consider the Ilgen et al. (1979) and Ashford and Cummings (in press) models of performance feedback in some detail and contrast their implications for employee motivation.

FEEDBACK AS A COMMUNICATION PROCESS

A process model of the effects of work performance feedback on recipients is shown in Figure 6.1 (Ilgen et al., 1979). As just noted, this model

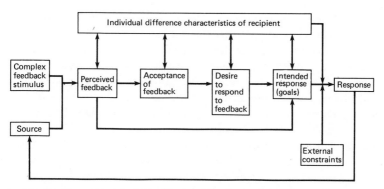

Figure 6.1. A process model of the effects of feedback on recipients. (This figure and subsequent figures from Ilgen *et al.*, 1979, are reprinted from D. Ilgen, C. Fisher, & M. Taylor. Consequences of individual feedback on behavior in organizations. *Journal of Applied Psychology*, 1979, *64*, p. 352. Copyright 1979 by the American Psychological Association. Reprinted by permission of the publisher and author.)

views feedback as a particular type of communication process. As such, the basic elements of the system are the source of the feedback, the feedback message itself, the recipient of the feedback, and their main and interactive impact on feedback process and reaction.

Source

Ilgen *et al.* (1979) note that the source, while technically not a part of the feedback, creates behavioral and attitudinal effects that are generally confounded with effects created by the feedback, per se. Thus, to understand the effects of feedback, it is important to examine possible source effects also.

There are three general categories of feedback sources: others, the task, and self. Others are those nonself individuals who have observed the recipient's behaviors or output and have some type of information about its effectiveness. In organizational settings this category consists most frequently of supervisory personnel, with co-workers, subordinates, and nonorganizational members with whom the recipient has contact as part of the work role (such as customers) also common.

The task itself can provide feedback to a work performer. In many jobs feedback is an inherent part of the task activities, particularly where the task predominantly involves motor activity or countable output. In other jobs, augmented feedback mechanisms can be added (see Annett, 1969; Bilodeau, 1966) to make the available task feedback more salient or timely.

Augmented feedback as a source would refer to mechanistic, not interpersonal, sources of additional task feedback.

Work performers may be able to evaluate their own job performance and, thus, to provide themselves with feedback. It is likely that several factors, such as the measurability of task output, the amount of the individual's experience on the task, and the individual's level of self-esteem, affect the extent to which individuals make such evaluations and the extent to which they utilize them (Ilgen et al., 1979).

It is likely that different feedback sources would elicit differential recipient response. To understand better the impact that a source has, Ilgen et al. (1979) introduce two characteristics of sources from the communications and social influence literature, namely, credibility and power. Credible sources are perceived by the recipient to possess the expertise to judge his or her behavior accurately and to be trustworthy. Power is the degree of control that the source has over potential rewards and sanctions for the recipient. Power and credibility are theoretically independent, although they may covary in many situations; both are predicted to have positive relationships with the recipient's attempt to behave in concordance with feedback.

Message

In general, the message is *the* feedback (i.e., information about the appropriateness of past performance [Ilgen et al., 1979]). A message or instance of performance feedback does not stand alone. It is more appropriate to think about the increment information value of feedback (Annett, 1969). A work performer may be relatively knowledgeable or relatively ignorant about the appropriateness of his or her past work performance. The information value of the same feedback message will differ greatly depending on the accuracy and extent of the performer's current performance knowledge.

Although feedback is often described in terms of two primary functions, directing and motivational, Annett (1969) and Ilgen et al. (1979) note that, in practice, it is hard to separate the effects of these two functions. The directing function is an informational one, informing the recipient of the particular work behaviors that are appropriate. The motivational function is concerned with relating behaviors with rewards or outcomes, both positive and negative. Ilgen et al. (1979) argue that those concerned with behavior in organizational settings should view performance feedback from a broad motivational framework within which feedback can serve both to direct behavior and either to influence future performance goals or to reward or punish.

Recipient

The recipient of the performance feedback is the work performer. Ilgen *et al.* (1979) describe the recipient as a processor of performance information who receives this information as a source-and-message couplet. That is, for the individual, work performance feedback represents a confounding of source and message. The process model presumes that characteristics of the recipient interact with source and message characteristics to produce a reaction to the performance feedback by the recipient.

Feedback Process and Reaction

As Figure 6.1 reveals, Ilgen *et al.* (1979) hypothesize that the recipient's reaction to feedback involves a four-part process leading to the actual behavioral response or responses on the part of the recipient. Source, message, and recipient characteristics may affect each of these four parts of the process. The four parts or stages of the recipient's processing of and reaction to performance feedback are perception of feedback, acceptance of feedback, desire to respond to feedback, and the intended response.

PERCEIVED FEEDBACK. The accuracy with which the recipient perceives the feedback from any given source is labeled· as *perceived feedback* in the Ilgen *et al.* (1979) model. Ilgen *et al.* suggest that such source factors as type (supervisor, peers, task, self, etc.), psychological closeness to the recipient, credibility, and power may affect how accurately a recipient perceives the message from the particular source. Such factors may differentially affect the degree of attention paid to the source by the recipient and, thus, influence the accuracy of the perception. They also identified three message factors that appear to affect perceptions of accuracy. These message factors are the temporal interval between the individual's behavior and the feedback about the behavior (timing), the positive or negative tone of the information about behavior (sign), and how often feedback is given to the recipient (frequency). Characteristics of the recipient also are suggested by Ilgen *et al.* as influences on the accuracy of perceived feedback. They stress the importance of self-perceptual sets or frames of reference as influences on the selective sensing and interpreting of feedback from various sources.

ACCEPTANCE OF FEEDBACK. Ilgen *et al.* (1979) use *acceptance* to refer to the recipient's *belief* that the feedback is an accurate portrayal of his or her performance, regardless of the veridicality of this belief. Characteristics of the source, message, and recipient are hypothesized by the Ilgen *et al.* model to influence the acceptance of feedback.

Source credibility, the degree of credibility attributed to a source by the recipient, was identified by Ilgen *et al.* as the principal source characteristic affecting the acceptance of feedback. They suggest that credibility, in turn, is influenced by the recipient's perception of the source's *expertise*, the recipient's *trust* in the source's motives, the *congruence* of the feedback with the source's role, and by the *reliability* of the source.

The most important message characteristic in terms of its impact on the acceptance of feedback is the *sign* of the feedback. Generally, positive or favorable feedback is more readily accepted by the recipient than is negative or unfavorable feedback. Ilgen *et al.* interpret this finding with a self-image or self-esteem framework. They argue that favorable feedback is consistent with most individuals' self-images and, therefore, is easily accepted.

Message *consistency*, or the extent to which the feedback received from a given source is either all positive or all negative, is also a major influence on the acceptance of feedback. One interpretation of this effect is that the individual infers that one's own performance is the primary cause of consistent feedback, and, thus, accepts the feedback. However, inconsistent feedback may be attributed to causes beyond the control of the individual and, thus, is not accepted by the recipient.

Ilgen *et al.* suggested that certain recipient characteristics may affect acceptance of feedback. Individuals with an internal rather than external *locus of control* (Rotter, 1966) may be more likely to accept feedback about performance. Recipient *age*, or age-correlated factors such as *experience* or *seniority*, appears to be inversely related to the willingness to accept feedback. It was suggested that older (more experienced, more senior) work incumbents may rely more on his or her own past experience and knowledge as a source of feedback and less on external sources.

DESIRE TO RESPOND. The willingness to respond to feedback in a manner congruent with that feedback (e.g., maintaining behavior for which positive feedback was received or improving that performance for which negative feedback was received) is labeled as *desire to respond to feedback* by Ilgen, *et al.* (1979). They again consider source, message, and recipient characteristics that may affect the willingness to respond to feedback.

The source characteristic of most importance in influencing the desire to respond to feedback would appear to be *power*. Ilgen *et al.* define *power* as the extent to which the recipient perceives that the source has control over outcomes and rewards valued by the recipient. Increased source power would be expected to enhance recipient compliance even if the feedback were not accepted.

Several message characteristics were identified by Ilgen *et al.* as influencing the desire to respond to feedback. These were the timing, the frequency, and the sign of the feedback message. These factors also were noted as being an important influence on the perception of feedback. With regard to the desire to respond, these three message characteristics are generally confounded in a particular study and are rarely investigated separately from each other. The discussion that follows recognizes this confounding and addresses these variables in combination.

Frequency of feedback is usually associated with improved performance (Ilgen *et al.*, 1979). However, this is too simplistic a generalization, because it ignores the sign and timing of the feedback. The sign and frequency of feedback are probably confounded in many instances. Sources are more likely to give positive feedback than negative feedback. Also, if feedback is usually associated with performance improvement, then the recipient's performance should improve over time, resulting in a greater and greater proportion of favorable performance and feedback. Timing may also be confounded with sign and frequency. Sources are more likely to give positive feedback more quickly following the appropriate behavior than they are to give negative feedback following behavior appropriate for such feedback. The work of Gordon (1970, 1972) suggests that poor performance is less frequent in most work settings than adequate or good performance by supervisors (and others). The low reliability of such evaluations could also affect the frequency and timing of feedback that might be given about such performance.

Ilgen *et al.* (1979) regard the view that feedback enhances performance, because it serves as a reinforcer of appropriate work behaviors, as not very helpful in the understanding of feedback effects. They favor a more cognitive orientation that focuses on the informational value of feedback rather than its possible reinforcement value. This cognitive orientation is compatible with currently popular approaches to work motivation such as those based on expectancy theory (e.g., Naylor, Pritchard, & Ilgen, 1980; Porter & Lawler, 1968; Vroom, 1964).

Viewing feedback as providing information about the likelihood that various outcomes or rewards may be received given certain types or levels of work performance appears to be fruitful. Since actual rewards cannot generally be administered to the work performer at the completion of each work unit, an important function of feedback is to lead the work performer to anticipate a reward at some time in the future (i.e., to serve as an *incentive*). Feedback can provide descriptive and evaluative information about past performance that can be used by the work performer to establish perceived relationships (or *instrumentality beliefs*) between performance and rewards that are received. The absence of such feedback is likely to result in the individual establishing incorrect perceptions about the relationship between rewards and behaviors.

Feedback may also serve to strengthen an individual's belief about his or her ability to perform a task successfully. Various motivational theories consider this belief to be most important in the activation and direction of behavior. For example, similar concepts are labeled as *expectancy beliefs* in expectancy theory (Mitchell, 1974; Porter & Lawler, 1968), as the need for *competence* (White, 1959), and as *personal efficacy* (Bandura, 1977). All of these concepts share the basic idea that individuals will not (or be less likely to) attempt performance levels that are viewed as impossible to achieve. Providing feedback about an individual's success (or partial success) may serve to increase the individual's belief that more effort expenditure will result in more successful performance. It is suggested by Ilgen *et al.* (1979) that feedback should be positive, should provide an increment of information beyond what the individual already knows, and, perhaps, should not be so frequent as to appear to be controlling (Deci, 1975).

Research on the personality characteristics of recipients that may affect their desire to respond to feedback has yielded a rather consistent pattern of results (Ilgen *et al.*, 1979). Feedback that emphasizes the work performer's competence and control over the task appears to impact positively on individuals whose personal needs are satisfied through the successful performance of the task itself. These individuals are characterized by such personality factors as internal locus of control, high self-esteem, and high need for achievement. For those individuals whose personal needs may be better satisfied by factors external to the task itself are likely to be influenced more by feedback concerned with the relationship between task performance and various rewards and outcomes. Such individuals are likely to have an external locus of control and strong affiliative needs.

INTENDED RESPONSE. In the Ilgen *et al.* (1979) model the desire to respond to feedback is the major input to the establishment of the response that the recipient intends to make. Performance or response intentions may be thought of as the goal or target set by the recipient. This goal may not always be met; hence, the actual response or performance level is likely to differ in some way from the intended response.

A more extended discussion of goals and their relationship to feedback will be presented later in this chapter. Focusing now just on source, message, and recipient effects on the intended response reveals that relatively little research from this perspective examined this component of Ilgen *et al.*'s process model. Since in general the more control the work performer has over goals, the better the performance (Steers & Porter, 1974), the self as a source of goals and feedback may enhance the intended response. Data on other sources are lacking. The work of Locke (e.g., see reviews by Locke, 1975 and by Locke, Cartledge, & Koeppel, 1968) suggests that an important message factor is goal difficulty. Generally, more difficult goals result in higher levels of performance. In terms of recipient factors affecting the intended response, it could be inferred that individuals with strong intrinsic motivation would be expected to intend to respond at a higher level than those individuals motivated more strongly by factors other than the task itself.

FEEDBACK AS A RESOURCE FOR THE INDIVIDUAL WORK PERFORMER

Ashford and Cummings (in press) argue that our understanding of the experience of the individual in the feedback process and of the nature of feedback in organizations has been constrained by the past emphasis on the performance enhancement effects of feedback information. These authors suggest that it is necessary to move away from the view that feedback is only an organizational resource or tool that organizational management can use to motivate, direct, and enhance the work performance of subordinates. A basic premise of Ashford and Cummings is that feedback is a valuable resource for the individual work performer, as well as for the organization. As a valued resource, feedback then becomes something that is sought by the individual, not merely received in a passive way.

The Value to the Individual of Seeking Feedback

Feedback must have value for the individual work performer if it is to be reasonable to consider it as an individual resource. Ashford and Cummings (in press) suggest that feedback may satisfy several motives and, thus, that it is reasonable for individuals to seek feedback in the work environment. These possible motives are discussed in the following sections.

ERROR CORRECTION. Through feedback an individual can obtain information about the quantity and quality of his or her performance. This information is useful in correcting errors of performance that may be preventing the individual from achieving various goals (both performance and nonperformance) that the individual desires. The individual should, thus, be motivated to seek feedback in order to have a greater chance of achieving these desired goals.

DRIVE TO SELF-EVALUATE. Ashford and Cummings (in press), following Festinger (1954), argue that individuals have an inherent drive to evaluate themselves. Individuals will first attempt to evaluate themselves by comparison to objective, nonsocial referents such as the percentage of "correct" behaviors. However, to the extent that such objective referents are not present or are difficult to interpret, individuals will make comparisons with others. Indeed, Festinger (1954) states that the subjective evaluation of the adequacy of one's performance and abilities is a major source of satisfaction deriving from social interrelationships. This suggests that the individual *actively* makes these social comparisons and seeks feedback as the basis for such comparisons.

EFFECTANCE MOTIVATION. As defined by White (1959), *effectance* is a motivation to achieve some sense of mastery over one's environment. This mastery leads to competence, a capacity to interact effectively with the environment. The individual has, then, a motivation to interact in a competent way with his or her environment. Feedback information that is available in a task situation becomes a necessary, although not sufficient, condition for achieving competence (i.e., no sense of mastery can be achieved without the individual having feedback information available and using it). Thus, again Ashford and Cummings (in press) argue that an individual inevitably *seeks* feedback so as to achieve effectance and competence.

It can be noted that effectance motivation is conceptually similar to further motivational constructs proposed by other theorists. In particular, it appears to be highly related to Bandura's (1977) *personal efficacy*, to Rotter's (1966) *internal versus external locus of control*, to *need for achievement* (e.g., Atkinson & Feather, 1966), and to *expectancy beliefs* postulated by valence–instrumentality–expectancy theories of work motivation (e.g., Porter & Lawler, 1968; Vroom, 1964). Thus, there appears to be theoretical convergence on the importance of knowledge about one's mastery over, or ability to control, one's environment, including the work situation.

UNCERTAINTY REDUCTION. Another possible motive for the seeking of feedback information can be derived from the theoretical and empirical work on curiosity and information seeking (e.g., Berlyne, 1960, 1966; Lanzetta, 1971). It is argued that individuals experience conflict when they are faced with a stimulus situation for which the appropriate response is not clear. This conflict, in turn, motivates the seeking of additional information to reduce the uncertainty or ambiguity of the situation. To the extent that there is uncertainty about the relevance of a given behavior for the attainment of an individual's goal or goals, it would be predicted that the individual would actively seek feedback pertinent to the appropriateness of the particular behavior and, perhaps, alternative behaviors.

The several possible motives for the active seeking of performance feedback suggest strongly that performance information can (and should) be considered as a resource for the individual work performer. The various motives certainly do not have equal impact, either within or between individuals, but their scope would argue that these motives, taken as a set, would have a nonzero effect on most, if not all, individuals.

In addition to the motives just discussed, it is apparent that feedback is a resource that can be useful for the individual in the attainment of performance and nonperformance goals. The literature on feedback has been predominantly concerned with performance goals, yet it is clear, and has long been recognized (e.g., March & Simon, 1958), that individuals have a myriad of goals, some congruent with organizational goals, others inconsistent, and some parallel to or coexisting with the performance goals. These goals include performance in the current job, advancement, job security, personal growth, interpersonal growth, impression management, and so forth (Ashford & Cummings, in press). The various goals held by an individual form a frame of reference against which the individual can evaluate his or her competence. Feedback of various types and from various sources may be necessary for the individual to judge goal attainment adequately.

A Model of Feedback as a Resource

The model of feedback as a resource to the individual suggested by Ashford and Cummings (in press) is shown in Figure 6.2. The individual work performer is placed within an information environment (cf. Hanser & Muchinsky, 1978). The information environment contains two types of information comprising *feedback*, along with much other information. The types of information relevant to feedback are designated *referent*, which tells the individual what behaviors are required for successful performance on the job, and *appraisal*, which tells the individual the extent to which he or she is performing the job successfully (Greller & Herold, 1975).

As shown in Figure 6.2, this model of feedback posits that four functions influence a central, cognitive or *thinking* function of the individual. A *motivating* function is the basic source of energy for the system, creating the desire or need for performance and personally relevant feedback infor-

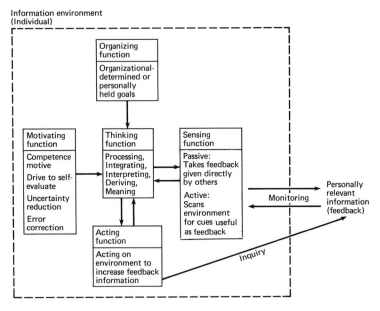

Figure 6.2. The individual as a seeker of feedback within an information environment. (From S. Ashford & L. L. Cummings. Feedback as an individual resource: Personal strategies for creating information. *Organizational Behavior and Human Performance, 32*, in press.

mation. Previously discussed motives, such as the drive to self-evaluate, competence motivation, uncertainty reduction, and error correction, are included here (Ashford & Cummings, in press). The more these motives are present in an individual, the greater the extent to which the individual will seek feedback.

Organizationally determined and personally held goals are hypothesized to serve an *organizing* function. The effort expenditure arising from the motivating function must be directed if it is to be useful. These goals direct the individual to seek information appropriate to learning more about goal attainment.

Once the motivating and organizing functions are influencing the cognitive or thinking function, means or strategies for seeking feedback must be activated. Ashford and Cummings (in press) suggest two information-attaining functions, the *sensing* function and the *acting* function. The sensing function monitors the environment and takes in information. It can be relatively passive and receive feedback information explicitly directed toward the individual work performer from some source. It may also be relatively active and scan or search the environment for cues or information that may be useful as feedback. The sensing function, however, only observes the environment in some fashion; it does not initiate active inquiries about performance and other behavior.

The acting function serves to attempt to increase the amount of feedback information available to the individual work performer. The individual, through the acting function, directly asks relevant sources in the environment about the effectiveness of task performance.

Ashford and Cummings (in press) note that sensing requires less effort than acting. This suggests that individuals will generally use the sensing function more frequently than, and prior to, the use of the acting function. However, if the environment is particularly ambiguous with regard to feedback cues and/or the individual's motivation to obtain feedback is very strong, the acting function is likely to be used more than the sensing function because of the presumed higher quality of the feedback information obtained by the acting function.

The quality of the feedback information obtained by direct inquiry is presumed by Ashford and Cummings to be higher than that obtained by observing one's work situation. This presumption is based on the substantially lower amount of inference required of the individual work performer when processing feedback obtained from direct inquiry. The use of situational cues, on the other hand, generally requires the observer to interpret these cues in relation to one's effectiveness. These interpretations are likely to be biased by the individual's implicit theories of social perception and personality (cf. Ross, Lepper, & Hubbard, 1975).

There may be factors that reduce the presumed greater accuracy of feedback obtained from direct query. As Ilgen et al. (1979) noted, the sign of the feedback message is an important variable in several respects. Of particular relevance here is the finding that sources may distort unfavorable information when required to give feedback to work performers (Fisher, 1978) or even avoid giving the negative feedback if possible (Meyer, 1976). These findings suggest that favorable feedback obtained by direct query may be more accurate than such performance information inferred from observations of the work environment, but that this may not hold for unfavorable feedback. We need to know more about conditions that enhance and inhibit the bias in giving negative feedback to others.

A factor that may serve to inhibit direct inquiry regarding work behavior is the public nature of such queries (Ashford & Cummings, in press). The public asking for feedback involves more risks than merely observing the work environment for feedback cues. The potential (or actual) source who is asked may interpret the query in a variety of ways, not all of them favorable to the inquirer. For example, such action could be interpreted as indicating insecurity on the part of the work performer or as revealing the individual's desire to improve his or her performance. We know very little about what influences these inferences or attributions about the motives and other qualities of those asking for feedback.

FEEDBACK AS A COMMUNICATION PROCESS AND FEEDBACK AS AN INDIVIDUAL RESOURCE: IMPLICATIONS AND DISCUSSION

The feedback models suggested by Ilgen et al. (1979) and Ashford and Cummings (in press) can perhaps be better viewed as complementary rather than competitive. A number of practical as well as research issues can be fruitfully discussed within the frameworks of these two models. The remainder of this section examines a selected set of issues concerning feedback from the perspectives of feedback as a communication process and feedback as an individual resource. These issues are also related to the question of how to design a performance measurement system to provide information of value in feedback. These two models aid in the design of such systems by placing the performance information in the broader context of the social and psychological variables present in the appraisal situation.

Feedback and Goal Setting

Both Ilgen *et al.* (1979) and Ashford and Cummings (in press) stress the importance of goals, but the emphases and foci of the two perspectives are somewhat different. The differences in emphasis are consistent with the general perspectives of the two models. Ilgen *et al.* are principally concerned with the relationship between the *specificity* of feedback received by the individual work performer and the *specificity* of goals (or intended responses) that are established. In general, specific goals have been found to result in better performance than general goals (e.g., Locke, 1967, 1968; Steers & Porter, 1974). Ilgen *et al.* hypothesize that feedback specificity and goal specificity interact as indicated in Figure 6.3.

Figure 6.3 suggests that the most improvement in performance would be expected when there is both specific feedback and specific goals. This allows the recipient to evaluate his or her performance easily with respect to the goal (assuming that specificity and meaningfulness of the feedback covary). Specific feedback combined with general goals is likely to result in ambiguity on the part of the recipient with regard to whether the goal was achieved. Ilgen *et al.* hypothesize that this ambiguity would lead the recipient, over time, to redefine goals in more specific terms. Ashford and Cummings would be likely to agree with this, as the increased specificity of goals should result in uncertainty reduction for the work performer.

General feedback to an individual work performer who has specific goals is likely to be interpreted by the individual in terms of the performer's frame of reference (Ilgen *et al.*, 1979) (i.e., the individual is likely to transform the general feedback into more specific feedback regarding his or her goals). Since general feedback usually takes the form of one undifferentiated point (i.e., performance is good or performance is bad), the recipient of the feedback is most likely to interpret the feedback as meaning that his or her various specific goals are either all being attained or all not being attained. General feedback does not recognize or address differ-

		Goals	
		Specific	General
Feedback	Specific	Feedback is easily understood and applied to future performance	Performance evaluation is difficult
	General	Feedback is interpreted in terms of the performer's frame of reference	Feedback is difficult to interpret and apply

Figure 6.3. Interaction of goal and feedback specificity. (From Ilgen *et al.*, 1979, p. 365.)

ential goal attainment. In the case of less than adequate performance, general feedback particularly does not serve well Ashford and Cummings's (in press) motive of error correction. The inadequacy of general feedback for error correction is even more pronounced when the goals themselves are general.

Goal difficulty and the *degree of control* the individual work performer has over the goals that are set have also been found to influence performance. Locke (1968) has noted that more difficult goals lead to higher performance levels than less difficult ones. This finding has been corroborated by a large amount of experimental evidence (e.g., Latham & Baldes, 1975; Umstot, Bell, & Mitchell, 1976), although with a caveat that very difficult goals may be viewed as difficult and stifle motivation (Steers & Porter, 1974).

The degree of control that one has over goals was identified by Steers and Porter (1974) as a potentially important factor in affecting subsequent performance. They noted, however, that the results of research looking at participation in goal setting (the principal way that degree of control has been operationalized) were contradictory in whether participation was effective or not in increasing performance. Locke and Schweiger (1979), following an extensive review of the participation in decision-making literature, concluded that participative decision making had no consistent impact on goal setting and task performance when compared to assigned goals.

According to Locke (1968), the critical factor may not be participation in goal setting but the *acceptance* of goals by the work performers. Goals must be accepted by the individual in order for the individual to be motivated toward their attainment. The apparent lack of impact of participation in goal setting on performance may be that the acceptance of assigned goals in the various research studies was relatively high and, thus, participation could not substantially increase goal acceptance. Work performers may often be willing to accept goals set by others, if the goals are not unreasonable, because having *any* goal may reduce ambiguity and uncertainty. Relatively specific goals assigned by others may provide an important and desired source of feedback to the individual and, thus, be accepted (cf. Ashford & Cummings, in press).

Locke (1968) and Ashford and Cummings (in press) argue that individuals will set personal goals (both performance and nonperformance) if goals are not developed in some other function (e.g., assigned or mutually set with supervisor). These personal goals may be in conflict with the implicit goals of the supervisor or organization. It appears that making these often implicit goals explicit should enhance performance and, at least for most work performers, also enhance individual satisfaction. Ilgen *et al.* (1979) note that too little feedback is usually the norm in most organizations. This suggests that too few goal-related discussions also occur between supervisors and subordinates in most organizations.

Negative Feedback

As noted earlier, Ilgen *et al.* (1979) indicate that the sign of a feedback message (i.e., its positive or negative nature) contributes importantly to the reaction of a recipient to the feedback. Generally, negative feedback is less likely to be perceived accurately and is less well accepted than positive feedback. If we note the motives that work performers have for seeking feedback (Ashford & Cummings, in press), it is easy to understand these findings. For most individuals the competence motive and the drive to self-evaluate are concerned with demonstrating to oneself (and, perhaps, to others) that one is a capable individual, deserving of respect and positive regard. Negative feedback does not positively contribute to the development of these feelings of achievement and self-worth. The consequences of negative feedback are more frequently hostility, ego-defensiveness, and rationalization.

Kay, Meyer, and French (1965) investigated the relationship between negative comments from the supervisor in a feedback session and defensive comments of the subordinate. The general finding was that, as the number of negative feedback comments increased, the number of defensive comments of the subordinate increased. However the relationship was not linear, but rather a curvilinear, positively accelerated one as shown in Figure 6.4, adapted from Landy and Trumbo (1980).

Kay *et al.* (1965) also noted that a common way that supervisors try to "cushion" the impact of negative feedback may lessen the favorable effects of positive feedback. Often, supervisors create a "praise/criticism/praise sandwich." Some positive comments are first given by the supervisor so that the subordinate is in a "proper" frame of mind when the negative feedback is given. Then, the feedback session ends with a few more positive comments so that the subordinate leaves the session with a more favorable attitude. The result of this sequencing of comments is that the subordinate quickly learns the pattern. The first positive comments are a signal that criticism is to follow, and the final positive comments are a

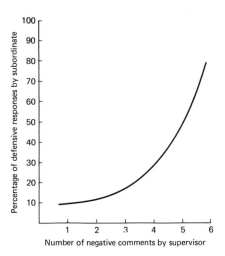

Figure 6.4. Hypothetical relationship between negative comments by supervisor and defensive responses by subordinate. (From Landy & Trumbo, 1980, p. 135.)

signal that the critical comments are over, at least for now. Thus, the favorable feedback is not well attended to by the subordinate and the possible beneficial effects on the subordinate's behavior are lost.

As Latham and Wexley (1981) have noted, the previously discussed unfavorable consequences of negative feedback or criticism have led some to the conclusion that criticism should be completely avoided. This does not seem to be a realistic course of action as it appears inevitable that some criticism be given. It appears more worthwhile to examine the conditions that lead to better acceptance of negative feedback. Indeed, the writings of Ashford and Cummings (in press) would suggest that negative feedback is potentially useful to the individual in helping to satisfy the motives of error correction and uncertainty reduction.

A number of authors have addressed this issue, and their suggestions are summarized here. Several authors (e.g., Ilgen *et al.*, 1979; Kay *et al.*, 1965; Landy, Barnes, & Murphy, 1978; Latham & Wexley, 1981) have suggested that more frequent feedback sessions are desirable. In reference to negative feedback, more frequent sessions would permit fewer criticisms per session. Figure 6.4 suggests that individuals can tolerate a few criticisms with relatively little defensiveness, but that increasing the number of critical comments beyond a few has a disproportionate impact on the amount of defensiveness displayed by the recipient.

Latham and Wexley (1981), Burke, Weitzel, and Weir (1978), Landy *et al.* (1978), and Ilgen *et al.* (1979) have recommended that negative feedback be presented with specific examples to justify the criticisms. They also note that the negative feedback be paired with a specific plan for improving the performance problem. Again, the need to match specific feedback with specific goals (and with a way to reach those goals) is stressed.

Ilgen *et al.* (1979) and Landy *et al.* (1978) note that the credibility and expertise of the source appear to be important for favorable reactions to performance feedback. Acceptance of feedback, particularly negative feedback, is not likely unless the recipient believes that the source is knowledgeable about both the job requirements and the performance of the recipient. Thus, it would appear that the source should not be too removed, either physically or hierarchically, from the recipient. In most cases, for formal performance appraisal sessions at least, the supervisor is the obvious source.

The view of Ashford and Cummings (in press) that feedback is actively sought by individual work performers raises some additional issues. Some of the motives for seeking feedback suggested by Ashford and Cummings can generally be better satisfied by positive rather than negative information, particularly competence motivation and the drive to self-evaluate. It could be argued that uncertainty reduction could be served by either positive or negative feedback and that for only the motive of error correction is negative feedback likely to be more useful. Thus, positive feedback satisfies more of the motives for seeking feedback, in general, and is likely to be sought more frequently than negative feedback. It can be hypothesized that one factor affecting the individual's choice of a source to monitor or to query is the expectation of the sign of the feedback from that source. Triandis (1971) presents a functional theory of attitudes that suggests that the possible use or uses of potential information determines whether we seek it or not. This appears to account for the observed selectivity in information exposure that occurs in many facets of everyday life. This also supports the hypothesis that an individual will generally seek positive information about his or her performance, although Korman's (1970, 1976) theory of self-consistency would argue that low self-esteem individuals would seek negative information about their performance.

We do not know much about how people develop their expectations about the sign of the feedback that a particular source is likely to give to them. We can only fall back on the faithful "it is learned." However, even this does suggest some hypotheses. Work performers with little experience in work, the organization, the job, or the work group are not as likely as the more experienced performer to obtain only (or a high proportion of) positive feedback. Since less experienced individuals, on the average, do not perform as well as more experienced workers, the increased amount of negative feedback may be useful in error correction. However, what are the effects on the individual's self-esteem and perception of competence? It is probably necessary for the supervisor to give frequent and positive (if at all possible) feedback to the new employee to prevent the individual from being overwhelmed by negative feedback.

If more experienced individuals are able to seek and obtain positive feedback with a high success rate, it may be hypothesized that they become less accepting of negative feedback over time. Individuals develop a self-stereotype of their work performance. This stereotype is likely to be positive in tone. Particularly for those individuals who value work highly, performance information inconsistent with this stereotype may be rejected rather than assimilated (cf. Sherif, Sherif, & Nebergall, 1965). Thus, for example, Meyer and Walker (1961) found that older (probably also more experienced since age and experience are generally positively correlated) workers used feedback less than younger ones.

Finally, several writers have suggested that participation by the recipient in the appraisal session is useful for gaining acceptance and for subsequent productivity increases (e.g., Burke et al., 1978; Latham & Wexley, 1981). As noted earlier, Locke and Schweiger (1979) concluded that participation in goal setting had no positive impact on later performance when compared to assigned goals. Their review did suggest that satisfaction of the recipient was often enhanced by the participation. Participation in an appraisal session may serve to provide information to the source (usually the supervisor) about possible performance constraints existing in the work situation and to clarify role definitions and expectations for the recipient. Thus, participation by the recipient in the appraisal session may be useful even if performance enhancement does not result.

Links between Performance Feedback and Rewards

Although positive feedback (praise) is generally rewarding and negative feedback (criticism) is not, feedback by itself is not usually viewed as sufficient reward or punishment to alter work behavior in any substantial or long-term way. Rather, as the saying goes, "talk is cheap." Praise from a supervisor is fine for a while, but may become dissatisfying if no other rewards are forthcoming. Similarly, criticism with no other sanctions becomes interpreted by the work performer as "bark, but no bite." It appears that feedback must be linked in some fashion to the organizational reward system if it is to remain meaningful to the recipient.

It should be noted that the linkages between work behavior and feedback and between feedback and rewards need not be perfectly deterministic in the sense of every behavior leading to a *specific* feedback comment that leads to a *particular* reward or punishment for the work performer. Rather, what is necessary is that the work performer perceive that the performance feedback is reasonable, based on his or her work behaviors (the feedback is *accepted*, Ilgen et al., 1979), and that various organizational (and, perhaps, interpersonal) rewards or sanctions are distributed in general accordance with the feedback. This accordance should be both ipsative and normative (i.e., the work performer should receive "more" of a reward when his or her performance is "better" than it is at other time periods [own performance rewarded ipsatively] and those work performers whose performance is "better" than that of other performers should receive "more" of the reward than the "poorer" performers do [normative reward]).

Meyer, Kay, and French (1965) have noted some possible difficulties that may occur if a single feedback session is used to discuss both future performance goals and extrinsic rewards to be received by the work performer (e.g., pay increases). Meyer et al. found that the discussion of rewards tended to dominate these sessions such that little time was spent on setting goals. Thus, they recommended that separate sessions, not separated too much in time, be held for goal-setting purposes and for discussion of salary increases. Landy et al. (1978) recently reported no effect of salary discussions on employee reactions to performance appraisals. However, this is a potential problem that should be monitored and alleviated by separate sessions if it is present.

Ilgen et al. (1979) note that some evidence suggests that explicit contingencies between behavior and rewards can lead to a perceived loss of control over one's behavior (e.g., Deci, 1975). Fisher (1978) reported results indicating that a sense of personal control over one's behavior and a sense of personal competence (cf. Ashford & Cummings, in press) are necessary for an individual to be intrinsically motivated in the work setting. We know little about how to resolve an apparent dilemma. Feedback, or, at least, positive feedback, should enhance perceptions of competence, but it may denote loss of control to the worker, particularly if it is linked to organizational rewards. Ilgen et al. (1979) stress that feedback should be positive and incrementally informative (i.e., providing information about performance not redundant with that already possessed by the recipient) in order to maximize perceptions of competence. Just when feedback becomes controlling rather than informative remains a research question as yet unanswered. Given that most individuals desire more feedback than they are currently getting and that research findings are casting doubt on the pervasiveness of the negative impact of contingent rewards on intrinsic motivation (e.g., Farr, 1976; Farr, Vance, & McIntyre, 1977; Wimperis & Farr, 1979), loss of personal control may not be a serious problem in most work settings.

A final point regarding the linkage of feedback and organizational rewards is implied by Ashford and Cummings (in press). They stress that each work performer has a (unique) array of organizationally determined and personally held goals. Thus, a reward for Person A may not be a reward for Person B. From the logic of a cognitive approach to work motivation, rewards need to be individualized (cf. Lawler, 1971, 1973). This complicates life considerably for the supervisor who is attempting to link feedback and rewards, but to ignore individual differences in goals may result in behavior-feedback-reward links that really please no one.

FUTURE RESEARCH NEEDS

Although a multitude of specific research needs arise when one looks at what we currently know about the effects of feedback, several general research areas stand out to us as being of particular importance. We will briefly mention these here.

How do individuals integrate feedback from several sources, particularly when the various messages are not perfectly congruent? Both Ilgen et al. (1979) and Ashford and Cummings (in press) note that several different potential sources of feedback exist, but neither deal in any detail with the question of information integration. Greller (1980) and Greller and Herold (1975) have made important steps in learning more about work performers' perceptions of feedback sources, but much additional research in this area is needed.

What are the long-term effects of subordinate expectations on the reaction to feedback from a supervisor? Little feedback research is longitudinal; indeed, much of this research is retrospective, which allows for memorial biases to occur. Ilgen, Peterson, Martin, & Boeschen (1981) recently examined pre- and postfeedback session data from supervisor–subordinate pairs employed by an industrial organization. Their data revealed that supervisors and subordinates often disagreed about the appraisal process and the content of the feedback message. Subordinate postsession perceptions tended to be biased in the direction of their presession expectations. These are most interesting data and replications and extensions are needed.

Does specificity of feedback actually improve the acceptance of feedback, particularly negative feedback? Although highly touted as a technique, Ilgen *et al.* (1979) could find no empirical tests contrasting specific with general feedback. Even though specificity has many logical advantages over generality, it is likely that the effect is not that simple. Indeed, data from the learning and training areas suggest that too much specificity can be detrimental to learning and performance (Goldstein, 1974). The increased amount of information provided by highly specific feedback may overwhelm the individual and lead to confusion, particularly if the individual is not experienced in the task.

What are the relative merits of formal versus informal feedback? Many authors (e.g., Latham & Wexley, 1981) advocate that informal feedback be incorporated into the supervisor's regular style of management. This makes good sense for several reasons. From the perspective of Ashford and Cummings (in press), individuals are seeking feedback more or less continuously, and reserving supervisory feedback to one or two formal sessions per year poorly serves this seeking of information. More informal feedback would also shorten the delay between the individual's actual instance of work behavior and the related feedback. Much evidence exists that feedback is more effective when such delays are minimal (cf. Latham & Wexley, 1981). Finally, supervisors are already generally giving informal feedback to subordinates, but may not be aware of it! "Formalizing" informal feedback, by training supervisors in its use, may alleviate possible negative effects of the current, spontaneous form of informal feedback that is likely to exist in most work settings. Despite the logic of informal feedback, we do not know what functions it better serves and what functions are better dealt with in a formal feedback session.

How do we give feedback to groups? Nadler (1979) has formulated some beginning steps toward the understanding of feedback given to a group rather than to an individual, but we need to know more, as he indicates. As many tasks become team projects rather than individual endeavors, this is increasingly important.

SUMMARY

Theoretical and applied interest in performance feedback is growing. The traditional view of feedback as a communication sequence with a source and recipient of a feedback message has provided us with a framework for considering such independent variables as source characteristics, recipient characteristics, and message characteristics, and such dependent variables as feedback perceptions, feedback acceptance, and intended responses or goals. This approach has primarily focused, however, on performance improvement as a result of feedback as the most important measure of feedback effectiveness.

A more recent perspective has examined feedback as a valued resource. Thus, the focus is on feedback seeking by work performers. Formal feedback processes in organizations are only one possible source of performance information. Feedback is likely to be elicited by the work performer by observation, inference, or direct questioning. From the resource perspective, the giving of feedback is costly (in time, effort, and possible interpersonal difficulties) to the source and is done only when the source anticipates a benefit greater than the cost. The benefits to the source and to the work performer should not be viewed as only performance improvement. The goals of the various parties are likely to be varied and to include such things as perceptions of self-worth, social acceptance, achievement, and satisfaction, in addition to performance change.

Viewing feedback as a communication sequence *and* as a valued resource complements each other and directs our thinking and research in potentially valuable directions. Much still remains to be learned about the many factors affecting the giving and receiving of feedback.

chapter seven

Performance Evaluation for Research and Administrative Purposes

In Chapter 6 we dealt with the issue of evaluation for motivational purposes. Since performance feedback can provide information that relates to the conditions surrounding rewards and punishments, performance information has the potential for affecting both worker motivation and satisfaction. In addition, the quality of that information as well as the manner by which it is presented to the individual can have effects on such things as work-group dynamics, supervisor–subordinate relations, and organizational climate. Each of these potential spheres of influence is important enough by itself to warrant efforts directed toward gathering accurate performance information in an effective manner.

In addition to the issues relating to individual workers and the information that they receive regarding their performance—the microanalytic issues—there are other broader macroanalytic issues that are influenced by the quality and quantity of performance data. These issues tend to be more important for aggregate organizational health and well-being than for individual worker effectiveness. These issues might be conveniently placed in two categories—research and administration.

In years past, research was thought to be something more appropriate for universities, "think tanks," and federal agencies than for private-sector employers. Both legal and economic constraints have made this view a thing of the past. The Uniform Guidelines on Employee Selection represent personnel "law" in the United States and require organizations to demonstrate the validity of decision rules for hiring and promotion, if those rules are shown to have a negative effect on a protected group (as defined by race, sex, color, religion, or national origin). To demonstrate validity, it is necessary to carry out some form of research. This research may be of the empirical variety in which data are gathered and analyzed for the purposes of argument. The research may also be of a nonempirical variety: The organization might systematically review the efforts of other organizations and develop a series of decision rules that are logically consistent. In most cases, this research involves performance measurement in some way. For example, if an organization wanted to demonstrate test validity empirically, it would probably correlate test scores with some measure of performance. Similarly, if the organization wanted to demonstrate test validity logically, it would probably conduct research aimed at demonstrating a relationship between the content of a test and the level of performance demanded by the job. We will examine the use of performance data for validation in some detail shortly.

Another potential research application of performance data is utility or cost-benefit analysis. Most organizations are concerned not only with the *absolute* effectiveness of certain personnel decision rules but also the *relative* effectiveness of those rules. In other words, while two strategies may have equal effects on performance, they may not be equal in their costs. For example, in hiring employees, we might either conduct a brief interview or give an extensive test battery. The former technique is considerably cheaper than the latter. Nevertheless, if interviews are not helpful in selecting effective employees, the cost is irrelevant. To assess the benefits of alternatives, it is necessary to assess performance accurately. The same argument can be easily extended to cover the case of training evaluation, the evaluation of the effectiveness of an incentive scheme for production workers, etc. Ultimately, some measure of performance effectiveness is required to carry out the cost-benefit research. We will discuss this research application of performance data in a later section of this chapter and in some detail in Chapter 9.

Most nonpsychologists are familiar with the administrative uses of performance data. The use of yearly performance reviews for making salary decisions about individuals, the examination of past performance to chose one of three applicants for promotion, the review of the effectiveness of specific employees to make decisions about necessary training or development, and so forth, are all examples of the administrative use of performance data. In these cases, performance information about single individuals is used to make decisions about them. Unlike the research uses, the performance data are not used to identify general strategies. Instead the data are used to make a decision about Individual A at Time 1. We will look at some of these administrative uses of performance data and how these data might be used more effectively. But before describing specific research and administrative uses of performance information, we would like to consider the broader issue of the similarities and discrepancies between research and administration.

COMMON FOUNDATIONS OF
RESEARCH AND ADMINISTRATION

In most cases, performance information that can be used to demonstrate the equity of administrative decisions can also be used to demonstrate the integrity of personnel decision systems. A valid performance measurement device will allow for equitable salary increases. An assessment center that adequately evaluates the current skill levels of management applicants permits a more accurate decision with respect to who will be hired or promoted. Keep in mind that a valid performance measurement system does not necessarily yield fair and equitable individual decisions—it simply permits them. Conversely, a performance evaluation system that is invalid (i.e., is incapable of producing numbers that are

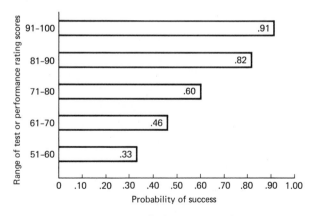

Figure 7.1. Individual expectancy chart.

accurate representations of actual performance) is unlikely to provide a firm foundation for fair and equitable individual decisions.

It is this issue—the fairness of decisions for the individual as contrasted with the fairness of decisions for the organization or institution—that helps to highlight the compatibility of research activities and administrative necessities. A useful concept for describing the concept of fairness is that of *expectancy of success*. One can contrast individual expectancies with institutional expectancies. For example, Figure 7.1 displays the probability that an individual with a given score X (say a test score or supervisory rating) will be successful. Thus, Figure 7.1 suggests that an individual with a score between 81 and 90 has a probability of .82 of being "successful" at the job in question. Another way of stating the same relationship might be that 82% of people chosen who had scores between 81 and 90 would be successful. This information can be used to determine whether an individual is being equitably treated with respect to hiring and/or promotion. Now consider Figure 7.2. This is an institutional expectancy chart. It suggests the impact of varying cut-off scores on overall effectiveness in an organization. It provides much less individual employee information but does an excellent job of helping an organization determine a valid decision rule for hiring or promotion.

Examining Figure 7.2, we can see that if we hire only people with a score of 91 or above, we can expect 91% of them to be successful. If we become slightly less demanding in terms of test performance and hire individuals who score 81 or above, we can expect a success rate of 87%. If we require a score of only 51 or above, we can expect 54% of the people to

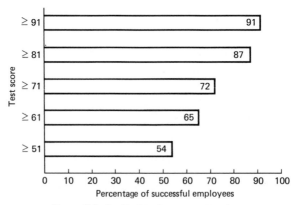

Figure 7.2. Institutional expectancy chart.

be successful. As you can see, the information gained from Figure 7.1, the individual expectancy chart, is different from that supplied by Figure 7.2, the institutional expectancy chart.

These two types of expectancies highlight the different meanings of "fairness." The object of an effective performance measurement system is to allow for decisions that simultaneously maximize the organizational and individual equity or benefit.

DIFFERENCES BETWEEN RESEARCH AND ADMINISTRATION

There are two major differences between the use of performance data for research purposes and the use of those data for administrative decisions. The first of these differences concerns the time frame. In most cases, research involves collecting data for a period of time, analyzing those data, and ultimately developing a plan or course of action based on that analysis. Regardless of whether the purpose of the research is economic (e.g., evaluating the cost effectiveness of a training program) or psychometric (e.g., establishing the predictive validity of a test or the reliability of a performance evaluation device) the passage of time usually plays a role in some manner or form.

On the other hand, administrative uses of performance data are contemporaneous. We are usually in the position of having to make a decision now—today—this minute. On November 13, each manager in the company must forward recommendations concerning salary increases; the decision concerning who will be promoted to district sales manager must be made no later than June 1; a reduction in the work force of 10% must be realized by January 1. Research usually involves prediction of some kind. If the prediction turns out to be accurate, the prediction rule is incorporated into the day-to-day operations of the organization and it becomes an administrative procedure. This administrative procedure is usually applied as if the prediction rule from which it was derived was perfectly accurate, an assumption that is never the case.

There is a second difference between research and administration. This difference was touched on in the earlier discussion of expectancy charts. Administration usually deals with the individual as the unit of analysis. It is a personal rather than statistical exercise. We are interested in which of the three applicants will be chosen for the job, which production workers will be tapped for first-level supervisory training, which workers will receive large bonuses and which small ones. We are interested in these individuals *by name*. We will somehow be "treating" each of them differentially. As you can see (and have probably experienced), administration can become an artistic exercise rather easily. On the other hand, research typically deals with mythical groups or statistical concepts. For example, our expectancy chart tells us something about the probability of success for *all people with scores of 92*; a training evaluation tells us something about the *expected effect* of a training program on people similar to those who were in the evaluation sample. Research depends on impersonality for its strength. It must be structured in such a way that it can transcend personal issues or concerns.

ADMINISTRATIVE USES OF PERFORMANCE DATA

There are many administrative decisions that might be based on information about past performance. The term *past performance* is rather general and might conceivably include performance over the course of an individual's career aggregated across organizations that have employed the individual; past performance might also include past test performance. We would like to limit our consideration of performance to include only behaviors that are directed toward satisfying one or more requirements of a particular job or position. Furthermore, we would like to assume that we are holding organizational membership constant so that we are talking about a decision that is being made within an organization and is being made with data gathered by or for that organization. This is a realistic constraint since most organizations do not have access to performance data from other organizations with which the individual might have been associated (except through self-report or anecdotal channels). With those constraints in mind, the most common administrative uses of performance information are promotion, identification of training needs, access to training opportunities, economic decisions, separation decisions, and lateral transfer or placement. We will deal with each of these categories in sequence.

Promotion

All of us would like to believe that there is some consistency to behavior. Managers and psychologists alike would like to believe that the best predictor of future behavior is past behavior. Personality theorists and researchers are currently engaged in heated debate with respect to what *type* of consistency might be sought in behavior, but few would argue that behavior is intraindividually *in*consistent. This presumed consistency suggests that to predict whether or not a given individual will prove effective in a particular position, we should examine that individual's past performance. Thus, most promotional decisions are based to a certain extent on a review of past performance. Though this would seem to be a reasonable strategy, it is a useless or even harmful strategy unless one important constraint is placed on that review of past behavior. The review should be directed toward assessing the adequacy of performance on dimensions that are also present in the anticipated job or position. Thus, if an individual is being considered for a promotion from janitor to security guard, the efficiency with which that individual moved a broom or mop would not be expected to have much predictive value for later performance as a guard. On the other hand, the ease with which the individual interacted with others in the work environment might be very useful in predicting future success in a security position.

To assure that the information to be used is relevant, it is critical that a job analysis of both positions be available. In this way, it is possible to determine which performance dimensions of the individual's current position can also be found in the new position. We can then be more discriminating in our examination of past performance. Figure 7.3 presents an

Performance components

Job title	Communication: Oral	Communication: Written	Attention to details	Use of tools	Interpersonal relations	Use of equipment	Planning
Laborer				X	X		
Machine operator I	X			X	X		
Machine operator II	X		X	X			X
Foreman	X	X			X		
Shift supervisor	X	X	X		X		X
⋮							
Plant manager	X	X	X		X		X

Figure 7.3. Performance components of various job titles in production department.

idealized version of the scheme that an organization might use to determine which behaviors to review for promotional purposes. As you can see from this figure, some behaviors can be used on a more uniform basis than others. These behaviors typically involve social rather than technical skills.

When little or no thought is given to the relationship between job demands and undifferentiated performance review is used as a basis for promotional decisions, the inevitable result is what has come to be known as the "Peter Principle" (Peter & Hull, 1969). This principle asserts that individuals will rise to their level of incompetence. If an individual is promoted as a reward for past behavior with no regard for the salience of that behavior for the position to which the individual was promoted, it is likely that the individual will eventually end up in a position for which he or she is spectacularly unprepared. This is particularly true when the promotions come rapidly. To be fair, one of the reasons why organizations allow the Peter Principle to operate is that their compensation scheme is not sufficiently flexible to allow for substantial wage or salary increases without a change in job titles. Thus, often the only way to reward a good performer economically is to change the person's job title (and more importantly, their pay class).

Ghiselli (1969) proposed an interesting constraint on the use of past performance data in making promotions. He suggested that the organizational structure, in particular the span of control, should play some role in the ultimate value of performance information for promotional purposes. He speculated that if the individual in question came from a small group of peers (small span of control unit), then "superior" performance would not have the same meaning as if the individual had come from a much larger group. If we were to translate this argument into statistical terms, he was saying that since the standard error of the performance was much greater in the smaller group (since it was based on a smaller N size), we would be less confident that the individual was truly "superior." On the other hand, in a large group, we would be more confident that the "top" performer was really outstanding (since in this case the standard error would be smaller). We might also infer a basic motivational argument from his proposition: Competition for promotion is greater in organizations with large spans of control than small ones, since the number of promotions available is often larger when spans of control are smaller (assuming a constant work force size). Ghiselli also suggested that the manner by which organizations ultimately fill vacancies affects the value of performance information, but in a less direct way. He suggested that open procurement systems (those that allow individuals to enter into vacant positions from the outside) place more pressure on individuals for high levels of performance than closed procurement systems (in which promotions occur solely from within the organization). This in turn makes it more likely that good performance evaluation histories imply good performance in some real sense. To summarize, Ghiselli suggests that records of past performance will be most useful in making promotional decisions when the individual in question was one of many under the same supervisor and when the organization allowed lateral entry for filling upper-level nonentry-level positions.

Needs Analysis

A second common administrative use of performance information is the identification of training needs in individual employees. When this process is used for single individuals it is often referred to as diagnostic counseling and intervention; when the process refers to groups of individuals within the organization it is often called *needs analysis*. The role of performance information is central to the development of the training program or intervention. There are three concepts that are useful for a discussion of how this information can be used to advantage. These concepts are consistency, consensus, and distinctiveness. These terms were introduced by Kelley (1967) and used by Green and Mitchell (1979) in applying attribution theory to leader behavior. In considering ineffective performance, *distinctiveness* concerns the issue of the specificity of the ineffectiveness. Is the poor performance peculiar to one aspect of the job (e.g., communications) or to many aspects? *Consistency* refers to a temporal aspect of poor performance. Is the performance consistently below expectations or is it more sporadic and unpredictable, sometimes above average and other times less adequate? The third concept, *consensus*, deals with the pervasiveness of the problem in the work force. Is the problem common to all individuals with a particular job title or in a common job family, or is it peculiar to only specific individuals?

The answers to the distinctiveness, consistency, and consensus questions will play a major role in determining the scope and direction of the training effort. For example, if there is a high degree of distinctiveness, training might be rather narrow, dealing with only limited aspects of the job duties. If there is a high degree of consistency, the poor performance might be more difficult to deal with and require a substantial period of "relearning." If there is high consensus, it might be more appropriate to use group rather than individual intervention techniques. These are just examples of how the concepts of consistency, consensus, and distinctiveness affect the use of performance data in determining training needs. There are also combinations of these "conditions" that have implications for training efforts. Consider the diagram presented in Figure 7.4. The three dimensions correspond to the consistency, consensus, and distinctiveness components. This figure allows us to present an idealized version of how performance information might be brought to bear on training issues.

The easiest way to demonstrate a potential administrative strategy is through an analysis of variance approach. Let us consider the consistency dimension to be Factor A, the consensus dimension to be Factor B, and the distinctiveness dimension Factor C. For the sake of simplicity, let us assume that we have been gathering performance information on 100 employees, distributed over 10 jobs. Furthermore, let us assume that we have been gathering this information systematically every 3 months for 10 years. Although an actual analysis of these data would be a bit complicated due to nesting and repeated measures, conceptually we might look for significant main effects and/or interactions. These various factors and possible interpretations of their statistical significance appear in Table 7.1. As you can see from Table 7.1, if Factor A were to be significant, it would imply that poor performance has a cyclic or temporal character to it. It might be that poor performance is more likely to occur in the summer than in the fall, winter, or spring. If Factor A were measured in terms of days

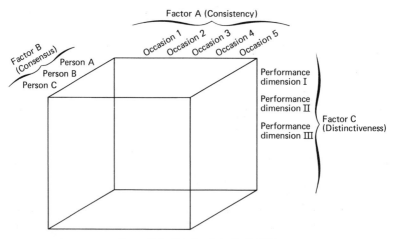

Figure 7.4. Facets of performance.

Table 7.1
Analysis of Performance Problems

Factor	Interpretation
A	Temporal aspects to performance (e.g., mid-week slump, pre-holiday slump)
B	Poor performance in subgroups (e.g., third shift production workers)
C	Distinct performance deficiency (e.g., poor attention to detail)
A × B	Cyclical periods of poor performance in certain subgroups (e.g., shipping department in winter)
A × C	Periodic appearance of specific type of poor performance (e.g., most quality, control errors on Friday)
B × C	Specific type of poor performance in certain subgroups (e.g., fork truck drivers ignore shipping labels)
A × B × C	Periodic specific performance problems in subgroups (e.g., receptionists unfriendly on Fridays)

of the week rather than quarters, it might mean that poor performance is more likely to occur on Friday than on any other day of the week. Similarly, a significant main effect for Factor B, the consensus factor, might imply that poor performance is peculiar to specific subgroups of individuals rather than the entire employee population. The inferences would depend on how the data were grouped. Finally, a significant main effect for Factor C would indicate that poor performance is related to specific dimensions of performance rather than all aspects of the work behavior.

In most applied situations, it is likely that several of the interactions will prove significant. In other words, it would not be surprising to find that the B × C interaction was significant. This would imply that individuals in particular jobs (e.g., shipping clerks) have more trouble on one dimension of performance (e.g., checking and verifying) than do other employees. This would suggest a training program directed to a specific subgroup and limited to specific aspects of behavior.

An approach such as the one above begs a number of questions. In the first place it assumes that performance on the jobs in question can be measured. Next, it assumes that we are able to gather longitudinal performance data on employees. Additionally, it assumes that performance can be "decomposed" into several constituent elements. Finally, it assumes that we have a hardware and software system that will allow such an analysis. That last issue is the easiest to deal with and we will treat it in some detail later in the chapter. Most organizations realize the need for some type of Management Information System (MIS). This is a big label for a rather basic concept. An organization should have the capacity to collect, store, and retrieve information pertaining to its members in an effective way. Part of that information should address the effectiveness of those members in carrying out assigned duties. With the current state of development of minicomputers and accompanying software/analysis packages, there is little excuse for organizations not to realize the full potential of a Management Information System. The other three problems (i.e., measuring specific aspects of performance over time) will be solved by a sensitive and responsive performance evaluation system. We have elaborated on the characteristics of that type of system in other parts of this book. Thus, at least in principle, we have an excellent opportunity to take full administrative opportunity of performance information in developing and applying training programs.

Access to Training

An administrative decision that is becoming more common is the identification of those individuals in an organization who will be permitted to seek further training. In management positions, this might be thought of as those allowed to get on the "fast track," and those with "potential for rapid development." A more pedestrian version of the same issue might be those individuals who will be permitted to take training (in-house or external) at company expense. In some organizations, this is considered to be a fringe benefit offered to all members, whereas in other organizations such access to training is considered a reward bestowed on those individuals who have earned it. Many organizations ask that supervisors evaluate subordinates on a dimension called "promotion potential." This dimension would, in turn, provide the organization with information that would allow for the discrimination among individuals with respect to admission to assessment centers, management development programs, and other training and development experiences. It should be obvious that there are disadvantages to such a strategy that must be considered (e.g., favoritism, self-fulfilling prophecy effects) but those are issues that should be part of another discussion.

Salary Decisions

This is the administrative area that probably receives most attention vis-à-vis the use of performance information for individual decisions. There is little doubt that most organizations in the United States (and in other similar capitalist free-enterprise environments) aspire to function as meritocracies. All other things being equal, most managers believe that there should be a relationship between effectiveness and pay for their subordinates. Furthermore, they would like this to be a relationship that holds at the individual level as well as the group level. In other words, managers would like to have the flexibility to reward employees differentially based on some measure of effectiveness. Unfortunately, there are some constraints on that ideal. Agreements with organizations representing employees in some aggregate form (such as labor unions) make this differential treatment difficult. Further, individual accomplishments are often difficult or impossible to measure due to interdependent work tasks, increasing degrees of automation, and other factors in the work structure and process. Finally, the economic resources of most organizations are fixed or limited, thus constraining rewards in both relative and absolute terms.

Even considering the constraining influences just mentioned, it is possible to tie economic rewards to performance to some extent. This implies the use of performance information. There are two basic models that cover contingent reward schemes. Put as simply as possible, the first model assumes that individuals should be paid in direct proportion to how well they do their assigned duties. In systems such as this, one often hears comments such as, "If that employee is the best damned floor sweeper that ever lived, there is no reason why his or her pay can't be the same as the best machine operator that ever lived." The second model accepts the meritocracy ethic but moderates it with what might be termed the "contribution" factor. In this model, the individual's rewards are weighted by the contribution of that individual's job title to the ultimate profitability or viability of the organization. Individual job titles that have little direct impact on "return on investment" indexes are allocated less of the fixed economic resource (often referred to as the "nut" or "bogey" in administrative circles) than are job titles with a greater impact on profitability.

If we accepted the first model of the distribution of rewards, we might simply arrange all of the individuals in the organization along some overall dimension of effectiveness and split up the available money in some manner that ties absolute amount of increase to position on the effectiveness continuum. Notice that the rewards are allocated on an absolute dollar basis with this model. If rewards are distributed on a "percentage of salary or wage" basis, we have built in the constraints of the second model. Instead of using a global estimate of effectiveness, we might statistically average the performance measures for individuals across aspects of performance, standardize those averages across individuals, and allocate rewards accordingly. Another strategy might be to compare or contrast each individual in the organization with every other individual in that organization (using some variation of a pair-comparison methodology) on some dimension of "value" or "effectiveness," scale individuals, and distribute rewards accordingly.

The second model implies the same basic operations with respect to the use of performance information, but it imposes a weighting scheme on the eventual rewards. The most common mechanism for imposing this weighting scheme is the concept of a pay class and its accompanying steps. Job classification assigns each job in the organization to a pay class. This class is defined by the upper and lower limits of the pay of someone in the class. The class is further broken down into a series of steps of increasing value within the class. In this system, managers might complete a "merit review" of an employee to determine whether or not that individual should be advanced to the next pay step. This review would include all of the aspects of performance that we have outlined earlier (objective measures, personnel measures, and judgmental measures).

As Lawler (1971) and others have pointed out, the most common problem encountered in using performance data for making individual compensation decisions is the perception of inequity on the part of the employee. This is either because they are led to believe that the entire increase is based on merit principles (rather than the more likely combination of cost of living, value of the job, and merit considerations) or because they are unaware of the performance data that were considered in making the allocations. Both of these problems highlight the need for education of employees with respect to administrative decision making. It is important for managers to be aware of the pitfalls of the "pay for performance" philosophy. But despite the fact that these pitfalls have been around for quite some time, there seems to be little dimunition in efforts to base economic rewards on performance. This is amply demonstrated by recent efforts of the United States government to reintroduce the concept of merit into civil service through the Civil Service Reform Act. It is unlikely that the meritocracy ethic will disappear in either private- or public-sector work environments. As a result, we would argue strongly that performance information—systematically gathered on salient dimensions of the job in question—forms the foundation for the application of that principle.

Terminations

In most employment settings, terminations are the most traumatic and time-consuming administrative decisions that must be made. Organizations are justifiably concerned that the decision to fire an employee be fair. If the decision is not fair, the individual might reasonably be expected to demand reconsideration or compensation from the organization on an individual basis (through a lawyer privately retained), on a representative basis (through a grievance formally filed by a labor union), or on a class membership basis if appropriate (through a Human Relations Commission or other offices concerned with personnel law). Equally important to the organization, if the decision is unfair, is the fact that they might be losing an outstanding employee and replacing him or her with someone less adequate. For those reasons, it should be clear that termination decisions (excluding layoffs caused by market or economic conditions) should be performance based. To use performance information effectively to make this type of decision, three things must be done: (a) the critical aspects of the job that the individual holds must be determined; (b) performance standards for the job must be set (i.e., absolute minimum requirements for effective performance on the critical aspects of that job); and (c) the individual in question must be accurately and reliably described with respect to those dimensions. Common sense suggests that individuals be given specific counseling and remedial opportunities prior to a termination decision. Furthermore, when an employee first joins an organization (or assumes a new job title), he or she might reasonably expect to be informed about the conditions that might lead to a termination decision. Nevertheless, when such a decision must be made, the organization is being unfair both to the individual in question and itself if that decision is not performance based.

Lateral Job Placement

The assignment of individual employees to jobs at the same organizational level as they currently occupy might be considered a specific case of the more general promotion strategy described earlier. The strengths and weakness of performance information for this decision are identical. If consideration is being given to moving Individual A from Job 1 to Job 2, this consideration should be based on (a) the extent to which Job 1 is similar to Job 2; and (b) the effectiveness of Individual A in Job 1. This type of decision is becoming more common with the introduction of concepts such as "matrix organizations," where individuals are moved from project to project or team to team based on their skills and the team needs. In those instances, the scheme implied by Figure 7.3 would be an important part of the decision-making process. The only change that would be required would be to replace the job titles on the horizontal axis with team-project designations.

There are many other administrative decisions that might be made based on performance information. We have considered only the most common of them. Nevertheless, it should be clear that performance data can and should be central to most of these decisions. The characteristic most common to each of these decisions is that it involves the manner in which the organization will treat specific individuals. We will now consider the implications of performance data for more abstract and less personal purposes—research activities.

RESEARCH USES OF PERFORMANCE DATA

As we indicated earlier, research uses of performance data emphasize statistical rather than personal realities, tend to involve substantial amounts of data, and often involve the passage of time in some respect. There are three primary research programs that we will examine: Psychometric research related to the prediction of success, training evaluation, and cost-benefit analysis.

Performance Data for Prediction

In the early years of applied psychology, it was common for criterion development and/or selection to follow rather than precede predictor selection. The psychologist or manager would first look about for a test or other selection device that appeared to be relevant for selecting people for the job in question. After a device was identified, a criterion or performance measure would be chosen to "validate the test." Guion (1961) has described this procedure in this way:

1. The psychologist has a hunch (or insight) that a problem exists and that he can help solve it.
2. He reads a vague, ambiguous description of the job.
3. From these faint stimuli he formulates a fuzzy concept of the ultimate criterion.
4. Being a practical psychologist, he may then formulate a combination of several variables that will give him—as nearly as he can guess—a single, composite measure of "satisfactoriness."
5. He judges the relevance of this measure, the extent to which it is neither deficient nor contaminated.
6. He may judge the relative importance of each of the elements in his composite and assign some varying amount of weight to each.
7. He then finds that the data required for his carefully built composite are not available in the company files, nor is there any immediate prospect of having such records reliably kept.

8. Therefore, he will then select "the best available criterion." Typically, this will be a rating and the criterion problem, if not solved, can at least be overlooked for the rest of the research [p. 142].

As you can see, the tail was wagging the dog! Today, there is much more emphasis on picking a criterion or measure of performance that defines one or more characteristics of the job. This, of course, is the purpose of job analysis. Assuming that criterion measures have been identified on the basis of a job analysis, performance data can then be collected that are operational definitions of those measures. Thus, at some point, we should be in the possession of performance data for N individuals. At that point, there are several things that might be done with those data. If we are interested in the validation of a selection strategy, we might choose either a concurrent or predictive variation of that theme. In a concurrent approach, we would gather some predictor information at approximately the same time as the performance data were collected. If a predictive design had been chosen, we would have already gathered predictor information at some earlier point and would have completed data gathering with performance information. From that point on, the process is a relatively straightforward one. We would carry out analytic operations intended to discover whether systematic changes in predictor scores were associated with systematic changes in performance scores. As long as performance can be quantified, the type of performance information is of no consequence for the analysis. One might use ratings, quantity estimates, quality estimates, or absences. One might even attempt to identify predictors of voluntary or involuntary termination. Thus, an individual's score might be anything from a rating on a 10-point scale through a binary score, 1 or 0, representing whether the individual had stayed with or left the organization over the course of some time period.

In addition to the classical criterion-related validity uses of performance data, there is also the use of performance data for content-oriented validity designs. The most common of these strategies is a demonstration of content validity. The task of the research in this case is to show that (a) the performance data represent a sample of the criterion domain identified in the job analysis; and (b) the criterion data have adequate psychometric credibility. The first requirement, the relationship between the requirements of the job and the performance measures chosen to define those requirements operationally, is the topic of another discussion. It does not directly relate to the use of performance information. The second issue, psychometric credibility, is a central research issue. It implies that actual performance data be gathered and analyzed. Once again, it would be necessary to show that the performance indexes are reliable and sensitive. The difference between this and the criterion-oriented validity strategies would be that in this case, one would not attempt to demonstrate a relationship *between* a predictor and a criterion; instead, the task would be to demonstrate that performance can be measured in some credible way and that those measures are systematically related to critical aspects of the job as defined in the job analysis.

Training Evaluation

At a basic level, the use of performance data for the evaluation of a training program is identical to its use for validation. We are trying to show that the performance of certain individuals is expected to be higher than the performance of other individuals. Specifically, we are hypothesizing that training improves performance and that those who excel in training will also excel in performance on the job. The goal of training is straightforward: We are trying to "treat" trainees so that they will be more effective. The purpose of training evaluation is to see if we actually accomplished that goal.

In training evaluation, we are faced with a choice among criteria in addition to the typical demands for reliable and sensitive measurements. Kirkpatrick (1959) identified four "levels" of criteria for training evaluation: reaction, learning, behavior, and results. Reaction criteria involve the trainees' impressions of the training program. Learning criteria address how much was actually learned in the period of training. Behavioral criteria refer to measures of performance when the individual is on the job. Results criteria refer to effectiveness in organizational terms such as percentage decrease in turnover or percentage decrease in scrap. For present purposes, performance data would be useful for evaluating behavioral and results criteria. As was the case in validation, the actual form of those data are less important than the psychometric characteristics of the indexes.

One important characteristic of training evaluation is the establishment of performance base rates prior to training. To assess the impact of training realistically, we should have some clear notion of what performance was like before training was introduced. Table 7.2 presents some typical designs for evaluating the impact of training. Each of these designs implies that we have pretraining performance data on at least some of the trainees. In addition, the designs suggest that we gather performance data on both

Table 7.2
Some Designs for Evaluating the Impact of Training

A quasi-experimental design proposed by Campbell and Stanley[a]

Group	Time 1	Time 2	Time 3
I	Measure—Train	Measure—No train	Measure
II	Measure—No train	Measure—Train	Measure

The four-group design proposed by Solomon[b]

Group	Time 1 (before)	Training period	Time 2 (after)
Experimental	Measure	Train	Measure
Control 1	Measure	Placebo activity	Measure
Control 2	Measure	No training	Measure
Control 3	No	No training	Measure

[a]Based on Campbell, D. T., and Stanley, J. C. *Experimental and quasi-experimental designs for research*. Chicago: Rand-McNally, 1963.
[b]Based on Solomon, R. L. An extension of control group design. *Psychological Bulletin*, 1949, *46*, 137–150.

trainees and various "control" subjects or employees. It should be obvious that if the performance data are unreliable or insensitive, we are not likely to be able to identify systematic training effects. Figures 7.5 and 7.6 describe the role of performance data in concrete terms. In Figure 7.5, the performance evaluation might include the number of grievances filed by the union, the satisfaction of work group members with supervisors, and the relative productivity of work groups. In Figure 7.6, the performance data would consist of gross sales and customer satisfaction. In both cases, it would be impossible to assess the effectiveness of the training without good performance measures.

Cost-Benefit Analysis

In most situations, we have the option of choosing from alternative strategies in making personnel decisions. For example, in selection, we might use interviews, application blanks, test results, or combinations of those components in making hiring decisions. While validity is a critical concern, so is the relative expense of the strategy. Given equal validities, we would choose the strategy that produced the greatest "gain" for the lowest price. The "gain" portion of this equation relates directly to perfor-

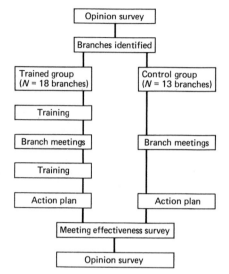

Figure 7.5. Overview of employee study design. (From Smith, P. E., 1976, p. 352.)

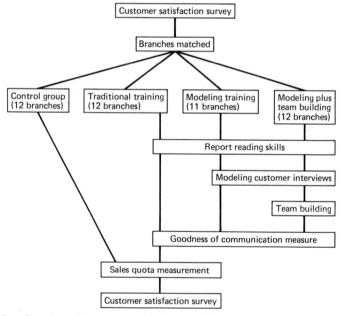

Figure 7.6. Overview of customer satisfaction modeling training design. (From Smith, P. E., 1976, p. 355.)

mance evaluation. We must have performance data to calculate that gain. With performance information in hand, we can then assess the potential of that decision strategy for yielding high performers, as well as the relative cost for administering that decision strategy. Although it is common for organizations to weight the relative costliness of various alternatives for making selection decisions, it is much less common for those organizations to consider the relative gains produced by these alternative schemes. Performance data afford us that luxury. We will not discuss cost-benefit analysis in any great detail here since Chapter 9 deals with that topic. But you should recognize the fact that cost-benefit analysis is a form of research and that it depends on good performance data.

IMPLICATIONS OF THE UNIFORM GUIDELINES FOR PERFORMANCE EVALUATION

Perhaps the single greatest influence on the development and use of performance assessment in the United States in the past decade has been the Uniform Guidelines on Employment Selection (1978). These guidelines have been adopted by the United States government in an attempt to eliminate unfair discrimination in employment settings. These guidelines affect virtually every organization in the country, either directly or indirectly. Even though the guidelines address themselves primarily to predictors or selection devices (tests, interviews, etc.), they clearly affect performance measures in certain circumstances as well. For example, whenever past performance evaluations are used to make a promotion decision, they are functioning as predictors; similarly, whenever criterion-related validity studies are conducted, it is necessary to establish the credibility of the performance measures used to validate the selection device. The guidelines specifically state:

> Whatever criteria are used should represent important or critical work behavior(s) or work outcomes. . . . The bases for the selection of the criterion measures should be provided, together with references to the evidence considered in making the selection of criterion measures. A full description of all criteria on which data were collected and means by which they were observed, recorded, evaluated, and quantified should be provided. If rating techniques are used as criterion measures, the appraisal form(s) and instructions to the raters should be provided as part of the validation evidence or should be explicitly described and available. All steps taken to insure that criterion measures are free from factors which would unfairly alter the scores of members of any group should be described [Uniform Guidelines, 1978, pp. 38300–38301].

It should be clear from these requirements that criterion measures must be carefully developed and evaluated. These legal demands closely parallel the standards for criteria set by the professional community. The following suggestions are presented by Division 14 of the American Psychological Association:

1. Criteria should be related to the purposes of the investigation.
2. All criteria should represent important work behaviors or work outputs on the job or in job relevant training as indicated by an appropriate review of information about the job.
3. The possibility of bias or other contaminations should be considered.
4. If evidence recommends that several criteria be combined to obtain a single variate, there should be a rationale to support the rules of combination.
5. It is desirable . . . that criterion measures be highly reliable [adapted from American Psychological Association, 1980, pp. 3–4].

These two sets of suggestions, the EEOC guidelines and the Division 14 principles, make clear the central role of performance indexes in both administration and research. Administratively, the rules by which specific individual decisions are made (e.g., promotional decisions) must be credible and based on performance data that are carefully gathered and analyzed. In terms of research, it is critical that criterion-related validation studies use appropriately defined and carefully gathered performance data.

As you might expect, there have been numerous fair employment practice court cases that have hinged on the issue of performance measurement. These cases have been reviewed by Arvey (1979) and Cascio and Bernardin (1980). Feild and Holley (1980) have completed an analysis of the verdicts in selected employment discrimination cases involving performance evaluations. Their analysis provides a nice heuristic device for examining what would seem to be the points of vulnerability in performance measurement, at least as far as interpretation of legal requirements is concerned. Feild and Holley reviewed 66 cases that were heard after 1971 on the basis of 13 dimensions. These dimensions were

1. Purpose of the appraisal system (promotion versus layoffs, transfers, discharges, etc.)
2. Job analysis used as basis for development of the performance appraisal system
3. Type of appraisal system used (trait versus behavioral)
4. Presence of reliability information
5. Frequency of appraisals

6. Number of evaluators used for providing performance information
7. Presence of training programs for evaluators
8. Specific appraisal instructions given to performance evaluators
9. Provisions for discussion of evaluation results with employee
10. Evidence provided with respect to the validity of the appraisal system
11. Basis for employment discrimination charge (race versus sex)
12. Type of organization (industrial versus nonindustrial)
13. Geographical location of organization

The subsequent analysis led to the conclusion that the following variables seemed to be related to whether the decision of the court-favored the employer or the employee: (a) type of organization; (b) provision of written instructions; (c) whether system was trait or behavior oriented; (d) whether a job analysis was used to develop the system; and (e) whether appraisal results were reviewed with employees. It is clear from this review and analysis that issues involving the adequacy of a performance evaluation system have in the past, and will continue in the future, to affect the legality of administrative practices and the credibility of personnel research.

SPECIAL CONSIDERATIONS

Management Information Systems

If performance data are to be used to their fullest potential, some form of automated storage and retrieval system needs to be used. One of the reasons why performance evaluation has such a poor reputation among employed groups is because of its historically haphazard character. Consider all of the things that must be done with those data: test validation, cost-benefit analysis, training evaluation, counseling, promotion, salary changes, etc. These decisions and uses comprise many different levels of aggregation. Test validation may be done with a sample of all hourly employees hired over the past 6 years; cost-benefit analysis might be done on a selection scheme intended to reduce absenteeism among those living more than 25 miles from the plant; counseling information is needed on an individual basis; salary changes are predicated on a "bogey" or fixed fund assigned to a particular job title. It is not uncommon for many of these activities to be going on simultaneously, and, whereas it might take weeks for several clerks to analyze these data, it takes literally seconds for a computer program to do the same task. We have alluded to the value of a management information system with performance data as a component in our discussions of the concepts of consistency, consensus, and distinctiveness of poor performance. Similar arguments may be made for the value of such a system for research purposes.

At the most basic level, an organization should have the capacity to use electronic data processing equipment to manipulate numbers representing performance. The equipment should allow for analyses by plant, department, shift, work group, individual, and by performance dimension. The basic data unit would be the individual worker. These data units could be combined or aggregated to yield higher level units such as work group or shift. Figure 7.7 presents an example of a data card that might be used to store the appropriate performance data for an individual worker. Other cards might be used to store predictor information, demographic data, and historical data describing the individual worker's career with the organization. We use the term *card* in a figurative rather than literal sense. It is now easier to store data directly through CRTs and other direct entry console devices than use the intermediate medium of a punched card. Nevertheless, regardless of how the data are entered, once in storage the personnel manager should never have to manipulate records or forms again. Of course, the data files must be regularly updated and "cleaned" of irrelevant information, but there should be few other data maintenance needs. By using performance data similar to those appearing in Figure 7.7, one should be able to counsel, validate, reward, promote, terminate, train,

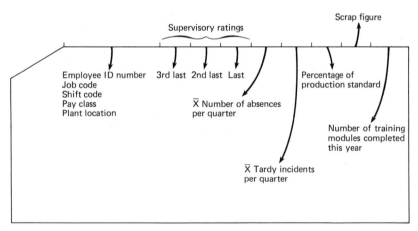

Figure 7.7. Idealized performance components of a Management Information System.

etc. Obviously, more data are necessary for specific uses. For example, validation requires predictor data, training evaluation requires training scores, and counseling requires data about other employees in similar job titles for comparative purposes. Nevertheless, to be used efficiently, basic performance data should form an integral part of a comprehensive management information system.

Combining Performance Data

A final issue bearing on the use of performance data concerns what we do with various pieces of information. Do we collect and average them somehow to create some overall or summary statistic, or do we maintain the distinctiveness of each piece? In technical terminology, we are considering multiple versus composite criteria. As a concrete example, let us consider a company that is faced with the necessity of assigning a percentage of their workers to special training in preparation for diversification. Since the company is relatively young, there is little variability in seniority. After a meeting of upper-level managers, the company decides to use a combination of production quality, production quantity, and initiative in making the decision. Furthermore, they decide that the quantity of production is twice as important as the quality of production, which in turn is twice as important as initiative. Consequently, the final equation might look like this:

$$4 \times \text{Quantity} + 2 \times \text{Quality} + \text{Initiative} = Y.$$

They would then arrange all of the employees from high to low on the basis of Y scores. They might then assign the top 20% of that distribution to training. The Y scores would represent a composite criterion. A new index representing performance level would have been formed by weighting and combining three performance measures.

On the other hand, a composite index that resulted from the combination strategy just described would be useless for counseling purposes. There would be no way of distinguishing one worker from another with respect to idiosyncratic strengths and weaknesses. For example, it would be impossible to determine if an individual was in the lower 20% of the distribution due to quality problems, quantity problems, or lack of initiative. As a result, the only advice that could be given to the individual would be some general exhortation to do better on every dimension. The point that we are trying to make is that it is better to gather individual pieces of information and combine them only for specific purposes. Different uses of performance data require different forms of information. The principle should be to try to retain as much information as possible. A composite index can always be computed when needed.

SUMMARY

In at least one respect, industrial psychologists and managers are similar. They both have an inordinate interest in understanding and predicting the behavior of workers. In this book, the behavior of interest is work performance. An appreciation of the antecedents and consequences of worker performance is useful from several perspectives. Two of those perspectives are research and administration.

Research activities and administrative activities are at once similar and dissimilar. In one sense, research is the raw product for administration. They are inextricably bound together. Administrative decision making is governed by rules. These rules should be based on past incidents of success and failure. When these past incidents are collected and analyzed to identify patterns, research is being conducted. When the patterns have been identified and a rule has been formed, the application of that rule is administration. Thus, even though research is past and future oriented, and administration is present oriented, they share a common goal—improved efficiency.

The administrative uses of performance data include almost any occasion when decisions are being made about individual workers. These decisions might relate to promotion, transfer, training assignments, or salary increases. As long as management can articulate some level or pattern of performance that is more desirable than some other level or pattern, performance data can be used to make administrative decisions. To the extent to which management is unsure of desirable behavior or prefers to make decisions on some basis other than merit, performance data are useless.

Research uses of performance data would include prediction and evaluation. A popular truism in psychology is that the best predictor of future behavior is past behavior. If this is the case, our capacity to anticipate behavior will critically depend on our capacity to describe ongoing behavior. Similarly, criterion-related validation designs depend on a criterion—a measure of performance. Such studies simply cannot be carried out in the absence of performance measures and data. In training programs, our goal is to "treat" the trainee in such a manner that behavior after training is different from behavior before training. To evaluate the effectiveness of our training, it is necessary to describe pre- and posttraining performance.

As we have seen in earlier chapters, there are many threats to accurate performance measurement. In recent years, research in the area of unfair discrimination in hiring has included consideration of adequacy of performance measurement. This trend is likely to continue. Most organizations will be well served if they develop a comprehensive management information system to handle employee data, including performance information. The multiple goals of counseling, administration, and research will more likely be met with such a system for data storage and retrieval.

part four

New Areas
for Examination
and Application

Although psychologists have been studying aspects of performance measurement for over 50 years, it is only in the last decade that any real progress has been made in identifying obstacles to the understanding and effective utilization of performance data. Chapter 8 examines emerging theories in social and cognitive psychology that may shape the next decade of research in performance measurement. Chapter 9 describes an innovative application of utility theory to performance measurement. Chapter 10 presents some general concluding thoughts regarding what we know and what we need to know about performance measurement.

Cognitive Aspects of the Process Model of Performance Rating: Theory and Research

Because of the relative paucity of published work concerned with either theoretical issues or empirical data directly relevant to the cognitive aspects of our process model of performance rating, Chapters 4 and 5 included little discussion of the cognitive components. In this chapter, we examine theory and data from other areas of psychology that may be useful for our purposes. We believe that a better understanding of the rating process and improvement in the use of ratings can occur if more attention is paid to the fundamental cognitive processes involved when one individual evaluates another. Thus, we think it is important to acquaint those interested in performance rating with recent concepts in cognitive and social psychology that are germane to the rating process.

We first present a brief review of the cognitive components of our process model of performance rating, followed by a discussion of recent findings and theory relevant to each cognitive component of the model. Finally, we suggest some potential applications of cognitive research results to the better understanding of the performance rating process.

COGNITIVE COMPONENTS OF
THE PROCESS MODEL: A BRIEF REVIEW

The process model of performance rating, presented in detail in Chapter 4, contains two basic cognitive components that are shown in Figure 8.1. The two components are presented in their temporal sequence. The first component is labeled as observation–storage and the second as retrieval–judgment. Obviously, the "black-box" approach of Figure 8.1 is not very informative regarding the cognitive operations of performance rating.

In Chapter 4 we attempted to describe more specifically the cognitive processes of relevance to performance rating. That attempt is shown again in Figure 8.2. As Figure 8.2 indicates, the cognitive operations involved in performance rating begin with some type of information input. We have labeled this input as *observation* since often the work performer is directly observed or watched by the rater. Input can come from sources other than the direct observation of the work performer, of course. These other sources can include production records, product examination, or discussions with other individuals in the work setting. The observation is not random; it is directed by what we have labeled as *stimulus preprocessing*. Rating instructions and training, as well as the nature of the rating form itself, focus the rater on certain aspects of the work performer's behavior and output. Also, the rater may have a personal "theory" of performance for the job in question and, thus, is directed to look for certain information that he or she believes is diagnostic about the level of job performance demonstrated by the individual. These various factors tend to bias the rater toward attending to certain aspects of job performance rather than others. These biases may be relatively common across raters, in the case of the efforts of rater training and instructions, or they may be relatively unique, in the case of personal theories of performance.

Performance observations are likely to be quite numerous, and the rater must quickly process the information in some fashion to avoid a condition of information overload. We propose that the initial processing of observa-

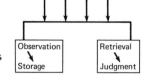

Figure 8.1. Basic cognitive components of the process model of performance rating.

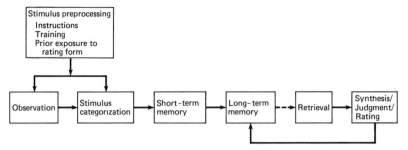

Figure 8.2. A more detailed view of the cognitive component in the rating process.

tion data is essentially an act of categorization. The performance information could be categorized according to a number of category systems. For example, new performance information could be classified according to dimensions of work performance, such as quantity of performance or quality of performance, or to general evaluative categories such as good or bad, or to whether the new performance was consistent or inconsistent with the previous performance of the individual. Later, we will examine in more detail the nature of category systems that are likely to be used by raters. Important here is the idea that performance information has been reduced in complexity and amount by categorization so that the rater can more efficiently deal with it.

After performance information has been categorized, it enters short-term memory from which it *may* enter long-term memory. Although cognitive theorists may argue over the exact nature of memory structure and process, for our purposes there is at least heuristic value in considering there to be two major components of memory, short term and long term. Not all information in short-term memory enters long-term memory. Some type of mechanism acts to select a limited amount of information from short-term memory for entrance into long-term memory. Once in long-term storage, information may exist there indefinitely, although its retrieval may not always be possible. Even if information is stored indefinitely in long-term memory, it is important to note that *what* is stored in the long-term memory of the rater is *not* a one-to-one representation of the original job performance of the work performer due to processes of observation, categorization, and selection.

At the time of performance evaluation, stored information about the performance of the ratee must be recalled or retrieved from memory. The probability of recall of stored performance information is not invariant. Factors such as the relative recency of the information, the perceived relevance of the information for the judgment at hand, the consistency of the information, and the structure and content of the rating instrument are likely to have some impact on the likelihood of recalling a specific bit of information about the job performance of the ratee. A question of interest in recent research in memory functions is whether people generally recall a series of specific facts about a past event or person or whether they recall more general "traits" or aggregations of facts and then infer specific details from the more general.

Finally, once the rater has remembered "something" about the ratee, the actual judgment or evaluation must be made. Typically, the rater must assess any information in terms of its general diagnosticity for the judgment required. It is likely here that a rater's personal "theory" of work performance is quite influential in the weighting of information. There may also be general judgmental biases that tend to influence the evaluation judgments of most raters. Of particular interest are likely to be information-seeking strategies used by raters to accumulate sufficient (at least in a perceived sense) information to make an adequate judgment.

The application of the research and theory in cognitive psychology to performance judgments is quite recent. The development and transfer of cognitive concepts are, thus, exploratory and may at first seem fragmented. It may therefore be helpful to consider a few ideas central to much of the relevant cognitive literature before looking in more detail at various selected parts of that literature.

An overriding concept that pervades recent theory and research in cognitive psychology is the cognitive *simplification* of the environment. There is simply too much information in our environment to attempt to process it in an all-inclusive, one-to-one fashion. However, we cannot function well by simply focusing only on that small portion of environmental information that we could process detail by detail. That strategy misses too much important information. Rather, it appears that we use strategies that allow us to process more of the total information with less attention to each detail. These strategies include the use of categories for pooling objects and people and the development of sets of typical characteristics for objects in a category. A more important concept is that the use of these simplification strategies is typically *automatic* in the sense that no conscious effort is needed to call these strategies into use. We use them without thinking and, thus, may not always be aware of biases that these strategies can induce. There is a price for being able to process more information. The price is the likelihood that we will frequently err in matters of detail and make major errors at times. However, we are sufficiently correct on enough occasions to be rewarded for using these strategies. It is important, however, that we remain sensitive to the possibility of error.

With this brief review of the cognitive components of the rating process, we can turn our attention to a more detailed but still selected examination of recent theory and data in cognitive psychology that appear to have relevance for performance rating. The discussion is organized around the major components of cognition.

OBSERVATION

The observation component in performance appraisal is importantly influenced by basic psychological processes such as perception, attention, and recognition. Feldman (1981) has reviewed current research and theory related to these processes, and research results from several lines of inquiry suggest that both object and social perception may be affected by automatic and conscious (or controlled) cognitive and sensory processes (e.g., Abelson, 1981; Langer, 1978; Nisbett & Wilson, 1977; Schneider & Shiffrin, 1977; Shiffrin & Schneider, 1977). Automatic processes occur without the individual thinking about what he or she is doing at the time. As a result of these processes, a person may respond to or be affected by features of the environment or of other people without awareness of the cues at the time of the response.

Feldman (1981) suggests that we automatically code other people in terms of certain common characteristics, such as race, gender, height, or style of dress, and that we categorize individuals in terms of those characteristics in a nonthinking or unintentional way. However, those categorizations may have important consequences for how we evaluate and interpret the behavior of the individuals.

Taylor and Fiske (1978), McArthur (1980), and Hamilton (1979) have noted that the salience or prominence of a particular type of information may be affected by various situational circumstances. It appears that a most important factor in determining salience may be the distinctiveness of a person or object vis-à-vis other individuals or objects in the situation. Studies by Langer, Taylor, Fiske, and Chanowitz (1976) have found that subjects stared longer at (paid more attention to) individuals with a novel, distinctive feature than at individuals without such a feature, except when normative pressure from another person precluded such staring. Additional research by Taylor, Fiske, Close, Anderson, and Ruderman (1977) examined the perceptual and attributional consequences of this differential attention to a distinctive person. They investigated the impact on observers' judgments about an individual when that individual was the sole minority group member (e.g., the only black in an otherwise white group, or the only female in an otherwise male group) or was part of a fully integrated group (e.g., three blacks and three whites or three females and three males). Taylor *et al.* (1977) found that the sole minority group member was perceived as having been prominent in a group discussion, received more extreme ratings or evaluative trait ratings, and was more likely to be perceived as having played a special role within the group than the same individual saying the same lines in the discussion within an integrated group.

Given that in many work situations blacks and women are truly minority group members (often there may be only a single black or woman in a work group), performance evaluators (most typically white and male) are likely to attend more to the behavior of the black or female employee, at least partially because of what appear to be automatic attentional processes. This increased attention, per se, is not likely to have a consistent impact on the direction of performance ratings (cf. Taylor *et al.*, 1977). The directionality of any shift in the mean ratings for minority group members may be affected by expectations and predispositions of the rater.

Feldman (1981) hypothesizes that, to the degree that the behavior of an individual's work performance is consistent with the rater's expectations, the behavior is noted and stored automatically. Attentional processes are controlled or directed only when some type of "problem" arises, such as when an individual's behavior is not consistent with expectations, when the inferential task for which the observation is being made is changed, when errors of inference are noted, or when a new individual enters the work situation.

The existence of automatic attentional processes has important implications for the understanding of performance ratings. Most, if not all, attempts to improve ratings through observational training have assumed that observation was only a controlled process. The preceding discussion suggests that an automatic process is the norm and that the controlled process is abnormal for the observer. Thus, it is likely to be difficult to make substantial changes in the ways that most raters observe work behavior or in what they attend to. These automatic processes also highlight the importance of rater expectations about performance. It may be that an approach to improving rater performance lies in altering their expectations to a more common ground based on the nature of the task to be performed.

Some research has shown that observational purpose does have an effect on the information that is encoded by an observer (e.g., Cohen & Ebbsen, 1979; Hoffman, Mischel, & Mazze, 1981; Jeffery & Mischel, 1979). These data suggest that instructions or training might modify the information observed and further processed by a rater either by conscious, controlled strategies or by eliciting an automatic attentional process consistent with the purpose of the observation.

CATEGORIZATION AND STORAGE

Because of the large amount of information available from the observation process, an individual must initially deal with this information in a most efficient manner if it is to be maintained in a useful fashion. Much recent research on human perception and cognition suggests that this initial processing of information (from any and all sensory modes) involves categorization.

The traditional view of categorization processes was that we develop and use a set of categories, each of which has a number of necessary properties. That is, each member of a particular category possesses all of a set of attributes that define the category. Thus, all squares are closed figures with four sides of equal length and with four right angles. This concept of a category is compatible with research results from laboratory studies of the learning of "artificial" categories or concepts (e.g., Bruner, Goodnow, & Austin, 1956). The term *artificial* is used here to indicate that the categories were defined by the experimenters and were not natural objects. For example, a category in Bruner *et al.* (1956) might have been defined as stimuli with green squares surrounded by a single border. In retrospect, we see that those artificial categories were, indeed, defined by a specific number of necessary attributes, but that this was forced on the subjects by the experimental methodology. What occurs with categories in the real world outside the constraints of experimental methods?

Rosch (1973) and her associates (Rosch & Mervis, 1975; Rosch, Mervis, Gray, Johnson, & Boyes-Braem, 1976) have argued that natural categories or concepts are not defined by a restricted set of features. If we consider the category of "furniture," what physical attributes are shared by a chair, a table, a lamp, a filing cabinet, and an ashtray? It is difficult to think of an attribute that is possessed by all of these category members and that is not trivial (e.g., they are solid or made up of atoms and molecules). We might argue that lamps and ashtrays are not really furniture, but subjects do often place these in this category if they are required to list as many examples of furniture as they can. This raises another point. Some objects are better examples of a category than are others. This is another distinction between the traditional and current views of categories. In the traditional view, all category members were equally good examples of the category.

Rosch and Mervis (1975) suggest that members of a category share a *family resemblance* to one another, much as members of a family tend to resemble each other to a greater extent than unrelated individuals. Thus, each category member possesses some attributes belonging to some, but not all, of the other category members. (This view of a category has also been labeled as a "fuzzy set," indicating that the category does not have firm or fixed boundaries, but rather variable ones.) The number of attributes that a category member shares with other members affects the *family resemblance* or *typicality* of that member. Members with a stronger family resemblance or greater typicality are judged as "better" examples of the category than those members with weaker resemblance or less typicality (Rosch & Mervis, 1975).

Rosch's (1973) views about object categories mesh well with research and theory about "person" categories (Cantor & Mischel, 1977, 1979). Cantor and Mischel have proposed that we develop *prototypes*, an abstract analogue summarizing family resemblances among category members, as a means of typing persons. These prototypes constitute a type of knowledge structure that can influence judgments and behaviors concerning individual or classes of persons. Once an evaluation has categorized an individual (or group) as belonging to a particular prototype, subsequent responses to and expectations about that individual (or group) are likely to be biased by the attributes comprising the prototype. (A prototype, used in this way, is not very different from a stereotype. However, as noted by Nisbett and Ross [1980], the term *stereotype* carries excess baggage in its usual meaning of denoting bigotry and unfair bias. The use of *stereotype* also often connotes impressions commonly held by majority group members about ethnic, racial, or religious minority groups. This may cause one to lose sight of the facts that prototypes may be based on other types of characteristics and that different individuals may have relatively unique conceptions of what characteristics constitute those of the prototype and of who is a member of a given prototype.) Person prototypes allow an individual to structure and organize one's knowledge about the probable behavior, attitudes, and other attributes of individuals and groups; this structuring undoubtedly simplifies and reduces what one needs to learn, store, and recall about specific individuals (Cantor & Mischel, 1979).

Much of the research on person prototypes has focused on two questions: (*a*) what are the characteristics of person categories at different levels of abstraction; and (*b*) what are the rules used to identify prototypical exemplars of person categories? Cantor and Mischel (1979) have provided a review of relevant past research and have reported on some of their own work in these areas. We will summarize their conclusions here.

Characteristics of Person Categories

It is obvious that people can be classified into categories of varying levels of inclusiveness or abstraction. These levels could be thought of as steps in a hierarchical taxonomy of persons. Figure 8.3 presents a hypothetical hierarchical prototype taxonomy that could represent several ways of categorizing organizational members. (Obviously, many other possible categories exist.) It is likely that several levels of abstraction are used to categorize people, because the various levels can be differentially useful depending on the purpose of the categorization and on how the information available from the category is to be used by the categorizer. Specific and relatively subordinate (within the hierarchy of the taxonomy) levels (such as Absentee in Figure 8.3) may be useful for making rather molecular behavioral predictions about an individual in a particular situation, whereas the relatively general and superordinate levels (e.g., Member of Organization X in Figure 8.3) may be better suited for broad conceptions about the configuration of attributes that would describe the (likely) central characteristics of an individual and indicate how this person may differ from other general types of people (Cantor & Mischel, 1979).

Cantor and Mischel (1979) examined the number and type of attributes used to describe prototypes at three levels (subordinate, middle, and superordinate) or a hierarchy of person categories. Four superordinate categories were used. They were (with some subordinate level examples in parentheses): (*a*) the committed person (antiwar protester, nun); (*b*) the

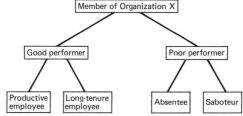

Figure 8.3. A hypothetical example of a simple hierarchical employee prototype taxonomy.

extraverted person (circus clown, press agent for a movie star); (c) the cultured person (donater to an art museum, gourmet); and (d) the emotionally unstable person (acrophobic, torturer). Subjects were asked to list within 2.5 minutes the attributes that they believed to be characteristic of and common to the members of a person category. Each subject did this for four categories from a single level in the hierarchy. A comprehensive list of attributes for each category at each level that had been given by at least 20% of the subjects was compiled. Independent subjects then estimated the percentage of members of each person category for which each attribute on the comprehensive list would be true. Final attribute lists were compiled for each category. These final lists contained those attributes that received a mean category member accuracy estimation of at least 50%.

The final attribute lists were examined for the number of attributes occuring (remembering that all had been judged to be true of at least 50% of the members of the category) for each level in the hierarchy. The data revealed that the subordinate-level categories were each represented by the most attributes, followed by the middle-level categories, and then by the superordinate-level categories. Thus, the categories lower in the hierarchy were richer than those higher in the sense that the larger number of attributes associated with these categories allowed one to know and predict more about members of the category. Categories can also differ in the degree to which their associated attributes overlap with, or are independent of, the associated attributes of other categories at the same hierarchical level. To the extent that category attributes overlap, the categories are less distinct and serve less well as a means of contrasting the members of different categories. Categories at the superordinate level were most distinct, as assessed by the degree of overlap on the attribute lists, followed by the middle-level categories, and then by the subordinate-level categories.

Cantor and Mischel (1979) did a content analysis of the final attribute lists at the three hierarchical levels to see if the levels differed in terms of the types of attributes characterizing category members. The attributes were classified into one of four categories: (a) physical appearance or possessions; (b) socioeconomic status; (c) traits; and (d) behavioral attributes. The most frequently occurring type of attribute at all three hierarchy levels was the traits class. Approximately 75% or more of the total attributes were traits. Socioeconomic and physical attributes were relatively rare, and behavioral attributes comprised 15–20% of the total. Behavioral and physical attributes were more pronounced at the subordinate and middle hierarchy levels than at the superordinate level.

Identification of Category Prototypes and
Category Membership

Cantor and Mischel (1979) suggest that it is often easy to categorize an object or person. However, because the nature of the boundaries of categories are often "fuzzy," and because category members need not share a common set of attributes, these decisions are often difficult. Cantor and Mischel hypothesize that we classify people according to a prototype matching process (e.g., a person is assigned to that person category whose prototype best matches the characteristics of the person). Following Rosch (1978) and Tversky (1977), they suggest that the categorization process includes both a judgment of the degree of association between the person's attributes and those of the category prototype and a judgment of the number of the person's shared attributes with other conceptually related categories.

When the decision maker has considerable knowledge about the "target" person, Cantor and Mischel suggest that the decision maker abstracts common elements (or attributes) from the large existing store of specific behavior and may ignore surface inconsistencies. When one must make a categorical judgment based on only limited knowledge of the target person, then the focus of the decision making may be a search for particular, highly typical category attributes and for the extent that these attributes are exhibited by the person consistently and in unusual or nonnormative situations. When little information is known about the target person, then less attention is paid to whether the person's attributes overlap with those of related categories or to whether how well they match the central or most important attributes of the particular category in question.

Implications of Category Prototypes for Storage of
Information about Persons

The importance of the existence of person prototypes (or, indeed, any categorical system) lies in how they are used to store and retrieve information about other persons. We will address issues relevant to storage here and discuss the retrieval of such information in a later section.

The use of person prototypes allows us to forego having to store "laundry lists" of information about each and every person we know (either directly or indirectly). Indeed, through prototypes we may be able to make at least somewhat accurate predictions about the characteristics of people whom we do not know, if we can assign the unknown persons to prototypes. By storing an association between a person and a prototype that is already associated with a set of attributes, we also link the person to this set of attributes at the "cost" of only a single learned link or association.

This does not imply that we do not store information about a person that may be inconsistent with the prototype or category to which we have assigned the person. Obviously, we do. Note that inconsistency can occur in two ways. A piece of information can be inconsistent if it is not a typical attribute of the prototype. Another piece of information may be inconsistent because it is contradictory with a typical attribute. Inconsistent information of the first type may become a part of the prototype if it is a stable characteristic of the person and present (or at least not contradicted) in other specific persons assigned to the category. If inconsistent, contradictory information is perceived as a stable attribute of the person; then it is likely that we would reassign the person to another category or attempt to discount the information in some way (e.g., perceiving that an external factor "forces" the person to have that characteristic).

As noted in Feldman (1981), research evidence suggests that consistent information (and people) will be processed in an automatic way (i.e., without conscious, directed effort). Since our tendency to abstract categories exists, it is most likely that the bulk of our encounters with other people are consistent and, thus, are subject to automatic processing and storing of information. Only inconsistent information may demand controlled processing.

Of importance are the findings of Hoffman *et al.* (1981), Jeffery and Mischel (1979), and Cohen and Ebbeson (1979), which suggest that the purpose for which information will later be used affects the manner in which the information is organized. An event can be encoded in different ways or according to different schemata, depending on how the observer plans to use the information in the future. Apparently, some schemata provide more relevant information for certain judgments. For example, Hoffman *et al.* found that subjects reading and categorizing a number of behavioral episodes with the purpose of recalling the episodes later or of empathizing with the principal character in the episodes tended to organize the material primarily in terms of the character's *goals* (the disposition to act toward a specific end). However, those subjects whose purpose was to form a general personality impression of the principal character or to predict the future behavior of the character tended to organize the episodes in terms of the character's *traits* (the disposition to behave in a particular style or manner). Most of the research on category prototypes has focused on traits and on other attributes of the target person, not including goals. Whether goals can be consistently linked to trait-oriented categories is not certain and represents an area for future research.

Implications for Performance Appraisal

Feldman (1981) has described several of the implications that information storage strategies using person prototypes have for performance appraisal. Additional information about an individual that is reasonably consistent with the existing category is assimilated automatically in terms of that category. This information processing, in turn, makes the category itself more accessible and salient to the individual (e.g., Wyer & Srull, 1980). Thus, the category is more likely to be activated in the future. This self-feeding system can result in the more pronounced use of a category without necessarily any directed control or intent on the part of the receiver or processor of the information.

It is quite probable that raters will differ in the number and nature of person categories that they use (cf. Hastorf, Schneider, & Polefka, 1970). It is also likely that different person categories will be salient for different raters because of cultural factors (Triandis, 1964) and individual difference variables such as degree of prejudice and cognitive complexity (Feldman & Hilterman, 1975). These differences in the type and salience

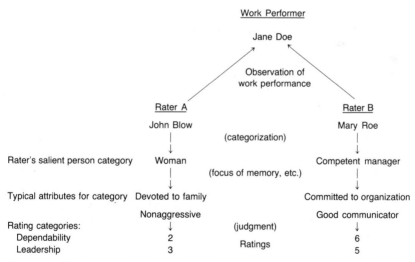

Figure 8.4. A hypothetical example of impact of salient person category on performance ratings. Note that the ratings are made on a 7-point scale with 7 = excellent.

of categories available to raters are likely to have an important role in the determination of subsequent evaluations. Some raters will attend to certain aspects of the behavior of the work performance because those aspects are the attributes most typifying a particular person category of high salience to those raters. Other raters may ignore these attributes and focus on other characteristics more typical for *their* salient person category. Figure 8.4 is a hypothetical example of the possible effects these categorization processes might have on performance ratings.

INFORMATION RECALL AND SEARCH

After information about an individual work performer has been stored, the rater must recall such information at the actual time of performance rating. The particular judgment specified by the rating instrument focuses an information search and recall process in which the rater recalls pertinent (as defined by an interaction of task, situation, rater, and person category factors) information available in memory and decides whether it is sufficient for the rater to make the required judgment.

There is considerable research evidence to suggest that recall of information about a person is not done simply in terms of specific instances of the behavior of the person. The assignment of a person to a category, as described in the previous section, influences the recall of information about that person (Feldman, 1981). Wyer and Srull (1980) have incorporated the notion of category prototypes into a model of memory and information processing.

Wyer and Srull hypothesize that behavioral information about a person may be held for some period of time in what they term a "work space." During this period of time, one has direct access both to the category the target person is assigned to and to the behavioral information. After some period of time, the categorical information only is retained in one or more "storage bins." Recall after some duration is limited to the target person's category; behavioral details are not stored. When recall of information about the target person occurs, the prototype of the category is remembered and its attributes are described as being true of the target person whether or not relevant behavioral information has been observed by the recaller.

Data consistent with the Wyer and Srull model have been presented by a number of researchers. Cantor and Mischel (1977) found that subjects "recalled" traits that were consistent with a given prototype when these traits had not been previously observed in the target persons. Carlston (1980) and Hastie and Kumar (1979) reported that their subjects recalled specific behaviors congruent with trait inferences they had previously made about the target persons. Similarly, Hamilton, Katz, and Leirer (1980) and Hastie (1980) obtained results indicating that general impressions about the personality of target persons facilitated the recall of trait-congruent behaviors. Higgins, Rhules, and Jones (1977) found that subjects' reproductions of stimulus information became polarized over time and that subjects tended to recall selectively trait categories (and not specific information items) that reflected a reduced category accessibility. The results of Hoffman *et al.* (1981) that subjects may use organizing schemes other than traits (e.g., the goals of the target person) is not inconsistent with the model of Wyer and Srull. Rather, these data suggest that it may be better to view categorization processes as involving more than just traits and physical attributes of category members and to remember that prototypical goals are a possible addition.

Related to Wyer and Srull's (1980) model is the concept of *script* (Abelson, 1981; Schank & Abelson, 1977). A script is defined as a conceptual representation of stereotyped event sequences (Abelson, 1981). A script includes a body of inferences that the person can make about what events have occurred or are likely to occur and the probable consequences of those events. For our purposes, we will just focus on one implication of the script concept, namely, the impact of scripts on the recall of past events.

Abelson (1981) has noted that a major test of the script concept is whether our memory for incompletely presented events (or an incomplete script) is recalled in terms of the complete script or in terms of the experientially correct but incomplete set of events. Studies by Bower, Black, and Turner (1979) and Graesser, Woll, Kowalski, and Smith (1980) have found a strong tendency for the false recognition of script events that had not been presented. Abelson has called this *gap filling*, and it is consistent with the view that our long-term memory of a scripted situation is of a generic script, modified by explicit memories of unusual events.

Inconsistent versus Consistent Category Information

Abelson's (1981) script view of our memory for past events raises an important issue. How do we remember events or attributes that are inconsistent with the script or category prototype? Much of what has been presented in this chapter suggests that we tend to recall consistent information, but may not encode and/or recall inconsistent information and may even distort it in some fashion to make it consistent with the category or script. It is clear, however, that we do remember, at least some of the time, the unusual, the unexpected, and the inconsistent. How can this phenomenon be reconciled with the category or script view of how we encode and recall the past?

Feldman (1981), drawing on the work of Schneider and Shiffrin (1977), Shiffrin and Schneider (1977), Langer (1978), Nisbett and Wilson (1977), and Schank and Abelson (1977), has suggested that inconsistent information results in a controlled processing of the information, whereas the consistent information is processed automatically (without conscious decision making) via categories and scripts. In Feldman's view, even controlled processing involves categories and scripts, but the individual must actively make judgments and inferences about the information and target person. By actively processing the inconsistent information, we may make it more salient and, thus, more available for recall.

Cohen (1981) has recently reported that subjects explicitly given the occupation of a target person (as a type of category) were better able to recall both category-consistent and category-inconsistent behaviors of the target person than subjects not given the occupational information. It may be that two processes are at work here. While the category availability ought to help automatically organize the consistent information about the category prototype, it may also help to highlight the inconsistent information that is then processed in a controlled fashion. Subjects without the occupational category must spend time and cognitive effort on making a categorization decision and are, therefore, more likely to fail to encode behavior, both consistent and inconsistent, of the target person.

Cohen (1981) has suggested that category-consistent information is more likely to be recalled than category-inconsistent information when the subject is faced wtih a potential information overload and when there is a relative balance of consistent and inconsistent information. A script or category may reduce the information load on the subject by minimizing the need to process consistent information consciously in either encoding or retrieval. Hastie and Kumar (1979) found that category-inconsistent attributes of a target person were less likely to be recalled selectively as the proportion of category-consistent and category-inconsistent features of the target became approximately equal. The relative salience of the inconsistent information may be reduced in the equal proportion condition.

Information Search

When faced with a decision or judgment task (in our most relevant case, a performance evaluation task), the evaluator must in some fashion assemble information or data that he or she believes to be relevant to or diagnostic for the given decision or judgment. As argued previously in this chapter, an initial impression of the target person may often be elicited automatically by the category to which the target has been assigned by the evaluator. Even when the evaluator tests the validity of this initial impression, the process of testing the impression (and, hence, the resulting additional information) may be biased (Feldman, 1981). Several studies (e.g., Einhorn & Hogarth, 1978; Snyder & Cantor, 1979; Snyder & Swann, 1978a, 1978b) have found that processes used to obtain additional information are biased to provide evidence *confirming* the initial impression (i.e., the evaluator seeks information that will support and not contradict the prior judgment).

It is inevitable, however, despite the bias toward obtaining confirming evidence, that information inconsistent with the initial impression or judg-

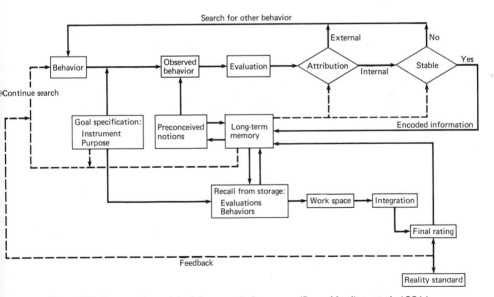

Figure 8.5. Proposed model of the appraisal process. (From Meglino *et al.*, 1981.)

ment is encountered in at least some evaluation or decision situations. How do we handle these discrepancies? There is evidence (cf. Ross, 1977) that a single item of inconsistent information tends to be discounted and that the more discrepant or inconsistent the single item is the greater the tendency is discount it. However, additional information inconsistent with the initial categorization or impression is likely to trigger the controlled precessing strategy (Feldman, 1981). The controlled process operates until the evaluator has resolved the information inconsistency through an attributional or recategorization process.

Meglino, Cafferty, DeNisi, and Youngblood (1981) have proposed a performance appraisal model, focusing on cognitive factors, that incorporates many of the previously discussed concepts about information search and recategorization. Their model is shown in Figure 8.5. The two principal bases for their model are Wyer and Srull's (1980) information-processing model and attribution theory (cf. Feldman, 1981; Kelley, 1967).

The model of Meglino et al. is also consistent with the category prototype concepts discussed earlier in this chapter. These are labeled as preconceived notions in their model and are seen as interacting with long-term memory and influencing the observation of the ratee's behavior. Like Wyer and Srull (1980), Meglino et al. hypothesize that the encoded information about behavior has been transformed several times from the actual behavior of the ratee via cognitive processing. Inferences about new information and the determination of the adequacy of the existing information are based on the attributions of the rater. The rater judges whether the observed behavior of the ratee is attributable to a factor external to the ratee (e.g., a rule, a machine, or another person) or to an internal factor (e.g., the ratee's ability or effort). If the attribution is to an external factor, then the observed behavior is not diagnostic about the ratee and the rater seeks other behavioral information. If the attribution is to an internal factor, then an additional attribution about the stability of the observed behavior is made by the rater. If the behavior is attributable to a stable internal characteristic (e.g., the ability level of the ratee), then the behavior is encoded into memory from which it can be recalled for purposes of making a final performance rating and also for purposes of making future attributions about the ratee's behavior. If the behavior is attributable to an unstable internal factor (e.g., the effort level of the ratee), then the search for information is continued and the behavior is not encoded. (This later point represents a weakness of the Meglino et al. model, as information about the consistency and level of work-related effort is stored by raters and often serves as an input to the final rating. The model must be modified to allow attributions about effort to become encoded by the rater.)

Information search continues in the Meglino *et al.* model until constrained by time and cost factors or until the rater ceases the search because he or she believes that the information stored about the performance of the ratee is sufficient to make the final rating. The process whereby the rater determines sufficiency is not specified in any detail and needs to be explicated in future theory and research.

JUDGMENT PROCESSES

After information has been gathered and stored as described in the previous sections, the rater must make a final judgment. This judgment represents an integration of the various pieces of information considered by the rater to be relevant to the particular decision that is to be made. (Judgments about very specific aspects or dimensions of work performance obviously should require integration of less information than do judgments about global or overall performance.) Clearly, cognitive activities that might be considered as judgments or decisions take place earlier in the rating process and have been discussed in previous sections of this chapter. Here we will attend principally to the integrative aspects of information processing and to the final judgment processes.

It should also be noted that the final evaluation recorded on an appraisal form may not necessarily conform to the outcome of the performance judgment process. There may be contextual variables that bear on the decision of what to record other than the judge's evaluation of the ratee's work performance (e.g., whether the judge must allow the ratee to see the actual appraisal ratings or whether the judge must work closely in the future with the ratee). For ease of presentation, we will often ignore these contextual factors in this discussion, but these factors may still bear heavily on the final recorded rating.

It is impossible, given the scope of this chapter, to review in any systematic fashion the abundant literature dealing with human judgement and decision making. Instead, we will focus on several selected approaches to the study of human judgment that appear to have particular relevance to performance ratings. For more comprehensive and detailed coverage of the judgment literature, refer to Hammond, McClelland, and Mumpower (1980); Slovic, Fischhoff, and Lichtenstein (1977); Nisbett and Ross (1980); and Einhorn and Hogarth (1981), among others.

Approaches Based on Decision Theory

A number of more specific approaches for studying human judgment are based on economic decision theory and have as their basic parameters concepts of the *probability* of the occurrence of a decision alternative and the *utility* of the alternative to the decision maker. Edwards (1954) noted the congruence of economists' and psychologists' interests in human decision making and stimulated an extensive research effort by many psychologists aimed at the description of the actual decision behavior of individuals and how that behavior departs from the optimal or rational behavior predicted by use of Bayes' theorem.

Bayes' theorem is a normative model that specifies certain internally consistent relationships among judgments. The basic tenets of the Bayesian approach are that judgments should be expressed in terms of subjective or personal probabilities and that the optimal revision of such judgments, in the light of new information, should be made via the following equation (Slovic & Lichtenstein, 1971):

$$p(H_i|D) = \frac{p(D|H_i)p(H_i)}{\sum_i p(D|H_i)p(H_i)} \qquad (8.1)$$

In Eq. (8.1), H_i are several mutually exclusive and exhaustive hypotheses and D is a new datum; $p(H_i/D)$ is the posterior probability that H_i is true (taking into account the new datum, D, as well as previous data); $p(D/H_i)$ is the conditional probability that the datum D would be observed if hypothesis H_i were true; and $p(H_i)$ is the prior probability of hypothesis H_i, conditional on the information available before the new datum D (Slovic & Lichtenstein, 1971).

Research has found that individuals tend to violate the normative decision behavior prescribed by decision theory. For example, Slovic and Lichtenstein (1971), reviewing Bayesian research on judgment, noted that in single-stage inference or judgment tasks conservatism is usually found (i.e., subjects when integrating probabilistic information tend to produce posterior probabilities of the likelihood of an event or alternative that lie closer to the prior probabilities than to those specified by Bayes' theorem). Thus, individuals do not modify previously held beliefs as much on the basis of newly learned information as Bayes' theorem suggests would be optimal in single-stage decisions. However in cascaded inference Slovic *et al.* (1977) note that the opposite occurs. Cascaded inference refers to problems with several stages, with inference at each subsequent stage dependent on data that are themselves inferences on judgments made about unreliable observations or other data. In these problems, subjects' posterior probabilities are more extreme than those prescribed by Bayes' theorem (cf. Peterson, 1973). In fact, the data on human decision making have led Kahneman and Tversky (1972) to conclude that humans do not closely follow Bayes' theorem in the evaluation and integration of information in judgment tasks.

JUDGMENT BY HEURISTICS. The growing evidence that people are not Bayesian has spurred much research interest in how people do process information. Seminal articles by Tversky and Kahneman (1971, 1973, 1974; Kahneman & Tversky, 1972, 1973) have demonstrated that three judgmental heuristics affect probabilisitc judgments in a number of different tasks. They have labeled these heuristics as representativeness, availability, and anchoring.

Representativeness refers to the application of resemblance or "goodness of fit" criteria to problems of judgment or categorization (Nisbett & Ross, 1980). In making a judgment, an individual assesses how similar, or representative, the important features of an object, person, or concept are to the typical features or attributes of members of a category. For example, consider the following two sequences of digits: (*a*) 11112222; and (*b*) 74163627. If asked to judge how likely it is that each of these sequences was drawn from a table of random numbers, most people would be confident that (*b*) came from such a table, but also confident that (*a*) did not. Actually, either sequence is equally likely to have been taken from a random number table, but (*b*) conforms more to (is more representative of) our conception of what a random series should look like.

Availability refers to how accessible objects are in the processes of perception, memory, or construction from imagination. Availability influences judgments of frequency of particular objects or the likelihood of particular events (Nisbett & Ross, 1980). For example, Kahneman and Tversky (1973) asked subjects to judge whether there are more words in the English language that start with the letter *r* or that have *r* as the third letter in the word. Subjects generally judge that more words start with *r* than have it as the third letter. Actually, the reverse is true. However, it is easy to generate many words beginning with *r*, but much harder to do so with words in which the third letter is *r*. Our storage and retrieval of words may be much like a dictionary and, thus, the availabilities of the two kinds of words are vastly different and our judgment is so swayed.

Anchoring refers to the use of a natural starting point or anchor as a first approximation to the judgment. Subsequent information results in an adjustment to the initial anchor, but typically the adjustment is imprecise and insufficient (Slovic *et al.*, 1977). For example, we might be asked to estimate the IQ of an outstanding collegiate athlete. We might think of a "dumb jock" and estimate initially 80. Later, when we are told that he has a 3.5 grade-point average, we would, no doubt, upgrade our estimate of his IQ. However, it is likely that we would not raise our estimate to as high a value as we might have given based on the grade-point average information only (and not knowing that he was a star athlete).

It should be noted that the heuristics of representativeness, availability, and anchoring are involitional (Naylor, Pritchard, & Ilgen, 1980) or automatic (Feldman, 1981) (i.e., they are not deliberately selected by the individual). They are simplifying strategies that can be attributed to organismic characteristics or tendencies of a nonmotivational or nonintentional kind (Naylor *et al.*, 1980). Indeed, Nisbett and Ross (1980) have noted that most individuals are not aware of their use of such heuristics even following judgments that clearly reveal such use. They note further that a considerable amount of conscious effort is required to avoid using these heuristics when they are not appropriate, even by subjects quite cognizant of the definitions of and judgmental errors caused by the inappropriate use of these three decision strategies.

Naylor *et al.* (1980) have also described some volitional heuristics that are voluntary strategies used by individuals principally to minimize cognitive effort. These include *judgment by habit* (i.e., making judgments similar to those we have made in the past) and *judgment by rules* (i.e., making judgments based on instructions or rules given to us by others, social groups, or by our culture). Volitional heuristics have not been researched much in the context of judgment, but these appear to be as important as the involitional heuristics in their effect on judgments (Naylor *et al.* 1980).

Approaches Based on Attribution Theory

Perhaps the dominant theoretical perspective in social psychology for the past decade has been attribution theory. There are a number of attribution theories (Kelley & Michela, 1980), but instead of discussing each theory, we will focus on the central themes of this approach. The central elements of attribution theories are that people attempt to understand and to interpret behavior (both their own and that of others) in terms of its causes, and that one's reactions to a given behavior are significantly affected by these causal interpretations.

Research on aspects of attribution theory has been considerable. Kelley and Michela (1980) report that a computer-assisted search yielded over 900 relevant references from the decade of the 1970s. We cannot systematically cover such a large amount of research here and will selectively address a few findings of special relevance to performance evaluation.

ANTECEDENTS OF ATTRIBUTIONS. Jones and Davis (1965) suggest that there are three major classes of antecedent variables that effect attributions. These classes were labeled as information, beliefs, and motivation. *Information* is concerned with the consequences of the action or behavior observed (in another or in oneself) in comparison to the consequences of other possible actions or behaviors. The intention governing the action is indicated to the observer or to oneself by those of its consequences not common to other actions. The fewer common consequences that exist, the less ambiguous or uncertain is the inferred intention. *Beliefs* about what other people would do in the same situation (what the socially desirable action is) also affect attributions. If the observer (or self) believes that few other people would have acted as the particular actor did, then it is more likely that a trait or disposition will be inferred for that actor than if the action was socially desirable. *Motivation* refers to whether the observer's (or self's) welfare is affected by the action of the actor. If the action does affect the perceiver's welfare, then dispositional attributions are more likely to be made.

Further evidence (e.g., Frieze & Weiner, 1971; Hayden & Mischel, 1976; Himmelfarb, 1972) suggests that an observer is more confident of trait or dispositional attributions if he or she observes *consistent* action or behavior of the actor in inconsistent or dissimilar situations, but that an inconsistent action of a person is likely to be attributed to situational differences.

INTEGRATING INFORMATION. The previous section suggests that the consistency of an actor's behavior as an impact on the kind of attribution made about the causes of such behavior. Clearly, most people are not perfectly consistent in their behavior, but we do make inferences that predict behavioral consistency. How do we arrive at predictions about behavior from fallible or unreliable data? We will consider several integration strategies that appear to be important, namely, similarity, discounting, salience, and primacy. Others are noted in Kelley and Michela (1980).

The *similarity* strategy assumes that properties of the cause are similar to properties of the observed effect (Shultz & Ravinsky, 1977). This is probably related to the representativeness heuristic suggested by Tversky and Kahneman (1974). For example, we tend to favor complex causal explanations for important effects. *Discounting* refers to attributing the behavior of an individual to nondispositional factors, such as the environment or another person. As noted earlier, inconsistent behavior is often attributed to situational causes. Also, behavior that is perceived to be constrained, rather than voluntary, is discounted as being diagnostic about the actor's traits or characteristics (Kelley, 1972).

Salience refers to the finding (e.g., Taylor & Fiske, 1975) that an effect is attributed to the cause (which may be a person) that is most salient in the perceptual field at the time the observer notes the effect. Salience has been found to be affected by relative uniqueness of a person or factor (e.g., Taylor, Fiske, Etcoff, & Ruderman, 1978), by "vividness" (Nisbett & Ross, 1980), emotional interest (e.g., Walster, 1966), concreteness (e.g., Enzle, Hansen, & Lowe, 1975), and the temporal, spatial, and sensory proximity of information (Nisbett & Ross, 1980). The most prevalent explanation for the impact of salient or vivid information is related to the information-processing strategies employed by people (Kelley & Michela, 1980; Nisbett & Ross, 1980), particularly the availability heuristic (Tversky & Kahneman, 1973).

The *primacy* effect is the tendency of a person to scan and interpret a sequence of information until an attribution or causal inference is made and then to disregard later information or to assimilate it into the earlier attribution (Kelley & Michela, 1980). This is congruent with our earlier discussion concerning categorization processes and characteristics of prototypes.

TYPES OF ATTRIBUTIONS. We have alluded to the types of attributions made about the behavior of others and of ourselves. Here we will be more specific about some of the research findings regarding the different types of attributions made about the causes of behavior.

ACTORS' VERSUS OBSERVERS' ATTRIBUTIONS. A general finding of attributional research is that actors tend to attribute their own behavior to situational characteristics, but that observers tend to attribute the same behavior to trait or dispositional characteristics of the actors (Ross, 1977). Although Ross (1977) has termed the tendency of observers to attribute the behavior to traits as "the fundamental attribution error," it is not clear that such a tendency can be termed an "error" with great certainty (Harvey, Town, & Yarkin, 1981). The accuracy of social judgments and perceptions such as causal attributions is difficult to ascertain, particularly in natural settings (cf. Cronbach, 1955). For our purposes it is sufficient to note this tendency for observers (such as performance raters) to see characteristics of

Locus of Control

	Internal	External
Stability — Stable	Ability or skill	Task difficulty
Stability — Unstable	Effort or motivation	Chance or luck

Figure 8.6. Causal attributions classified by stability and locus of control. (Adapted from B. Weiner, I. Frieze, A. Kukla, L. Reed, S. Rest, & R. M. Rosenbaum, Perceiving the causes of success and failure. In E. E. Jones, D. Kanouse, H. Kelley, R. Nisbett, S. Valins, & B. Weiner (Eds.). *Attribution: Perceiving the Causes of Behavior.* Morristown, N.J.: General Learning Corporation, 1972, p. 96. © 1971 General Learning Corporation. Reprinted by permission of Silver Burdett Company.

the actor (or the work performer) as causing observed behavior (such as work performance).

STABILITY AND LOCUS AS DETERMINANTS OF ATTRIBUTIONS. Weiner, Frieze, Kukla, Reed, Rest, and Rosenbaum (1972) have proposed a 2 × 2 classification of causal attributions based on factors of *stability* and *locus of control*. Stability is simply dichotomized as (relatively) "stable" and (relatively) "unstable." The locus of control of the causal factor can be either "internal" (to the actor) or "external." (Note that this use of "locus of control" should not be confused with the personality characteristic of the same name.) Figure 8.6 presents the Weiner *et al.* classification and the principal causal attribution made for each of the four cells.

If the cause of an action is perceived to be internal to the actor and relatively stable, then the attribution is to the *ability* or *skill* of the actor. If it is perceived to be internal but relatively unstable, then the attribution is to the actor's *effort* or *motivation* level. If external and stable, then the attribution is to *task difficulty* (or simplicity). If the cause of the behavior is perceived to be external and unstable, then the attribution is to *luck* or *chance*.

COGNITIVE PROCESSES IN PERFORMANCE EVALUATION: SUMMARY AND IMPLICATIONS

The literature on cognitive processes in human judgments and social cognition appears to be a rich source of theoretical concepts applicable to

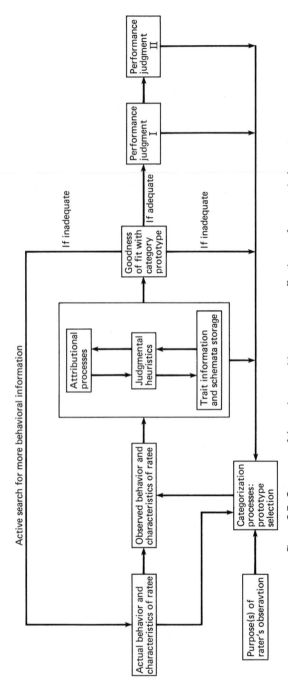

Figure 8.7. Summary of the major cognitive processes affecting performance judgment.

performance evaluations. Figure 8.7 is an attempt to summarize the major cognitive processes that function when we make judgments about others. (We have omitted in Figure 8.7 other noncognitive factors that affect performance judgments for the sake of greater clarity. Also, our present knowledge makes any given arrangement of and set of interconnections among all cognitive and noncognitive factors little more than a guess.)

The actual job performance and related behaviors and characteristics of the ratee, in addition to the purpose or purposes of the rater's observation, influence the range of category possibilities and the initial categorization of the ratee. The initial category selected and the actual behaviors and characteristics of the ratee affect the observed behavior and characteristics of the ratee. These are assumed to be relatively automatic processes, following Feldman (1981) among others. The observed behavior and characteristics serve as the input to an information-processing complex comprised of attributional processes, judgmental heuristics, and trait information and schemata storage. It is presumed that specific behaviors are not likely to be stored (Carlston, 1980; Hastie & Kumar, 1979). The output from the information-processing complex is assessed for its goodness of fit with the typical attributes of the category prototype. If the fit is adequate, a performance judgment, appropriate to the format of the evaluation instrument, is made. If the fit is inadequate, two processes occur. An active (or controlled, following Feldman, 1981) search for additional information is begun and the initial categorization is questioned to determine if recategorization is warranted. These two processes continue until there is an adequate fit between the output of the information-processing complex and the category prototype. (The adequacy of the fit is probably not fixed but is variable and influenced by factors such as the purpose of the judgment and time and effort constraints placed on the rater.) When an adequate fit is obtained, then the judgment occurs. A performance judgment is presumed to be stored and, thus, influences later observation of behavior, information processing, and, consequently, future judgments (cf. Lingle & Ostrom, 1979).

SUMMARY AND IMPLICATIONS

The view presented in this chapter, and summarized in Figure 8.7, that performance evaluators process information concerning work performance based on category prototypes and that they use judgmental heuristics that often lead to biases and errors in decision making suggests a different conception of the rater than has been (implicitly) held by most researchers of the rating process. The traditional view considered raters to be basically rational processors of information who needed only the proper rating instrument to produce psychometrically sound judgments. As we have discovered that there is no ideal rating instrument (see Chapter 4), we have also learned in this chapter that people do not tend to treat each person as an individual, recalling accurately the specific behaviors of each. Instead, we see that people attempt to simplify their cognitive load through the use of person categories, the storage of traits rather than behaviors, and the use of judgment heuristics, such as availability, representativeness, and anchoring. These simplifying strategies are used because much of the time they work well: The decisions or judgments are at least adequately accurate enough for the particular purpose. However, sometimes the strategies fail. A function of rater training probably should be to sensitize raters to these strategies and their limitations (cf. Einhorn & Hogarth, 1978).

Cooper (1981a, 1981b) has argued from a viewpoint similar to that taken in this chapter that halo in ratings is strongly influenced by cognitive distortions that support the development and maintenance of "illusory" theories that raters hold about how work performance dimensions covary. Cooper further argues that the elimination of these illusory covariation theories is difficult because of the same cognitive distortions. These distortions include the discounting of inconsistent information, the tendency to look for confirming but not disconfirming information, the failure to maintain and attend to accurate "hit" rates regarding the correctness of past judgments, and the relative cognitive ease of making judgments of "similar" rather than judgments of "different."

Cooper (1981b) has reviewed various techniques that have been tried to reduce halo and suggest that those techniques more consistent with the cognitive distortion perspective have been the more successful in reducing halo. These techniques include increasing the familiarity of the raters with the ratees, using multiple raters to "cancel" out idiosyncratic theories of illusory covariation, obtaining ratings or global aspects of work performance (that can be used to control statistically the effect of a general overall evaluative factor on the other more specific dimension ratings), and obtaining ratings on salient but performance irrelevant factors. Cooper also notes that the workshop method of rater training (e.g., Ivancevich, 1979; Latham et al., 1975) has shown some success in reducing halo.

Feldman (1981) has suggested that we should determine what category systems successful (accurate) raters use and what their category prototypes look like. Field research is needed to understand how categorical decisions are made and what determines the salience of information in organizational settings. Field studies should be augmented by laboratory research that can better control the situational factors that may confound results in the real-world settings. If successful, results from such research could be the basis for training raters in a particular organization in the use of appropriate categories and their prototypes.

The automatic nature of much of the processing of information makes the elimination of evaluation biases and errors difficult. We can probably partially alleviate some of these problems by reducing the memorial load on the rater through performance diaries, by encouraging and training raters in systematic observation and performance sampling techniques, and by giving raters feedback on the accuracy of their judgments whenever possible through comparisons with objective performance data or with other raters' judgments (Feldman, 1981).

Not enough attention has been given in past research to the cognitive aspects of performance ratings. We trust that in the near future it will be possible to place a chapter such as this near the front of a book on work performance measurement rather than near the end!

chapter nine

The Utility of
Performance Measurement

This book began with at least two implicit assumptions. The first assumption was that performance evaluation is a valuable part of the process by which organizations attempt to direct themselves. The second assumption was that performance evaluation was possible—from both the organizational and psychometric perspective. We feel that we have adequately supported both of these assumptions. Clearly there are conditions that can destroy the psychometric credibility of performance indexes. Similarly, it is not uncommon that a performance measurement system with the finest psychometric "pedigree" is not accepted by the intended users of that system and is subsequently subverted or ignored. But if we assume that a system has been well developed, and we further assume that the organizational conditions are right for its acceptance, there may still be some issues that would obviate its use. These issues may be grouped under the heading of *cost-benefit considerations*.

A BRIEF OVERVIEW

Personnel research often comes under attack because of its superficial concern for the cost effectiveness of personnel decision procedures. It is not so much that researchers are unaware of the issues involved but rather that tradition and basic measurement problems have precluded traditional cost-benefit analyses. Hull (1928) was an early advocate of the "targeted" approach to the application of individual differences data. He demonstrated that there were differences between jobs with respect to the ratio of the best to poorest worker. For example, the best to poorest ratio for the job title *machine operator* might be 5:1, whereas the best to poorest ratio for the job title *machine tender* might be 1.3:1. The implication is that the benefits to be derived from improving job performance will depend to some extent on the job title we happen to be dealing with at any given point. Similarly, Taylor and Russell (1939) introduced two other factors that might affect the benefits to be derived from a valid selection procedure. These factors were the selection ratio (the number of applicants per job opening) and the base rate (the percentage of applicants who would be successful even if the selection device or test were not used to make hiring decisions). Brogden and Taylor (1950) extended the earlier work by rescaling the dependent variable—performance—in dollar terms. The concept was similar to the early Hull notion of best to worst ratios. It simply took those ratios and turned them into economic indexes. Cronbach and Gleser (1965) were able to restate some of Brogden and Taylor's earlier work with the result that the role of the validity coefficient became clearer with respect to the effectiveness of a selection device. They were also instrumental in introducing the notion of *cost* to the cost-benefit analyses. This is an important detail, since it is relatively simple to squander the economic benefits of a personnel procedure by making that procedure enormously expensive. Finally, some comparatively recent work (Schmidt, Hunter, McKenzie, & Muldrow, 1979) has explored means for making the necessary cost-benefit analyses more defensible and feasible. In addition, the cost-benefit logic has been extended to cover the selection interview (Cascio, 1980).

With such a rich history, it is difficult to understand why the cost-benefit approach has not been more central to personnel research and application. The reasons for the underwhelming popularity of the cost-effectiveness paradigm are probably twofold:

1. Until recently, most applications of cost-benefit analyses have been in the area of the use of traditional tests for selection decisions. Since testing itself has been under attack for some time from other quarters (most notably, in the United States from the federal government as represented by the Equal Employment Opportunity Commission), it is not surprising that procedures correlative to testing are also languishing.

2. Until recently, several of the procedures that were central to cost-benefit analysis were of questionable repute. Specifically, many criticized the inflexibility and inherent weaknesses of the standard cost-accounting procedures that had been used to develop the dollar values of the jobs in question.

Presently, cost-benefit analyses are enjoying a renewal of enthusiasm. Alternatives to cost accounting are being explored and the cost-effectiveness paradigm has been applied outside of the boundaries of the basic selection decision. In this chapter, we will review some of the earlier work that led up to these advances and apply the notion of cost effectiveness to the performance evaluation paradigm.

HISTORICAL REVIEW OF UTILITY THEORY

The general conceptual definition of utility is the quality or state of being useful. For all practical purposes, the terms *utility* and *cost effectiveness* are identities in free-enterprise systems (capitalisms). Techniques that are profitable (and help ensure continued survival for the organization) are, by definition, high in utility. This might not be the case in a culture where worker well-being is a national goal (for example in a social democracy such as Sweden). In that case, a system might be marginally profitable yet of high utility. Actually, the differences between the capitalist and noncapitalist utility calculations are more a matter of who incurs the costs and who realizes the benefit rather than any structural differences in calculations. In the capitalist model, it is the organization that is thought to incur losses and realize benefits. In the social democratic model, it is the individual worker's cost-benefit ratio that is in question. Nevertheless, the great similarity between the language of cost effectiveness and the language of utility theory requires some arbitrary choice of a standard nomenclature. Throughout the rest of the chapter, we will use the term *utility* to convey the desire to maximize the positive economic advantages of a personnel strategy to an organization, while simultaneously minimizing negative economic consequences of that same strategy.

The Standard Deviation of Job Performance

Clark Hull was an early and articulate advocate of understanding the implications of individual differences for making personnel decisions. In 1928, he wrote a book entitled *Aptitude Testing* in which he outlined his notion of the role of aptitude differences in work performance. He argued that individuals commonly differ with respect to their efficiency on jobs. It was not unusual to claim that different people had different aptitudes and thus should be differentially placed. Munsterberg (1914) and others had made that argument some time earlier. Hull was pointing out that *within* jobs there were substantial differences in performance level between the best and the poorest worker. Table 9.1 shows Hull's results from examining several different occupations. It is equally interesting to note the differences between jobs; for example, between polishing spoons (where the ratio is 1:5.1) and trimming heels (where the ratio is 1:1.4). The implication of the between-job differences is that there might be systematic differences between jobs in terms of the degree to which they allow individual ability differences to manifest themselves. This is an important consideration since it suggests that we might realize a greater utility from concentrating on one job rather than another. This last suggestion is somewhat revisionist with respect to Hull's propositions. Nevertheless, it does not run counter to his data or arguments. He was trying to make a relatively simple point: People are reliably different. We would simply

Table 9.1
The Ratio of the Least Efficient to the Most Efficient Individual
Actually Engaged in a Variety of Gainful Occupations[a]

Source	Vocation	Criterion	Ratio of poorest to best worker
Loveday and Munro	Heel trimming (shoes)	Number of pairs per day	1:1.4
Elton	Loom operation (silk)	Percentage of time loom kept in operation	1:1.5
Pollock	Hosiery maters	Hourly piecework earnings	1:1.9
Wyatt	Loom operation (fancy cotton)	Earnings	1:2
Loveday and Munro	Bottom scoring (shoes)	Number of pairs per day	1:2
Pollock	Knitting-machine operators	Pounds of women's hose per hour	1:2.2
Scott and Clothier	Office boys	Weekly salary	1:2.3
Hertzberg and Thiel	Elementary teachers	Ratings of superiors	1:2.5
Farmer	Polishing spoons	Time per 36 spoons	1:5.1

[a]Hull, C. L. *Aptitude Testing.* New York: Harcourt, 1928, p. 35.

add another relatively simple point: Job demands may be reliably different as well. We will come back to this latter point toward the end of this chapter.

Hull's notion was intuitively appealing. It suggested that utility might be gained by moving the mean of the performance distribution up toward the high end of the performance scale. This might be most easily accomplished by substituting more able workers for their less able colleagues. Practically, this implied that through valid selection procedures greater numbers of high performers could be added to the work force, thus increasing the mean value of the performance distribution. Consider the two distributions in Figure 9.1. The figure on the left represents "random" selection (i.e., no valid selection device is being used). The figure on the right represents a performance distribution that might be expected if a moderately valid selection strategy is being used. The performance distribution on the right has been constructed by simply replacing five 15th percentile employees with five 85th percentile workers. As you can see, the mean of the distribution has shifted to the right as a result. This is merely an exercise in the possible rather than the probable. As we shall see shortly, there are many other factors that combine to determine the ultimate utility of a personnel strategy. Nevertheless, Figure 9.1 directly illustrates the impact of substituting valid for nonvalid procedures in personnel selection.

Now look at Figure 9.2. It differs in one important respect from Figure 9.1. The ratio of the best to worst worker is considerably lower in absolute

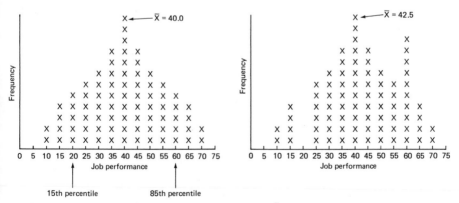

Figure 9.1. Effect on performance distribution mean ($\bar{X}$) of movement of cases from 15th percentile to 85th percentile (range = 40 units).

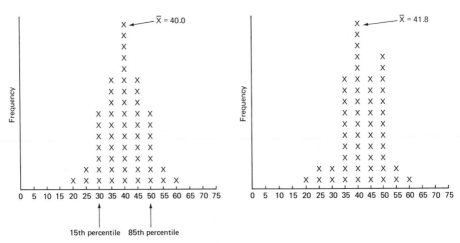

Figure 9.2. Effect on distribution mean ($\bar{X}$) of movement of cases from 15th percentile to 85th percentile (range = 20 units).

terms. These absolute terms are indicated by the continuum above the percentile equivalents in the figure. Compare the left sides of Figures 9.1 and 9.2 As you can see, the performance equivalent for the 15th percentile in Figure 9.1 is 15 units per hour. The performance equivalent in Figure 9.2 for the 15th percentile is 30 units per hour. Similarly in Figure 9.1, the performance equivalent for the 85th percentile is 60 units per hour, whereas the performance equivalent for the 85th percentile in Figure 9.2 is 45 units per hour. This means that the actual range of performance is greater in Figure 9.1 than in Figure 9.2 since the range bounded by the 15th and 85th percentiles in Figure 9.1 is 40 units (60 minus 20), but the range bounded by the 15th and 85th percentiles is only 20 units (50 minus 30) in Figure 9.2. In other words, the ratio of the best to poorest worker in Figure 9.1 would be higher (7:1) than the best to poorest ratio for Figure 9.2 (3:1). A comparison of these two figures suggests that more might be gained by concentrating on the "job" depicted by Figure 9.1 than the one portrayed in Figure 9.2. This suggestion can be confirmed by examining the right-hand sides of each of these figures. As you can see, the mean of the performance distribution moves farther to the right when five 15th percentile workers are replaced with five 85th percentile workers in Figure 9.1 than is the case when the case substitution is made in Figure 9.2. These figures provide a simple illustration of the relationship of utility to the potential range of performance.

As seen from the information contained in Table 9.1, the operational definition of the best to poorest index was somewhat loose. In one case it might have been earned income, whereas in another case it might have been units produced. This was something of a problem since the unit of measurement itself might introduce unwarranted variability (or un- necessarily restrict variance). As a result of such difficulties, there was a need for a common metric for indexing job performance. Brogden and Taylor (1950) suggested a dollar metric. They suggested that the worth of performance in dollar terms could be calculated through traditional cost- accounting methods. This involved estimating the worth of the output of the job in question.

The Brogden and Taylor approach to measuring performance in dollar terms required a rather extensive cost-accounting analysis of the output of a large number of individual workers in order to estimate the actual vari- ability of performance. Hull had suggested that a ratio be constructed from the output of the best and the poorest worker. While this was, by definition, the range of performance, it was hardly an accurate estimate of the average variability of performance unless one could assume a perfectly normal distribution of performance. If normality held, one could break the range into a specified number of units of equal size (e.g., six, if the sample of workers in the job in question was relatively large) and consider each unit to be equal to the standard deviation of performance. Such methods required great faith in the reliability and representativeness of the performances labeled "best" and "worst."

Brogden and Taylor suggested that the output of many workers be measured and then converted to a dollar metric, from which the standard deviation of the resulting distribution could be computed. This value would be a more accurate representation of the variability in performance in economic terms. Although this value also depends, to some degree, on normality (or at least the symmetry) of the distribution for its meaning, the sampling problems presented by choosing only the best and the worst performances for anchoring the performance continuum were eliminated.

Despite the fact that Hull's propositions with respect to individual differences in aptitudes would seem to combine nicely with Brogden's suggestions for transforming performance into a dollar metric, the tech- niques have been only sporadically applied in industrial settings. There are several reasons for this. First, and probably most salient, is the fact that many jobs are not easily described in terms of the worth of their output. This is particularly true in service occupations. For example, how would you go about assessing the dollar value of a bank clerk's performance, or the economic effectiveness of a lifeguard. A second reason for the unenthusiastic response to the approach was undoubtedly the distrust of cost-accounting procedures when applied to human endeavor. Many felt that unreasonable assumptions and estimates were made in the process of arriving at the final "dollar figure" for each job.

This measurement problem effectively suppressed widespread application of utility analyses until recently. Schmidt, Hunter, McKenzie, and Muldrow (1979) developed a method of estimating the dollar value of jobs that was more direct than the Brogden cost-accounting procedures and that met the demands of a ratio scale of measurement. This method will be discussed in some detail shortly.

Other Factors That Affect the Utility of Selection

Although the standard deviation of performance played an obvious role in the relative utility of a selection device, it was not the only influence to be considered. There were several others that were thought to affect utility. Among them were (a) the validity of the device; (b) the number of applicants per position (technically referred to as the selection ratio); (c) the cost of testing; and (d) the probability of hiring a relatively successful work force without using the selection device in question. To put these factors in perspective, it was assumed that valid predictors (i.e., those with significant correlations with performance indexes) yielded higher utility than nonvalid predictors. Similarly, it was assumed that the more selective one could be the higher the probability of hiring a person who would ultimately be a successful worker (assuming a valid predictor). It was naturally assumed that the cost of testing had to be minimized in order to realize any gain from using the selection device. Finally, it was assumed that the lower the probability of randomly hiring a successful performer, the greater the utility of a valid selection strategy.

It should be apparent that several of these factors interact. For example, as the selection ratio increases, so does the cost of selection, since many more applicants must be examined. It is actually these interactions that will ultimately determine the utility of a procedure. Several personnel researchers have produced nomographs describing these intricate relationships. One of these is presented in Figure 9.3. This nomograph helps illustrate the anticipated increase in job performance associated with varying selection ratios, validities, and best to poorest worker ratios.

Cronbach and Gleser (1965) introduced similar interactive models in their discussion of the utility of differential placement. They proposed

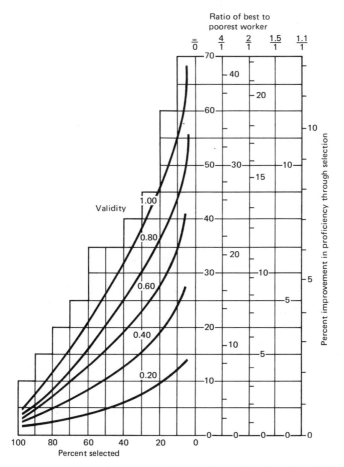

Figure 9.3. Percentage increase in job proficiency. (From E. E. Ghiselli & C. W. Brown. *Personnel and industrial psychology* [2nd ed.]. New York: McGraw-Hill, 1955, p. 147. Copyright 1955 by McGraw-Hill. Reprinted with permission.)

that the overall utility of a personnel decision system could be improved by sequencing selection decisions and using appropriate cost-benefit decision rules. Figure 9.4 describes a differential placement system suggested by Dunnette (1963) and based on principles suggested by Cronbach and Gleser (1965).

It may seem unnecessarily circuitous to review in detail the history of utility principles in selection research in order to apply these principles to performance evaluation. We have presented the review for two reasons:

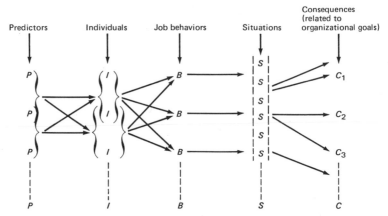

Figure 9.4. Dunnette's selection model. (Adapted from M. D. Dunnette. A modified model for selection research. *Journal of Applied Psychology*, 1963, *47*, p. 32. Copyright 1963 by the American Psychological Association. Adapted by permission of the author.)

1. Personnel decisions are not made in a vacuum. Selection systems ultimately affect training systems; training systems have an impact on performance evaluation systems; performance evaluation has an eventual impact on selection. We will deal with the systems approach to personnel decision making toward the end of this chapter. For that reason, it is important for the reader to appreciate the application of utility principles to the full range of personnel decisions.

2. The application of utility principles to performance evaluation systems represents a rather sizeable extension of the concepts. For that reason, it will be necessary to take certain liberties with certain utility concepts. It is important for the reader to be able to evaluate the reasonableness of these extensions in order to accurately assess the value of these extensions.

The Schmidt, Hunter, McKenzie, and Muldrow Solution to the Cost-Accounting Dilemma

Schmidt *et al*. (1979) reasoned that if "job performance in dollar terms is normally distributed, then the difference between the value to the organization of the products and services produced by the average employee (50th percentile) and those produced by an employee at the 85th percentile in performance is equal to the Standard Deviation of performance in dollar terms (SD_y) [p. 619]." This is based on a property of the normal curve. By definition, the absolute difference between the raw score equivalent of the 50th and 85th percentiles is equal to one standard deviation (or one z score unit). The same is true of the difference between the 15th and the 50th percentiles. Although this thought was hardly revolutionary, the method that was used to arrive at these estimates was.

Schmidt *et al.* decided that it would be easier to get estimates of how much it would cost to have a substitute perform the work of the person in question than to get direct estimates of the value of the output of that person. Supervisors were asked to estimate the value of computer programmers at various levels of proficiency. The instructions and questions are as follows:

> The dollar utility estimates we are asking you to make are critical in estimating the relative dollar value to the government of different selection methods. In answering these questions, you will have to make some very *difficult judgments*. We realize they are difficult and that they are judgments or estimates. You will have to ponder for some time before giving each estimate, and there is probably no way you can be absolutely certain your estimate is accurate when you do reach a decision. But keep in mind three things:
>
> > (1) The alternative to estimates of this kind is application of cost accounting procedures to the evaluation of job performance. Such applications are usually prohibitively expensive. And in the end, they produce only imperfect estimates, like this estimation procedure.
> >
> > (2) Your estimates will be averaged in with those of other supervisors of computer programmers. Thus errors produced by too high and too low estimates will tend to be averaged out, providing more accurate final estimates.
> >
> > (3) The decisions that must be made about selection methods do not require that all estimates be accurate down to the last dollar. Substantially accurate estimates will lead to the same decisions as perfectly accurate estimates.
>
> Based on your experience with agency programmers, we would like for you to estimate the yearly value to your agency of the products and services produced by the average GS 9-11 computer programmer. Consider the quality and quantity of output typical of the *average programmer* and the value of this output. In placing an overall dollar value on this output, it may help to consider what the cost would be of having an outside firm provide these products and services.
>
> > Based on my experience, I estimate the value to my agency of the average GS 9-11 computer programmer at _____ dollars per year.
>
> We would now like for you to consider the *"superior"* programmer. Let us define a superior performer as a programmer who is at the 85th percentile. That is his or her performance is better than that of 85% of his or her fellow GS 9-11 programmers, and only 15% turn in better performances. Consider the quality and quantity of the output typical of the superior programmer. Then estimate the value of these products and services. In placing an overall dollar value on this output, it may again help to consider what the cost would be of having an outside firm provide these products and services.

Based on my experience, I estimate the value to my agency of a superior GS 9-11 computer programmer to be _____ dollars per year.

Finally, we would like you to consider the "*low performing*" *computer programmer*. Let us define a low performing programmer as one who is at the 15th percentile. That is, 85% of all GS 9-11 computer programmers turn in performances better than the low performing programmer, and only 15% turn in worse performances. Consider the quality and quantity of the output typical of the low performing programmer. Then estimate the value of these products and services. In placing an overall dollar value on this output, it may again help to consider what the cost would be of having an outside firm provide these products and services.

Based on my experience, I estimate the value to my agency of the low performing GS 9-11 computer programmer at _____ dollars per year [From F. L. Schmidt, J. E. Hunter, R. McKenzie, & T. Muldrow. Impact of valid selection procedures on work-force productivity. *Journal of Applied Psychology*, 1979, *64*, p. 621. Copyright 1979 by the American Psychological Association. Reprinted by permission of the publisher and author.].

Since estimates of both the 15th and 85th percentile were obtained, it was possible for Hunter, Schmidt, and Pearlman (1979) to verify that the performance distribution was, in fact, normal. It is interesting to note that the supervisors who completed the questionnaire had no problems in making the requested estimates. They did not complain that the task was silly or impossible. Furthermore, the data confirmed that the estimates were psychometrically sound and met the condition necessary for inclusion in eventual utility calculations. The difference between the 85th and 50th percentile points was $10,871, whereas the difference between the 15th and 50th percentiles was $9,955. The difference between these two estimates was not significantly different, a condition necessary for the assumption of normally distributed estimates. These data were based on the responses of 105 supervisors. Hunter *et al.* (1979) claimed two distinct advantages for their method:

1. Estimates of the costs of having an outside organization provide the service in question are commonplace in many settings and provide a good mental standard for the judgments of the supervisors.
2. The fact that a large number of judges are used prevents individual biases and idiosyncracies from unduly influencing the estimates of SD_y.

THE FULL UTILITY MODEL

We have given you glimpses of the various facets of utility analysis to this point. To briefly recapitulate, we have suggested that the ultimate utility of a personnel decision system will be determined by varying levels of the following factors:

1. Validity of the system
2. Selection ratio
3. Dollar value of the performance being considered
4. Probability of success for individuals chosen without consideration for the x system under examination
5. Cost of the proposed system

We have presented these arguments in something of a vacuum. Typically, an organization is not deciding to accept or reject a systematic selection strategy. Instead, the decision is usually whether to replace or augment a system currently in use. Thus, one might be evaluating the utility of replacing a general intelligence test with a specific work-skills test; similarly, one might be considering the utility of adding an interview to a traditional paper-and-pencil testing program. In this situation, one is concerned not with utility in some absolute sense, but rather with a concept known as *utility gain* (or loss). Utility gain implies some additional value above or beyond that which is currently being realized from the personnel system that is in place. Thus, we are faced with a comparison of the relative differences between costs of the old and the new system and the benefits of the old and new systems. It is this framework that we will now pursue. We will present each of the elements that comprise a utility analysis in some detail. We will then consider the application of utility analysis to performance evaluation. Next, we will consider the research questions that must be answered before utility analysis can become an integral part of the introduction (or modification) of a performance evaluation system. Finally, we will suggest some directions in utility research that will enable the practitioner to choose among alternative systems for improving the mean performance of a work force.

Schmidt *et al.* (1979) have combined the work of Brogden and Taylor (1950) with the formulations of Cronbach and Gleser (1965) to construct a general equation that allows one to calculate the anticipated utility gain (or loss) to be expected from the introduction of a new selection device. This equation is as follows:

$$\Delta U = tN_s\ (r_1 - r_2)\ SD_y \phi/p\ -\ N_s\ (C_1 - C_2)/p \qquad (9.1)$$

A brief description of each of these components follows.

ΔU: This represents the expected gain in dollars that might be realized from the introduction of a new system.

t: This term represents the tenure of the average employee in the job title in question. By looking at the equation, one can see that the longer an employee stays, the greater the expected gain in dollars for the organization from the employee's successful performance. Since entry-level testing is a nonrecurring activity, this value does not appear on the right-hand or "cost" side of the equation.

N_s: In a selection paradigm, this number represents the number of individuals selected in a given year. The equation tells us that this number affects both the anticipated benefits and the anticipated costs. This value plays a critical role in determining whether a resulting utility change is positive or negative.

r_1: This value is the validity coefficient of the proposed new procedure or test. Hunter *et al.* (1979) suggest that the best way to determine this value is to synthesize the results of previous studies using the particular predictor under examination.

r_2: This value is also a validity coefficient; it is the validity of the current procedure or test. It is calculated in the same manner as r_1. If no procedure is currently in use (which implies that individuals are hired on a random basis), this value is assumed to be .00.

SD_y: This term represents the standard deviation of performance expressed in dollar terms. We have already described the importance of this component in some detail. It was this component that was both the curse and the salvation of utility analysis. If it can be estimated with some credibility, utility analysis becomes a major strategy in scientific personnel administration. If this term cannot be reasonably calculated, utility analysis represents a trivial exercise with little direct or obvious value. We have described the methods suggested by Schmidt *et al.* for calculating these estimates. At this point, these methods are both intuitively appealing and psychometrically promising. A brief glance at the utility equation tells us that this term has a multiplicative effect on the anticipated benefit component of the equation. The larger this value the greater the benefit. Remember our earlier description of the relationship between SD_y and the attempt to move the mean of the performance distribution toward the successful end of the continuum: the greater the value of SD_y, the more room for movement or improvement. We were able to demonstrate this effect in Figures 9.1 and 9.2.

p: This value is the selection ratio or the number of positions to be filled divided by the number of applicants. As the number of applicants increases relative to the number of positions, we can be more selective and thus we are more likely to be able to pick the best possible applicant. This is the benefit consideration. Nevertheless, as the selectivity increases, so does the cost of selection, since we are examining many more applicants for each position than would be the case with a fewer number of applicants. We can see from the equation that p has a direct effect on both the benefit and cost components. The determining factor in the ultimate contribution of p turns out to be C, the cost of examining the applicants.

ϕ: This value is directly related to the anticipated test score of those actually selected given the assumption of a normal distribution of test scores. Specifically, it is the height of the ordinate of the normal curve at point p.

C_1: This value represents the per applicant cost of the procedure or test under consideration. This might include the costs of developing the procedure or instrument, printing costs, administration costs, and a general overhead or indirect cost component.

C_2: This value represents the per applicant cost of the procedure that is currently being used. If C_1 exceeds C_2, the benefits of the new system must outweigh the benefits of the old system in order to realize a utility gain. Conversely, if C_1 is less than C_2, one might accept a lesser benefit of the new system if the cost differential can result in a utility gain. The best of circumstances would be a combination of greater benefits and lesser costs for a new system.

We have now completely described at least one general method for considering the utility of a personnel procedure. We have dealt almost exclusively with a selection paradigm. Now that we have provided a general view of the history and operations of this type of analysis, we would like to consider an application of utility propositions to the major theme of this book—performance evaluation. In the next section, we will argue that performance evaluation and feedback may be every bit as effective as valid selection devices in improving the mean performance of a work force. We will begin with a brief review of some relevant logic and research. Following that, we will translate the utility model presented earlier into a performance evaluation context. Finally, we will present an application of the approach in a real-world context.

THE ROLE OF PERFORMANCE MEASUREMENT AND FEEDBACK IN PERSONNEL SYSTEMS

There seems to be little doubt about the need for accurate measurement of employee performance in most, if not all, organizational settings. Performance evaluation serves many varied and important functions including assessing criteria for selection procedures and other personnel decisions, identifying strengths and weaknesses in job incumbents, specifying the requisite components for training programs, and providing the necessary information for feedback. In this section we would like to focus on this latter function of a performance evaluation system, providing employees with information about their past performance. For a complete discussion of the area of performance rating, refer to Landy and Farr (1980) and Jacobs, Kafry, and Zedeck (1980).

The positive influence of knowledge of results on both learning and subsequent performance is one of the more robust findings within the psychological literature (Adams, 1968; Ammons, 1956; Annett, 1969; Bilodeau & Bilodeau, 1961; Locke, Cartledge, & Koeppel, 1968; Locke, Shaw, Saari, & Latham, 1981). Although the data regarding the effects of feedback on rates of learning seem to be more numerous, there are a substantial number of studies investigating the facilitating effects of feedback about previous performance on follow-up measures of performance.

Feedback is simply information received by an individual that indicates the correctness, accuracy, or adequacy of past behavior (Ilgen, Fisher, & Taylor, 1979). From this definition, it follows that feedback serves at least two functions. First, feedback directs. When the feedback indicates certain deficiencies in *what* is being done, the message being transmitted is one that indicates to the employee that subsequent behavior should change in a direction designed to reduce the noted inadequacies. On the other hand, feedback can also serve a motivational function. When information about previous performance is used to focus an employee's attention on achieved levels of performance or *how much* is being done, the message the employee is receiving is one that instructs him or her to orient future efforts toward increasing subsequent performance. The former function of feedback may be viewed as primarily a qualitative orientation, whereas the latter represents a quantitative emphasis.

This distinction of feedback function has been made by Locke, Cartledge, and Koeppel (1968) with respect to knowledge of results. "KR [Knowledge of results] may facilitate performance in at least two ways: (a) by cueing or informing the subject (*S*) as to the type, extent, and direction of his errors; *S* can generally use such information to correct his errors or to improve his method of performing the task; and (b) by motivating *S* to try harder or persist longer at the task [p. 474]." Locke, Cartledge, and Koeppel (1968) point out that the effectiveness of the motivating function of knowledge of results depends on the goals an individual sets in response to the knowledge contained in the feedback. In delineating his theory of goal setting, Locke has consistently stated that it is not the knowledge of past results that effects performance, but rather the goals or intentions people form in light of that knowledge (Locke, 1967; Locke & Bryan, 1969; Locke, Bryan, & Kendall, 1968).

PERCENTAGE IMPROVEMENT ESTIMATES OF THE EFFECT OF FEEDBACK ON PERFORMANCE

Several studies in the applied psychological literature offer information regarding the impact of feedback on subsequent performance. Hundal (1969) examined the effect of three levels of feedback specificity on the productivity of 18 industrial workers performing the task of grinding metallic objects to specified sizes and shapes. The results of this study indicated that as feedback became more specific, subsequent performance improved. Within the context of this study, subjects in the no-feedback condition showed performance increases of 4%, subjects in the partial-feedback condition improved performance by 7%, and subjects in the specific-feedback condition increased performance by 16%.

Seligman and Darley (1977) looked at the relationship between feedback and performance in a very different setting. These authors examined the degree to which information about daily electricity consumption could lead to energy conservation. The study involved 99 physically identical three-bedroom homes, where it was observed that during the summer months central air-conditioning was the largest single source of electricity use. Accordingly, it was possible to estimate each household's expected electric consumption in terms of the average daily outdoor temperature. In this study, feedback was given as a percentage of actual consumption over predicted consumption and was displayed to the homeowners four times a week for a month. Results from this study indicated that during the feedback period the feedback group used 10.5% less electricity than a control group.

In a similar study, Hayes and Cone (1977) examined three methods for reducing electricity consumption. These methods included giving subjects information about ways to reduce consumption, giving feedback about daily electricity use, and offering monetary payments in accordance with the amount of energy conserved. Although the results of this study show that the payment condition was most effective in reducing electricity consumption, both information and feedback resulted in substantial reductions in electricity use. For two separate time periods, offering information results in 9 and 30% reductions in electricity use. For the feedback intervals, electricity use was down 15 and 21%.

In a study of goal setting, Latham and Baldes (1975) collected data on 36 logging trucks over a 12-month interval. After the third month, truckers were given information regarding sepcific objectives for subsequent performance. As a result of the information conveyed, performance increased about 30%. While this study was designed to specifically test hypotheses regarding goal setting, the results indicate that information about expected levels of future performance may facilitate performance. As was argued earlier, effective feedback not only should offer information about past performance but also should indicate what is anticipated with respect to future performance.

While the above empirical studies document the efficacy of feedback on subsequent performance, still other information is available. In a review of the knowledge of results literature, Locke, Cartledge, and Koeppel (1968) identify several studies indicating a beneficial effect of feedback on performance. Rather than duplicating the findings of this work, we will simply refer the reader to the article for a complete discussion of this topic. However, it is important to note that estimates of performance improvement as a result of feedback range from 8 to 26% across a variety of studies and tasks.

CORRELATIONAL ESTIMATES FOR THE EFFECT OF FEEDBACK ON PERFORMANCE

Locke, Bryan, and Kendall (1968, Experiment 2) had 30 undergraduate students assemble a number of identical objects from Tinker Toy sets. Each subject was instructed to complete as many objects as possible under the condition that one object must be completed before beginning another. Subjects were placed in either a piece-rate or hourly incentive condition. In both conditions, subjects were given information about the number of objects completed and asked about final goal levels during a rest period halfway through the task. The aspect of this study that is of special interest to us is the relationship between goals set during the halfway mark and second half performance with the effect of performance in the first half partialed out. This partial correlation reflects the subject's ability to use information from feedback in establishing levels of anticipated performance that are not effected by previous levels of performance. Locke, Bryan, and Kendall (1968) interpret this partial correlation of .57

($p < .01$) as indicating that subjects are setting goals that reflect their level of motivation. It might be suggested that this value reflects the degree to which subjects can match anticipations about future performance with actual performance; that is, given information about performance, subjects set goals that reflect their intentions regarding performance.

A reanalysis of data from the Hundal (1969) study described earlier provides even more direct evidence regarding the impact of feedback on subsequent performance. By looking at the relationship between level of feedback and performance after feedback and partialing out levels of performance prior to feedback, we can directly estimate the efficacy of feedback. The partial correlation obtained from this analysis was .52 ($p < .05$) indicating that as the feedback increased productivity scores increased. This result extends the Locke, Bryan, and Kendall (1968) propositions. It would appear that feedback has a facilitating effect regardless of whether workers set goals or are simply assigned goals.

A study by Erez (1977) examined impact of feedback and goal setting on clerical tasks. The data consisted of initial performance levels, feedback about previous performance, goal level or intentions with respect to performance, and performance in a retest phase. The latter variable was treated as a dependent variable in a stepwise regression analysis. When retest performance was examined, the *feedback and goal setting main effects* and *Feedback × Goal Setting Interaction* accounted for 19% more variance than the *previous performance* component ($p < .01$).

Umstot, Bell, and Mitchell (1976) investigated the effect of setting goals on performance of subjects working on a task requiring the transfer of information from maps to computer cards. Umstot *et al.* (1976) found a significant main effect for goal setting that accounted for 14% of the variance in performance. They also investigated the impact of adding additional goals and found that the percentage of variance in performance that could be accounted for by goal setting increased to 26% with these additional goals.

Finally, in a study by Becker (1978), 80 families were asked to set goals regarding reduced electricity consumption. Half of the families were asked to set a goal of 20% reduction, whereas the other half were given a goal of 2% reduction. Within each group, families were either given no feedback about electricity usage or were given feedback three times per week. An additional 20 families served as controls. The results of this study indicate that only the feedback group with the 20% reduction goal actually reduced electricity consumption. This implies that both feedback and goal setting are important.

In summary, the results of these brief and selective literature reviews suggest that feedback can and does have an effect on subsequent performance. The term *feedback* includes two distinct components, knowledge of results about past performance and setting goals or establishing intentions about future performance. The data presented suggest that feedback may result in increases of performance varying from 10 to 30%. Additionally, measures of association indexing the relationship between feedback and subsequent performance suggest correlations ranging from .30 to .50.

Feedback is not a standard process. It varies from one person to another, from one situation to another, and from one time to another. Thus, things like the reason for the feedback, the management style of the supervisor giving the feedback, and the frequency of the feedback all play a role in its final impact on performance. Unfortunately, in our literature review, we were unable to uncover any firm estimates of the impact of these contextual variables. Since the utility equations require such estimates, we have been limited to using the studies described earlier for the validity figure (r). This is not meant to imply that procedural or contextual variables are unimportant. They certainly must play some role. We just do not yet know how much they combine with substantive information to yield an impact on performance.

AN APPLICATION OF UTILITY CONCEPTS TO PERFORMANCE MEASUREMENT

As we have seen, Schmidt *et al.* (1979) make a good argument with respect to the utility of predictors. The same argument might be made with respect to criteria. This may be an important extension since scientific personnel selection is not the only personnel decision strategy. In the United States, some employers have chosen to pull back from standardized testing because of the implications of the Uniform Guidelines. Although "quota hiring" is hardly the norm, many personnel practitioners have the feeling that the elimination of adverse impact rather than the maximization of performance is the major goal of a selection program. This specific example reflects a general attitude of minimizing costs and ignoring benefits within a cost-benefit analysis framework. Perhaps this attitude is not merely capricious but actually the result of a lack of specificity on the part of personnel researchers and practitioners regarding the potential effectiveness of proposed programs. Additionally, many organizations do not add significant numbers of employees during a single year. While these organizations can still maximize their selection decisions, these decisions will not have any dramatic short-term impact on profitability. Finally, many labor–management agreements act as an artificial stabilization agent in the work picture, reducing still further the number of openings in a given work force.

Thus, although the utility of a selection strategy is clearly important in many settings, the "profitability" of the organization might often depend on additional parts of the personnel system. We are not arguing that the utility of the various components of a personnel system are mutually exclusive; certainly the dynamic nature of behavior in general and work behavior in particular is sufficient to counter that argument. Rather, we are arguing that in particular contexts, it is reasonable to concentrate on parts of the personnel system in addition to selection. For this demonstration, we will concentrate on performance evaluation and feedback.

ASSUMPTIONS ABOUT FEEDBACK

As we have seen in the previous section, there is a clear implication in the applied literature that performance evaluation and feedback have an impact on work behavior. This is a reasonable hypothesis that is supported both by applied research and more fundamental research in learning theory. A general working hypothesis might be that knowledge of results improves performance. But as we have pointed out in a review of the performance rating literature (Landy & Farr, 1980), the term *knowledge of results* begs an enormous number of questions. There is a good deal of research directed toward identifying the most efficient ways of actually providing that knowledge. While we recognize the importance of this area of research, it is not our intention to address the efficiency of performance feedback directly. In order to consider the utility of selection procedures, it was necessary for Schmidt and his colleagues (Schmidt *et al.*, 1979) to assume that there was a relationship between a given test score and subsequent performance. We must, similarly, assume that there is a relationship between feedback and performance. The literature review presented in the earlier section is evidence of the acceptability of that assumption. There are other assumptions that will be necessary as we become more specific in our utility framework, but we will deal with them as they arise.

Some Necessary Translations

Since the utility arguments that we presented earlier were tied to the selection paradigm, it is necessary to make a few adaptations to describe accurately the value of utility models for the performance evaluation and feedback area. As we will see, some components translate more easily than others. We will deal with them one at a time.

ΔU: The expected gain in dollars from the introduction of a new system of some sort is not dependent on the substance of that system. A dollar gained or lost from a new training or selection technique is worth just as much as a dollar gained or lost from a performance appraisal system. This is the dependent variable in the equation. In the selection system, the value of ΔU is determined by comparing the relative costs and benefits of a current selection system to a proposed one. In the performance paradigm, the comparison is between the costs and benefits of a current evaluation and feedback system compared to those anticipated from a proposed system.

t: This value represents the tenure in years of the employee in the organization. In the selection paradigm, it is considered only as a multiplier of the benefit components since it is a one-time-only cost (i.e., a test is administered only at the time of application not once a year for as long as the employee remains in the organization). The situation is somewhat different in the performance evaluation paradigm. It is generally accepted by those who value performance evaluation that it should be conducted once a year and possibly more often. This implies that the costs of the system are directly proportional to the tenure of the employee. Thus, for the performance context, the term t should appear in both benefit and cost components of utility calculations. On the cost side, it should be transformed to represent the number of evaluations conducted over the anticipated employment period for the average employee.

N_s: In the selection context, this value represents the number of individuals actually hired. In the performance context, this value would represent the number of people receiving evaluation and feedback. As is the case in selection systems, the greater the number of people who receive the "treatment," the greater both the benefits and the costs to the organization. In the case of performance evaluation, we might reasonably assume that all individuals will receive evaluation and feedback.

r_1 and r_2: These terms represented the new and the old validities in the selection paradigm. In the context of performance evaluation, it makes more sense to think of a "treatment effect" of a procedure rather than its "validity" (although conceptually the term validity is just as appropriate as "treatment effect"). Hunter, Schmidt, and Pearlman (1979) have suggested that the term d_t (where the subscript "t" might be thought to stand for "treatment") be substituted for the validity components (r_1 and r_2) of the selection equation. This term is meant to represent the difference in true scores between the average "treated" individual and the average "untreated" (or control) individual. In our case, this would be the difference in true performance scores between the mean of those receiving evaluation and feedback and those not receiving such treatment. This translation is covered in great detail in both Hunter *et al.* (1979) and Landy, Farr, and Jacobs (1982). For the present demonstration, it is sufficient to say that the value of d_t is usually twice that of the corresponding r_1/r_2 difference. We will drop the r values from further discussion and substitute d_t.

SD_y: This term requires no translation. It is an estimate of the pooled standard deviation of performance (in dollar terms) of the population of workers under examination (both "treatment" and control).

p: In the selection paradigm, the value represents the selection ratio. Since we assume that all workers will eventually receive evaluation and feedback, this term can be dropped from further consideration.

ϕ: As was the case with p, since all workers will receive feedback, this term can be dropped in the performance context.

C_1: This value represents the per employee cost of the new evaluation and feedback procedure. This would include any recurring costs of evaluation and feedback such as production costs for forms or nonproductive administrative time for supervisors and subordinates. In addition, this value might also include some "amortized" indexes such as the one-time-only development costs of the new system (staff development cost, consultant cost, etc.).

C_2: This value represents the per employee cost of the previous procedure. In many organizations, this cost might be expected to be quite low since routine evaluations are often accomplished in an extremely casual manner. It is not uncommon for a manager to complete evaluations on as many as 15 subordinates in less than 1 hour. Needless to say, these evaluations are not extensively discussed with the subordinates in question. Even in this case, one must consider the cost of forms and supervisory time.

A DEMONSTRATION

To this point we have presented theory and idealized situations. The value of the utility approach might be best appreciated by applying it to a concrete problem and examining the economic impact of improved performance evaluation and feedback. To set the stage for the demonstration, it is necessary to accept certain values for the various components of the utility gain formula. By now you should be familiar with the general equation and the meaning of the components so they will be listed simply for the purpose of identifying critical values that will be inserted in the utility gain formula.

For the demonstration, we have chosen an organization that has recently installed a comprehensive performance evaluation, feedback, and goal-setting system. Prior to its introduction, there was no formal system for accomplishing performance review. The organization is a large, multi-division manufacturing organization. We will concern ourselves primarily with the job title "manager," the first level of middle management. There are approximately 500 such managers currently employed in the organization. We will estimate the gain to the organization over a 1-year period of time. The values to be used in the calculation will be as follows:

$N = 500$: All managers will be exposed to the appraisal and feedback.

$d_t = .60$: In our literature review, we concluded that the "validity" of evaluation and feedback was about .30. Since d_t is about twice the value of r, it is equal to .60.

$SD_y = \$20,000$: In conversations with executive officers of the organization, it was estimated (using procedures similar to those suggested by Schmidt et al., 1979) that the difference in value to the organization between a 15th percentile and 50th percentile manager was $20,000; similar values were arrived at for the difference between 50th and 85th percentile managers. Of course, it was more difficult to estimate this value for managers with substantially different area responsibilities (e.g., marketing versus manufacturing) than it would have been to estimate the value for computer programmers, but it was accomplished without undue difficulties.

$C_1 = \$700$ per employee: In calculating this value, we considered the costs of developing the program, the time required for training evaluators, the time required of supervisors for carrying out and feeding back the results of the evaluation, and the "down time" of the manager being evaluated. These costs are probably overestimates of actual costs.

$C_2 = \$00$: Since there had been no prior procedure, there was no prior cost.

Given these values, the utility of introducing a performance evaluation and feedback system would be approximately 5.3 million dollars for 1 year. This value is impressive and becomes more so when you realize that the average tenure of the managers in question is 4 or more years. This means that over the organizational lifetime of a given manager, the expected gain is much larger, possibly as much as three times as great!

OBSTACLES TO THE APPLICATION OF UTILITY CONCEPTS

It would be delightful if we could crank out anticipated utility gain figures for every procedure from changing the color of the walls in the restrooms to installing new equipment at every work station, but we are not yet able to do that. There are still a few obstacles to overcome. These obstacles fall into two general categories—measurement considerations and traditional methods.

Measurement Considerations

The demonstration just presented, as well as the earlier ones by Schmidt *et al.* (1979) have dealt with limited job titles. It may be that some job titles defy the calculation of SD_y. Another problem is the estimation of d_t, the impact of the proposed procedure. It will be necessary to carry out a comparative evaluation of the effectiveness of the proposed procedure before any reasonable conclusion can be drawn.

Traditional Methods

Perhaps an even greater obstacle will be the simple fact that utility analysis has always been the toy of the production staff and has been off-limits to those not directly involved in the production of goods or services. In particular, personnel managers have often been placed in the position of arguing that their expenditures are not unnecessarily high or frivolous without recourse to the anticipated benefit side of the cost-benefit equation. The procedures that we have described might help the personnel manager to get out of the closet and to argue on an even footing with colleagues in production departments when budget planning time rolls around. As we have tried to show, the calculations are not in themselves demanding or intimidating. Furthermore, the estimates that the personnel manager will be required to make are no more arbitrary than those which are universally made in traditional cost-accounting procedures by industrial engineers.

A FINAL COMMENT

We would be remiss if we did not carry the utility approach to its logical conclusion. Once SD_y has been accurately estimated, there is nothing to prevent one from assessing the relative effectiveness of alternative approaches to increasing the mean value of performance in the employee population. We might consider choosing from recruitment, selection, training, performance evaluation, or motivational strategies. We might consider mixing and matching them or using sequential decision rules for determining the most cost-effective combinations of personnel system components. For example, consider Table 9.2. In this table, we present hypothetical data based on utility analyses of several alternative approaches to improving performance. As you can see, the choice reduces to a comparative analysis of the present level of success in the employee population and the cost-benefit characteristics of the program being considered. If only 10% of the current employees are considered "successful," one might choose to increase the validity of selection. If such a strategy is not feasible (due to the unavailability of valid selection devices for the job in question), one might next consider the feasibility of installing an MBO system. The same logic can be applied to other comparisons. We are suggesting that utility analysis become a regular part of the evaluation of all components in a personnel decision system.

SUMMARY

Whenever a personnel manager makes a decision involving a worker, a "treatment" is being applied. This treatment is being applied both to the individual and the organization. For example, consider a promotion. The organization is being affected by virtue of the fact that the talent at one organizational level is being increased. The individual is being affected by virtue of the fact that he or she is receiving a reward, a challenge, and a new set of suitable responsibilities. In some ideal sense, everyone expects benefits to accrue to the organization from this treatment. Furthermore, although somewhat peripheral in a classical cost-benefit approach, the individual also gains from the treatment, independent of the gain to the organization. The same logic can be applied to decisions involving selection, training, salary increases, layoffs, and terminations. Each of these decisions can be recast in cost-benefit terms. The decision is directed toward a goal of increasing benefits or reducing costs.

Performance evaluation and feedback are "treatments." They have the same goal as administering tests or presenting training programs. The intention of performance appraisal systems is to improve the overall level of performance in the organization. We assume that people desire to improve and only require information and instruction to accomplish that improvement. The effect of performance has been well documented in the psychological literature. This effect might be thought of as the "validity" of feedback. We estimate that the lower bound for the validity of feedback systems is approximately .30. This value compares favorably with the validities of many paper-and-pencil tests, particularly in light of the fact that this is most likely an underestimate of the true validity.

Utility theory was introduced to personnel psychology almost 40 years ago. The goal of utility analysis is the calculation of the benefits (in dollars) to be realized from the introduction of a personnel decision system. The systems most often studied in the past were selection systems. A major stumbling block to the full use of utility models was the determination of the dollar value of performance. Traditional cost-accounting methods were cumbersome and required some questionable assumptions in the case of human performance. A recent technique developed by Hunter *et al.* (1979) solved the most serious problems in translating performance to a dollar basis. This breakthrough coupled with the estimates of the validity of performance measurement and feedback permits us to calculate the anticipated gain from using effective performance measurement systems. A demonstration of the use of utility theory showed that in an organization with 500 middle-level managers, a gain of 5.3 million dollars could be realized in 1 year from the introduction of a performance appraisal system at that managerial level. This gain would be magnified for each year of use of the system.

Such demonstrations are useful from several perspectives. In the first place, they permit personnel managers to join their production colleagues in projecting benefits as well as costs. In the past, the personnel staff could only comment on how little or how much a particular program would cost. Now they can balance costs against benefits as is done in line departments. In addition, utility calculations permit comparison of alternative treatments. It is possible to project the utility gain from introducing training and diminishing testing, or vice versa. Such an approach also permits the calculation of incremental gains to be realized from combining various personnel strategies such as selection and training, or training and performance feedback. We predict that utility calculation will become a standard tool of the personnel manager in the years to come. This will help strengthen the bond between research and practice.

chapter ten

Concluding Comments

There has been an enormous amount of research and theorizing in the area of performance measurement in the past 3 decades. As is the case with many topics, we are discovering as much about what we do not know as what we do know. Fortunately, both research and theory building are becoming more sophisticated. This suggests that the next decade should bring enormous progress. In this final chapter, we will identify some areas that we feel need closer examination and will also try to identify those areas where substantial progress has already been made. This chapter is not, however, a summary but rather a *pot pourri* of themes that emerge from the preceding chapters.

THE MULTIPLE ROLES OF PERFORMANCE MEASUREMENT AND FEEDBACK

We have proposed that performance measurement can serve three major functions in an organization. It can facilitate effective personnel decisions (administration), provide the empirical foundation for derivation of these decision rules (research), and improve the motivation of members of the organization (counseling). Let us briefly consider whether or not these purposes are currently being served.

Research

In this area, the results have been pleasing. It is obvious that criterion-related validity is impossible without one or more specific measures of performance. To a lesser extent, training evaluation has also depended on some measure of performance, often in the form of pre- and posttraining measures of the same behavior. But in some senses, the success has been almost too complete. It has only been recently that the validity of the performance measure has been questioned in validation studies. In the typical validation study of the 1960s, if a correlation coefficient between a predictor and criterion turned out to be nonsignificant, the hunt was renewed for a valid predictor. It was assumed that the criterion was "valid" (i.e., a reasonable representation of the performance demands of the job). It is likely that many good tests have been abandoned over the years due to misplaced trust in a performance measure. Thus, while research uses of performance information are common and well documented, the effectiveness of this activity ultimately depends on the extent to which performance has been adequately defined through job analysis techniques.

Counseling

Performance measurement has the capacity to make an enormous impact on the individual worker. Every manager has encountered the desire for feedback among workers at all levels. People want to know how they are performing. This information therefore serves several purposes for them. It confirms that certain task-related strategies are effective, points out areas in which new strategies are needed, represents the potential for social approval and improved self-esteem, and serves as a distant signal of forthcoming rewards and punishments. To a large extent, this promise of value has remained unfulfilled. The most common complaint of the worker is that they receive no feedback of any kind. No matter how well performance is measured, counseling demands feedback.

There are several possible explanations for the stunted development of the counseling function of performance measurement. The first is the most obvious: Supervisors are afraid to provide honest feedback. They are uncomfortable in the position of "judge." They often have terrible information to work with and, thus, are vulnerable to charges of ignorance. The workers may refuse to accept the system in any form. The counseling system itself is often linked to reward–punishment decisions and becomes a source of dissatisfaction. There are some steps that might be taken to improve the situation. One might begin with a good job analysis. There is no substitute for knowing the most important and frequently demanded job activities when measuring performance. In addition, if supervisors are being asked to function in pedagogical roles, they should be given training in the clinical skills so necessary to this art. For example, they might be taught techniques for developing and discussing intraindividual performance profiles and for avoiding interindividual value judgments. Also, much could be done to engage the individual being evaluated in the information-gathering phase of the process. The employee could be asked to complete a personal assessment as a basis for discussion with the supervisor. Any or all of these techniques can help strengthen performance-based counseling.

Administration

As with counseling, administrative decision making based on performance information could be better. Some of the decisions that are commonly affected by performance information are salary–wage adjustments, promotions, and layoffs. Like any score, the performance score that represents any given worker (whether it is a rating or a production count) has a standard error. This means that we have varying amounts of confidence in our knowledge of the range of that score. This is seldom taken into account in administrative decision making. Differences between individuals that represent fractions of a standard error are taken to be "real." The fact is that many performance measurement systems pretend to be something they are not, and the people whose lives are being affected by these decisions are painfully aware of the pretense.

If the administrative uses of performance information are to become more effective (and credible), certain facts must be faced. The first of these facts is that the standard-error concept should influence our use of performance data for decisions that involve single individuals. Conceptually, the issue is tied to the number of observations of the individual in question and the number of other individuals being evaluated. Realistically, the typical situation would probably allow for the development of some small number of performance-level categories (5–10). The individuals being evaluated would then be placed in one of those categories based on performance data. Within categories, other devices might be used to make finer distinctions, devices such as work samples or knowledge tests. One might even develop a multiple-hurdle framework for performance measurement in which the grossest measures of performance (those with least discriminating power) are used to identify broad performance groupings and the most refined measures (those with good discriminating power) are used to identify performance levels within these groupings. This would be necessary from a cost-benefit standpoint, since the most refined measures are also likely to be the most administratively expensive.

We can see from the considerations just presented that there is still room for improvement in the use of performance information for each of the three major purposes. In part, the weaknesses stem from the failure to carry out a procedure basic to many forms of measurement—sampling.

What Is Being Measured?

For the sake of discussion, let us assume that there are three sampling dimensions to a single data point—people, variables, and occasions. In this case, let us say that the data point represents performance of a particular person. That data point belongs to one and only one person. We would feel very uneasy in generalizing to the performance of all people in the organization or to the organization as a whole from this one data point. To make such general statements, we would want to sample more people from the population of members of that organization.

Let us move on to the next sampling parameter—variables. When we consider the performance data of an individual, we are assuming that the individual would have received the same scores on any similar or parallel measuring instrument. To the extent that the individual would not have received identical scores, we are limited in our inferences to "performance" in the more general sense. We are stuck with the operational definition provided by the instrument currently used. At the very least this means that when we are using this performance information for administration, research, or counseling, we must limit our considerations to the narrow definition of the instrument rather than any broader conceptual meaning. We can broaden our base of inference only by broadening the scope of our instrument or by demonstrating that the instrument or measure is representative of a much broader domain from which it was sampled.

Finally, we are left with the most concrete parameter of sampling—observations. We would like to believe that we collect and store performance information on a systematic basis. We do not. Even if we did, it might be better to gather it on a random basis rather than a stratified one, given the ultimate use of the information. Evaluators seldom use any specific scheme for collecting information. This means that inferences from the information must be limited by the method used to gather the information. We cannot generalize to "the" performance of a given individual or group as if the occasion were irrelevant. We could only do that if we had systematically sampled various occasions. The remedy for this weaknesses is obvious. Develop a sampling plan for performance measurement. The plan should guarantee that there are a sufficient number of observations and that they are representative of the period of time under consideration. Representativeness could be guaranteed by randomization or stratification.

If we are to take the issue of measurement seriously in the performance domain, we must realize that we are constrained by the rules of any kind of measurement. These rules imply adequate sampling, a condition that is seldom met.

WHO "OWNS" PERFORMANCE?

An issue that often arises in the context of measuring production quantity is that of credit. In a work setting with semiautomated machines and workers who are dependent on each other during the various stages of production, how is credit assigned for output (i.e., who "owns" performance)? There are many possible owners. Credit might justifiably be assigned to a plant, a department, a shift, a work group, a supervisor–subordinate dyad, or to an individual. In most instances, there are multiple owners. For example, in a semiautomated environment, production rate is probably owned by the plant, the shift, and the work group. On the other hand, the quality of production may be owned by the work group and the individual. Absence might be owned by the shift and the individual. In this model, we are suggesting that various levels of aggregation are necessary to understand various aspects of performance. We commonly cast performance in individual terms, but this may be more wishful thinking than reflection of reality. The following equation might be a reasonable representation of the potential variance components in any particular example of performance.

$$\text{Performance A} = \beta_{\text{Plant}} x_{\text{Plant}} + \beta_{\text{Department}} x_{\text{Department}} + \beta_{\text{Shift}} x_{\text{Shift}} + \beta_{\text{Group}} x_{\text{Group}} + \beta_{\text{Dyad}} x_{dyad} + \beta_{individual} x_{\text{Individual}}$$

In the performance-rating chapter, we dealt with the issue of various influences on the rating process. This obscured the larger issue of attribution. How can success and failure be accurately assigned to individuals and groups? This is an area in which considerable progress might be realized.

Technology

Rating is the most ubiquitous method of performance measurement. There are some things we know about it and some things we do not. What do we know? For one thing, we know that the act of evaluation is almost universal to the human species. As a result, performance evaluation should be compatible with naturally occurring activities. The real issue becomes one of superimposing a standardized format–procedure on that activity so that we are not faced with a Tower of Babel.

In our earlier discussions of rating, we concluded that the accuracy and effectiveness of performance appraisal was less a matter of format than procedure. There is no "one best rating format." Nevertheless, the procedures that are used to develop BARS rating systems are usually rigorous and appropriate. For that reason, we are inclined to recommend the development of BARS scales for performance rating not because the scales themselves are inherently better, but because the procedures that comprise scale development lend themselves to a comprehensive and accurate conceptualization of the performance parameters of the jobs or roles under examination. By extension, we might even suggest using the developmental procedures that are part of the BARS technique but a final format that is different from a BARS format.

Rating scales can be used effectively when performance judgments are to be made. But what about situations where actual behavior is under consideration? With some minor exceptions, there are few instruments available for observing and recording behavior. This may be particularly important in measuring the performance of new employees or those who have recently completed training. Perhaps we are more interested in knowing if patterns of behavior have been developed than we are in the actual results of those behaviors or general judgments of capacities or limitations. Detailed job analysis instruments such as the Position Analysis Questionnaire of McCormick and his colleagues (McCormick, Jeannerett, & Mecham, 1972) could help substantially in developing such observation scales. It may be that we simply have not observed people performing with sufficient detail and intensity to have a good feel for what we are trying to measure.

Raters

It is ironic that of all the performance that has been appraised in the past several decades the one performance area that has received least attention is "performance appraising." In the "physician heal thyself" spirit, we would suggest that much might be learned from doing a job analysis of the manager as performance evaluator. It should be possible to identify the most important and most frequently required behaviors of that task. Next, it should be possible to measure the performance of various individuals in their capacities as raters. This, in turn, could lead to an identification of the critical knowledges, skills, and abilities in rating tasks. We have no doubt that many of these skills would be labeled "cognitive" skills. They might include activities such as memorization, categorization, discrimination, generalization, judgment, or reasoning. Even though the performance appraisal literature is replete with references to cognitive psychology and information processing, relatively little is known about the cognitive demands that are represented in an appraisal task.

It should be possible to conduct needs analyses within organizations to identify areas for improvement in the performance evaluation arena. To put the issue in a slightly different light, if we decided to hire an individual who would carry out all of the performance evaluation tasks for the organization, we would go about selecting and training that individual in a way that departs radically from the procedures we currently use in obtaining ratings of subordinates from managers. Similarly, we would be more concerned about the social and physical environment in which our hypothetical "performance evaluator" works than we are in the case of the manager evaluating performance. Appraisal does not occur in a vacuum. It has a social context to it. We need to know much more about this context. In a sense, it represents a potential source of stress in the job of "evaluator," much like heat or noise or workload represents a potential stressor in a production environment. Put in its simplest form, we would be well advised to start thinking about performance evaluation as a job that a rater carries out, and then we might be better able to identify the significant task and environmental demands that are part of that job.

THE EVALUATION IMPERATIVE

As we proposed earlier in this chapter, evaluation is a naturally occurring phenomenon in our species. The issue is whether the tendency can be harnessed and used to the mutual advantage of the individual and the organization. It should be obvious that we believe that evaluation is a sine qua non for both individual and organizational effectiveness. Advances in thought, theory, and technology of performance measurement will help to ensure that organizational research, administration, and counseling efforts yield appropriate benefits.

Appendix:
Wherry's Theory of Rating

ROBERT J. WHERRY

INTRODUCTION

During World War II, the United States Army embarked on a program of personnel research that had a major impact on the field of applied psychology. Some of the best measurement specialists attacked the issues that would directly aid in improving military efficiency. One such issue was the accurate and reliable measurement of task performance. As was the case in the nonmilitary sector, there were many duties that did not lend themselves to performance measurement through observation of work output. Thus, judgment was required. Robert Wherry, a psychometrician, devoted his efforts to developing a theory of rating that might help illuminate the threats to the validity of performance as measured through supervisors' judgments.

Wherry drew upon his background in applied measurement to develop a series of postulates that might be used to derive testable corollaries relating to the accuracy and reliability of performance ratings. These postulates were based on both measurement theory and learning theory. His work was careful, direct, and useful. Unfortunately, it remained buried in file cabinets and was never published in scientific journals. This was a tragedy since it offered a blueprint for basic research in this area.

In the 1950s and 1960s, Wherry's students at Ohio State University were exposed to his work in classes and seminars. The technical reports describing Wherry's theory were used in these classes and occasionally found their way to individuals working in the area of performance rating. We received a copy from one of Wherry's former students, C. J. Bartlett, and used it to structure a preliminary literature review in the area. After our 1980 article in the Psychological Bulletin *(Landy & Farr, 1980) was published, we were deluged with requests for Wherry's technical reports. As a result, we contacted Wherry and asked him if he would consider preparing an Appendix for this book in the form of an abstracted version of his work for the United States Army. He agreed, and what follows is his description of the theory. Robert Wherry died recently after a long and productive career as an applied psychologist. We are delighted to be able to include his work in this book.*

FOREWORD

This report is the last of a series in a larger study on the construction of personnel evaluation instruments. The objective of the larger study was to discover what factors other than actual performance of the ratee affect ratings and to determine the extent to which these biases can be eliminated or at least minimized.

To meet this objective, a coordinated series of projects was undertaken. In the research projects of this series already completed:

1. The literature on control of bias in ratings was reviewed and reported in PRS Technical Research Report 898.
2. Material and items were gathered and prepared for experimental rating scales of instructors—PRS Technical Research Report 914.
3. Indexes of rating items (e.g., preference index, discrimination index) were developed and analyzed for use in constructing less biased rating scales—PRS Technical Research Report 915.
4. The general areas of instructor behavior (e.g., mastery of subject matter, skill in motivating students), as measured by the rating items chosen for study, were determined—PRB Technical Research Report 919.
5. Several forms of various types of rating scales (adjectival, checklist, forced-choice), were developed with scoring keys designed to reduce bias—PRB Technical Research Report 920.
6. Ratings on a forced-choice rating scale were found to be more closely related to objective measures of performance than were rat-

ings on scales in adjectival or checklist form—PRB Technical Research Report 921.

In the present report, the findings of the previous studies are incorporated into a theory of rating and of the control of bias. An equation for the rating response is mathematically expressed and the underlying postulates and theorems are made explicit. The corollaries of the theory may lead to better understanding of the differences in effectiveness of ratings in different situations and to better control of bias in ratings. It is hoped that the theoretical formulation will stimulate and be of use to further research on the important problem of accurate rating.

THE EQUATION OF THE RATING RESPONSE

Rating theory in the past has been either nonexistent or fragmentary. Although rating is recognized as a legitimate measurement process, unlike psychophysics, mental testing, or psychological scaling, it has no such body of theory. An extensive survey of the literature (Wherry, 1950) showed an abundance of platitudes and rules of thumb, a smattering of empirical findings, and a complete absence of any rational system or theory. This is an attempt to supply such a theory.

Since this is to be a psychological theory, we shall start with a job analysis of the rating process. The rater attempts to make a report on the past behavior of the ratee in some special area defined by the rating item. This area may vary from "general value to the organization" through "loyalty" down to "bites his finger nails"—to cite only a few examples of the different levels of response that may be required. This rating report usually covers some specified period of time such as the past year or past 6 months. The response may vary considerably in the degree of quantification required. It may consist of answering yes or no to the question of "the applicability of the description" or the "desirability of the observed behavior." It may consist of an extension of the 2-point scale to include 5 or 10 or 20 or even 100 categories.

Psychologically, this process is predominantly one of recall on the part of the rater. The desired material of recall is a summing up of the totality of pertinent past observations of the appropriate behavior of the ratee. In addition, if the ratings are to reflect the true value of the ratee, the behavior observed must have been an adequate reflection of the ratee's behavior. Thus, the accuracy of the rating depends on the following steps occurring in the following order: (*a*) performance by the ratee; (*b*) observation of the performance by the rater; and (*c*) recall of the observations by the rater. The accuracy of the rating is based on the adequacy of these three processes. The theory to be developed will attempt to express in quantitative fashion the relationship of these three phases to the final rating. From this quantitative relationship certain predictions will be made concerning rating phenomena.

The theory will be concerned with the potential accuracy of the ratings. It is of course recognized that the rater can deliberately falsify the report, but we will not deal primarily with such conscious bias. On the other hand, we will be mainly concerned with the role of unconscious bias and its elimination.

Although we stated that rating theory, as such, was practically nonexistent, we do not mean to imply that the theory to be developed here is entirely new. Indeed, the pieces are almost entirely old. It is only the organization and quantitative statement that might be claimed as a contribution. To cite all the sources that have contributed to this theory is beyond the power of the author, but the contributions of five writers— Mosier (1940), Gulliksen (1950), Helson (1947), Bartlett (1932), and Bellows (1941)—are so important that they will be briefly described before we begin the formal development of the theory.

Theoretical Background

Mosier (1940) attempted to show that mental test theory and psychophysical theory stem from the same basic type of data—the interaction of persons and stimuli. These basic data could be thought of as comprising a matrix in which the columns represent persons, the rows represent stimuli, and each cell contains a response, R_{ij}, which stands for the response of a person (i) to a stimulus (j). Mental testing was shown to be concerned with operations across rows (i.e., the responses of a given person to a number of stimuli). Psychophysics is concerned with responses across columns (i.e., the responses to a given stimulus of a number of persons). Mental testing attempts to scale persons, whereas psychophysics scales stimuli. On the basis of the proposed matrix, Mosier was able to demonstrate that the theorems of mental testing and of psychophysics must be transposable. Since our analysis of the rating process indicates a similarity to mental testing in the first phase and to psychophysics in the second phase, Mosier influenced the author to examine closely both test theory and perceptual theory for possible leads as to rating theory.

Gulliksen (1950) has collected and synthesized most of the rationale of mental test theory. By means of a few quite simple postulates and definitions he was able to derive most of the theorems of mental testing. His basic equation is one which states that a person's test score (X_i) is a joint function of true score (T_i) and of random error (E_i), or

$$X_i = T_i + E_i. \tag{1}$$

If we accept Mosier's transposability hypothesis, we can posit a similar equation to describe a psychophysical response to an object (X_o) as the sum of its true scale value (T_o) and a random error term (E_o), or

$$X_o = T_o + E_o. \tag{2}$$

This equation was indeed used by Mosier to derive some of the classical psychophysical theorems.

Helson (1947), however, has suggested that the equation of the psychophysical response is oversimplified. He proposed that any adequate explanation of the usual psychophysical results must include reference to what he calls the "adaptation level." This adaptation level is defined as

$$A = X^p X_b^q X_r^s \tag{3}$$

where the X without subscript refers to the actual stimulus presented, the X_b refers to the background stimulus, and the X_r refers to the residual effect of all previous stimuli encountered. The exponents p, q, and s are relative weights. This concept, considerably modified for the sake of simplicity, might be used to indicate that the psychophysical response might be more adequately reflected by the equation

$$X_o = T_o + B_o + E_o, \tag{4}$$

where B_o refers to some bias present in the observer's judgment due to past conditions. This may result in either an overevaluation or an underevaluation of a given stimulus or class of stimuli.

Bartlett (1932) has advanced a theory of memory that stresses the positive character of forgetting. Recall is in accordance with a "schema" or generalized pattern. Inconsistent details are obliterated in favor of the general concept, whereas supporting details are selected or even unknowingly invented. We shall assume that memory acts in this fashion when past behavior is to be recalled for the purpose of completing a rating scale. We shall also assume that this process in recall is closely related to the bias that enters into perception of observed behavior.

The Equation of a Rating Response

In line with the historical background just presented, the act of rating is seen as depending upon the following series of events that are allied to the concepts developed.

The first link in the chain is the actual behavior of the individual (X_A). As a first approximation, we might assume that this behavior is of the same nature as a mental test event, that is, it is composed of one part true ability (T) and another part random error (E_A). These two components are differentially weighted t_A and e_A, where the sum of the weights squared is equal to unity. Thus the actually performed event can be mathematically expressed, using standard scores, as

$$z_{X_A} = t_A z_T + e_A z_{E_A}. \tag{5}$$

This expression parallels Spearman's two-factor theory of intelligence. Obviously, the true equation should probably contain group or common factors as well as a general one, but for convenience we shall restrict our development to this simpler case.

As a second approximation we will add a third term to the equation to include what Bellows (1941) has called contamination due to environmental influences (I). A person's performance of a given act is influenced by the conditions under which it is performed. The prior instruction, the suitability of the tools provided, the work setting (lighting, ventilation, temperature), and the time (of day, of week, shift) may all influence the outcome. Thus we expand Eq. (5) to read

$$z_{X_A} = t_A z_T + i_A z_I + e_A z_{E_A}, \tag{6}$$

where

$$t_A^2 + i_A^2 + e_{E_A}^2 = 1.00.$$

This added element will also be useful in explaining the inadequacy of the usual work record as a test of ability. In mental testing it would be useful to explain the poorness of the usual oral examination or unstructured interview. It would also be useful in discussions of culture-free tests.

The second step in the series consists of the perception (X_p) of the ratee's behavior (X_A) by the rater or observer. To what is actually happening the rater will unconsciously add a bias component (B_p) and a new random error term (E_p). Before developing the entire equation we need to examine further the nature of the bias component. Following Helson's lead, we might expect this term to embrace three separate components:

1. An actual T component, with weight t_p, indicating an expectancy of ability equal to what actually possessed. A rater who had had only relevant contacts with the ratee and a great deal of such contact would have a relatively high weight for this component. With this component in B_p we can expect that a rater will give somewhat valid responses even when observing atypical behavior.

2. An areal, nonrelevant bias factor, B_{PA}, with weight b_{PA}, which is a kind of residual effect of all previous error and nonrelevant experiences aroused by seeing the ratee in stimulus situations that the rater classifies as belonging to a particular area of behavior. Thus, a particular bias for or against a given individual as a scholar, for example, differs from the bias held against that same individual as a disciplinarian, or as an organizer, or as a social companion.

3. An overall bias component, B_{PO}, with weight b_{PO}, a residual effect of all possible areal bias effects, pertinent or irrelevant, a kind of background against which all acts of the individual, regardless of stimulus, are evaluated.

If in addition we now assume that the observed happening X_A has a weight a_p and that the random error of perception E_p has a weight e_p, we can write in standard score terms:

$$z_{X_p} = a_p z_{X_A} + t_p z_T + b_{PA} z_{BPA} + b_{PO} z_{BPO} + e_p z_{E_p}, \tag{7}$$

where the sum of the weights squared again equals unity.

Substituting the previously derived value of z_{X_A} from Eq. (6) in Eq. (7) yields

$$z_{X_p} = a_p(t_A z_T + i_A z_I + e_A z_{E_A}) + t_p z_T + b_{PA} z_{BPA} \tag{7a}$$
$$+ b_{PO} z_{BPO} + e_p z_{Ep}.$$

Expanding and collecting like terms of z_T, we obtain

$$z_{X_p} = (a_p t_A + t_p) z_T + a_p i_A z_I + b_{PA} z_{BPA} + b_{PO} z_{BPO} \tag{7b}$$
$$+ a_p e_A z_{EA} + e_p z_{EA}.$$

The third step in any rating is the actual recall and reporting of the recollections of previously observed behaviors associated with the scale to be used. The act of recall will then contain one component that will be based upon the sum of p previous elements z_{X_p} or $\Sigma^p z_{X_p}$. But we know from Bartlett (1932) that memory is more than the sum of its parts. It is partly, sometimes largely, composed of an imposed schema or systematic bias factor of recall, B_R. This bias factor of recall can probably be best described as being composed of the same three types of components as were found in the bias of perception, namely, true, areal bias, and overall bias. The weights of these components may differ from those in perception, however. There will of course also be a random error factor, e_R, for recall. Expressing this paragraph mathematically gives us

$$z_{X_R} = a_R \left(\sum_{}^{p} z_{X_p} \right) + t_R z_T + b_{RA} z_{BRA} + b_{RO} z_{BRO} + e_R z_{ER}, \qquad (8)$$

where again the sum of the squares of all weights is unity, and substituting our previous equation for z_{X_p}

$$z_{X_R} = a_R \sum_{}^{p} [(a_p t_A + t_p) z_T + a_p e_A z_I + b_{PA} z_{BPA} + b_{PO} z_{BPO}$$
$$+ a_p e_A z_{EA} + e_p z_{Ep}] + t_R z_T + b_{RA} z_{BRA} + b_{RO} z_{BRO}$$
$$+ e_R z_{ER}. \qquad (8a)$$

To simplify this equation, we will first consider the effect of the operation of summing in the first term. We shall assume that the rater's weights and the z_T value for the ratee are constant. The remaining z terms will be considered as variables and the mean z values will be represented by the symbol $\bar{z}$ with proper subscript. Thus we would obtain

$$z_{X_R} = p a_R [(a_p t_A + t_p) z_T + a_p i_A \bar{z}_I + b_{PA} \bar{z}_{BPA} + b_{PO} \bar{z}_{BPO}$$
$$+ a_p e_A \bar{z}_{EA} + e_p \bar{z}_{Ep}] + t_R z_T + b_{RA} z_{BRA} + b_{RO} z_{BRO}$$
$$+ e_R z_{ER}. \qquad (8b)$$

Clearing the bracketed term, we would obtain

$$z_{X_R} = p a_R (a_p t_A + t_p) z_T + p a_R a_p i_A \bar{z}_I + p a_R b_{PA} \bar{z}_{BPA}$$
$$+ p a_R b_{PO} \bar{z}_{BPO} + p a_R a_p e_A \bar{z}_{EA} + p a_R e_p \bar{z}_{Ep} + t_R z_T$$
$$+ b_{RA} z_{BRA} + b_{RO} z_{BRO} + e_R z_{ER}. \qquad (8c)$$

Another assumption that will further simplify our equation is based on the postulated relation between the bias of perception and the bias of recall. We shall assume that the two bias terms of recall are identical with the mean values of the biases of perception, at least for the items recalled. Thus, we assume that

$$\bar{z}_{B_{PA}} = z_{B_{RA}} \tag{9}$$

and

$$\bar{z}_{B_{PO}} = z_{B_{RO}}. \tag{9a}$$

Making the indicated substitutions and collecting like terms gives:

$$z_{X_R} = (pa_{R}a_{p}t_A + pa_{R}t_p + t_R)z_T + pa_{R}a_{p}i_A\bar{z}_I + (pa_{R}b_{PA}$$
$$+ b_{RA})z_{B_{RA}} + (pa_{R}b_{PO} + b_{RO})z_{B_{RO}} + pa_{R}a_{p}e_A\bar{z}_{E_A}$$
$$+ pa_{R}e_{p}\bar{z}_{E_P} + e_{R}z_{E_R}. \tag{8d}$$

Summary

The definitions and equations just presented constitute the major postulates of the theory. Eq. (8d) may appear long and involved. It is replete with unknown constants. Despite certain simplifying assumptions, it is still quite complex. However, it represents fairly well the actually complex response that rating involves. We shall see in later sections that its consideration and manipulation lead to many believable and practical theorems and corollaries about ratings.

FACTORS AFFECTING THE ITEM WEIGHTS

In the preceding section we derived the rather complex equation (8d) to represent the final rating response. For the sake of brevity in future sections of this report, we will now substitute new complex weights to replace the composite weights in that equation. The following equivalents are therefore defined:

$$W_T = pa_{R}a_{p}t_A + pa_{R}t_p + t_R, \tag{10}$$

$$W_{B_{RA}} = pa_{R}b_{PA} + b_{RA}, \tag{11}$$

$$W_{B_{RO}} = pa_{R}b_{PO} + b_{RO}, \tag{12}$$

$$W_I = pa_{R}a_{p}i_A, \tag{13}$$

$$W_{E_A} = pa_{R}a_{p}e_A, \tag{14}$$

$$W_{E_P} = pa_{R}e_p, \text{ and} \tag{15}$$

$$W_{E_R} = e_R. \tag{16}$$

Substituting these new values in Eq. (8d) yields

$$z_{X_R} = W_T z_T + W_{BRA} z_{BRA} + W_{BRO} z_{BRO} + W_I \bar{z}_I + W_{EA} \bar{z}_{EA}$$
$$+ W_{EP} \bar{z}_{EP} + W_{ER} \bar{z}_{ER} \tag{8e}$$

The relative proportion of true score (z_T), Areal bias (z_{BRA}), Overall bias (z_{BRO}), Environmental influence (z_I), and Error (z_{EA}, z_{EP}, and z_{ER}) in a given rating will be a function of the squares of the seven weights defined in Eqs. (10) through (16). The variance—obtained by squaring, summing, and averaging—is given by the equation

$$\frac{z_{X_R}^2}{N} = \left[\frac{\begin{array}{c} W_T z_T + W_{BRA} z_{BRA} + W_{BRO} z_{BRO} + W_I \bar{z}_I \\ + W_{EA} \bar{z}_{EA} + W_{EP} \bar{z}_{EP} + W_{ER} \bar{z}_{ER} \end{array}}{N} \right]^2 . \tag{17}$$

Since each of the seven terms is unrelated to each of the others by definition, all cross product terms in the expansion will equal zero and all sums of squares of standard scores will equal unity. Hence

$$\frac{z_{X_R}^2}{N} = 1.00 = W_T^2 + W_{BRA}^2 + W_{BRO}^2 + W_I^2 + W_{EA}^2 + W_{EP}^2 + W_{ER}^2 . \tag{17a}$$

Thus as one weight increases the others must decrease.

The True Score Weight, W_T

The weight of the true score, W_T, is composed of three terms involving six constants. Its equation is

$$W_T = p a_R a_p t_A + p a_R t_p + t_R \tag{10}$$

Since W_T increases as each of these constants increases, we shall consider them in turn. The three t values are the most important since they do not appear in any of the other Ws, whereas the p and a values do appear in many of the others.

The Weight t_A

The weight t_A reflects the true component of every performance by the ratee. An inspection of Eq. (6) shows that t_A increases as i_A and/or e_A decrease. Attempts to minimize i_A, or at least to make it constant for all ratees, will increase the importance of t_A. Thus, we can deduce that the nature of the work situation is an important determiner of the accuracy of ratings. Hence, we can conclude that

THEOREM 1. *Tasks in which the performance is maximally controlled by the ratee rather than by the work situation will be more favorable to accurate ratings.*

Any increment or decrement of performance not due to the ability of the ratee can only be considered as a source of error or as an irrelevant fact contributing to bias. Only as the task permits the full and unimpeded expression of ability will it contribute maximally to the true component, t_A. From this theorem we can draw several corollaries:

COROLLARY 1a. *Tasks in which the raw material, tools, working conditions (light, heat, etc.) are constant from worker to worker will lead to more accurate ratings of ability than will those in which such factors are variable.*

This corollary concerning working conditions parallels the usual control of the testing situation in the administration of mental tests.

COROLLARY 1b. *Tasks that are man paced rather than machine paced will lead to more accurate ratings of ability.*

Machine-paced tasks would tend to make everyone equal in speed of performance, thus hiding individual differences. Machine-paced tasks would resemble the mental-testing situation in which items were all at one level of difficulty, thus serving to dichotomize but not to metricize the population.

COROLLARY 1c. *Positions in which output is restricted by union or other agreement will be less amenable to accurate rating than will those in which freedom of individual output is unlimited.*

The only tasks that enter into the final ratings are those that are selected through recall by the rating stimuli to recall. Thus we can also conclude that

THEOREM 2. *Rating scales or items that have as their behavioral referents those tasks that are maximally controlled by the ratee will lead to more accurate ratings than those that refer to tasks controlled by the work situation.*

The Weights t_p and t_R

The weights t_p and t_R will be considered together because of their similarity. They represent the true portions of the bias of perception and of the bias of recall respectively. They compete with the areal and overall bias and error weights in both perception and recall. The probability of a large true component in these bias responses is based on the same underlying conditions. The relative size of each t is probably a function of the proportion of previous contacts between rater and ratee that have been pertinent. Hence we can conclude that

THEOREM 3. *Raters will vary in the accuracy of ratings given in direct proportion to the relevancy of their previous contacts with the ratee.*

Biases, by definition, grow from irrelevant contacts, whereas the true component of the rater's bias in either perception or recall can increase only as the true observations are more predominant than are irrelevant experiences. An often verified empirical observation can be deduced as a corollary of this theorem

COROLLARY 3a. *Close personal friends and relatives of the ratee will be less accurate raters than will close associates on the job only.*

Close personal friends and relatives will be thrown into irrelevant nonshop contacts with the ratee to a much greater extent than will close associates on the job.

The Weight p

It will be recalled that p is the number of perceptions that contribute to recall at the time of rating. This constant serves to increase the relative strength of the first two terms of Eq. (10), and thus increases the role of t_A and t_p as opposed to t_R. Inspection of Eqs. (10) through (12) discloses that it occurs twice in the general weight for z_T but only once in the weights for the bias terms, thus tending to enhance z_T rather than $z_{B_{RA}}$ or $z_{B_{RO}}$. Thus we can conclude that numerous observations will tend to enhance the accuracy of ratings.

THEOREM 4. *Raters will vary in the accuracy of ratings given in direct proportion to the number of previous relevant contacts with the ratee.*

Since the error portions of even relevant contacts act to create bias, and since these errors tend to cancel out as the number of pertinent acts observed increases, from theorems (3) and (4) combined we deduce that

COROLLARY 4a. *Close job associates will be more accurate raters than will casual acquaintances or infrequent observers.*

COROLLARY 4b. *The longer the rater knows the ratee on the job, the greater the probability that the ratings will be accurate.*

COROLLARY 4c. *The greater the geographical proximity of the rater to the ratee's work place, the greater the probability of multiple pertinent experiences and hence the greater the probability of accurate ratings.*

Since p is the number of perceptions recalled rather than the number taking place, we know that the stimuli to recall may serve to partially determine the value of p.

THEOREM 5. *Rating-scale items that refer to easily observed behavior categories will result in more accurate ratings than will those which refer to hard-to-observe behaviors.*

COROLLARY 5a. *Rating items that refer to frequently performed acts will be rated more accurately than those that refer to acts performed rarely or at long intervals.*

The Weight a_p

The weight a_p serves to increase the influence of actually observed behavior as against bias or error in the act of perceiving. Any factor that will heighten sensory experience while it decreases the effects of previous experience or decreases error will increase a_p. From this we can deduce certain conditions that will increase this external aspect of perception.

THEOREM 6. *The rater will make more accurate ratings when forewarned about the types of activities to be rated, since this will facilitate the more proper focusing of attention on such pertinent behavior.*

COROLLARY 6a. *Courses for the instruction of raters will be more efficient if they include instruction in what to look for.*

COROLLARY 6b. *In lieu of such actual instruction, duties that normally involve direct supervisory relation to the ratee, as would be true for an immediate supervisor, will serve to increase rating accuracy.*

THEOREM 7. *If the perceiver makes a conscious effort to be objective, after becoming aware of the biasing influence of previous set, he or she may be able to reduce the influence of the bias.*

COROLLARY 7a. *Training courses for the rater should include instruction on the effect of set on perception and provide practice in objectivity of observation.*

COROLLARY 7b. *Deliberate direction of attention to the objective (measurable) results of behavior may serve to restrain the biasing effects of set.*

THEOREM 8. *If the perceiver is furnished an easily accessible check list of objective cues for the evaluation of performance, which can be referred to frequently, the perceiver should be better able to focus his or her attention properly.*

The Weight a_R

The weight a_R appears in two of the terms composing W_T. It represents the actual recall of previously perceived events as opposed to schema (bias) and error components. It can perhaps be best associated with the recall value of the rating stimulus and the rating situation. Starting with a consideration of the rating stimulus we can posit that

THEOREM 9. *Physical features of a scale that facilitate recall of the actual perception of behavior will increase the accuracy of ratings.*

COROLLARY 9a. *Longer, objective, descriptive statements will be more effective than single value words or simple phrases in defining the steps on an adjectival-type rating scale.*

COROLLARY 9b. *Overall ratings made after completion of a previous objective review (such as would be provided by the previous filling out of a checklist or forced-choice form) will be more accurate than those made without such a review.*

COROLLARY 9c. *The clearer (more self-explanatory) and more unambiguous the scale to be rated, the more likely that attention will be centered on the desired behavior.*

THEOREM 10. *The keeping of a written record between rating periods of specifically observed critical incidents will improve the objectivity of recall.*

The function of such a written record is twofold. It gives extra sensory reinforcement at the time of observation. It can also be reviewed just prior to the rating period, thus reviving and strengthening pertinent aspects of recall.

We earlier pointed out that the general rating situation can also affect the weight a_R. We therefore hypothesize that

THEOREM 11. *Any setting that facilitates the increase of bias, such as knowledge that the rating will have an immediate effect upon the recipient, will decrease the accuracy of raters, whereas any set that stresses the importance to the organization or to society as a whole will decrease perceived bias elements and thus increase accuracy.*

COROLLARY 11a. *Ratings obtained under experimental conditions (i.e., to be used only to improve instruments, methods, or the like for the good of the organization) will be more accurate than those obtained under actual on-the-job conditions where resulting administrative action will or may affect the ratee.*

COROLLARY 11b. *Ratings obtained in advance through a routine process will be more accurate than those especially secured at the time when an administrative action (such as promotion) is contemplated.*

THEOREM 12. *Knowledge that the rating given will have to be justified may serve unconsciously to affect the rating given.*

COROLLARY 12a. *Knowledge that the rating may have to be justified to the ratee may cause the rater to recall a higher proportion of favorable perceptions and thus lead to leniency.*

COROLLARY 12b. *Knowledge that the rating may have to be justified to the rater's superior may cause the rater to recall a higher proportion of perceptions related to actions known to be of particular interest to the superior whether such actions are pertinent or not.*

COROLLARY 12c. *To assure that neither of the distorting affects just mentioned shall take place alone, it is better to assure their mutual cancellation by requiring that both types of review shall take place.*

A third source of affects on a_R can be secured by preparation dating back to the time of perception of behavior, based on certain well-known determiners of recall.

THEOREM 13. *Since forgetting is largely a function of intervening activities interposed between learning and recall, ratings secured soon after the observation period will be more accurate than those obtained after a considerable lapse of time.*

COROLLARY 13a. *A rating should be secured immediately, whenever the ratee's supervisor is changed in the same job or when the ratee moves to a new position.*

THEOREM 14. *If observation is sufficiently frequent so as to constitute overlearning, the accuracy of recall will be improved.*

This theorem reiterates the importance of theorem (4) on the necessity for frequent relevant contact but for a different reason.

THEOREM 15. *Observation with intention to remember will facilitate recall.*

This theorem is related to or dependent upon theorem (6) since the rater must know what he or she is to try to remember.

Relation of the Weights W_T, t_A, t_p, t_R, p, a_p, a_R to Other Weights

Theorems 1–5 serve other purposes in addition to acting as a guide for increasing the weight W_T through the increase of its components, p, t_p, t_R, t_A, a_R, and a_p. Each of these six components is in turn linked to other basic weights which compose, along with a_R and a_p, the other major W values. Thus:

$$t_A^2 + i_A^2 + e_A^2 = 1.00,$$

$$a_P^2 + t_P^2 + b_{PA}^2 + b_{PO}^2 + e_P^2 = 1.00, \text{ and}$$

$$a_R^2 + t_R^2 + b_{RA}^2 + b_{RO}^2 + e_R^2 = 1.00.$$

From these relationships we see that i_A^2 and e_A^2 are inversely related to t_A^2, and that hence as an increased t_A increases W_T, the decreased value of e_A decreases the weight W_{E_A}, and the decreased value of i_A decreases the weight W_I. Also as a_P and t_P increase, b_{PA}, b_{PO} and e_P must decrease proportionately. Hence, as W_T increases due to those causes, the weights $W_{B_{RA}}$, $W_{B_{RO}}$, W_I, and W_{E_A} decrease. Again, as a_R and t_R increase, b_{RA}, b_{RO}, and/or e_R must decrease. Hence as W_T increases due to these causes, the weights $W_{B_{RA}}$, $W_{B_{RO}}$, W_I, and W_{E_R} decrease.

Relative Size of $W_{B_{RA}}$ and $W_{B_{RO}}$

The areal and overall bias weights are seen to increase in competition with each other. Their relative size will depend upon the ratio of b_{PA} to b_{PO} and of b_{RA} to b_{RO}. If we consider these two pairs of weights as competing with each other, we can hypothesize that

THEOREM 16. *Performances that are readily classified by the observer into a special category will have relatively larger areal and smaller overall bias components.*

COROLLARY 16a. *Jobs with simplified performance units requiring a single discrete aptitude will be rated with relatively more areal and less overall bias than will complex jobs requiring a complex pattern of aptitudes.*

THEOREM 17. *Rating items that are readily classified by the rater as referring to a given area of behavior will result in relatively larger areal and less overall bias than will items that suggest a complex pattern of behavior to the rater.*

COROLLARY 17a. *Rating items shown to be factorially unidimensional will result in relatively larger areal and relatively smaller overall bias than will items shown to have a complex factor pattern.*

Summary

The 17 theorems and 23 corollaries developed in this section suggest many practical methods for increasing the efficiency of ratings. They also should serve to explain why certain rating situations lead to more effective ratings than do others. Finally, several of the corollaries lead to practical suggestions for the training of raters.

THE EFFECT OF PLURAL RATINGS ON
THE WEIGHTS

This section of the original report dealt with the effect of adding new areas, items, and raters to the rating system. The effect of these changes on the various elements of the rating equation were explored and incorporated in a series of equations. These manipulations resulted in the development of a series of theorems.

THEOREM 18. *The effect of adding an increased number of unidimensional items to a single-item rating scale is a reduction in random error components, thus giving added relative emphasis to the true, areal bias, overall bias, and environmental contamination components.*

THEOREM 19. *The addition of a number of items, each from an independent area or factor, to a single-item rating scale will reduce the random error and areal bias components, thus giving added emphasis to true, environmental contamination, and overall bias components.*

COROLLARY 19a. *Of two rating scales, each composed of the same number of items, the one composed of independent items will be more effective than one composed of homogeneous items.*

THEOREM 20. *The addition of extra qualified raters, with identical irrelevant contacts with a ratee, on a single item produces the same effect as the addition of extra items with the same areal classification.*

THEOREM 21. *The addition of enough extra qualified raters, each with a completely different set of irrelevant contacts with the ratees will result in obtaining virtually true ratings in which areal and overall bias as well as error components have disappeared, even though each rater responds but to a single item.*

THEOREM 22. *The addition of extra items of each type to the items of a heterogeneous scale will reduce error variance, but will have no effect on areal or overall bias.*

THEOREM 23. *The use of several raters on a multi-item homogeneous scale of rating items has the same effect on error reduction as multiplying the number of items in the original scale by the number of raters used when all raters have identical irrelevant contacts with the ratees.*

THEOREM 24. *The use of several raters on a multi-item completely heterogeneous list of rating items, if all rater backgrounds are identical, will merely have the same effect as an increase in the number of independent items, thus reducing the error component but having little if any effect on the other components.*

THEOREM 25. *To the extent that irrelevant rater contacts with the ratees are somewhat different, the use of plural raters on a completely heterogeneous list of items will result in a reduction of both areal and overall bias.*

THEOREM 26. *The addition of several extra items to each area of a completely heterogeneous scale to be used by several raters will further reduce error but will have no added effect on the removal of bias.*

THEOREM 27. *The use of several raters on a scale composed of several items in each of several areas will further reduce error, but may or may not reduce bias components depending on the degree of correlation among the irrelevant backgrounds of the raters.*

RELIABILITY OF RATINGS

In a very real sense we were discussing reliability in the last two sections when we were discussing error elimination. To reduce error or bias is to increase true reliability. However, the true state of affairs may or may not be reflected by the reliability coefficient chosen. The reliability of a rating scale will be a function of the method of measurement to an even greater extent than would be the case for a psychological test or psychophysical scores.

The theorems that follow were developed by a series of mathematical equations, which we omit here to save space.

THEOREM 28. *The reliability of a rating item will be higher when determined by the test–retest, same-rater method than when tested by the test–retest, different-rater method, and this superiority will increase as the difference in irrelevant (nonwork) contacts of the raters increase.*

THEOREM 29. *The reliability of a single-item rating scale will be greater by the test–retest, same-rater method than when calculated by the item-alternate item, same-rater method.*

THEOREM 30. *The reliability of a single-item rating when determined by the item-alternate item, same-rater method may or may not be greater than when it is determined by the item-same item, alternate-rater method. The relative size of the two estimates depends on the relative size of the true and bias components and on the degree of similarity of the alternate items and alternate raters.*

THEOREM 31. *The reliability of a single-item rating will be lower when determined by an item-similar item, different-rater approach than by a method in which only the item or only the rater are not identical and even lower than when both are identical.*

THEOREM 32. *Intercorrelations among single-item ratings, even though the items are truly orthogonal, will not equal zero but, rather, will equal the product of the standard score weights of overall bias. This fact accounts for what has been called halo.*

THEOREM 33. *Halo will not disappear even when different raters are used unless the irrelevant contacts with the ratees of the different raters is completely without overlap.*

THEOREM 34. *A multi-item unidimensional scale is more reliable than a single item, but the relative proportion of true score to bias is not increased.*

THEOREM 35. *A multi-item completely heterogeneous scale will appear to be less reliable than an equally long unidimensional scale, but the loss will be due to bias reduction rather than to error increase.*

THEOREM 36. *Addition of several extra items to each area of a multidimensional test will increase reliability by decreasing error.*

THEOREM 37. *A multi-item unidimensional test will be more reliable when measured by the test–retest, same-rater method than by the rater–alternate rater, same-test method.*

THEOREM 38. *The reliability of a rating scale tells us very little about its value since the apparent reliability may be due to bias rather than to true score components.*

FACTORS FROM DIFFERENT TYPES OF SCALES

The various types of scales—adjectival, checklist, and forced-choice rating scales—were evaluated with respect to validity.

THEOREM 39. *In a forced-choice rating scale composed entirely of positively phrased items, the true score value assigned to the ratee is proportional to the number of valid items chosen from the pairs, whereas the extent to which the description is composed of irrelevant bias factors is proportional to the number of invalid items chosen.*

THEOREM 40. *In a forced-choice scale composed entirely of negatively phrased items, the ratee securing a large number of most like valid item responses is really a poor performer, whereas the ratee said to be like a large number of invalid descriptors has a less negative true performance.*

THEOREM 41. *The proper scoring technique for an evaluative forced-choice scale composed of both positive and negatively phrased pairs consists of assigning positive credit for the choice of positive valid items and for the choice of negative invalid items.*

THEOREM 42. *For checklist and adjectival rating scales, if the score on a series of less valid items is partialed out from the score for a series of more valid items, the resulting corrected score will be more truly representative of actual job performance.*

THEOREM 43. *The principal general factor, derivable from a set of intercorrelations based on biased rating items and scales and a biased criterion, will represent the bias components of the ratings.*

THEOREM 44. *A common factor with certain rating items having high loadings, whereas other scales or items have only chance loadings, and upon which the overall criterion has a sizeable loading, probably represents the true score component.*

THEOREM 45. *A common factor having high loadings on some scales but with only chance loadings on many others, including the overall criterion scale, probably represents an areal bias factor.*

THEOREM 46. *The true score of a ratee can best be predicted by multiple regression using the best validity coefficients of the items as criterion correlations.*

AN ADDITION TO THE THEORY

We have so far treated ratings as if they depended only on (*a*) performance; (*b*) observation; and (*c*) recall. However, before the ratings can be used they must also be evaluated. The description contained in the rating must be summarized with the elements properly evaluated. This summation can take one of two trends: It can either (*a*) express the overall fitness of the employee by some single number (when the rating is to be used for retention or salary raise); and/or (*b*) take the form of a profile that depicts the strong and weak areas of the employee's ability and performance (when the ratings are to be used for placement, training, promotion, etc.). None of the rating scales discussed so far succeeds in attaining either of these goals perfectly.

Actually, the forced-choice overall rating is probably the best producer of the single score representing the level of performance since it is the only one with built in bias elimination. When the biases of the rater are uncontrolled and he or she is forced to attempt such a summary, the rater is not able to do so successfully because each rater adopts some strategy for weighting the various areas of performance and no single strategy is adopted by a majority of the raters involved. Wherry and Naylor (1966) have demonstrated this fact for three different types of air force supervisors. Only if the biases of each single rater are offset by using a large number of raters can we trust the resulting validity coefficients. This finding probably accounts for the fact that peer nominations involving a wide variety of raters has so often been used in previous research studies. Actually, when forced-choice scales have been used, the scoring key must be kept secret and be based on all available adequate raters.

For the second purpose—an adequately differentiating profile of areal abilities—the overall evaluative forced choice is the poorest and can indeed not be used at all for that purpose. On the other hand, the adjectival scale was supposedly designed to obtain just such a profile, and the checklist scale could easily be adapted for that purpose by obtaining subscores for each area's items. In fact, neither of these scales results in such a *discriminating* profile of the various areas. The presence of overall bias and environmental contamination is usually so high that the supposedly independent scale scores correlate somewhere between .80 and 1. To obtain such truly discriminating profiles with independent measures of each area, Wherry (1959) developed what he called a Differential Forced-Choice Rating Scale. Items in that scale instead of having pairs of items, one valid and one not valid, consist of sets of items, one from each area, and all equated on preference index, general factor (bias) loading, and discrimination index. The set of items is to be rank ordered in terms of applicability to the ratee. Although such a rating scale will produce a differential profile of the type wanted, it of course cannot possibly be used to estimate the overall level of performance.

Many of the hypotheses presented in this theoretical work are testable. Many have already been borne out by previous researches. It is hoped that this theoretical formulation will stimulate further research. Such research should lead not only to better control of bias but also to better and more precise statement of the theory itself. The present theory is neither complete nor correct—no theory ever is. It is, however, a theory and if its formulation has brought many of the problems of rating into sharper focus and formed a basis for relating it to general psychological and measurement theory, it will have been worthwhile.

References

Abelson, R. P. Psychological status of the script concept. *American Psychologist*, 1981, *36*, 715–729.

Adams, J. A. Response feedback and learning. *Psychological Bulletin*, 1968, *70*, 486–504.

Allen, M. J., & Yen, W. M. *Introduction to measurement theory*. Monterey, Calif.: Brooks/Cole, 1979.

Alwin, D. An analytic comparison of four approaches to the interpretation of relationships in the multitrait-multimethod matrix. In H. Costner (Ed.), *Sociological methodology 1973–74*. San Francisco, Calif.: Jossey-Bass, 1974.

American Psychological Association, Division of Industrial-Organizational Psychology. *Principles for the validation and use of personnel selection procedures* (2nd ed.). Berkeley, Calif.: Author, 1980.

Amir, Y., Kovarsky, Y., & Sharan, S. Peer nominations as a predictor of multistage promotions in a ramified organization. *Journal of Applied Psychology*, 1970, *54*, 462–469.

Ammons, R. B. Effects of knowledge of performance: A survey and tentative theoretical formulation. *Journal of General Psychology*, 1956, *54*, 279–299.

Annett, J. *Feedback and human behavior*. Baltimore, Md.: Penguin Books, 1969.

Arvey, R. D. *Fairness in selecting employees*. Reading, Mass.: Addison-Wesley, 1979.

Arvey, R. D., & Hoyle, J. C. A Guttman approach to the development of behaviorally based rating scales for systems analysts and programmer/analysts. *Journal of Applied Psychology*, 1974, *59*, 61–68.

Ash, P. The parties to the grievance. *Personnel Psychology*, 1970, *23*, 13–37.

Ashford, S. J., & Cummings, L. L. Feedback as an individual resource: Personal strategies of creating information. *Organizational Behavior and Human Performance*, *32*, in press.

Atkinson, J. W., & Feather, N. T. *A theory of achievement motivation*. New York: Wiley, 1966.

Baker, E. M., & Schuck, J. R. Theoretical note: Use of signal detection theory to clarify problems of evaluating performance in industry. *Organizational Behavior and Human Performance*, 1975, *13*, 307–317.

Bandura, A. Self-efficacy: Toward a unifying theory of behavioral change. *Psychological Review*, 1977, *54*, 191–215.

Barnes, J. L. *Age as a perceptual cue in the performance appraisal process: The relationship between perceived age similarity and performance ratings of exempt employees*. Unpublished doctoral dissertation, The Pennsylvania State University, 1980.

Barnes, J. L., & Landy, F. J. Scaling behavioral anchors. *Applied Psychological Measurement*, 1979, *3*, 193–200.

Barnowe, J. T. Leadership and performance outcomes in research organizations: The supervisor of scientists as a source of assistance. *Organizational Behavior and Human Performance*, 1975, *14*, 264–280.

Barrett, R. S. Influence of supervisor's requirements on ratings. *Personnel Psychology*, 1966, *19*, 375–387.

Barrett, R. S., Taylor, E. K., Parker, J. W., & Martens, L. Rating scale content: I. Scale information and supervisory ratings. *Personnel Psychology*, 1958, *11*, 333–346.

Bartlett, C. J. The relationship between self-ratings and peer ratings on a leadership behavior scale. *Personnel Psychology*, 1959, *12*, 237–246.

Bartlett, F. C. *Remembering*. New York: Macmillan, 1932.

Bartol, K. M., & Butterfield, D. A. Sex effects in evaluating leaders. *Journal of Applied Psychology*, 1976, *61*, 446–454.

Bass, A. R., & Turner, J. N. Ethnic group differences in relationships among criteria of job performance. *Journal of Applied Psychology*, 1973, *57*, 101–109.

Bass, B. M. Reducing leniency in merit ratings. *Personnel Psychology*, 1956, *9*, 359–369.

Bassett, G. A. A study of the effects of task goal and schedule choice on work performance. *Organizational Behavior and Human Performance*, 1979, *24*, 202–227.

Bassett, G. A., & Meyer, H. H. Performance appraisal based on self-review. *Personnel Psychology*, 1968, *21*, 421–430.

Bayroff, A. G., Haggerty, H. R., & Rundquist, E. A. Validity of ratings as related to rating techniques and conditions. *Personnel Psychology*, 1954, *7*, 93–114.

Becker, L. J. Joint effect of feedback and goal setting on performance: A field study of residential energy conservation. *Journal of Applied Psychology*, 1978, *63*, 428–433.

Bellows, R. M. Procedures for evaluating vocational criteria. *Journal of Applied Psychology*, 1941, *25*, 499–513.

Bendig, A. W. A statistical report on a revision of the Miami instructor rating sheet. *Journal of Educational Psychology*, 1952, *43*, 423–429. (a)

Bendig, A. W. The use of student rating scales in the evaluation of instructors in introductory psychology. *Journal of Educational Psychology*, 1952, *43*, 167–175. (b)

Bendig, A. W. The reliability of self-ratings as a function of the amount of verbal anchoring and of the number of categories on the scale. *Journal of Applied Psychology*, 1953, *37*, 38–41.

Bendig, A. W. Reliability and number of rating scale categories. *Journal of Applied Psychology*, 1954, *38*, 38–40. (a)

Bendig, A. W. Reliability of short rating scales and the heterogeneity of the rated stimuli. *Journal of Applied Psychology*, 1954, *38*, 167–170. (b)

Berkshire, J. R., & Highland, R. W. Forced-choice performance rating—A methodological study. *Personnel Psychology*, 1953, *6*, 355–378.

Berlyne, D. E. *Conflict, arousal and curiosity*. New York: McGraw-Hill, 1960.

Berlyne, D. E. Curiosity and exploration. *Science*, 1966, 153, 25–33.

Bernardin, H. J. Behavioral expectation scales versus summated scales: A fairer comparison. *Journal of Applied Psychology*, 1977, *62*, 422–427.

Bernardin, H. J. Effects of rater training on leniency and halo errors in student ratings of instructors. *Journal of Applied Psychology*, 1978, *63*, 301–308.

Bernardin, H. J. *Rater training to enhance accuracy: A look at the big picture*. Paper presented at Performance Appraisal Conference, Old Dominion University, Norfolk, Va., April 1980.

Bernardin, H. J., Alvares, K. M., & Cranny, C. J. A recomparison of behavioral expectation scales to summated scales. *Journal of Applied Psychology*, 1976, *61*, 564–570.

Bernardin, H. J., Cardy, R. L., & Carlyle, J. J. Cognitive complexity and appraisal effectiveness: Back to the drawing board? *Journal of Applied Psychology*, 1982, *67*, 151–160.

Bernardin, H. J., & Kane, J. S. A second look at behavioral observation scales. *Personnel Psychology*, 1980, *33*, 809–814.

Bernardin, H. J., LaShells, M. B., Smith, P. C., & Alvares, K. M. Behavioral expectation scales: Effects of developmental procedures and formats. *Journal of Applied Psychology*, 1976, *61*, 75–79.

Bernardin, H. J., & Pence, E. C. Effects of rater training: Creating new response sets and decreasing accuracy. *Journal of Applied Psychology*, 1980, *65*, 60–66.

Bernardin, H. J., & Smith, P. C. A clarification of some issues regarding the development and use of behaviorally anchored rating scales (BARS). *Journal of Applied Psychology*, 1981, *66*, 458–463.

Bernardin, H. J., & Walter, C. S. Effects of rater training and diary-keeping on psychometric error in ratings. *Journal of Applied Psychology*, 1977, *62*, 64–69.

Berry, N. H., Nelson, P. D., & McNally, M. S. A note on supervisor ratings. *Personnel Psychology*, 1966, *19*, 423–426.

Bigoness, N. J. Effect of applicant's sex, race, and performance on employers' performance ratings: Some additional findings. *Journal of Applied Psychology*, 1976, *61*, 80–84.

Bilodeau, E. A., & Bilodeau, I. McD. Motor skills learning. *Annual Review of Psychology*, 1961, *12*, 243–280.

Bilodeau, I. McD. Information feedback. In E. A. Bilodeau (Ed.), *Acquisition of skill*. New York: Academic Press, 1966.

Blanz, F., & Ghiselli, E. E. The mixed standard scale: A new rating system. *Personnel Psychology*, 1972, *25*, 185–199.

Blood, M. R. Spin-offs from behavioral expectation scale procedures. *Journal of Applied Psychology*, 1974, *59*, 513–515.

Blum, M. L., & Naylor, J. C. *Industrial psychology*. New York: Harper & Row, 1968.

Blumberg, H. H., DeSoto, C. B., & Kuethe, J. L. Evaluations of rating scale formats. *Personnel Psychology*, 1966, *19*, 243–259.

Booker, G. S., & Miller, R. W. A closer look at peer ratings. *Personnel*, 1966, *43*, 42–47.

Borman, W. C. The rating of individuals in organizations: An alternate approach. *Organizational Behavior and Human Performance*, 1974, *12*, 105–124.

Borman, W. C. Effects of instructions to avoid halo error on reliability and validity of performance evaluation ratings. *Journal of Applied Psychology*, 1975, *60*, 556–560.

Borman, W. C. Format and training effects on rating accuracy and rater errors. *Journal of Applied Psychology*, 1979, *64*, 410–421.

Borman, W. C., & Dunnette, M. D. Behavior-based versus trait-oriented performance ratings: An empirical study. *Journal of Applied Psychology*, 1975, *60*, 561–565.

Borman, W. C., & Vallon, W. R. A view of what can happen when behavioral expectation scales are developed in one setting and used in another. *Journal of Applied Psychology*, 1974, *59*, 197–201.

Borresen, H. A. The effects of instructions and item content on three types of ratings. *Educational and Psychological Measurement*, 1967, *27*, 855–862.

Bower, G., Black, J., & Turner, T. Scripts in memory for text. *Cognitive Psychology*, 1979, *11*, 177–220.

Brehmer, B. Cue utilization and cue consistency in multiple-cue probability learning. *Organizational Behavior and Human Performance*, 1972, *8*, 286–296.

Brief, A. P. Peer assessment revisited: A brief comment on Kane and Lawler. *Psychological Bulletin*, 1980, *88*, 78–79.

Brogden, H. E., & Taylor, E. K. The dollar criterion: Applying the cost accounting concept to criterion construction. *Personnel Psychology*, 1950, *3*, 133–154.

Brown, E. M. Influence of training, method, and relationship on the halo effect. *Journal of Applied Psychology*, 1968, *52*, 195–199.

Brumback, G. A reply to Kavanagh. *Personnel Psychology*, 1972, *25*, 567–572.

Bruner, J. S., Goodnow, J. J., & Austin, J. G. *A study of thinking.* New York: Wiley, 1956.

Buckner, D. N. The predictability of ratings as a function of interrater agreement. *Journal of Applied Psychology*, 1959, *43*, 60–64.

Burke, R. J., Weitzel, W., & Weir, T. Characteristics of effective employee performance review and development interviews: Replication and extension. *Personnel Psychology*, 1978, *31*, 903–919.

Burnaska, R. F., & Hollmann, T. D. An empirical comparison of the relative effects of rater response biases on three rating scale formats. *Journal of Applied Psychology*, 1974, *59*, 307–312.

Cameron, K. Measuring organizational effectiveness in institutions of higher education. *Administrative Science Quarterly*, 1978, *23*, 604–632.

Cameron, K. & Whetten, D. A. *Organizational effectiveness: A comparison of multiple models.* New York: Academic Press, 1983.

Campbell, D. T. Systematic error on the part of human links in communication systems. *Information and Control*, 1958, *1*, 334–369.

Campbell, D. T., & Fiske, D. W. Convergent and discriminant validation by the multitrait–multimethod matrix. *Psychological Bulletin*, 1959, *56*, 81–105.

Campbell, D. T., Hunt, W. A., & Lewis, N. A. The relative susceptibility of two rating scales to disturbances resulting from shifts in stimulus context. *Journal of Applied Psychology*, 1958, *42*, 213–217.

Campbell, D. T., & Stanley, J. C. *Experimental and quasi-experimental designs for research.* Chicago: Rand McNally, 1963.

Campbell, J. P. Psychometric theory. In M. D. Dunnette (Ed.), *Handbook of industrial and organizational psychology.* Chicago: Rand McNally, 1976.

Campbell, J. P., Dunnette, M. D., Arvey, R. D., & Hellervik, L. V. The development and evaluation of behaviorally based rating scales. *Journal of Applied Psychology*, 1973, *57*, 15–22.

Campbell, J. P., Dunnette, M. D., Lawler, E. E., III, & Weick, K. E., Jr. *Managerial behavior, performance, and effectiveness.* New York: McGraw-Hill, 1970.

Cantor, N., & Mischel, W. Traits as prototypes: Effects on recognition memory. *Journal of Personality and Social Psychology*, 1977, *35*, 38–48.

Cantor, N., & Mischel, W. Prototypes in person perception. In L. Berkowitz (Ed.), *Advances in experimental social psychology* (Vol. 12). New York: Academic Press, 1979.

Carlston, D. E. The recall and use of traits and events in social information processes. *Journal of Experimental Social Psychology*, 1980, *16*, 303–328.

Carter, G. C. Measurement of supervisory ability. *Journal of Applied Psychology*, 1952, *36*, 393–395.

Cascio, W. Responding to the demand for accountability: A critical analysis of three utility models. *Organizational Behavior and Human Performance*, 1980, *25*, 32–45.

Cascio, W. F., & Bernardin, H. J. *An annotated bibliography of court cases relevant to employment decisions*. Mimeo, Tampa, Fla., 1980.

Cascio, W. F., & Valenzi, E. R. Behaviorally anchored rating scales: Effects of education and job experience of raters and ratees. *Journal of Applied Psychology*, 1977, *62*, 278–282.

Centra, J. A. *The influence of different directions on student ratings of instruction* (ETS RB 75-28). Princeton, N.J.: Educational Testing Service, 1975.

Centra, J. A., & Linn, R. L. *Student points of view in ratings of college instruction* (ETS RB 73-60). Princeton, N.J.: Educational Testing Service, 1973.

Chadwick-Jones, J. K., Brown, C., Nicholson, J., & Sheppard, C. Absence measures: Their reliability and stability in an industrial setting. *Personnel Psychology*, 1971, *24*, 463–470.

Chadwick-Jones, J. K., Nicholson, N., & Brown, C. *Social psychology of absenteeism*. New York: Praeger, 1982.

Chaney, F. B. A cross-cultural study of industrial research performance. *Journal of Applied Psychology*, 1966, *50*, 206–210.

Chaney, F. B., & Teel, K. S. Improving inspector performance through training and visual aids. *Journal of Applied Psychology*, 1967, *51*, 311–315.

Cheloha, R. S., & Farr, J. L. Absenteeism, job involvement, and job satisfaction in an organizational setting. *Journal of Applied Psychology*, 1980, *65*, 467–473.

Cleveland, J. N., & Landy, F. J. The influence of rater and ratee age on two performance judgments. *Personnel Psychology*, 1981, *34*, 19–29.

Cleven, W. A., & Fiedler, F. Interpersonal perceptions of open-hearth foremen and steel production. *Journal of Applied Psychology*, 1956, *40*, 312–314.

Cohen, B., & Chaiken, J. M. *Police background characteristics and performance*. New York: Rand Institute, 1972.

Cohen, C. E. Person categories and social perception: Testing some boundaries of the processing effects of prior knowledge. *Journal of Personality and Social Psychology*, 1981, *40*, 441–452.

Cohen, C., & Ebbesen, E. B. Observational goals and schema activation: A theoretical framework for behavior perception. *Journal of Experimental Social Psychology*, 1979, *15*, 305–329.

Connolly, T., Conlon, E. J., & Deutsch, S. J. Organizational effectiveness: A multiple-constituency approach. *Academy of Management Review*, 1980, *5*, 211–217.

Cooper, W. H. Conceptual similarity as a source of illusory halo in job performance ratings. *Journal of Applied Psychology*, 1981, *66*, 302–307. (a)

Cooper, W. H. Ubiquitous halo. *Psychological Bulletin*, 1981, *90*, 218–244. (b)

Cornelius, E. T., III, Carron, T. J., & Collins, M. N. Job analysis models and job classification. *Personnel Psychology*, 1979, *32*, 693–708.

Cotton, J., & Stoltz, R. E. The general applicability of a scale for rating research productivity. *Journal of Applied Psychology*, 1960, *44*, 276–277.

Cox, J. A., & Krumboltz, J. D. Racial bias in peer ratings of basic airmen. *Sociometry*, 1958, *21*, 292–299.

Cozan, L. W. Forced choice: Better than other rating methods? *Personnel*, 1959, *36*, 80–83.

Crano, W. D., & Brewer, M. B. *Principles of research in social psychology*. New York: McGraw-Hill, 1973.

Cravens, D. W., & Woodruff, R. B. An approach for determining criteria of sales performance. *Journal of Applied Psychology*, 1973, *57*, 242–247.

Creswell, M. B. Effects of confidentiality on performance ratings of professional personnel. *Personnel Psychology*, 1963, *16*, 385–393.

Cronbach, L. J. Coefficient alpha and the internal structure of tests. *Psychometrika*, 1951, *16*, 297–334.

Cronbach, L. J. Processes affecting scores on understanding of others and assumed "similarity." *Psychological Bulletin*, 1955, *52*, 177–193.

Cronbach, L., & Gleser, G. *Psychological tests and personnel decisions*. Urbana: University of Illinois Press, 1965.

Cronbach, L. J., & Meehl, P. E. Construct validity in psychological tests. *Psychological Bulletin*, 1955, *62*, 281–302.

Crooks, L. A. (Ed.). *An investigation of sources of bias in the prediction of job performance: A six-year study*. Princeton, N.J.: Educational Testing Service, 1972.

Cummings, L. L., & Schwab, D. *Performance in organizations: Determinants and appraisals*. Glenview, Ill.: Scott, Foresman and Company, 1973.

Dawes, R. M., & Corrigan, B. Linear models in decision making. *Psychological Bulletin*, 1974, *81*, 95–106.

Deci, E. L. *Intrinsic motivation*. New York: Plenum Press, 1975.

DeJung, J. E., & Kaplan, H. Some differential effects of race of rater and combat attitude. *Journal of Applied Psychology*, 1962, *46*, 370–374.

Dickinson, T. L., & Tice, T. E. A multitrait–multimethod analysis of scales developed by retranslation. *Organizational Behavior and Human Performance*, 1973, *9*, 421–438.

Dickinson, T. L., & Tice, T. E. The discriminant validity of scales developed by retranslation. *Personnel Psychology*, 1977, *30*, 217–228.

Dickinson, T. L., & Zellinger, P. M. A comparison of the behaviorally anchored rating and mixed standard scale formats. *Journal of Applied Psychology*, 1980, *65*, 147–154.

Dipboye, R. L., Arvey, R. D., & Terpstra, D. E. Sex and physical attractiveness of raters and applicants as determinants of resumé evaluations. *Journal of Applied Psychology*, 1977, *62*, 288–294.

Dunnette, M. D. A note on *the* criterion. *Journal of Applied Psychology*, 1963, *47*, 251–254.

Dunnette, M. D., & Borman, W. C. Personnel selection and classification systems. *Annual Review of Psychology*, 1979, *30*, 477–525.

Eckerman, A. C. An analysis of grievances and aggrieved employees in a machine shop and foundry. *Journal of Applied Psychology*, 1948, *32*, 255–269.

Edwards, A. L. *Techniques of attitude scale construction*. New York: Appleton-Century-Crofts, 1957.

Edwards, W. The theory of decision making. *Psychological Bulletin*, 1954, *51*, 380–417.

Einhorn, H. J. Expert measurement and mechanical combination. *Organizational Behavior and Human Performance*, 1972, *7*, 86–106.

Einhorn, H. J., & Hogarth, R. M. Confidence in judgment: Persistence of the illusion of validity. *Psychological Review*, 1978, *85*, 395–416.

Einhorn, H. J., & Hogarth, R. M. Behavioral decision theory: Processes of judgment and choice. *Annual Review of Psychology*, 1981, *32*, 53–88.

Elmore, P. B., & LaPointe, K. Effects of teacher sex and student sex on the evaluation of college instructors. *Journal of Educational Psychology*, 1974, *66*, 386–389.

Elmore, P. B., & LaPointe, K. A. Effect of teacher sex, student sex, and teacher warmth on the evaluation of college instructors. *Journal of Educational Psychology*, 1975, *67*, 368–374.

Enzle, M. E., Hansen, R. D., & Lowe, C. A. Humanizing the mixed-motive paradigm: Methodological implications from attribution theory. *Simulation and Games*, 1975, *6*, 151–165.

Erez, M. Feedback: A necessary condition for the goal setting-performance relationship. *Journal of Applied Psychology*, 1977, *62*, 624–627.

Farr, J. L. Task characteristics, reward contingency, and intrinsic motivation. *Organizational Behavior and Human Performance*, 1976, *16*, 294–307.

Farr, J. L. *Comments on the papers by Bernardin and by Ilgen.* Paper presented at the Conference on Performance Appraisal, Old Dominion University, Norfolk, Va., April, 1980.

Farr, J. L., Enscore, E. E., Dubin, S. S., Cleveland, J. N., & Kozlowski, S. W. J. *Behavior anchored scales: A method for identifying the continuing education needs of engineers.* Final Report, Grant No. SED-78-21940, National Science Foundation. University Park, Pa.: Department of Psychology, The Pennsylvania State University, 1980.

Farr, J. L., O'Leary, B. S., & Bartlett, C. J. Ethnic group membership as a moderator of the prediction of job performance. *Personnel Psychology*, 1971, *24*, 609–636.

Farr, J. L., Vance, R. J., & McIntyre, R. Further examinations of the relationship between reward contingency and intrinsic motivation. *Organizational Behavior and Human Performance*, 1977, *20*, 31–53.

Feigl, H., & Scriven, M. (Eds.). *The foundations of science and the concepts of psychology and psychoanalysis.* Minneapolis: University of Minnesota Press, 1956.

Feild, H. S., & Holley, W. H. *The relationship of performance appraisal system characteristics to verdicts in selected employment discrimination cases.* Mimeo, Auburn University, 1980.

Feldman, J. M. Beyond attribution theory: Cognitive processes in performance appraisal. *Journal of Applied Psychology*, 1981, *66*, 127–148.

Feldman, J. M., & Hilterman. R. J. Stereotype attribution revisited: The role of stimulus characteristics, racial attitude, and cognitive differentiation. *Journal of Personality and Social Psychology*, 1975, *31*, 1177–1188.

Ferguson, L. W. The value of acquaintance ratings in criteria research. *Personnel Psychology*, 1949, *2*, 93–102.

Festinger, L. A theory of social comparison processes. *Human Relations*, 1954, *7*, 117–140.

Finn, R. H. Effects of some variations in rating scale characteristics on the means and reliabilities of ratings. *Educational and Psychological Measurement*, 1972, *32*, 255–265.

Fisher, C. D. The effects of personal control, competence, and extrinsic reward systems on intrinsic motivation. *Organizational Behavior and Human Performance*, 1978, *21*, 273–288.

Fiske, D. W., & Cox, J. A., Jr. The consistency of ratings by peers. *Journal of Applied Psychology*, 1960, *44*, 11–17.

Fitzgibbons, J., & Moch, A. *Employee absenteeism: A summary of research.* Washington, D.C.: Educational Research Service, Inc., 1980.

Fox, H., & Lefkowitz, J. Differential validity: Ethnic group as a moderator in predicting job performance. *Personnel Psychology*, 1974, *27*, 209–223.

Frank, L. L., & Hackman, J. R. Effects of interviewer-interviewee similarity on interviewer objectivity in college admissions interviews. *Journal of Applied Psychology*, 1975, *60*, 356–360.

Freeberg, N. E. Relevance of rater-ratee acquaintance in the validity and reliability of ratings. *Journal of Applied Psychology*, 1969, *53*, 518–524.

Friedlander, F. Performance and orientation structures of research scientists. *Organizational Behavior and Human Performance*, 1971, *6*, 169–183.

Friedman, B. A., & Cornelius, E. T., III. Effect of rater participation in scale construction on the psychometric characteristics of two rating scale formats. *Journal of Applied Psychology*, 1976, *61*, 210–216.

Frieze, I. H., & Weiner, B. Cue utilization and attributional judgments for success and failure. *Journal of Personality*, 1971, *39*, 591–605.

Gaudet, F. J. *Solving the problems of employee absence*. New York: American Management Association, 1963.

Ghiselli, E. E. *Theory of psychological measurement*. New York: McGraw-Hill, 1964.

Ghiselli, E. E. The efficacy of advancement on the basis of merit in relation to structural properties of the organization. *Organizational Behavior and Human Performance*, 1969, *4*, 402–413.

Ghiselli, E. E., & Brown, C. *Personnel and industrial psychology*. New York: McGraw-Hill, 1955.

Ghiselli, E. E., Campbell, J. P., & Zedeck, S. *Measurement theory for the behavioral sciences*. San Francisco: W. H. Freeman and Co., 1981.

Ghiselli, E. E., & Siegel, J. P. Leadership and managerial success in tall and flat organization structures. *Personnel Psychology*, 1972, *25*, 617–624.

Goldstein, I. L. *Training: Program development and evaluation*. Monterey, Calif.: Brooks/Cole, 1974.

Goldstein, I. L., & Mobley, W. H. Error and variability in the visual processing of dental radiographs. *Journal of Applied Psychology*, 1971, *55*, 549–553.

Goodman, P. S., Pennings, J. M., & Associates. *New perspectives on organizational effectiveness*. San Francisco, Calif.: Jossey-Bass, 1977.

Gordon, L. V., & Medlund, F. F. The cross-group stability of peer ratings of leadership potential. *Personnel Psychology*, 1965, *18*, 173–177.

Gordon, M. E. The effect of the correctness of the behavior observed on the accuracy of ratings. *Organizational Behavior and Human Performance*, 1970, *5*, 366–377.

Gordon, M. E. An examination of the relationship between the accuracy and favorability of ratings. *Journal of Applied Psychology*, 1972, *56*, 49–53.

Graesser, A. C., Woll, S. B., Kowalski, D. J., & Smith, D. A. Memory for typical and atypical actions in scripted activities. *Journal of Experimental Psychology: Human Learning and Memory*, 1980, *6*, 503–515.

Grant, D. L. A factor analysis of managers' ratings. *Journal of Applied Psychology*, 1955, *39*, 283–386.

Green, S. G., & Mitchell, T. R. Attributional processes of leaders in leader-member interactions. *Organizational Behavior and Human Performance*, 1979, *23*, 429–458.

Greenhaus, J. H., & Gavin, J. F. The relationship between expectancies and job behavior for white and black employees. *Personnel Psychology*, 1972, *25*, 449–455.

Greller, M. Evaluation of feedback sources as a function of role and organizational level. *Journal of Applied Psychology*, 1980, *65*, 24–27.

Greller, M., & Herold, D. Sources of feedback: A preliminary investigation. *Organizational Behavior and Human Performance*, 1975, *13*, 244–256.

Grey, J., & Kipnis, D. Untangling the performance appraisal dilemma: The influence of perceived organizational context on evaluative processes. *Journal of Applied Psychology*, 1976, *61*, 329–335.

Guilford, J. P. *Psychometric methods* (2nd ed.). New York: McGraw-Hill, 1954.

Guilford, J. P., Christenson, R. R., Taaffe, G., & Wilson, R. C. Ratings should be scrutinized. *Educational and Psychological Measurement*, 1962, *22*, 439–447.

Guion, R. M. Criterion measurement and personnel judgments. *Personnel Psychology*, 1961, *14*, 141–149.

Guion, R. M. *Personnel testing*. New York: McGraw-Hill, 1965.

Gulliksen, H. *Theory of mental tests*. New York: Wiley, 1950.

Gupta, N., Beehr, T. A., & Jenkins, G. D. The relationship between employee gender and supervisor-subordinate cross-ratings. *Proceedings of the Academy of Management*, 1980, *40*, 396–400.

Hackman, J. R., & Porter, L. W. Expectancy theory predictions of work effectiveness. *Organizational Behavior and Human Performance*, 1968, *3*, 417–426.

Hamilton, D. L. A cognitive-attributional analysis of stereotyping. In L. Berkowitz (Ed.), *Advances in experimental social psychology* (Vol. 12). New York: Academic Press, 1979.

Hamilton, D. L., Katz, L., & Leirer, V. Organizational processes in impression formation. In R. Hastie, T. Ostrom, E. Ebbesen, R. Wyer, D. Hamilton, & D. Carlston (Eds.), *Person memory: The cognitive basis of social perception*. Hillsdale, N.J.: Lawrence Erlbaum, 1980.

Hammond, K. R., McClelland, G. H., & Mumpower, J. *Human judgment and decision making*. New York: Praeger, 1980.

Hamner, W. C., Kim, J. S., Baird, L., & Bigoness, W. J. Race and sex as determinants of ratings by potential employers in a simulated work sampling task. *Journal of Applied Psychology*, 1974, *59*, 705–711.

Hanser, L. M., & Muchinsky, P. M. Work as an information environment. *Organizational Behavior and Human Performance*, 1978, *21*, 47–60.

Harris, W. A., & Vincent, N. L. Comparison of performance of sales training graduates and nongraduates. *Journal of Applied Psychology*, 1967, *51*, 436–441.

Harvey, J. H., Town, J. P., & Yarkin, K. L. How fundamental is "the fundamental attribution error"? *Journal of Personality and Social Psychology*, 1981, *40*, 346–349.

Harvey, R. J. The future of partial correlation as a means to reduce halo in performance ratings. *Journal of Applied Psychology*, 1982, *67*, 171–176.

Hastie, R. Memory for behavioral information that confirms or contradicts a personality impression. In R. Hastie, T. Ostrom, E. Ebbesen, R. Wyer, D. Hamilton, & D. Carlston (Eds.), *Person memory: The cognitive basis of social perception*. Hillsdale, N.J.: Lawrence Erlbaum, 1980.

Hastie, R., & Kumar, P. A. Person memory: Personality traits as organizing principles in memory for behaviors. *Journal of Personality and Social Psychology*, 1979, *37*, 25–38.

Hastorf, A. H., Schneider, D. J., & Polefka, J. *Person perception*. Reading, Mass.: Addison-Wesley, 1970.

Hayden, T., & Mischel, W. Maintaining trait consistency in the resolution of behavioral inconsistency: The wolf in sheep's clothing. *Journal of Personality*, 1976, *44*, 109–132.

Hayes, S. C., & Cone, J. D. Reducing residential electrical energy use: Payments, information, and feedback. *Journal of Applied Behavioral Analysis*, 1977, *10*, 425–435.

Hellriegel, D., & White, G. E. Turnover of professionals in public accounting: A comparative analysis. *Personnel Psychology*, 1973, *26*, 239–250.

Helson, H. Adaptation level as a frame of reference for prediction of psychophysical data. *American Journal of Psychology*, 1947, *60*, 1–30.

Hemphill, J. Dimensions of executive positions. *Ohio State Studies in Personnel. Research Monographs*, Ohio State University, Bureau of Business Research, 1960, *98*.

Heneman, H. G., III. Comparisons of self-and superior ratings of managerial performance. *Journal of Applied Psychology*, 1974, *59*, 638–642.

Heron, A. The effects of real-life motivation on questionnaire response. *Journal of Applied Psychology*, 1956, *40*, 65–68.

Higgins, E. T., Rhules, W. S., & Jones, C. Category accessibility and impression formation. *Journal of Experimental Social Psychology*, 1977, *13*, 141–154.

Himmelfarb, S. Integration and attribution theories in personality impression formation. *Journal of Personality and Social Psychology*, 1972, *23*, 309–313.

Hoffman, C., Mischel, W., & Mazze, K. The role of purpose in the organization of information about behavior: Trait-based versus goal-based categories in person cognition. *Journal of Personality and Social Psychology*, 1981, *40*, 211–225.

Hollander, E. P. The reliability of peer nominations under various conditions of administration. *Journal of Applied Psychology*, 1957, *41*, 85–90.

Hollander, E. P. Validity of peer nominations in predicting a distant performance criterion. *Journal of Applied Psychology*, 1965, *49*, 434–438.

Huck, J. R., & Bray, D. W. Management assessment center evaluations and subsequent job performance of white and black females. *Personnel Psychology*, 1976, *29*, 13–30.

Hulin, C. L. The measurement of executive success. *Journal of Applied Psychology*, 1962, *46*, 303–306.

Hulin, C. L. Some reflections on general performance dimensions and halo rating error. *Journal of Applied Psychology*, 1982, *67*, 165–170.

Hull, C. L. *Aptitude testing*. New York: Harcourt, 1928.

Hundal, P. S. Knowledge of performance as an incentive in repetitive industrial work. *Journal of Applied Psychology*, 1969, *53*, 224–226.

Hunter, J. E., Schmidt, F. L., & Pearlman, K. *Assessing the impact of intervention programs on workforce productivity*. Washington, D.C.: U.S. Office of Personnel Management, 1979.

Ilgen, D. R. Attendance behavior: A re-evaluation of Latham and Pursell's conclusions. *Journal of Applied Psychology*, 1977, *62*, 230–233.

Ilgen, D. R., Fisher, C. D., & Taylor, M. S. Consequences of individual feedback on behavior in organizations. *Journal of Applied Psychology*, 1979, *64*, 349–371.

Ilgen, D. R., & Hollenback, J. H. The role of job satisfaction in absence behavior. *Organizational Behavior and Human Performance*, 1977, *19*, 148–161.

Ilgen, D. R., Peterson, R. B., Martin, B. A., & Boeschen, D. A. Supervisor and subordinate reactions to performance appraisal sessions. *Organizational Behavior and Human Performance*, 1981, *28*, 311–330.

Isard, E. S. The relationship between item ambiguity and discriminating power in a forced-choice scale. *Journal of Applied Psychology*, 1956, *40*, 266–268.

Isley, R. N., & Caro, P. W. Use of time-lapse photography in flight performance evaluation. *Journal of Applied Psychology*, 1970, *54*, 72–76.

Ivancevich, J. M. The performance to satisfaction relationship: A causal analysis of stimulating and nonstimulating jobs. *Organizational Behavior and Human Performance*, 1978, *22*, 350–365.

Ivancevich, J. M. Longitudinal study of the effects of rater training on psychometric error in ratings. *Journal of Applied Psychology*, 1979, *64*, 502–508.

Ivancevich, J. M. A longitudinal study of behavioral expectation scales: Attitudes and performance. *Journal of Applied Psychology*, 1980, *65*, 139–146.

Jacobs, R., Kafry, D., & Zedeck, S. Expectations of behaviorally anchored rating scales. *Personnel Psychology*, 1980, *33*, 595–640.

Jacobson, M. B., & Effertz, J. Sex roles and leadership: Perceptions of the leaders and the led. *Organizational Behavior and Human Performance*, 1974, *12*, 383–396.

James, L. R. Criterion models and construct validity for criteria. *Psychological Bulletin*, 1973, *80*, 75–83.

Jay, R., & Copes, J. Seniority and criterion measures of job proficiency. *Journal of Applied Psychology*, 1957, *41*, 58–60.

Jeffery, K. M., & Mischel, W. Effects of purpose on the organization and recall of information in person perception. *Journal of Personality*, 1979, *47*, 397–419.

Jenkins, G. D., & Taber, T. A Monte Carlo study of factors affecting three indices of composite scale reliability. *Journal of Applied Psychology*, 1977, *62*, 392–398.

Johnson, D. M. Reanalysis of experimental halo effects. *Journal of Applied Psychology*, 1963, *47*, 46–47.

Johnson, G. A. The relative efficacy of stimulus vs. reinforcement control for obtaining stable performance change. *Organizational Behavior and Human Performance*, 1975, *14*, 321–341.

Jones, E. E., & Davis, K. E. From acts to dispositions. In L. Berkowitz (Ed.), *Advances in experimental social psychology* (Vol. 2). New York: Academic Press, 1965.

Jurgensen, C. E. Intercorrelations in merit rating traits. *Journal of Applied Psychology*, 1950, *34*, 240–243.

Jurgensen, C. E. Item weights in employee rating scales. *Journal of Applied Psychology*, 1955, *39*, 305–307.

Kafry, D., Jacobs, R., & Zedeck, S. Discriminability in multidimensional performance evaluations. *Applied Psychological Measurement*, 1979, *3*, 187–192.

Kahneman, D., & Tversky, A. Subjective probability: A judgment of representativeness. *Cognitive Psychology*, 1972, *3*, 430–454.

Kahneman, D., & Tversky, A. On the psychology of prediction. *Psychological Review*, 1973, *80*, 237–251.

Kalleberg, A. L., & Kluegel, J. R. Analysis of the multitrait–multimethod matrix: Some limitations and an alternative. *Journal of Applied Psychology*, 1975, *60*, 1–9.

Kane, J. S., & Lawler, E. E., III. Methods of peer assessment. *Psychological Bulletin*, 1978, *85*, 555–586.

Kane, J. S., & Lawler, E. E., III. Performance appraisal effectiveness: Its assessment and determinants. In B. M. Staw (Ed.), *Research in organizational behavior* (Vol. 1). Greenwich, Conn.: JAI Press, 1979.

Kane, J. S., & Lawler, E. E. In defense of peer assessment: A rebuttal to Brief's critique. *Psychological Bulletin*, 1980, *88*, 80–81.

Kaufman, G. G., & Johnson, J. C. Scaling peer ratings: An examination of the differential validities of positive and negative nominations. *Journal of Applied Psychology*, 1974, *59*, 302–306.

Kavanagh, M. J. The content issue in performance appraisal: A review. *Personnel Psychology*, 1971, *24*, 653–668.

Kavanagh, M. J. Rejoinder to Brumback "The content issue in performance appraisal: A review." *Personnel Psychology*, 1973, *26*, 163–166.

Kavanagh, M. J., MacKinney, A. C., & Wolins, L. Issues in managerial performance: Multitrait–multimethod analysis of ratings. *Psychological Bulletin*, 1971, *75*, 34–49.

Kay, B. R. The use of critical incidents in a forced-choice scale. *Journal of Applied Psychology*, 1959, *43*, 269–270.

Kay, E., Meyer, H. H., & French, J. R. P. Effects of threat in a performance appraisal interview. *Journal of Applied Psychology*, 1965, *49*, 311–317.

Keaveny, T. J., & McGann, A. F. A comparison of behavioral expectation scales and graphic rating scales. *Journal of Applied Psychology*, 1975, *60*, 695–703.

Kelley, H. H. Attribution theory in social psychology. In Levine, D. (Ed.), *Nebraska Symposium on Motivation* (Vol. 15). 1967, 192–238.

Kelley, H. H. Attribution in social interaction. In E. E. Jones, D. E. Kanouse, H. H. Kelley, R. E. Nisbett, S. Valins, & B. Weiner, (Eds.), *Attribution: Perceiving the causes of behavior*. Morristown, N.J.: General Learning Press, 1972.

Kelley, H. H., & Michela, J. L. Attribution theory and research. *Annual Review of Psychology*, 1980, *31*, 457–501.

Kidd, J. S., & Christy, R. T. Supervisory procedures and work-term productivity. *Journal of Applied Psychology*, 1961, *45*, 388–392.

Kilbridge, M. Turnover, absence, and transfer rates as indicators of employee dissatisfaction with repetitive work. *Industrial and Labor Relations Review*, 1961, *15*, 21–32.

Kingstrom, P. O., & Bass, A. R. A critical analysis of studies comparing behaviorally anchored rating scales (BARS) and other rating formats. *Personnel Psychology*, 1981, *34*, 263–289.

Kirchner, W. K. Predicting ratings of sales success with objective performance information. *Journal of Applied Psychology*, 1960, *44*, 398–403.

Kirchner, W. K. Relationships between general and specific attitudes toward work and objective job performance for outdoor advertising salesmen. *Journal of Applied Psychology*, 1965, *49*, 455–457. (a)

Kirchner, W. K. Relationships between supervisory and subordinate ratings for technical personnel. *Journal of Industrial Psychology*, 1965, *3*, 57–60. (b)

Kirchner, W. K., & Reisberg, D. J. Differences between better and less effective supervisors in appraisal of subordinates. *Personnel Psychology*, 1962, *15*, 295–302.

Kirkpatrick, D. L. Techniques for evaluating training programs. *Journal of the American Society of Training Directors*, 1959, *13*, 3–9, 21–26.

Kirkpatrick, J. J., Ewen, R. B., Barrett, R. S., & Katzell, R. A. *Testing and fair employment*. New York: New York University Press, 1968.

Klieger, W. A., & Mosel, J. N. The effect of opportunity to observe and rater status on the reliability of performance ratings. *Personnel Psychology*, 1953, *6*, 57–64.

Klimoski, R. J., & London, M. Role of the rater in performance appraisal. *Journal of Applied Psychology*, 1974, *59*, 445–451.

Klimoski, R. J., & Strickland, W. J. Assessment centers—valid or merely prescient. *Personnel Psychology*, 1977, *30*, 353–361.

Klores, M. S. Rater bias in forced-distribution ratings. *Personnel Psychology*, 1966, *19*, 411–421.

Komaki, J., Barwick, K. D., & Scott, L. R. A behavioral approach to occupational safety: Pinpointing and reinforcing safe performance in a food manufacturing plant. *Journal of Applied Psychology*, 1978, *63*, 434–445.

Korman, A. K. Toward a hypothesis of work behavior. *Journal of Applied Psychology*, 1970, *54*, 31–41.

Korman, A. K. A hypothesis of work behavior revisited and an extension. *Academy of Management Review*, 1976, *1*, 50–63.

Kraut, A. I. Intellectual ability and promotional success among high level managers. *Personnel Psychology*, 1969, *22*, 281–290.

Kraut, A. I. Prediction of managerial success by peer and training-staff ratings. *Journal of Applied Psychology*, 1975, *60*, 14–19.

Lahey, M. A., & Saal, F. E. Evidence incompatible with a cognitive compatibility theory of rating behavior. *Journal Applied Psychology*, 1981, *66*, 706–715.

Lamouria, L. H., & Harrell, T. W. An approach to an objective criterion for research managers. *Journal of Applied Psychology*, 1963, *47*, 353–357.

Landy, F. J. Discussion. In S. Zedeck (Chair), *A closer look at performance appraisal through behavioral expectation scales.* Symposium presented at the meeting of the American Psychological Association, San Francisco, August 1977.

Landy, F. J., Barnes, J., & Murphy, K. Correlates of perceived fairness and accuracy in performance appraisal. *Journal of Applied Psychology*, 1978, *63*, 751–754.

Landy, F. J., Barnes-Farrell, J., & Cleveland, J. Perceived fairness and accuracy of performance evaluation: A follow-up. *Journal of Applied Psychology*, 1980, *65*, 355–356.

Landy, F. J., & Farr, J. L. Police performance appraisal. *JSAS Catalog of Selected Documents in Psychology*, 1976, *6*, 83. (Ms. No. 1315)

Landy, F. J., & Farr, J. L. Performance rating. *Psychological Bulletin*, 1980, *87*, 72–107.

Landy, F. J., Farr, J. L., & Jacobs, R. R. Utility concepts in performance measurement. *Organizational Behavior and Human Performance*, 1982, *30*, 15–40.

Landy, F. J., Farr, J. L., Saal, F. G., & Freytag, W. R. Behaviorally anchored scales for rating the performance of police officers. *Journal of Applied Psychology*, 1976, *61*, 752–758.

Landy, F. J., & Guion, R. M. Development of scales for the measurement of work motivation. *Organizational Behavior and Human Performance*, 1970, *5*, 93–103.

Landy, F. J., Hedrick, K. L., & Bellamy, R. *The reliability of absence measures.* Unpublished manuscript, Pennsylvania State University, 1982.

Landy, F. J., & Trumbo, D. A. *The psychology of work behavior* (Rev. ed.). Homewood, Ill.: Dorsey Press, 1980.

Landy, F. J., Vance, R. J., & Barnes-Farrell, J. L. Statistical control of halo: A response. *Journal of Applied Psychology*, 1982, *67*, 177–180.

Landy, F. J., Vance, R. J., Barnes-Farrell, J. L., & Steele, J. W. Statistical control of halo error in performance ratings. *Journal of Applied Psychology*, 1980, *65*, 501–506.

Langer, E. J. Rethinking the role of thought in social interaction. In J. H. Harvey, W. J. Ickes, & R. F. Kidd (Eds.), *New directions in attribution research* (Vol. 2). Hillsdale, N.J.: Lawrence Erlbaum, 1978.

Langer, E. J., Taylor, S. E., Fiske, S., & Chanowitz, B. Stigma, staring, and discomfort: A novel-stimulus hypothesis. *Journal of Experimental Social Psychology*, 1976, *12*, 451–463.

Lanzetta, J. T. The motivational properties of uncertainty. In H. I. Day, D. E. Berlyne, & D. E. Hunt (Eds.), *Intrinsic motivation: A new direction in education.* Toronto: Holt, Rinehart & Winston of Canada, 1971.

Latham, G. P., & Baldes, J. J. The "practical significance" of Locke's theory of goal setting. *Journal of Applied Psychology*, 1975, *60*, 122–124.

Latham, G., Fay, C., & Sarri, L. The development of behavioral observation scales for appraising the performance of foremen. *Personnel Psychology*, 1979, *32*, 299–311.

Latham, G. P., & Kinne, J. D. Improving job performance through training in goal-setting. *Journal of Applied Psychology*, 1974, *59*, 187–191.

Latham, G. P., & Locke, E. A. Increasing productivity with decreasing time limits: A field replication of Parkinson's law. *Journal of Applied Psychology*, 1975, *60*, 524–526.

Latham, G. P., & Pursell, E. D. Measuring absenteeism from the opposite side of the coin. *Journal of Applied Psychology*, 1975, *60*, 369–371.

Latham, G., Saari, L., & Fay, C. BOS, BES, and baloney: Raising Kane with Bernardin. *Personnel Psychology*, 1980, *33*, 815–821.

Latham, G. P., & Wexley, K. N. Behavioral observation scales for performance appraisal purposes. *Personnel Psychology*, 1977, *30*, 255–268.

Latham, G. P., & Wexley, K. N. *Increasing productivity through performance appraisal*. Reading, Mass.: Addison-Wesley, 1981.

Latham, G. P., Wexley, K. N., & Pursell, E. D. Training managers to minimize rating errors in the observation of behavior. *Journal of Applied Psychology*, 1975, *60*, 550–555.

Lawler, E. E., III. The multitrait–multirater approach to measuring managerial job performance. *Journal of Applied Psychology*, 1967, *51*, 369–381.

Lawler, E. E., III. *Pay and organizational effectiveness: A psychological view*. New York: McGraw-Hill, 1971.

Lawler, E. E., III. *Motivation in work organizations*. Monterey, Calif.: Brooks/Cole, 1973.

Lawler, E. E., III., Hall, D. T., & Oldham, G. R. Organizational climate: Relationship to organizational structure, process, and performance. *Organizational Behavior and Human Performance*, 1974, *11*, 139–155.

Lawshe, C. H. A quantitative approach to content validity. *Personnel Psychology*, 1975, *28*, 563–575.

Lay, C. H., Burron, B. F., & Jackson, D. N. Base rates and informational value in impression formation. *Journal of Personality and Social Psychology*, 1973, *28*, 390–395.

Lee, D., & Alvares, K. Effect of sex on descriptions and evaluations of supervisory behavior in a simulated industrial setting. *Journal of Applied Psychology*, 1977, *62*, 405–410.

Lefkowitz, J. Effect of training on the productivity and tenure of sewing machine operators. *Journal of Applied Psychology*, 1970, *54*, 81–86.

Lepkowski, J. R. Development of a forced-choice rating scale for engineer evaluation. *Journal of Applied Psychology*, 1963, *47*, 87–88.

Leventhal, L., Perry, R. P., & Abrami, P. C. Effect of lecturer quality and student perception of lecturer's experience on teacher ratings. *Journal of Educational Psychology*, 1977, *69*, 360–374.

Levine, E. L. Introductory remarks for the symposium "Organizational applications of self-appraisal and self-assessment: Another look." *Personnel Psychology*, 1980, *33*, 259–262.

Lewis, N. A., & Taylor, J. A. Anxiety and extreme response preferences. *Educational and Psychological Measurement*, 1955, *15*, 111–116.

Lingle, J. H., & Ostrom, T. M. Retrieval selectivity in memory based impression judgments. *Journal of Personality and Social Psychology*, 1979, *37*, 180–194.

Lissitz, R. W., & Green, S. B. Effect of the number of scale points on reliability: A Monte Carlo approach. *Journal of Applied Psychology*, 1975, *60*, 10–13.

Locke, E. A. Motivational effects of knowledge of results: Knowledge or goal setting? *Journal of Applied Psychology*, 1967, *51*, 324–329.

Locke, E. A. Toward a theory of task motivation and incentives. *Organizational Behavior and Human Performance*, 1968, *3*, 157–189.

Locke, E. A. Personnel attitudes and motivation. *Annual Review of Psychology*, 1975, *26*, 457–480.

Locke, E. A., & Bryan, J. F. Knowledge of score and goal level as determinants of work rate. *Journal of Applied Psychology*, 1969, *53*, 59–65.

Locke, E. A., Bryan, J. F., & Kendall, L. M. Goals and intentions as mediators of the effects of monetary incentives on behavior. *Journal of Applied Psychology*, 1968, *52*, 104–121.

Locke, E. A., Cartledge, N., & Koeppel, J. Motivational effects of knowledge of results: A goal-setting phenomenon. *Psychological Bulletin*, 1968, *70*, 474–485.

Locke, E. A., & Schweiger, D. M. Participation in decision-making: One more look. In B. M. Staw (Ed.), *Research in organizational behavior* (Vol. 1). Greenwich, Conn.: JAI Press, 1979.

Locke, E. A., Shaw, K. N., Saari, L. M., & Latham, G. P. Goal setting and task performance: 1969–1980. *Psychological Bulletin*, 1981, *90*, 125–152.

London, M., & Poplawski, J. R. Effects of information on stereotype development in performance appraisal and interview context. *Journal of Applied Psychology*, 1976, *61*, 199–205.

Lord, F. M., & Novick, M. R. *Statistical theories of mental test scores*. Reading, Mass.: Addison-Wesley, 1968.

Maas, J. B. Patterned scaled expectation interview: Reliability studies on a new technique. *Journal of Applied Psychology*, 1965, *59*, 431–433.

McArthur, L. Z. What grabs you? The role of attention in impression formation and causal attribution. In E. T. Higgins, C. P. Herman, & M. P. Zanna (Eds.), *Social cognition: The Ontario symposium on personality and social psychology*. Hillsdale, N.J.: Lawrence Erlbaum, 1980.

McCormick, E. J. *Job analysis: Methods and applications*. New York: Amacom, 1979.

McCormick, E. J., & Bachus, J. A. Paired comparison ratings: I. The effect on ratings of reductions in the number of pairs. *Journal of Applied Psychology*, 1952, *36*, 123–127.

McCormick, E. J., & Ilgen, D. R. *Industrial psychology* (7th ed.). Englewood Cliffs, N.J.: Prentice-Hall, 1980.

McCormick, E. J., Jeanneret, P. R., & Mecham, R. C. A study of job characteristics and job dimensions as based on the Position Analysis Questionnaire (PAQ). *Journal of Applied Psychology Monograph*, 1972, *56*, 347–368.

McCormick, E. J., & Roberts, W. K. Paired comparison ratings: II. The reliability of ratings based on partial pairings. *Journal of Applied Psychology*, 1952, *36*, 188–192.

McCormick, E. J., & Tiffin, J. *Industrial psychology* (6th ed.). Englewood Cliffs, N.J.: Prentice-Hall, 1974.

McGregor, D. An uneasy look at performance appraisal. *Harvard Business Review*, 1957, *35*, 89–94.

McGregor, D. *The human side of enterprise*. New York: McGraw-Hill, 1959.

Mai-Dalton, R. R., Feldman-Summers, S., & Mitchell, T. R. Effect of employee gender and behavioral style on the evaluations of male and female banking executives. *Journal of Applied Psychology*, 1979, *64*, 221–226.

Mandell, M. M. Supervisory characteristics and ratings: A summary of recent research. *Personnel Psychology*, 1956, *32*, 435–440.

March, J. G., & Simon, H. A. *Organizations*. New York: Wiley, 1958.

Meglino, B., Cafferty, T., DeNisi, A., & Youngblood, S. *A cognitive view of the performance appraisal process*. Paper presented at the 89th Annual Convention of the American Psychological Association, Los Angeles, August 1981.

Meyer, H. H. Methods for scoring a check-list type rating scale. *Journal of Applied Psychology*, 1951, *35*, 46–49.

Meyer, H. H. *Performance review discussion: Making it constructive*. Paper presented at the

Annual Convention of the American Psychological Association, Washington, D. C., August 1976.

Meyer, H. H. Self-appraisal of job performance. *Personnel Psychology*, 1980, *33*, 291–295.

Meyer, H., Kay, E., & French, J. R. Split roles in performance appraisal. *Harvard Business Review*, 1965, *43*, 123–129.

Meyer, H. H., & Walker, W. B. A study of factors relating to the effectiveness of a performance appraisal program. *Personnel Psychology*, 1961, *14*, 291–298.

Miller, G. A. The magical number seven, plus or minus two: Some limits on our capacity for processing information. *Psychological Review*, 1956, *63*, 81–97.

Miner, J. B. Management appraisal: A review of procedures and practices. In H. L. Tosi, R. J. House, & M. D. Dunnette (Eds.), *Managerial motivation and compensation*. East Lansing: Michigan State University, Graduate School of Business Administration, 1972.

Mischel, H. N. Sex bias in the evaluation of professional achievements. *Journal of Educational Psychology*, 1974, *66*, 157–166.

Mitchell, T. R. Expectancy models of job satisfaction, occupational preference, and effort: A theoretical, methodological, and empirical appraisal. *Psychological Bulletin*, 1974, *81*, 1053–1077.

Moore, L. F., & Lee, A. J. Comparability of interviewer, group, and individual interview ratings. *Journal of Applied Psychology*, 1974, *59*, 163–167.

Mosier, C. I. Psychophysics and mental test theory: Fundamental postulates and elementary theorems. *Psychological Review*, 1940, *47*, 355–366.

Mowday, R. T., Porter, L. W., & Steers, R. M. *Employee-organization linkages: The psychology of commitment, absenteeism, and turnover*. New York: Academic Press, 1981.

Muchinsky, P. M. Employee absenteeism: A review of the literature. *Journal of Vocational Behavior*, 1977, *10*, 316–340.

Mullins, C. J., & Force, R. C. Rater accuracy as a generalized ability. *Journal of Applied Psychology*, 1962, *46*, 191–193.

Munsterberg, H. *Psychology: General and applied*. New York: D. Appleton and Company, 1914.

Murphy, K. R. Difficulties in the statistical control of halo. *Journal of Applied Psychology*, 1982, *67*, 161–164.

Murphy, K. R., Martin, C., & Garcia, M. Do behavioral observation scales measure observation? *Journal of Applied Psychology*, 1982, *67*, 562–567.

Myers, J. H. Removing halo from job evaluation factor structure. *Journal of Applied Psychology*, 1965, *49*, 217–221.

Nadler, D. A. The effects of feedback on task group behavior: A review of the experimental literature. *Organizational Behavior and Human Performance*, 1979, *23*, 309–338.

Naylor, J. C., Pritchard, R. D., & Ilgen, D. R. *A theory of behavior in organizations*. New York: Academic Press, 1980.

Naylor, J. C., & Wherry, R. J., Sr. The use of simulated stimuli and the "JAN" technique to capture and cluster the policies of raters. *Educational and Psychological Measurement*, 1965, *25*, 969–986.

Neibel, B. W. *Motion and time study* (7th ed.). Homewood, Ill.: Irwin, 1982.

Newman, J. E. Predicting absenteeism and turnover: A field comparison of Fishbein's model and traditional job attitude measures. *Journal of Applied Psychology*, 1974, *59*, 610–615.

Newman, R. I., Hunt, D. L., & Rhodes, F. Effects of music on employee attitude and productivity in a skateboard factory. *Journal of Applied Psychology*, 1966, *50*, 493–496.

Nisbett, R., & Ross, L. *Human inference: Strategies and shortcomings of social judgment*. Englewood Cliffs, N.J.: Prentice-Hall, 1980.

Nisbett, R. E., & Wilson, T. D. Telling more than we can know: Verbal reports on mental processes. *Psychological Review*, 1977, *84*, 231–259.

Norman, W. T., & Goldberg, L. R. Rater, ratees, and randomness in personality structure. *Journal of Personality and Social Psychology*, 1966, *4*, 681–691.

Nunnally, J. C. *Psychometric theory* (2nd ed.). New York: McGraw-Hill, 1978.

Obradovic, J. Modification of the forced-choice method as a criterion of job proficiency. *Journal of Applied Psychology*, 1970, *54*, 228–233.

Overall, J. E. Reliability of composite ratings. *Educational and Psychological Measurement*, 1965, *25*, 1011–1022.

Pace, R. W. Oral communication and sales effectiveness. *Journal of Applied Psychology*, 1962, *46*, 321–324.

Parker, J. W., Taylor, E. K., Barrett, R. S., & Martens, L. Rating scale content: 3. Relationship between supervisory and self-ratings. *Personnel Psychology*, 1959, *12*, 49–63.

Passini, F. T., & Norman, W. T. Ratee relevance in peer nominations. *Journal of Applied Psychology*, 1969, *53*, 185–187.

Payne, R. B., & Hauty, G. T. The effect of psychological feedback on work decrement. *Journal of Experimental Psychology*, 1955, *50*, 343–351.

Peter, L., & Hull, R. *The Peter Principle*. New York: William Morrow, 1969.

Peters, D. L., & McCormick, E. J. Comparative reliability of numerically anchored versus job-task anchored rating scales. *Journal of Applied Psychology*, 1966, *50*, 92–96.

Peterson, C. R. Introduction to special issue on hierarchical inference. *Organizational Behavior and Human Performance*, 1973, *10*, 315–317.

Porter, L. W., Crampon, W. J., & Smith, F. S. Organizational commitment and managerial turnover: A longitudinal study. *Organizational Behavior and Human Performance*, 1976, *15*, 87–98.

Porter, L. W., & Lawler, E. E., III. *Managerial attitudes and performance*. Homewood, Ill.: Dorsey Press, 1968.

Prien, E. P., & Ronan, W. W. Job analysis: A review of research findings. *Personnel Psychology*, 1971, *24*, 371–396.

Pulakos, E. D., & Wexley, K. N. The relationship among perceptual similarity, sex and performance ratings in manager-subordinate dyads. *Academy of Management Journal*, 1982, in press.

Pursell, E. D., Dossett, D. L., & Latham, G. P. Obtaining valid predictors by minimizing rating errors in the criterion. *Personnel Psychology*, 1980, *33*, 91–96.

Ritti, R. R. Control of "halo" in factor analysis of a supervisory behavior inventory. *Personnel Psychology*, 1964, *17*, 305–318.

Roach, D. E., & Wherry, R. J. Performance dimensions of multi-line insurance agents. *Personnel Psychology*, 1970, *23*, 239–250.

Robinson, D. D. Prediction of clerical turnover in banks by means of a weighted application blank. *Journal of Applied Psychology*, 1972, *56*, 282.

Ronan, W. W., & Prien, E. P. *Toward a criterion theory: A review and analysis of research and opinion*. Greensboro, N.C.: Creativity Institute of the Richardson Foundation, 1966.

Ronan, W. W., & Prien, E. P. *Perspectives on the measurement of human performance*. New York: Appleton-Century-Crofts, 1971.

Rosch, E. On the internal structure of perceptual and semantic categories. In T. E. Moore (Ed.), *Cognitive development and the acquisition of language*. New York: Academic Press, 1973.

Rosch, E. Principles of categorization. In E. Rosch & B. B. Lloyd (Eds.), *Cognition and categorization*. Hillsdale, N.J.: Lawrence Erlbaum, 1978.

Rosch, E., & Mervis, C. B. Family resemblances: Studies in the internal structure of categories. *Cognitive Psychology*, 1975, *7*, 573–605.

Rosch, E., Mervis, C. B., Gray, W. D., Johnson, D. M., & Boyes-Braem, P. Basic objects in natural categories. *Cognitive Psychology*, 1976, *8*, 382–439.

Rose, G. L. Sex effects on effort attributions in managerial performance evaluation. *Organizational Behavior and Human Performance*, 1978, *21*, 367–378.

Rosen, B., & Jerdee, T. H. The influence of sex role stereotypes on evaluations of male and female supervisory behavior. *Journal of Applied Psychology*, 1973, *57*, 44–48.

Ross, L. The intuitive psychologist and his shortcomings. In L. Berkowitz (Ed.), *Advances in experimental social psychology* (Vol. 10). New York: Academic Press, 1977.

Ross, L., Lepper, M. R., & Hubbard, M. Perseverance in self perception and social perception: Biased attributional processes in the debriefing paradigm. *Journal of Personality and Social Psychology*, 1975, *32*, 880–892.

Rothaus, P., Morton, R. B., & Hanson, P. G. Performance appraisal and psychological distance. *Journal of Applied Psychology*, 1965, *49*, 48–54.

Rothe, H. F. The relation of merit ratings to length of service. *Personnel Psychology*, 1949, *2*, 237–242.

Rothe, H. F. Output rates among industrial employees. *Journal of Applied Psychology*, 1978, *63*, 40–46.

Rothe, H. F., & Nye, C. T. Output rates among coil winders. *Journal of Applied Psychology*, 1958, *42*, 182–186.

Rotter, G. S., & Tinkleman, V. Anchor effects in the development of behavior rating scales. *Educational and Psychological Measurement*, 1970, *30*, 311–318.

Rotter, J. B. Generalized expectancies for internal versus external control of reinforcement. *Psychological Monographs*, 1966, *80*(1, Whole No. 609).

Rusmore, J. T. Position description factors and executive promotion. *Personnel Psychology*, 1973, *26*, 135–138.

Saal, F. E. Mixed standard rating scale: A consistent system for numerically coding inconsistent response combinations. *Journal of Applied Psychology*, 1979, *64*, 422–428.

Saal, F. E., Downey, R. G., & Lahey, M. A. Rating the ratings: Assessing the psychometric quality of rating data. *Psychological Bulletin*, 1980, *88*, 413–428.

Saal, F. E., & Landy, F. J. The mixed standard rating scale: An evaluation. *Organizational Behavior and Human Performance*, 1977, *18*, 19–35.

Sauser, W. I., Jr., & Pond, S. B., III. Effects of rater training and participation on cognitive complexity: An exploration of Schneier's cognitive reinterpretation. *Personnel Psychology*, 1981, *34*, 563–577.

Schank, R., & Abelson, R. P. *Scripts, plans, goals, and understanding*. Hillsdale, N.J.: Lawrence Erlbaum, 1977.

Schein, V. E. The relationship between sex role stereotypes and requisite management characteristics. *Journal of Applied Psychology*, 1973, *57*, 95–100.

Schein, V. E. Relationships between sex role stereotypes and requisite management characteristics among female managers. *Journal of Applied Psychology*, 1975, *60*, 340–344.

Schmidt, F., Hunter, J., McKenzie, R., & Muldrow, T. Impact of valid selection procedures on work-force productivity. *Journal of Applied Psychology*, 1979, *64*, 609–626.

Schmidt, F. L., & Johnson, R. H. Effect of race on peer ratings in an industrial setting. *Journal of Applied Psychology*, 1973, *57*, 237–241.

Schmitt, N., & Hill, T. Sex and race composition of assessment center groups as a determinant of peer and assessor ratings. *Journal of Applied Psychology*, 1977, *62*, 261–264.

Schmitt, N., & Lappin, M. Race and sex as determinants of the mean and variance of performance ratings. *Journal of Applied Psychology*, 1980, *65*, 428–435.

Schneider, D. E., & Bayroff, A. G. The relationship between rater characteristics and validity of ratings. *Journal of Applied Psychology*, 1953, *37*, 278–280.

Schneider, W., & Shiffrin, R. M. Controlled and automatic human information processing: I. Detection, search, and attention. *Psychological Review*, 1977, *84*, 1–66.

Schneier, C. E. Operational utility and psychometric characteristics of behavioral expectation scales: A cognitive reinterpretation. *Journal of Applied Psychology*, 1977, *62*, 541–548.

Schneier, C. E., & Beusse, W. E. The impact of sex and time in grade on management rating in the public sector: Prospects for the Civil Service Reform Act. *Proceedings of the Academy of Management*, 1980, *40*, 329–333.

Schultz, D. G., & Siegel, A. I. The analysis of job performance by multidimensional scaling techniques. *Journal of Applied Psychology*, 1964, *48*, 329–335.

Schwab, D. P., & Heneman, H. G. Age stereotyping in performance appraisal. *Journal of Applied Psychology*, 1978, *63*, 573–578.

Schwab, D. P., Heneman, H. G., III, & DeCotiis, T. Behaviorally anchored rating scales: A review of the literature. *Personnel Psychology*, 1975, *28*, 549–562.

Scott, W. E., Jr., & Hamner, W. C. The influence of variations in performance profiles on the performance evaluation process: An examination of the validity of the criterion. *Organizational Behavior and Human Performance*, 1975, *14*, 360–370.

Seligman, C., & Darley, J. M. Feedback as a means of decreasing residential energy consumption. *Journal of Applied Psychology*, 1977, *62*, 363–368.

Shapira, Z., & Shirom, A. New issues in the use of behaviorally anchored rating scales: Level of analysis, the effects of incident frequency, and external validation. *Journal of Applied Psychology*, 1980, *65*, 517–523.

Sharon, A. T. Eliminating bias from student ratings of college instructors. *Journal of Applied Psychology*, 1970, *54*, 278–281.

Sharon, A. T., & Bartlett, C. J. Effect of instructional conditions in producing leniency on two types of rating scales. *Personnel Psychology*, 1969, *22*, 251–263.

Sherif, C. W., Sherif, M., & Nebergall, R. E. *Attitude and attitude change*. Philadelphia, Pa.: Saunders, 1965.

Shiffrin, R. M., & Schneider, W. Controlled and automatic human information processing: II. Perceptual learning, automatic attending, and a general theory. *Psychological Review*, 1977, *84*, 127–190.

Shultz, T. R., & Ravinsky, F. B. Similarity as a principle of causal inference. *Child Development*, 1977, *48*, 1552–1558.

Slovic, P., Fischhoff, B., & Lichtenstein, S. Behavioral decision theory. *Annual Review of Psychology*, 1977, *28*, 1–39.

Slovic, P., & Lichtenstein, S. C. Comparison of Bayesian and regression approaches to the study of information processing in judgment. *Organizational Behavior and Human Performance*, 1971, *6*, 649–744.

Smith, P. C. Behaviors, results, and organizational effectiveness: The problem of criteria. In M. D. Dunnette (Ed.), *Handbook of industrial and organizational psychology*. Chicago: Rand McNally, 1976.

Smith, P. C., & Kendall, L. M. Retranslation of expectations: An approach to the construction of unambiguous anchors for rating scales. *Journal of Applied Psychology*, 1963, *47*, 149–155.

Smith, P. E. Management modeling training to improve morale and customer satisfaction. *Personnel Psychology*, 1976, *29*, 351–359.

Smulders, P. G. Comments on employee absence/attendance as a dependent variable in organizational research. *Journal of Applied Psychology*, 1980, *65*, 368–371.

Snyder, M., & Cantor, N. Testing hypotheses about people: The use of historical knowledge. *Journal of Experimental Social Psychology*, 1979, *15*, 330–342.

Snyder, R. A., Raben, C. S., & Farr, J. L. A conceptual model for the systemic evaluation of human resource development programs. *Academy of Management Review*, 1980, *5*, 431–444.

Snyder, M., & Swann, W. B., Jr. Behavioral confirmation in social interaction: From social perception to social reality. *Journal of Experimental Social Psychology*, 1978, *14*, 148–162. (a)

Snyder, M., & Swann, W. B., Jr. Hypothesis-testing processes in social interaction. *Journal of Personality and Social Psychology*, 1978, *36*, 1202–1212. (b)

Solomon, R. L. An extension of control group design. *Psychological Bulletin*, 1949, *46*, 137–150.

Spielberger, C. D. (Ed.). *Police selection and evaluation.* New York: Hemisphere, 1979.

Spool, M. D. Training programs for observers of behavior: A review. *Personnel Psychology*, 1978, *31*, 853–888.

Springer, D. Ratings of candidates for promotion by co-workers and supervisors. *Journal of Applied Psychology*, 1953, *37*, 347–351.

Srinivasan, V., Shocker, A. D., & Weinstein, A. G. Measurement of a composite criterion of managerial success. *Organizational Behavior and Human Performance*, 1973, *9*, 147–167.

Staugas, L., & McQuitty, L. L. A new application of forced-choice ratings. *Personnel Psychology*, 1950, *3*, 413–424.

Steers, R. M., & Porter, L. W. The role of task-goal attributes in employee performance. *Psychological Bulletin*, 1974, *81*, 434–452.

Steers, R. M., & Rhodes, S. R. Major influences on employee attendance: A process model. *Journal of Applied Psychology*, 1978, *63*, 391–407.

Stone, E., Rabinowitz, S., & Spool, M. D. Effect of anonymity on student evaluations of faculty performance. *Journal of Educational Psychology*, 1977, *69*, 274–280.

Suchman, E. E., & Scherzer, A. L. *Current research in childhood accidents.* New York: Association for the Aid of Crippled Children, 1960.

Suci, G. J., Vallance, T. R., & Glickman, A. S. A study of the effects of "likingness" and level of objectivity on peer rating reliabilities. *Educational and Psychological Measurement*, 1956, *16*, 147–152.

Svetlik, B., Prien, E., & Barrett, G. Relationships between job difficulty, employee's attitude toward his job, and supervisory ratings of the employee effectiveness. *Journal of Applied Psychology*, 1964, *48*, 320–324.

Taylor, E. K., & Hastman, R. Relation of format and administration to the characteristics of graphic scales. *Personnel Psychology*, 1956, *9*, 181–206.

Taylor, E. K., Parker, J. W., Martens, L., & Ford, G. L. Supervisory climate and performance ratings, an exploratory study. *Personnel Psychology*, 1959, *12*, 453–468.

Taylor, E. K., Schneider, D. E., & Clay, H. C. Short forced-choice ratings work. *Personnel Psychology*, 1954, *7*, 245–252.

Taylor, E. K., & Wherry, R. J. A study of leniency in two rating systems. *Personnel Psychology*, 1951, *4*, 39–47.

Taylor, F. W. *Principles of scientific management.* New York: Harper & Row, 1947.

Taylor, H. C., & Russell, J. T. The relationship of validity coefficients to the practical effectiveness of tests in selection: Discussion and tables. *Journal of Applied Psychology*, 1939, *23*, 565–578.

Taylor, J. B., Haeffele, E., Thompson, P., & O'Donoghue, C. Rating scales as measures of clinical judgment: 2. The reliability of example-anchored scales under conditions of rater heterogeneity and divergent behavior sampling. *Educational and Psychological Measurement*, 1970, *30*, 301–310.

Taylor, S. E., & Fiske, S. T. Point of view and perceptions of causality. *Journal of Personality and Social Psychology*, 1975, *32*, 439–445.

Taylor, S. E., & Fiske, S. T. Salience, attention, and attributions: Top of the head phenomena. In L. Berkowitz (Ed.), *Advances in experimental social psychology* (Vol. 11). New York: Academic Press, 1978.

Taylor, S. E., Fiske, S. T., Close, M. Anderson, C., & Ruderman, A. J. *Solo status as a psychological variable: The power of being distinctive.* Unpublished manuscript, Harvard University, 1977.

Taylor, S. E., Fiske, S. T., Etcoff, N. L., & Ruderman, A. J. Categorical and contextual bases of person memory and stereotyping. *Journal of Personality and Social Psychology*, 1978, *36*, 778–793.

Tenopyr, M. L. The comparative validity of selected leadership scales relative to success in production management. *Personnel Psychology*, 1969, *22*, 77–85.

Terborg, J. R., & Ilgen, D. R. A theoretical approach to sex discrimination in traditionally masculine occupations. *Organizational Behavior and Human Performance*, 1975, *13*, 352–376.

Thornton, G. C. Psychometric properties of self-appraisals of job performance. *Personnel Psychology*, 1980, *33*, 263–271.

Thornton, G. C., & Zorich, S. Training to improve observer accuracy. *Journal of Applied Psychology*, 1980, *65*, 351–354.

Toole, D. L., Gavin, J. F., Murdy, L. B., & Sells, S. B. The differential validity of personality, personal history, and aptitude data for minority and nonminority employees. *Personnel Psychology*, 1972, *25*, 661–672.

Torgerson, W. S. *Theory and methods of scaling.* New York: Wiley, 1958.

Travers, R. M. W. A critical review of the validity and rationale of the forced-choice technique. *Psychological Bulletin*, 1951, *48*, 62–70.

Triandis, H. C. Cultural influences upon cognitive processes. In L. Berkowitz (Ed.), *Advances in experimental social psychology* (Vol. 1). New York: Academic Press, 1964.

Triandis, H. C. *Attitude and attitude change.* New York: Wiley, 1971.

Turner, W. W. Dimensions of foreman performance: A factor analysis of criterion measures. *Journal of Applied Psychology*, 1960, *44*, 216–223.

Tversky, A. Intransitivity of preferences. *Psychological Review*, 1969, *76*, 31–48.

Tversky, A. Features of similarity. *Psychological Review*, 1977, *84*, 327–352.

Tversky, A., & Kahneman, D. Belief in the law of small numbers. *Psychological Bulletin*, 1971, *76*, 105–110.

Tversky, A., & Kahneman, D. Availability: A heuristic for judging frequency and probability. *Cognitive Psychology*, 1973, *5*, 207–232.

Tversky, A., & Kahneman, D. Judgment under uncertainty: Heuristics and biases. *Science*, 1974, *185*, 1124–1131.

Uhrbrock, R. S. Standardization of 724 rating scale statements. *Personnel Psychology*, 1950, *3*, 285–316.

Uhrbrock, R. S. 2000 scaled items. *Personnel Psychology*, 1961, *14*, 375–420.

Uhrbrock, R. S., & Richardson, M. W. Item analysis. *Personnel Journal*, 1933, *12*, 141–154.

Umstot, D. D., Bell, C. H., Jr., & Mitchell, T. R. Effects of job enrichment and task goals on satisfaction and productivity: Implications for job design. *Journal of Applied Psychology*, 1976, *61*, 379–394.

Uniform Guidelines on Employee Selection Procedures. *Federal Register*, 1978, *43*(166), 38290–38309.

Vance, R. J., & Kuhnert, K. W. *Cognitive complexity and rating behavior*. Paper presented at the Annual Meeting of the Midwestern Psychological Association, St. Louis, May 1980.

Vance, R. J., Kuhnert, K. W., & Farr, J. L. Interview judgments: Using external criteria to compare behavioral and graphic scale ratings. *Organizational Behavior and Human Performance*, 1978, *22*, 279–294.

Vroom, V. H. *Work and motivation*. New York: Wiley, 1964.

Wagner, E. E., & Hoover, T. O. The influence of technical knowledge on position error in ranking. *Journal of Applied Psychology*, 1974, *59*, 406–407.

Walster, E. Assignment of responsibility for an accident. *Journal of Personality and Social Psychology*, 1966, *3*, 73–79.

Waters, L. K., & Waters, C. W. Peer nominations as predictors of short-term sales performance. *Journal of Applied Psychology*, 1970, *54*, 42–44.

Weiner, B., Frieze, I., Kukla, A., Reed, L., Rest, S., & Rosenbaum, R. M. Perceiving the causes of success and failure. In E. E. Jones, D. E. Kanouse, H. H. Kelley, R. E. Nisbett, S. Valins, & B. Weiner, (Eds.), *Attribution: Perceiving the causes of behavior*. Morristown, N.J.: General Learning Press, 1972.

Wells, W. D., & Smith, G. Four semantic rating scales compared. *Journal of Applied Psychology*, 1960, *44*, 393–397.

Wendelken, D. J., & Inn, A. Nonperformance influences on performance evaluation: A laboratory phenomenon? *Journal of Applied Psychology*, 1981, *66*, 149–158.

West, L. J. Fatigue and performance variability among typists. *Journal of Applied Psychology*, 1969, *53*, 80–86.

Wexley, K. N., & Pulakos, E. D. Sex effects on performance ratings in manager-subordinate dyads: A field study. *Journal of Applied Psychology*, 1982, *67*, 433–439.

Wexley, K. N., Sanders, R. E., & Yukl, G. A. Training interviewers to eliminate contrast effects in employment interviews. *Journal of Applied Psychology*, 1973, *57*, 233–236.

Wherry, R. J. *The control of bias in rating: Survey of the literature* (Personnel Research Board Report 898). Washington, D.C.: Department of the Army, Personnel Research Section, 1950.

Wherry, R. J. *The control of bias in rating: A theory of rating* (Personnel Research Board Report 922). Washington, D.C.: Department of the Army, Personnel Research Section, February 1952.

Wherry, R. J. An evaluative and diagnostic forced-choice rating scale for servicemen. *Personnel Psychology*, 1959, *12*, 227–236.

Wherry, R. J., & Naylor, J. C. Comparison of two approaches—JAN and PROF—for capturing rater strategies. *Educational and Psychological Measurement*, 1966, *26*, 267–286.

White, R. W. Motivation reconsidered: The concept of competence. *Psychological Review*, 1959, *66*, 297–333.

Whitla, D. K., & Tirrell, J. E. The validity of ratings of several levels of supervisors. *Personnel Psychology*, 1953, *6*, 461–466.

Willingham, W. W. Interdependence of successive absolute judgments. *Journal of Applied Psychology*, 1958, *42*, 416–418.

Wimperis, B. R., & Farr, J. L. The effects of task content and reward contingency upon task performance and satisfaction. *Journal of Applied Social Psychology*, 1979, *9*, 229–249.

Windle, C. D., & Dingman, H. F. Interrater agreement and predictive validity. *Journal of Applied Psychology*, 1960, *44*, 203–204.

Wright, P. The harassed decision maker: Time pressures, distractions, and the use of evidence. *Journal of Applied Psychology*, 1974, *59*, 555–561.

Wyer, R. S., Jr., & Srull, T. K. Category accessibility: Some theoretical and empirical issues concerning the processing of social stimulus information. In E. T. Higgins, C. P. Herman, & M. P. Zanna (Eds.), *Social cognition: The Ontario symposium on personality and social psychology*. Hillsdale, N.J.: Lawrence Erlbaum, 1980.

Yukl, G. A., & Latham, G. P. Consequences of reinforcement schedules and incentive magnitudes for employee performance: Problems encountered in an industrial setting. *Journal of Applied Psychology*, 1975, *60*, 294–298.

Yukl, G. A., & Latham, G. P. Interrelationships among employee participation, individual differences, goal difficulty, goal acceptance, goal instrumentality, and performance. *Personnel Psychology*, 1978, *31*, 305–323.

Zavala, A. Development of the forced-choice rating scale technique. *Psychological Bulletin*, 1965, *63*, 117–124.

Zedeck, S., & Baker, H. T. Nursing performance as measured by behavioral expectation scales: A multitrait–multirater analysis. *Organizational Behavior and Human Performance*, 1972, *7*, 457–466.

Zedeck, S., Imparato, N., Krausz, M., & Oleno, T. Development of behaviorally anchored rating scales as a function of organizational level. *Journal of Applied Psychology*, 1974, *59*, 249–252.

Zedeck, S., Jacobs, R., & Kafry, D. Behavioral expectations: Development of parallel forms and analysis of scale assumptions. *Journal of Applied Psychology*, 1976, *61*, 112–115.

Zedeck, S., & Kafry, D. Capturing rater policies for processing evaluation data. *Organizational Behavior and Human Performance*, 1977, *18*, 269–294.

Author Index

Numbers in italics refer to the pages on which the complete references are listed.

Subject Index

ORGANIZATIONAL AND OCCUPATIONAL PSYCHOLOGY